D0010401

firefly

THE OFFICIAL
COMPANION

VOLUME TWO

Features and Interviews by Abbie Bernstein, Bryan Cairns, Karl Derrick & Tara DiLullo

TITAN BOOKS

CONTENTS

STILL FLYING

An interview with Joss Whedon

What are some of your favorite incidents from filming?

I'm going to forget a bunch, but one that always comes to mind is the basketball game [in 'Bushwhacked']. Because I've always been extremely strict about how I shoot things and about how I write things. And Tim [who directed the episode] had written an entire scene, and I was like, 'But you're going to roll, right, and just let them mess around.' And we both knew instantly that we were not going to use any of our scripted dialogue. That was just [the actors]. I mean, a few of the gags were called upon, but mostly it was just 'Do what you can, have your fun.' And everybody was so socked into their characters, this being just the second episode, that the liveliness of that was something that I hadn't really ever allowed or been privileged to have from a troupe before. And then of course [in 'Serenity'], closing the doors on Mal and Jayne before they got in from the airlock was funny. I have to say, I argued strenuously against it, because I was terrified that something terrible would happen. I said, 'Let's close the doors a little earlier' and everyone was like, 'Don't tell them.' I'm like, 'But what if...' They're like, 'Dude, don't tell them. They'll be cool.' I'm such a wuss: 'I just don't know if that'll be cool...' And it was awesome [laughs], because everybody stayed in character. Jayne just pushed his way to the front. And most of my stories end up being about stuff like that. Nathan is hilarious and people are really fun to be around, but it was mostly about them bringing something, some energy or some moment or some piece of movement that I hadn't really prepared myself for. A show does unfold while you're shooting it. And watching every actor get so specific and so focused that every time I looked at one of them, I'd be like, 'This is their story — there is nobody else.' And the camera moved to somebody else, and I'd be, 'This is *their* story, there's nobody else.' And it's not an incident, it's more a general feeling, but it's part of what made me fight for the show so hard.

One of the things I ended up doing was, we blocked a scene without the cameramen, which other shows have done, but I hadn't actually heard about it at the time. We gave the cameramen their general measurements and then sent them away so that we could rehearse the scene, so that the camera operators would have no idea who was talking next, just to keep them on their feet, just to keep things alive.

The best thing that ever happened was definitely during 'The Message'. I think for some reason it wasn't on the gag reel. It was possibly the best piece of acting I've ever seen, which is the three-sixty [360 degree camera rotation] that Tim [as director] did while everyone was listening to the farewell message from Tracey [played by Jonathan M. Woodward]. And Nathan is standing with Zoe, looking kind of stricken — this is his old friend — and the camera pans around to Kaylee — and Nathan's sitting next to Kaylee, looking kind of stricken in another way. And he managed to duck under the camera and get to every single member of the cast and just look really sad [laughs]. And some of them just could not keep it together and some of them did. But I've got to tell you — it's hard to describe. And then when it finally panned down to the body in the coffin, Nathan was lying in [Woodward's] arms, looking stricken. It was unbelievable — not only hilarious, but technically proficient. He really put some thought into it. But that's Nathan.

One other incident, definitely one of my favorites: a big executive came onto the big set, took a look at everything and gave me the words of encouragement that stayed with me throughout the run of the show. He looked around and said, 'Don't fuck it up' [laughs].

In the scripts, how much of the dialogue was to foreshadow or give exposition, and how much was just for the sheer pleasure of hearing the characters be the characters — for example in 'Serenity', when Mal asks Jayne what will happen if he's offered enough money to betray the crew and Jayne says, 'That'll be an interesting day'?

You're working both. The fact of the matter is, he said that, and as it turned out, it *was* an interesting day, but

❖ Opposite: Jayne and Mal: they aim to misbehave...

❖ Below: *Firefly* creator Joss Whedon.

that doesn't mean that it necessarily had to happen. What you do when you build a show is, you open as many doors as possible, and then don't look in all of them [laughs]. And that goes for not just the audience, but you yourself. You have to control it, because some shows will just build mysteries without knowing where they're going and suddenly you realize that that's what they're doing and they become unbearable. But you do want to open every avenue possible — romance, conflict, trouble, excitement, revelation — without deciding exactly what's going to happen, because the show's going to evolve; relationships are going to evolve; storylines are going to evolve. That's the way they work.

The relationship between Wash and Zoe and Mal was always very charged. 'War Stories' was like, 'Let's take a run at that.' It's good, primal stuff. One of the *key* things when the show was being picked up, or not being picked up, was when I got a call that said, 'We will pick up the show, but Wash and Zoe can't be married. Because we think that maybe the Captain and Zoe could have some tension from the script we read, from 'The Train Job'.' That was the moment where I said, 'You know what? Now we're talking about two different shows, and I don't want you to pick it up, because first of all, having a happily married couple is something that interests me, it's a different dynamic than I've been seeing. Second of all, what's more devastating: your husband will find out or your boyfriend will find out? So the stakes are just higher.' So that was important to me and something we knew was going to be exciting, and when we made 'War Stories', it was very much 'Let's give that marriage its moment.'

'Objects in Space' was 'Let's get away from the nu-nus-ba-boo-boo-ba-crazy and let's open up River a little bit.' Not because people were like, oh, they hate her, because nobody was *watching*, so it's not like we had all this feedback, but just the feeling of, 'There's more there, let's start exploring that.' The thing is that every episode, you want everyone to shine. The 'Our Mrs. Reynolds' principle — the idea of having nine people in the show was so that you could just toss that pebble in the pond and the entire show could just be ripples. And everybody's take on something would be worth hearing about. That's why 'Out of Gas' and 'Our Mrs. Reynolds' are both key, because everybody's just being themselves, reacting to one extreme situation or another.

Did you run into problems with using the word 'humped'?

Never. I've always had it easy with language, because I'll always throw in a word that's not *quite* the word we're not supposed to use, but clearly means it. And I honestly don't think I ever had a language problem. I mean, I kept saying 'rutting' all the time and 'bunged', which if you really break it down, is even more impressive [laughs]. In the early days of *Buffy*, I used British terms. And on *Firefly*, I used British, but usually Elizabethan terms, or terms that were made up to be ever so slightly different, but never any that would actually raise alarms, because nobody actually really seemed to know what they *meant*. The one big restriction we had was, we couldn't say anything actually really dirty in Chinese. Because they were like, 'Mm, if this goes overseas, people will be able to understand what they're saying, so you can't cuss.' Originally, we had them cussing like sailors in Chinese, but they were like, 'No, you have to say something that can be understood [without offending speakers of Chinese].' And then we found, because Chinese is so short — basically, it's the opposite of German or Japanese, there are no syllables of any kind — that we have to write monologues just for somebody to have a few syllables. That was a problem.

In the 'Serenity' teleplay, Mal has the line in Chinese, 'Fuck everyone in the universe to death...'

Yes. Probably changed. But we did have 'the explosive diarrhea of an elephant', which is apparently more acceptable.

With its somewhat existential subtext, does 'Objects in Space' break the fourth wall in any way?

It's not meant to. It describes the walls, but it's very much meant to be an episode of the show and to be what is really happening in the lives of these people. Even though it contains elements of fantasy and some very strange

observations, it's all trying to live in a realistic world. I'm not a big fan of breaking the fourth wall, with very rare exceptions — on *Angel*, there was 'Spin the Bottle' and every now and then on *Buffy*, 'Dawn's in trouble — it must be Tuesday,' we'd do something like that. On a show like *Firefly*, which is in its infancy, we wouldn't go near that. Also, those shows [*Buffy* and *Angel*] take place in the modern world. Pop culture references, by their very nature, to an extent sort of break the fourth wall. *Firefly* was designed not to be able to *have* any pop culture references, so it would not be something I would be anxious to do. You spend so much time in a science-fiction show getting people to accept the world they're in, you don't want to mess with that.

Are there any episodes that you wanted to write and just did not have time to do?

Are you kidding? Here's the thing. There are episodes that I pitched to Nathan before we ever started shooting that burn up inside me, that I could spend three hours going over in my head meticulously, every moment, that

❖ Opposite top: Alan Tudyk and Jewel Staite prepare for a take.

❖ Opposite middle: Take 6 on the *Firefly* clapper board.

❖ Opposite below: Joss Whedon during filming.

❖ This page top: Nathan Fillion and Morena Baccarin on set.

❖ Middle: Sean Maher in front of the camera.

❖ Below: The Sino-American Alliance flag.

❖ Right: Mal and Wash on the bridge during 'Serenity'.

❖ Below left: The co-pilot's seat and steering yoke.

❖ Below right: One of Serenity's control panels.

though. The one good thing about being under constant threat of cancellation, as we were from the very beginning, is you make really good TV [laughs], because every time we thought, 'Here's an interesting idea — let's explore that somewhere along the line,' we'd get another smoke signal [that the show might be canceled] and we'd look at each other and go, 'We can't do this nice little idea. We have to punch everybody in the stomach. Right now, what's the most unbelievably cool thing we can think of — what's the most primal thing, what's the funniest, what's the most interesting?'

We were on our toes every second, because we figured, the one thing we had to fall back on was quality. That's all we had. And quite frankly, the first episodes wouldn't have been as strong, as frantic about trying to save it. And so, while I never got to make a lot of the episodes that I wished I had, I feel that the DVD box set is as strong as it is, pound for pound, partially for that reason. Which is not the way I'd *like* to live my creative life, but it did — we did make the best of it.

Was the storyline in *Serenity* — the *Serenity* movie rather than 'Serenity' the episode or Serenity the ship —

Or the battle.

Or the valley. Or the emotional condition. I think we've now exhausted them.

I believe there are the adult diapers.

we will never film. And there are more than a few. And that is again, part of how *Serenity* happened, because my desire to tell this story was overwhelming; but ultimately, TV and movies — a little bit different. And I knew if I made *Serenity*, I was not going to be telling those stories. Some of them are so dark, you can't believe it, and some of them are very beautiful. Most of them are both. But I had such paces to put these people through and never got the chance. I will say one thing,

Okay, or the diapers — were the elements of *Serenity* originally intended to eventually be part of *Firefly*, and if so, about where would they have come in?

My estimation was, towards the end of season two was going to be where we would find out about Miranda and the Reavers. This would not have led to any overthrow of the government, necessarily, but it would serve the uncracking of River's mind and rebuilding of her. I was giving it two seasons — could've ended up being one if we felt like we needed a little more momentum. But that was in the back of my head.

Would the Reavers ever have talked?

I certainly didn't intend them to. But I was still playing with different ideas about the Reavers. The idea that I used in the movie with the Reavers did not come right away. The idea of a planet being killed I had in my head. The idea that the Reavers had come from that, I didn't have until later in the process, until actually I was writing the movie. I think they would have been about the same [as they were in the film if they had been depicted on *Firefly*]. I had a whole thing worked out where Kaylee was going to go to a carnival and see one in a sideshow and then it was going to turn out to be a guy in a costume, because Mal explained that no Reaver would ever, *ever* let themselves be caught alive, that they'd eat themselves first. And I always wanted to keep that. It would have been a long damn while before we ever really caught sight of one. We had a lot of shows and ideas for shows, where we were constantly under threat of them, but they were in another ship, they were in another place, we didn't see them for a long while. And then once we saw them, oh,

the terrible, terrible things I was going to do. There are some things I won't say [laughs], because I will never give up on a story completely, but it wasn't going to be pretty.

What was in Inara's needle?

One of the things that I'm still going to keep for myself. It may be in the special edition once I finally wake up to reality. But my unreality occasionally opens in theaters, so...

How did you originally intend to end season one?

No idea. Because I really did think season two would be a good place to reveal River's troubles, so I didn't have anything in mind.

Can you talk at all about the episodes that you were prepping when *Firefly* got canceled?

❖ Above: Kaylee's room sign.

❖ Left: The galley set.

We really weren't [prepping anymore], because we had been given the order for three — we were filming the third when we got canceled — and we weren't concentrating on ideas. We had no impression that we were going to be told to make more. Now, had somebody said, 'Boom, you're on,' I'm sure we had some things floating around, but let me put it this way — I don't remember what they were.

We filmed 'Objects in Space' before we filmed 'Trash', 'The Message' and 'Heart of Gold'. There are in fact a couple of snafus. In 'Trash', River says, 'I can kill you with my brain', and in 'The Message', Jayne calls her 'a mind-reading genius', neither of which has been revealed until 'Objects in Space'. And we never aired those episodes ['Trash' and 'The Message'], we only aired 'Objects in Space'. But when we put them on DVD, we wanted 'Objects in Space' to be last, because it felt like more of a summing up, so you can look at those two things as kind of snafus, because originally they came after. But then they never came at all, at least not to network television.

While *Firefly* was airing in its first run, did you have any sense of how intense the fandom was?

Not huge [sighs]. I mean, there was a full-page ad in

❖ Right: Joss Whedon on set.

❖ Below: Joss hugs Jewel Staite on the final day of filming.

❖ Opposite: The *Firefly* crew.

Variety before the show was canceled, trying to keep it on. I was aware that there was a fanbase, but at that point, the only thing that mattered to [the network] was, how big was it? Not how vociferous was it, how big. At one point, I was asked, 'Why should we keep this show?' and my answer was, 'You're going to have a fanbase that loves it like they don't love other things [laughs], and I believe it'll grow — if you ever air it.' The kind of shows I make start out this way and then the word spreads and they become part of people's lives — people who are more dedicated than anything — but the network was interested in opening-weekend mentality and they weren't going to listen to that. So I was aware of [the fandom] to an extent. I knew what we were doing, for one thing, I knew how good it was, and that may sound like I'm all up in me, but this was an alchemy that went way beyond anything I could have imagined when I first thought of the show. From every single crewmember, from every actor — *every* actor, and that's a lot of actors — the energy was just phenomenal and I knew the shows were reflecting that and I'd heard from fans who were amazed by it. But the thing with the Internet is, you can convince yourself the entire world's talking about you from three guys posting over and over and over [laughs]. You can't really put a number on that. And if you can't put a number on it, an executive isn't going to be interested in it — not the executives who ultimately have the power in this situation.

It's been widely reported that Alan Tudyk gave you the red button that recalls the crew in 'Out of Gas' when *Firefly* ended. Did you press the red button to bring the cast back when *Serenity* got greenlit?

You know, it doesn't work. It turns out it was just a prop. It was really cute that Alan gave it to me, but it's not connected to anything. Disappointing, really. No, I think like Mal, I passed out right in front of it. And then I woke up and used the telephone.

Is there anything else you want to say about *Firefly*?

So much and I can't really remember anything, because it's been a part of me for a long time. It was a part of me when it was just a story in my head and then it was the most beautiful experience I could have imagined, because it sprang fully armored from Zeus's head, like Athena. I mean, the casting process was nightmarishly difficult, but once they were put together, you just couldn't imagine that there would be such an extraordinary band, people that I would hold so dear, characters that I would love so much, a world that visually would excite me that much and a staff that would be that creative and exciting. I mean, I had grips

coming up to me saying, 'I've been in this business for twenty-five years and I've never had so much fun.' I don't know why the grips were having fun [laughs], but they were. There was no above and below the line [status division between cast and crew], there was no attitude. The troubles we had with the network, which were constant, only brought us together, only made us feel more like a unit, a platoon or a family. I saw people who were veterans, who have been in this game forever, and I saw people who were just getting their first break, and they were having the same emotion, they were feeling the same about what they were

doing. The connection was just extraordinary. And I realize, and I've said this before, that none of that matters if it doesn't make it onto the screen. But it did. The energy between those people, the work that went into those scripts, the ease that the crew worked with and the amount of care that went into all of these episodes, it *did* show up. So it *does* matter. It wasn't just a party that we happened to film, it was a really concentrated effort by a lot of extraordinary artists to make something and I'm just swimmingly proud of it. Like the nine actors, like the crew, like the episodes, like everything else, it was more than the sum of its parts.

JAYNESTOWN

Written by Ben Edlund
Directed by Marita Grabiak

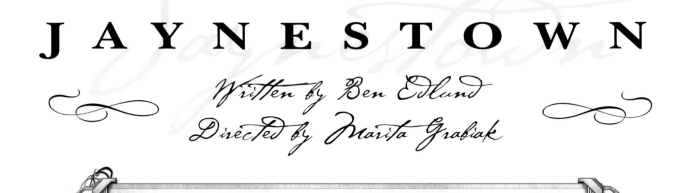

BEN EDLUND

Ben Edlund was known for creating the comic book and live-action satirical superhero series *The Tick* and had worked on the screenplay for the animated feature *Titan A.E.* before he was brought on board as a staff writer/producer on *Firefly*. His first credited episode was 'Jaynestown'.

Edlund says the idea for 'Jaynestown' came to him initially "when I was about to fall asleep, that there could be a way of reversing the Robin Hood myth: making everyone who took part in it seem like an utter piece of crap — starting with Jayne, of course. So the idea of there being a town that worshipped Jayne for all the wrong reasons, and how that might touch Jayne and also create problems for him, felt like a good story; when I pitched it to Joss, he was really happy with it.

"Jayne is such a bastard. And writing for a bastard is always fun. There were some abused/abusing childlike aspects to Jayne that you could almost sympathize with. He's a nightmare, there is something about him that makes you not want to see him succeed, but you don't want to see him fail, either. You don't want him gone, you just want him... punched."

Why are the planet's inhabitants farming mud? "I had read somewhere about high-tech ceramics. There were beginning to be quasi-synthetic ceramics in engine use and in other high-tech applications, so it made sense that there'd be a certain planet where there were valuable mineral sediment deposits. It just fit in with that frontier world and with the notion of fusing high-tech sci-fi with a really low-tech town of lumpen proletariat masses. I was trying, as always, to infuse ambient humor into an idea. There's something absurd about it, the whole culture of mud-covered people with their own songs [Edlund wrote 'The Hero of Canton'], their own bar and their own history of attempts at rebellion, which were usually fairly small and uncoordinated. They were in a position where they would support the idea of a Robin Hood."

Inara's profession provided the subplot. "We were thinking there would be something for her to do on this planet. The organic part of it is that she would have a client who is this frontier, rich person, who was lording the wealth over all these people. I think we had just been fooling around with the notion of her relieving someone of their virginity, since that's so sci-fi," Edlund laughs. "At least when I was a sci-fi fan. I'm sure a story about having my virginity relieved was just what I was looking for when I was a kid — easily until I was twenty!"

As for River's freaked-out reaction to Book's hair, "I think I always had the 'snow on the roof' thing in my script. But when I was done with the first draft, it went to Tim and Joss. I know that Joss had some refinements. He was very pleased, as I recall, about the run where River is using her crazy intellect/lack of propriety to 'fix the bible'. That was something that helped cement some kind of interaction between River and Book through this episode. Also, about that period, Joss wanted to make sure that someone pointed out Ron's amazing crazy hair when it was undone, because it was a free special effect — we used as many of those as we could get!" Edlund laughs.

"I think 'Jaynestown' is about tone and maybe getting a sense that there was a lighter side to being on a spaceship with a bunch of freaks — there's something fun and almost familial about it."

TEASER

INT. SERENITY - COMMON AREA

KAYLEE and SIMON enter from the passenger corridor, walking slowly as they talk. Kaylee is aglow with warm flirtation.

KAYLEE
Come on, it's true. Admit it.

SIMON
No, I won't, because it's not. I use swearwords, like anybody else.

KAYLEE
Oh really? Never heard you. When is it you do all your cussin'? After I go to bed?

SIMON
I swear. When it's appropriate.

KAYLEE
(laughs)
Simon! Whole point of swearin' is that it ain't appropriate.

INARA walks toward them, heading for the stairs up to the shuttle catwalk. She's dressed with stunning elegance.

KAYLEE (cont'd)
Hey there, 'Nara. Heading off for some glamorous romance?

Simon turns, momentarily stunned by her elegance.

INARA
(a little laugh)
Let's hope so.

SIMON
You look... very... very...

INARA
(smiles, then heads upstairs)
That's my job, Doctor. See you two tomorrow. Don't let Mal get you into too much trouble while I'm gone.

KAYLEE
Bye now! Have good sex!

Simon turns to her, abashed. Kaylee is innocent sincerity:

KAYLEE (cont'd)
What?

Then Simon catches sight of something through the infirmary window, shouts, and makes his way around to the door.

SIMON
AAAA!

Kaylee follows. Simon stands in shock. The infirmary has been ransacked. The contents of the cabinets cover every surface. JAYNE sits on the examination table, quietly taping a SMALL HANDGUN to his bare mid-section with medical tape.

KAYLEE
Now see, this'd be the perfect time for a swearword.

INT. SERENITY - INFIRMARY

Simon enters, shrill with agitation. Jayne doesn't look up.

SIMON
What happened in here?!

JAYNE
Needed to find some tape.

SIMON
So you had to tear my infirmary apart?!

JAYNE
(looks up at mess)
'Parently.

Simon starts putting it all away, fuming. Kaylee helps him.

SIMON
My god, you're like a trained ape! Without the training. No, apes are noble creatures, you're some sort of man-ape-thing that went horribly wrong.

JAYNE
(nonchalant)
Keep that tongue waggin', little man, might just have to rip it out an' flush it down the freshener.

Jayne pulls a length of tape with a loud rip, biting it off with his teeth. MAL appears at the door, looking at the gun taped to Jayne's middle.

MAL
Jayne, I told you, we're puttin' down at the Canton

factory settlement on Higgins' Moon.

JAYNE
Yep. That you did.

MAL
Canton don't let you bring guns into their town.

JAYNE
Yessir. That's why I ain't strappin' one to my hip.

MAL
No, that's why you ain't strappin' one anywhere.

JAYNE
Listen, Mal, I was in Canton a few years back, and I might have made me a coupla enemies there-abouts.

SIMON
(sarcasm)
Enemies? You? No! How can it be?

JAYNE
(ignores Simon)
I just don't like the idea of goin' in empty-handed is all —

MAL
Why're you still arguing what's been decided?

Mal stares at him, and leaves as Jayne glumly pulls the tape off, wincing.

EXT. SERENITY - NEARING HIGGINS' MOON

Higgins' Moon below: small, muddy brown, no place to raise a kid. Serenity rakes back, her belly glowing red as she hits re-entry. She makes a controlled tumble into the atmosphere.

INT. SERENITY - BRIDGE - DAY

WASH pilots, hits switches in preparation for landing, then hits the ship's com.

WASH
Okay Inara, we're atmospheric. You're good to go —

INT. INARA'S SHUTTLE - DAY

Inara works her controls, heating up the shuttle's engine, disengaging from Serenity.

INARA
Thanks, Wash. Shuttle disengaging in three, two, one...

We hear LOUD METAL CA-THUNKS as Serenity's locks on the shuttle are released.

EXT. SERENITY - HIGGINS' MOON ATMOSP-HERE - DAY

Inara's shuttle disengages, peeling away.

EXT. CANTON - ESTABLISHING - DAY

ANGLE OVER MUD BOG — which bubbles and farts in the FG. Beyond it, Serenity comes to rest on a landing field at the edge of a peninsula that

JAYNE'S COSTUMES

Costume designer Shawna Trpcic: "Your bounty hunter, your warrior, your guy just making it on the cusp. Anything from Robert De Niro's character in *Midnight Run* to every hardcore guy doing a thing — with the coats, again, we went to the past to define the future. It was a World War Two jacket, a World War One flight cap, modern-day army boots — pieces from a lot of different eras. I had a lot of fun with the graphics for Jayne's t-shirts. The costume production assistant was really good on the computer, and he and I were on the same page with our take on art. I would come to him with five or six different images and he would blend them all together on the computer and come up with a couple of different choices, then we'd show them to Joss and let him make the final decision. That was our way of making our tough guy a little more lyrical and a lot less of an echo of every other bad guy — with the goofy t-shirts. One of them did say 'soldier', but a lot of them said, 'fighting elves', all in Chinese. We had someone downstairs in the Fox library who could translate for us."

stretches out into the bog. Factory structures stand on the peninsula's far side.

EXT. SERENITY - CARGO RAMP - LANDING AREA - DAY

Mal walks down the ramp. Wash and ZOE stand at the bottom. Kaylee and Simon stand with BOOK and RIVER at the top of the ramp, looking around.

SIMON
Well. Canton really —
(breathes in)
— really stinks.

MAL
That's what makes it a great drop point. No one comes here that doesn't have to.

WASH
I vote we do this job really really fast.

MAL
Kessler's our man, he's holding the goods we're to deliver. We go in, we make contact. Easy peasy.
(turns to Zoe)
Zoe, you're holding down the fort. Call ahead to Bernoulli, tell him we'll have his merchandise there end of the week.

WASH
Don't I usually stay with the ship?

ZOE
I outrank you. Have fun.
(kisses him)

Zoe goes up the ramp.

SIMON
So, this is a place where they... they make mud?

KAYLEE
Yep. Clay, really. Be surprised how many things it ends up in.
(pats the ship)
Serenity's got more than a few ceramic parts in her.

SIMON
Really. Huh.
(looks out)
A mud-based economy. That's almost interesting.

KAYLEE
Cap'n...? Don't you think Simon should come with us?

SIMON
What? Kaylee, I don't think that's such a good —

KAYLEE
You said yourself this was an easy one. And he's got to get a little outlaw field experience sometime, if he's gonna be of any use 'cept doctorin'.

JAYNE
(snorts)
Fat chance of that.

Jayne stomps down the ramp, joining them. He's tying the flaps of his "thrilling heroics" hat under his chin. He pulls his goggles over his eyes. Wash sees his new look and raises his eyebrows. Book turns to Simon.

BOOK
You go on, boy. See the sights. I can watch over your sister. I believe we've been developing a rapport.

SIMON
I don't know. River can be —

BOOK
Go on. I'm a Shepherd after all. Should be able to keep my eye on a flock of one.

Book turns to River, who smiles at him sweetly, nodding.

MAL
We're not going far, Doctor. And you might maybe make yourself useful.

JAYNE
Come again?

Mal turns to Jayne, sees his hat/goggles, squints at him for a beat, then continues.

MAL
The management here don't take so kind to sight-seein'. Which is why we'll be posing as buyers. And there isn't a one of us looks more the part than the good Doctor.
(looks Simon over)
The pretty fits, the soft hands, definitely a mon-eyed individual, rich and lily-white and pasty all over —

SIMON
All right. Fine. I'll go. Just, stop describing me.

Mal smiles and guides Simon into the lead of their party.

MAL
You're the boss, boss.

JAYNE
He's the boss now?
(growls to himself)
Day keeps gettin' better and better.

EXT. CANTON MUDWORKS - DAY

Oh, it's muddy all right. Mud encrusts everything; the WORKERS, the pipelines that feed out of the mud-bog, the crappy structures, and THE FORE-MAN who oversees it all. He wears hip-high rub-berized boots, a MACHETE strapped in its sheath to one leg. Our crew passes through a chain-link fence which surrounds the area.

The Foreman sees them and turns. At his throat is a thin METAL COLLAR with two flat black discs, mounted over his larynx. He touches it, and his voice projects as if from a BULLHORN, gruff and confrontative.

FOREMAN
Area's employee-only! You best be headin' back to the Landing, 'less you got business here!

C A N T O N

Production designer Carey Meyer: "To create the large puddle of mud we used a big hole already at the location. We lined it with plastic and filled it with water and then added a chemical or a substrate to try to make it viscous. I remember the special effects guy, Bruce Minkus [also a *Buffy* alum], adding the stuff and saying, 'No, one gal-lon is going to make this whole huge pond super-viscous,' and ten barrels later, we were still adding and trying to come up with something that felt right.

"We created the interior of the bar, a little hole in the ground in the village, on stage. It's always an issue when you bring real dirt or products that can get airborne onto a stage. People get extremely wary and upset about it. We'd been through this issue a lot on *Buffy* — we were con-stantly in these environments that needed to look like dirt or mud or whatever. We decided, in this mud environment, to use actual dirt, just because it looks the best.

"We had done some sketches for the sweat boxes and Ben Edlund thought they looked too rustic, and so he did a little sketch for us — he's actually a very good artist. We went with his design and found some of those dividers that they use on construction sites to direct traffic — they're plastic and they fill them up with water. We used them to create barriers. We put them together like puzzle pieces and created what looked like a square box that had a lot of intri-cate shape to it, and then painted it up like metal and created little hatch doors and propped them up on a little precipice in the middle of this swamp."

SIMON
(too loudly)
YES!
(Foreman puzzled)
We're, uh — I — Yes. I'm looking to buy some mud.

Mal trades a look with Wash over Simon's awkwardness. But the Foreman shuts off his bullhorn collar and steps forward, all salesman smiles now.

FOREMAN
Well, then. Came to the right place.

He claps Simon on the back, his glove leaving a dusty handprint of dried mud on Simon's jacket.

EXT. CANTON MUDWORKS - FURTHER IN - DAY

The Foreman leads Simon on a tour of the plant. The others follow a distance behind, and by their looks this has been going on a bit long. MUD WORKERS shamble by, bent under heavy loads of mud-bricks; clearly back-breaking work.

FOREMAN
...And a 'course we can handle any volume here, got over two-thousand workers, mostly indentured, pay 'em next to nothin', so's we can pass them savings directly on to you-the-customer...

SIMON
Savings. Excellent, that's — because as I said before, I'll be needing quite a bit of it... I — I'm a buyer.

Simon struggles to hold his cover, but the Foreman isn't listening closely enough to notice. He rambles on:

FOREMAN
Yup. Best of its kind. We mix it and brick it raw on the premises, but you add the right catalysts, kiln it proper, this stuff is stronger'n steel ten times over, at half the weight.

SIMON
Yes, I — I've heard good things about the mud... Lot of people are talking about the mud...

Now the Foreman turns to him, a little quizzical.

WASH
(to Kaylee)
What happened to Simon? Who is this diabolical master of disguise?

KAYLEE
He's learning...

MAL
(calls to Simon)
'Scuse me, boss? I'm sure the Foreman's got things need attendin'. Why don't we wander a bit, take a look at the operation, then you can figure on whether we'll set up our account here?

SIMON
Yes?
(playing up role)
I mean, I make the decisions around here, uh —

employee...
(to Foreman)
I employ him. He is a person I employ. I'm the boss.

The Foreman gives him a somewhat confused look.

FOREMAN
O-kay... So you'll be wantin' to —?

SIMON
Yes, I think we'll wander for a bit.

FOREMAN
Fair enough. You come see me when you're done.

He walks off.

MAL
All right, let's head to worker-town.

As they pass by Simon, he reads from their looks that he didn't handle things so effectively. But Kaylee falls in step with him, brushing the mud off his jacket, smiling.

KAYLEE
I thought you did great.

EXT. CANTON WORKER-TOWN - DAY

The crew walks down a muddy lane between two rows of MUD DWELLINGS. Jayne looks back at Simon.

JAYNE
(to Mal)
Boy's gonna get us killed. Let's just do the deal and git.

MAL
His disguise ain't half so funny as yours. What are you supposed to be, anyway?

WASH
You haven't been here in years, Jayne. You really think you need that get-up? No one's gonna remember you...

Mal, in the lead, stops, seeing something O.S. Deadpan:

MAL
Think it's possible they might.

Before them stands a life-size mud-clay STATUE OF JAYNE on a pedestal. It's posed heroically, staring down in proud defiance. Jayne stares, in shock.

SIMON
Son of a bitch...

END OF TEASER

ACT ONE

EXT. CANTON TOWN SQUARE - DAY

Jayne, Mal and the others look up at Jayne's statue, still stunned speechless. Mal steps up next to Jayne; both are transfixed by the statue.

MAL
Jayne?

JAYNE
Yeah?

MAL
You want to tell me how come there's a statue of you, here, starin' at me like I owe him somethin'?

JAYNE
Wishin' I could, Cap'n.

MAL
No. Seriously. Jayne? You want to tell me how come there's a —

Jayne shoots furtive glances all around, keenly aware of his current visibility. His voice is an urgent whisper.

JAYNE
(interrupting)
Look, Mal, I got no ruttin' idea. I was here a few years back, like I said. Pulled a second-story, stole a lotta scratch from the Magistrate up on the hill. But things went way south, and I had to high-tail it. They don't put you on a pedestal in town square for that —

MAL
Yeah, 'cept I'm lookin' at some fair compellin' evidence says they do. Or maybe there's more went down here than you're lettin' on?

JAYNE
(hand to breast)
On my mother, Mal. I don't got the faintest notion.

The others stare up at the statue. Simon is deeply disturbed.

SIMON
This must be what going mad feels like.

WASH
I think they've really captured him, though, you know? Captured his essence.

KAYLEE
He looks sort of angry, don't he?

WASH
Kinda what I meant.

A LOUD STEAM WHISTLE blows — Jayne jumps near a mile.

FOREMAN (O.S.)
(distant, bullhorn)
Shift four, on duty. Shift four, on duty.

A new shift of mud farmers starts coming out of their homes, trudging toward the factory area.

JAYNE
Hey, I got an idea — 'Stead of hangin' around playin' art critic until I get pinched by The Man, how's about we move the hell away from this eerie-ass piece-a-work and get on with our 'creasingly eerie-ass day? How's that!?

Mal stands, staring at the statue.

MAL
I don't know. This here's a spectacle might warrant a moment's consideration.

Kaylee sidesteps by behind him, looking up, unsettled.

KAYLEE
Wherever I move to, his eyes keep... followin' me.

The 'Jaynestown' prop Adam Baldwin got away with: "It was the last day of location when we were shooting with the statue, and the light was gone and we were done. After I had knocked over the statue, someone encouraged me to 'take it home'. Well, it was too big to take home. 'Aw, you should take the head.' So I cocked the head off and held it up high. Everyone was like 'Yeahhhh!' I took it home because the guy who built it was there and he said he didn't care. The next day I got a call from the unit production manager going 'Where's the head?' 'Ahh... well, I have it.' 'Well, you have to bring it back. We need to do an insert shot of the thing.' If you ever see that episode, the insert shot was done to add the plaque that says 'Jayne Cobb'. You'll notice as it pans up past the neck, there's a crack they couldn't fix or didn't take the time to. I ended up donating the head, it made $1,500 for charity."

Jayne stomps off, teeth gritted with fury.

JAYNE
Come on, gorramn it! We got a job, let's go do it an' get outta here.

Jayne stops and turns, a distance away from the statue. But they can barely pull their eyes off it.

JAYNE (cont'd)
I crossed the Magistrate of this company-town, understand? An' he's not exactly a forgivin' sorta guy —

EXT. HIGGINS' HACIENDA - DAY

Inara, escorted by a company man, walks across the lawn of the Magistrate's estate.

MAGISTRATE HIGGINS, late fifties, tall, powerfully built under a few decades of doughy excess, stands with his VALET, ready to receive her. She does a graceful curtsey.

INARA
Magistrate Higgins, I may presume?

HIGGINS
You may. But I only make the people I own use my title.
(chuckles)
Mr. Higgins will do fine.

INARA
And you can call me Inara, Mr. Higgins.

HIGGINS
It's a rare pleasure, your visit to my little moon. Journey wasn't too taxing?

INARA
Not at all. I am refreshed and ready. Shall we begin at say, six o'clock?

HIGGINS
Perfect.
(starts to go)
I have a feeling it will take all your arts to deal with this particular problem.

INARA
Every "problem", Mr. Higgins, is an opportunity in disguise...

INT. SERENITY - DINING ROOM - DAY

River sits at the dining table. Book's bible is open in front of her, and she scribbles furiously into it, crossing out words, writing in the margins. Book walks in, speaks from across the room.

BOOK
What are we up to, sweetheart?

RIVER
Fixing your bible.

BOOK
I — uh — What?

He starts moving over to her.

RIVER
Bible's broken. Contradictions, faulty logistics — it doesn't make sense...

Now Book sees what she's doing. His bible's all fucked up, and there's a small stack of torn-out pages next to it.

BOOK
No, no, you can't...

River's still scribbling away as she chatters manically.

RIVER
So we'll integrate non-progressional evolution theory with God's creation of Eden — eleven inherent metaphoric parallels already there...

Eleven, important number, prime number, one goes into the house of eleven eleven times but always comes out one —

BOOK
River, just take it easy. You shouldn't —

RIVER
Noah's Ark is a problem —

She flips a page back and forth, frowning at it.

BOOK
Really.

RIVER
(rapid nod)
We'll have to call it early quantum state phenomenon — only way to fit five-thousand species of mammal on the same boat.

She tears the page out of the book.

BOOK
Gimme that!

Book snatches the bible up, somewhat possessively.

BOOK (cont'd)
River! You don't fix the bible!

River looks up at him, sweet, sincere, deadpan:

RIVER
(holds up torn-out pages)
It's broken. It doesn't make sense.

BOOK
It's not about making sense. It's about believing in something, and letting that belief be real enough to change your life. It's about "faith".
(gets up)
You don't fix faith, River. It fixes you.

He smiles, trying to gently take the crumpled, torn-out pages from her hand. She tugs back. They have a short tug-of-war then Book relents.

BOOK (cont'd)
Why don't you, ah, you hang on to those then.

INT. CANTON TAVERN - DAY

The kind of dirty dive that's actually made of dirt. Rugged, simple furnishings, with a crowd of mud-crusted off-duty WORKERS hunkered over their beers. A LOCAL BUSKER strums a battered GUITAR in one corner. MEADOWS, a young Mudder, sweeps up the bar with a dust broom. He looks at Jayne with some interest.

Our crew sits around a table. Mal has his back against the wall, taking in the view.

There're several clay bottles of beer on the table. Jayne pours himself a drink, as do the others.

JAYNE
Can't be a statue a' me. No reason for it. Flies in the face of every kinda sense.

BOOK'S BIBLE

Prop master Skip Crank: "Ron Glass was great. In almost every script it said: 'Book enters with his bible.' It was a tiny bible that Joss had picked out. I'd hand Ron this bible and he'd say 'No, not the bible!' I'd reply, 'Didn't you read the script?'

"Summer went through the whole routine of destroying Book's bible. Ron was really happy as he thought he'd never have to see the thing again. Then, later in the episode, she gives it back to him! Summer insisted that she taped all the pages back in herself. She really did want to do the whole thing.

"On Randy's truck we had probably the biggest bible you've ever seen. It was like two phone books taped together. For a joke, I went to see Ron with it and said, 'You know River tore up your bible? Well, here's your new one.' He said, 'No Way!'

"After we were canceled, I presented him with his original bible, and he cried. It was really sad."

WASH
Won't argue with that —
(drinks, spits it out)
Gaah! <Je shr shuh muh lan dong shi!?> [What is this garbage!?]

JAYNE
They call it Mudder's Milk.
(takes a big gulp)
Got all the vitamins, proteins, and carbs of your Grandma's best turkey dinner, plus fifteen-percent alcohol.

WASH
It's horrific!

SIMON
Worked for the Egyptians.

Jayne downs his glass and exhales, turning to Simon.

JAYNE
Whazzat?

SIMON
The ancient Egyptians, back on Earth-That-Was. It's not so different from the ancestral form of beer they fed to the slaves who built their pyramids. Liquid bread. Kept them from starving, and knocked them out at night, so they wouldn't be inclined to insurrection.

KAYLEE
Wow, Simon... That's so — so historical.

JAYNE
(to Simon)
Tell me, Little Miss Big-Words — you see a pyramid sittin' out there?

SIMON
No —

JAYNE
(rests his case)
Neither do I.
(pours a beer)
So here, let me pour you a big frosty mug of "shut-the-hell-up".

Jayne shoves a mug of beer at Simon.

Mal narrows his eyes at a relatively WELL-DRESSED MAN across the bar, who seems to be watching them.

MAL
(to himself)
Now what's a gussied-up fella like you doin' in a place like this?

The man sees he's being seen.

A YOUNG BOY (maybe thirteen) stands a short distance away from the crew's table, staring at Jayne with intense interest.

JAYNE
Shake your head, boy. Yer eyes are stuck.
(boy still staring)
GIT!
(boy runs off)

The well-dressed man walks up to their table. He stops at Mal.

WELL-DRESSED MAN
You wouldn't be looking for Kessler?

MAL
Just having a brew.

JOSS WHEDON

A town where Jayne is the local hero because he gave to the poor because he was trying to get the hell away in his ship [laughs] — how do you not do that? That was a huge amount of fun and I also thought they did some great stuff with that muddy town visually, but it was just pure romp. There's some emotion that happens during it, but it really was just how ridiculous would this be, and everybody was at the top of their game. It was too good a premise not to do, basically.

The man sits, close.

WELL-DRESSED MAN
I knew a Kessler.

MAL
"Knew"?

WELL-DRESSED MAN
He was a good middle-man. Low profile, didn't filch. But last week, the factory Foreman and his Prod crew heard he was moving contraband through town and gave him a peck a' trouble for it.

MAL
What kind of a "peck" was that?

WELL-DRESSED MAN
'Kind where they hacked off his hands and feet with machetes and rolled him into the bog.

WASH
They peck pretty hard 'round here.

MAL
Listen, I got a client offworld waiting for his delivery. If the goods are gone —

WELL-DRESSED MAN
Not to worry, your man's merchandise is safe in Kessler's hiding place. We just got to figure out how to get it cross town without being seen by the Foreman and his Prods. I'd advise we all just lay low for the moment —

The Busker starts singing.

BUSKER
JAAAYNE! The man they call JAAAYNE!

Jayne hears his name and sits straight up, horrified.

JAYNE
<Yeh-soo, ta ma duh — > [Hay-soose-mother-of-jumped-up —]

With lightning reflexes, Kaylee slaps her hand over his mouth; the applause of the mud workers (for the busker) helps cover Jayne's outburst.

Thus begins 'The Ballad of Jayne'. The mud workers erupt into the opening chorus, swinging their mugs in joyful song.

CROWD
He robbed from the rich, and gave to the poor, stood up to The Man, and gave him what for / Our love for him now, ain't hard to explain, THE HERO OF CANTON! THE MAN THEY CALL JAYNE!

The crowd gives way to the Busker, who sings a verse:

BUSKER
Our Jayne saw the Mudders' backs breaking / and he saw the Mudders' laments / and he saw the Magistrate taking / every dollar an' leavin' five cents / so he said, 'Can't do this to my people' / 'Can't crush them under your heel'./ Jayne strapped on his hat, and in ten seconds flat, stole everything there was fit to steal —

The crowd erupts again, REPEATING THE CHORUS. Over this, Mal and Jayne discuss this unsettling new wrinkle.

MAL
Umm... Jayne?

JAYNE
Yeah, Mal.

MAL
You got any light to shed on this development?

JAYNE
No, Mal.

Simon, seated by Kaylee, looks even more disturbed.

SIMON
No... This must be what going mad feels like...

He lifts up his beer and takes a deep drink.

The chorus ends and the Busker goes back to pickin', singing/story-telling another verse.

BUSKER
And here's what separates heroes / from common folk like you an' I. / The man they call Jayne, turned 'round his plane / and let that money hit sky. / He dropped it onto our houses. / He dropped it into our yards. / The man called Jayne,

'THE HERO OF CANTON'

Composer Greg Edmonson explains that it was 'Jaynestown' writer Ben Edlund who composed 'The Hero of Canton'. "The song had to be pre-recorded, so they had something to use during the filming of the scene." While he won't swear to it, Edmonson believes the actor singing lead in the episode is the same person singing on the soundtrack. "I'm pretty sure that they cast someone who could sing and he came in and sang. I know all the background singers were SAG singers who I use all the time; Craig Stull, who played on the main title, played guitar on that song. I didn't go to that recording session, because I was too busy trying to score another episode, so I think Craig called the singers that I knew and gave them instructions. I've worked with them all so many times before, I knew that it would turn out perfect, so I didn't have to sweat that one."

Edmonson did compose the music performed before the balladeer launches into 'Hero'. "The guitar music that precedes the song was just something that was meant to be played in a bar that really would just fit under the dialogue and not be too big a deal and would lead logically into the song."

THE HERO OF CANTON

Jayne.
The man they call Jayne...

He robbed from the rich
and he gave to the poor.
Stood up to The Man
and gave him what for.
Our love for him now
ain't hard to explain.
The hero of Canton,
the man they call Jayne!

Our Jayne saw the Mudders' backs breakin'.
He saw the Mudders' lament.
And he saw the Magistrate takin'
every dollar and leavin' five cents.
So he said, "You can't do that to my people,"
He said "You can't crush them under your heel.
So Jayne strapped on his hat
and in five seconds flat
stole everythin' Boss Higgins had to steal.

He robbed from the rich
and he gave to the poor.

Stood up to The Man
and gave him what for.
Our love for him now
ain't hard to explain.
The hero of Canton,
the man they call Jayne!

Now here is what separates heroes
from common folk like you and I.
The man they call Jayne
he turned 'round his plane
and let that money hit sky.

He dropped it onto our houses
he dropped it into our yards.
The man they called Jayne
he stole away our pain
and headed out for the stars!

Here we go!

He robbed from the rich
and he gave to the poor.
Stood up to The Man
and gave him what for.
Our love for him now
ain't hard to explain.
The hero of Canton,
the man they call Jayne!

stole away our pain / and headed out for the stars.

The crowd has erupted again, REPEATING THE CHORUS. Jayne seethes, facts dawning on him:

JAYNE
I'll be gorramned! That's where the cash went!
(to Mal and the rest)
I stole that money from Higgins, like the song says. Lifted me one of his hover-planes, but I got tagged by anti-aircraft. Started losin' altitude — had to dump them strongboxes of money to stay airborne.
(takes a drink)
Sixty-thousand, untraceable, an' I dropped it square in mud-farmer central!

The CHORUS ENDS, and the Busker plays a final bit of guitar, crescendoing as the crowd APPLAUDS. Wash looks at them all in disbelief.

WASH
We gotta go to the crappy town where I'm a hero...

INT. SERENITY - BOOK'S BERTH - NIGHT

Book steps into his berth and pulls out the sink, starting his pre-dinner ablutions. He starts to untie his bun of hair...

INT. SERENITY - COMMON AREA - EVENING

River walks from the common area into the passage leading to Book's berth.

INT. SERENITY - BOOK'S BERTH - NIGHT

Book splashes his face, bent over the sink.

RIVER (O.S.)
Hello?

BOOK
In here, River.

River steps into his doorway, looking down at the crumpled pages in her hands.

RIVER
I'm — I tore these out of your symbol, and they turned into paper — but I want to put them back, so —

BOOK
Sorry? What's that?

His hair is like a corona of grey fire around his head. River looks up, sees him, and drops the pages.

RIVER
(highest-pitched scream imaginable)

She runs off.

BOOK
River — ?

INT. SERENITY - CORRIDOR OUTSIDE BOOK'S BERTH - NIGHT

River runs by Zoe. Zoe hears Book inside.

BOOK (O.S.)
River — Come back —

ZOE
Book? What the hell happened to —
(as she turns, looks into Book's door)
AAA!

She startles at Book's hair.

INT. CANTON TAVERN - NIGHT

Jayne is hunched over his beer, looking ready to pop a nut. The crowd is lively and drunkish.

JAYNE
Captain, now they're off the subject of me, shouldn't we be gettin' the hell out of here?

MAL
I'd say that's a reasonable request, given the circumstance.

Jayne's up in a flash, stomping out. The others follow in his wake.

JAYNE
Ruttin' Mudders...

He pushes the front door open with a heave and stops dead:

EXT. CANTON TAVERN - NIGHT

The street in front of the tavern is filled with an affordable sea of MUD-WORKERS. At the front is the boy who Jayne chased off before. On sight of Jayne, they all cry:

CROWD
JAYNE!

Off Jayne and Mal's shocked expression, we BLACK OUT.

END OF ACT ONE

ACT TWO

EXT. CANTON TAVERN - NIGHT

A second after we left. Jayne stands, eyes aflame with alarm, as the crowd chants his name.

CROWD
JAYNE! JAYNE! JAYNE!

A beat of this, then Jayne turns, unceremoniously darting back into the bar. Wash turns to the others, mocking tremendous excitement.

WASH
I can't get enough of this local color!

INT. CANTON TAVERN - NIGHT

The crowd inside has stopped singing, confused. Meadows, the young man who's been sweeping the place, watches as Jayne pushes through them, bellying up to the bar, slams down his hat and goggles, desperate for drink.

JAYNE
Gimme some Milk.

The BARTENDER splashes a bottle of Mudder's Milk into a glass and Jayne takes a slug.

Meadows puts his broom down, stepping into the middle of the tavern behind Jayne, who's drinking down the Mudder's Milk.

MEADOWS
Don't you understand?! He's come back!
(crowd still lost)
It's Jayne!

Jayne's eyes dart like a wounded bull's in the ring. The bartender SLAPS the glass away from his lips.

JAYNE
What th —

BARTENDER
The hero of Canton won't be drinking that <shiong mao niao.> [panda urine.]

He pulls a dusty WHISKEY BOTTLE from below the bar and slams it down.

BARTENDER (cont'd)
He drinks the best whiskey in th' house.

Jayne, mystified, watches the bartender pour.

CROWD INSIDE BAR
(erupts into a CHEER)

They converge on him, slapping his back, shaking his hand. The brute has lost his connection to reality, just stands there as if in a strange dream.

Mal and the others push back into the crowded bar. The well-dressed man catches Mal by the sleeve, alarmed.

WELL-DRESSED MAN
'Hell is goin' on? This how people lay low where you're from?!

MAL
Not generally, no...

WELL-DRESSED MAN
Listen, friend, I came here to make sure a deal went down solid, not to get chopped up by the Canton Prod crew and fed to the bog!

Mal pulls the man's grasping hand from his arm, a touch riled by the contact. He's intuitively piecing out a new strategy.

MAL
Understand your concerns, friend. But this here is all part of our new plan.

KAYLEE
Captain? How exactly is this part of our —

MAL
(gritted teeth)
Still workin' the details...

MAL

"No matter how long the arm of the Alliance might get... we'll just get us a little further."

While the casting of Nathan Fillion as Malcolm Reynolds seems like the most perfect connection of actor to character ever, Fillion laughs at the assertion and dispels that common misconception held among fans. "Malcolm Reynolds is a pained man and he's obviously closed off." The actor explains that, in reality, he is the polar opposite of Mal so taking on the role was an absolute stretch for him. "It's not so much that he's not like me, but that he was such a challenge to play. I felt it was important that Joss knew this. I said, 'Just so you know, I love this character and I want to play him — he's not me. This is not the kind of person I am. I'm a happy, very lucky, excited individual. Life has been very, very kind to me.' I just thought that the distinction was important."

Fillion says bridging the gap between reality and character in playing Mal really came so much more easily than expected due to the caliber of the cast around him. The usual stresses of being a series lead never materialized for the actor, who says, "I didn't feel immediately like, 'Oh there is a lot of extra pressure on me to do something in particular in terms of leadership.' I had been a fan of many of the people that were cast. Gina Torres — I loved her work. Ron Glass, of course. Adam Baldwin... are you kidding? Alan Tudyk, when I saw he was cast I thought, 'What is he doing here? He's a movie star! Why is he slumming with us?'" He laughs, then adds seriously, "There would be moments all the time, when we would be on set dealing with adversity, there would be a problem and they would say, 'How can we help?' It became apparent that these fun, easy-going, relaxed people, who were extremely talented, who were there to do a job, were also very passionate and interested that we were also there for each other. I'm only too grateful to know these people. I respect their talent. I admire them." After a thoughtful pause, Fillion lights up and adds passionately, "There were also a lot of guest cast that came to *Firefly* and became a part of it

and gave of themselves and their passion. I might not have been able to impart to them how special they were. The guest cast are often unsung heroes and they were amazing and a part of the *Firefly* family. I want them to know how much I appreciate the work they did and how much they are included in the family."

While Reynolds had distinct relationships with all of the members of the Serenity family, when asked whom Malcolm revealed himself most to, Fillion readily answers, "Shepherd Book. The characters would come to Mal with bits or ideas, and maybe Mal would listen or have his own ideas. But whenever Book says something to Malcolm Reynolds, Malcolm Reynolds listens. He's one of the few people Mal listens to. He'll listen to Zoe, but his call is *the* call. He doesn't listen to Zoe because she has a bigger heart than he does. Book is very knowledgeable about a lot of things. Mal holds a lot of his feelings within him. He doesn't say a lot or tell a lot of who he is or how he is or why he is, nor does Book. That is something that Malcolm sees and doesn't press him about. So if Malcolm had a guide, it was Book."

With the series long over and one last adventure captured on film for the big screen, Fillion still looks at his time playing Malcolm Reynolds as one of the highlights, not only of his career, but also of his life. "I fell in love," the actor says of the show. "I told myself in 1997, 'Don't fall in love. Do your best. Always give 110 percent. Always swing at what they throw at you, but don't fall in love.' I lost it with *Firefly*. I lost the plan and was so in love. It was hard. We fought a war and were in a battle and being crushed and I kept telling people, 'Don't worry. We are making a great show. That's our ace in the hole.' But it was taken away from me. The parallel between that and Malcolm Reynolds' experience is only too poetic."

Still touched by the loss to this day, Fillion is winsome but never bitter. With his signature smile, he offers, "I'm the biggest *Firefly* fan you will ever meet. I have a place in my heart for that program and that film like no other person could, except for Joss. But my one advantage over Joss is that I got to live it. To be a fan and the Captain is a real interesting and fortunate place to be."

INT. INARA'S SHUTTLE - NIGHT

Inara has laid out a complex array of bowls and china on a low table in the main area of her shuttle. She's preparing for the COMPANION TEA CER-EMONY. She lights a candle, then flips open a pretty silver pocketwatch, nodding to herself as she checks the time. There is a knock at her O.S. door.

Magistrate Higgins steps into the doorway.

HIGGINS
Inara, allow me to introduce my son, Fess Higgins.

FESS HIGGINS, the Magistrate's twenty-six-year-old son, steps into the doorway. He's on the heavy side, but not unattractive, in his way. Inara smiles warmly.

INARA
Hello, Fess.
(to Higgins)
Mr. Higgins, this shuttle is a Place of Union. I'm sure you can appreciate —

HIGGINS
The lady said "hello", Fess. Don't just stand there looking at your shoes —

FESS
Dad —

Higgins forcefully guides Fess into the shuttle, stopping just short of the tea ceremony table.

HIGGINS
Get in there, son, make a man of yourself!

INARA
Mr. Higgins —

HIGGINS
(sees tea set-up)
What is this? I brought you here to bed my son, not throw him a tea party —

Inara is polite, but afire with firmness.

INARA
Sir, the Companion Greeting Ceremony is a ritual with centuries of tradition behind it. There are reasons for the way we do things.

HIGGINS
Listen, Inara, I called on you for one thing and one thing only. My son is twenty-six years old and he ain't yet a man. Twenty-six!
(looks at son with contempt)
And since he can't find a willin' woman himself —

Inara takes Higgins by the arm and starts gently but firmly guiding him out of the shuttle. He blusters but goes along.

INARA
Mr. Higgins, you are not allowed here.

HIGGINS
I — What?

INARA
As I said, this room is a consecrated Place of Union. Only your son belongs here.

HIGGINS
Well! This is — I —

She escorts him out the door. There's a WET SHLUP as Higgins' shoes hit the muddy ground.

INARA
Now you go on, and let us begin our work.

HIGGINS
Now you listen here, young lady —

Inara flashes a sweet smile and closes the door on him.

INARA
Goodnight, Mr. Higgins.

Inara resets an out-of-place hair, smoothes her countenance, and turns to Fess, now the portrait of hospitality.

INARA (cont'd)
Well. That's a bit more peaceful. Will you sit?

INT. CANTON TAVERN - NIGHT

Jayne leans against the bar, drink in hand, surrounded by adorers. He's starting to get into it. Meadows raises his mug.

MEADOWS
To Jayne —

CROWD
To Jayne!

They all drink. Jayne grins, despite himself, and swigs down his drink. The bartender fills it immediately. Jayne smiles wider, lifts his glass.

JAYNE
To the Mudders!

CROWD
To the Mudders!

They drink again.

Wash and Mal stand off to the side. Wash has a glass of whiskey in his hand. A MUDDER ELDER, in his sixties, finishes his drink and turns to Mal.

MUDDER ELDER
So, you're one of Jayne's men, eh?

Wash smiles. Mal's not pleased.

MAL
What? No —

MUDDER ELDER
Must be a heck of an honor, servin' under a man like that. Strong as a drafthorse, ain't he?

MAL
Listen, Mudhead, I don't —

CINEMATOGRAPHY

Director of photography David Boyd: "I had made it known to Carey Meyer early on that I loved ceilings in sets. He totally agreed and built ceilings into everything that he constructed. In the Mudders' bar ceiling, we designed holes, as if this were subterranean, and stuck lighting down through it in the form of very spotty lights. We put fans in these holes which turned very slowly. So we built in the fact that this place needed to be ventilated for some reason on this planet, and that light came from these strange sources. No one could or wanted to explain what they were, but they landed at odd angles, not from a sun, but from some other thing."

MUDDER ELDER
An' a heart as big as all outdoors...

Wash CHUCKLES, patting Mal on the back.

WASH
Yup, we're just happy he lets us stay.

At a table, Simon and Kaylee sit, drinking. Simon's actually a little plastered, and Kaylee's having the time of her life, nestled next to him.

SIMON
(a little slurred — more reminiscing than bitter)
You know, I've saved lives. Dozens. Maybe hundreds. I re-attached a girl's leg. Her whole leg. She

named her hamster after me. I got a hamster. He drops a box of money, he gets a town.

KAYLEE
Hamsters is nice —

SIMON
To Jayne! The box dropping, man-ape-gone-wrong-thing, hero of Mudville.

Kaylee laughs and drinks his toast with him.

KAYLEE
You know, you're pretty funny, even without cussin'...

Simon takes another sip and smiles at her, seeing her in the drunken light which makes all things sublime.

SIMON
You know... you're pretty... pretty.

Kaylee's smile drops. She wants to make sure she heard right.

KAYLEE
What? What did you say?

SIMON
(drunk smile)
Nothing. Just that you're pretty... Even when you're covered with engine grease, you're — maybe 'specially when you're covered with engine grease, you're —

Mal steps in over them, unintentionally cutting Simon off.

MAL
It's time to get out of this nuthouse. Got some plannin' to work out.

Kaylee's nightmare: boy-in-gear, Captain wants to go.

KAYLEE
Now, Captain?! But things are goin' so well!

MAL
(not quite getting it)
Um. I suppose, Jayne's certainly feelin' better about life. But we —

Kaylee gives Mal a fierce look.

KAYLEE
I said things are goin' well —

MAL
(gets it)
Oh. "Well". Well... I tell you what. Jayne's stuck here with his adoring masses, how about you and Simon hang around, keep an eye on him for me?

Simon raises his glass, oblivious to any sub-text at this point, drunker by the minute.

INT. SERENITY - CARGO BAY - NIGHT

Book and Zoe are crouched, Book's magnificent hair still out of its cage. River is inside the bay's secret compartment.

RIVER (O.S.)
(to herself, rapid)
They say the snow on the roof is too heavy — They say the ceiling will cave in — His brains are in terrible danger —

BOOK
River...? Please, why don't you come on out...

RIVER (O.S.)
No. Can't. Too much hair.

BOOK
(surprised)
Is — is that it?

He turns to Zoe, who nods.

ZOE
Hell yes, Preacher. If I didn't have stuff to get done, I'd be in there with her...

Book gives Zoe a look of mild affront and starts tying up his hair.

BOOK
(to River)
It's the rules of my order... Like the book, it symbolizes —

ZOE
(cuts him off)
Uh-huh. River, honey... He's putting the hair away now...

RIVER (O.S.)
Doesn't matter. It'll still be there... waiting...

WASH (O.S.)
Honey, we're home!

Mal and Wash walk into the cargo bay. Zoe goes to them.

ZOE
Where you guys been? Mal, Bernoulli's chompin' at the bit. Says he wants his merchandise yesterday —

MAL
Yeah, well, we got a couple of wrinkles to work out on the deal.

WASH
(bit buzzed on drink)
Did you know Jayne is a bonafide folk hero? Got a song and everything.

ZOE
(as in "get out")
<Hoo-tsuh.> [Shut up.]
(eyes Wash)
You been drinkin', husband.

MAL
That he has. Don't make it any less the case.

ZOE
You're telling me Jayne is a —

MAL
(nods)
It's true. True enough to use, anyways. We've talked a few pillars of the Mudder community into havin' a little 'Jayne Day' celebration in town square tomorrow... That should buy us enough distraction to get those stolen goods out from under the Foreman and his crew a' Prods...

ZOE
You're really gonna have to start again.

They stop by Book.

MAL
Shepherd, everything goin' okay?

BOOK
I, uh, I'm working on it, Captain.

RIVER (O.S.)
We need a snow shovel...

INT. INARA'S SHUTTLE - NIGHT

Fess sits next to Inara at the low table, sipping his tea.

FESS
(looking into his cup)
It's just... my father's always been so in control, of everything, of me, of everyone... I could never be like him, no matter who he pays to —
(reddens, looks up)
I'm sorry... This whole thing, it is embarrassing. My father's right again, I guess. And to have to bring you here, to —

INARA
Your father isn't right, Fess. It's not embarrassing to be a virgin. It's simply one state of being. And as far as bringing me here — Companions choose the people they're to be with very carefully... For example, if your father asked me to come here for him, I wouldn't have.

FESS
Really?

INARA
Really, Fess. But you're different from him.

She turns to him, stroking his cheek, looking into his eyes.

INARA (cont'd)
The more you accept that, the stronger you'll become...

She leans in and kisses him gently on the lips.

INT. CANTON TAVERN - NIGHT

Jayne now has a WOMAN on one arm, clinging to him. She's somewhere between robust and plain, but with a Janis Joplin carnality that suits him. He speaks to Meadows, who looks at him adoringly.

JAYNE
So the Magistrate, he let you folks keep all that cash?

MEADOWS
He did. And it pained him, that's for dead sure. When he found out, he sent his Prods in to take it back from us... But the workers resisted.

JAYNE
Fought the law, eh?

MEADOWS
(nods)
If the Mudders are together on a thing, there's too many of us to be put down... So in the end, he just called it a "bonus".

JAYNE
(rueful laugh)
One hell of a bonus...

MEADOWS
And then, when we put that statue of you up in town square, he rolled in, wanted to tear it down. But the whole town rioted...

This, the idea of violence in his name, touches our drunken Jayne so deeply, a tear comes to his eye.

JAYNE
(drunken emotion)
You guys started a riot? On account of me? Oh... I am truly touched, truly, truly touched by that. I mean, all of this has been swell and all, but that, my very own riot...
(almost chokes up)
...That's just about the nicest thing I ever heard...

MEADOWS
I can't believe you're back...

He throws a big arm over Meadows, squeezing him warmly.

JAYNE
How could I stay away?

INT. HIGGINS' HACIENDA - NIGHT

Higgins paces as the Foreman comes in, led by a VALET.

FOREMAN
Magistrate Higgins —

Higgins is only vaguely listening, lost in his dirty hopes.

HIGGINS
M'son's out there, I pray to God losin' his cherry...

FOREMAN
There's a problem in worker-town, sir.
(Higgins listening)
Jayne Cobb's come back.

Whatever we can do to subtly imply that ancient, boiling hatred has just snapped a nerve in this Higgins' head...

EXT. CANTON PRISON FIELD - NIGHT

Out on the bog. A catwalk stretches out to an area dotted with rusted steel boxes (not unlike the hotbox from *Cool Hand Luke*). Airholes poke through doors in their fronts.

Higgins and the Foreman are at one of the boxes. The Foreman carries a beat-up duffel bag.

The Foreman fumbles through some keys and opens the door. Rank darkness inside. CAMERA PUSHES IN on the small dark doorway. We hear rustling inside, the scratch of uncut nails along a wall.

HIGGINS
Evening, Stitch.

STITCH (O.S.)
(hissing exhale)
What do you want with me?

HIGGINS
Nothing. You've done your time. Paid your debt. Time you were on your way.

STITCH HESSIAN'S face pushes out of the shadows inside, fast. Half of it is a mass of scar tissue; one eye is missing.

He slithers out of the box, dropping heavily to his feet on the catwalk. He's a tall, creepy son-of-Manson, long bedraggled hair and beard, scarred

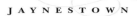

all over his sinewy body.

Higgins nods to the Foreman, who throws the duffel at Stitch.

HIGGINS (cont'd)
Here. I believe these were your personal effects...

Stitch looks in the duffel, surprised to pull out a SHOTGUN. Higgins turns, starting to walk away, then stops.

STITCH
You keep me in that box four years and then give me a loaded gun?

HIGGINS
Got the urge to use it, no doubt. But I'm not the one that brought you in on that robbery. I'm not the one who partnered up with you and then turned on you when his plan went south. How high up was that shuttle when he pushed you out? Thirty feet? Jayne Cobb cost you four years of your life, plus a perfectly good eyeball. And here's the poetical portion: he's back in town. This very day.

Stitch's body tenses with hideous rage. He COCKS his gun.

HIGGINS (O.S.)
Best of luck in your new life.

END OF ACT TWO

ACT THREE

INT. CANTON TAVERN - MORNING

The morning after. One or two MUDDERS lie passed out. Camera finds Kaylee and Simon. They're tangled up in each other, asleep. Kaylee has her hand on Simon's chest, under his shirt, which is half-unbuttoned. She wakes groggily, sees Simon next to her, and smiles, soaking him in.

Then Mal is above her. She turns and smiles at him, too, still half-asleep.

KAYLEE
(dreamy)
Hiya, Captain...
(snaps out of it)
Captain!!

This wakes up Simon, who gets his bearings quickly.

❖ Left: The lantern Higgins is carrying when he releases Stitch.

SIMON
Wha —? Kay —? — Mal! Mal, I, uh...

He starts untangling himself roughly from Kaylee's embrace.

SIMON (cont'd)
Captain, nothing happened — There was some drinking, but — We certainly didn't — I mean, I would never — not with Kaylee, I — I assure you, nothing inappropriate took place —

KAYLEE
What do you mean, not with me?

Kaylee, getting pissed, helps him untangle with a strong shove. Mal is uninterested.

MAL
Uh-huh... Where's my hero?

JAYNE
(singing)

He robbed from the rich, and gave to the poor, stood up to The Man, and gave him what for...

Jayne descends the stairs into the tavern from the rooms above. His arm around the woman from last night.

JAYNE (cont'd)
The living legend needs eggs!
(gives it thought)
Or another Milk, maybe...

MAL
No. The living legend is comin' with us. He has a little appearance to make.

JAYNE
He does?

MAL
That's right. This job here has gone way past long enough.

JAYNE
(to the woman)
You go on, now. Got me important hero-type stuff to do.

Kaylee follows them to the door. Simon gets up, to fall in line, but Kaylee turns on him.

KAYLEE
Where you goin'?

SIMON
What? I'm coming with y —

She pokes him in the chest, miffed enough to not want him around for a bit.

KAYLEE
I don't think so. No, maybe you ought to stay here. It's about the time for a civilized person to have his breakfast. That's the sorta thing would be appropriate, don't you think?

Simon turns to Mal, who shrugs. It's clear Simon is only an honorary member of the club; Kaylee outranks him. They turn and go, leaving Simon alone in the tavern.

SIMON
Mal...
(as they walk out)
Guys?

MAL
See you on the ship, Doc.

Simon shakes his head, still groggy, and sits down. After a beat, he turns to the bartender.

SIMON
Excuse me... Could I see a menu?

BARTENDER
(laughing snort)
"Menu"...

INT. INARA'S SHUTTLE - MORNING

Fess lies next to Inara in bed.

INARA
You're very quiet.

FESS
I'm sorry — I'm just — I just thought I'd feel... different, after... Aren't I supposed to be a "man" now?

INARA
A man's just a boy who's old enough to ask that question. Our time together, it's a ritual, a symbol. It means something to your father. I hope it was not entirely forgettable for you...

FESS
Oh, no, it was...

INARA
But it doesn't make you a man. That you do yourself.

This seems to sink in with Fess. We hear a loud RAPPING at the shuttle door.

HIGGINS (O.S.)
Fess! Fess Higgins, get out here!

EXT. CANTON BACKSTREET - DAY

Mal and Jayne walk along the lane of shanties we used once before. Kaylee walks a distance behind.

MAL
So that's where the little "Jayne" celebration we planned comes in... Should give us time to move the goods back onto Serenity...

JAYNE
I dunno. I mean, do you think we should be usin' my fame to hoodwink folks?

Mal stops, turning.

MAL
You better laugh when you say that.

JAYNE
No really, Mal. I mean, maybe there's somethin' to this — The Mudders... I think I really made a difference in their lives. Me, you know? Jayne Cobb.

MAL
I know your name, jackass.

JAYNE
Did you know they had a riot on my account?

Mal turns as Wash drives up on the MULE, with Zoe.

WASH
Morning, kids.

ZOE
Is that Jayne? Is that really him? Wash — pinch me, I must be dreamin'!

Mal hops on the Mule, as does Kaylee. He turns to Jayne.

JAYNE
Hell, I'll pinch ya.

MAL
Just get on over to town square, Jayne. Your fans are waiting.

They drive off.

EXT. CANTON WILDS - DAY

Wash drives the Mule to a deserted back area of Canton, and they all dismount.

They clamber through the reeds, and come upon a steep earth-cut. Down in it we see a pile of CRATES, covered with a mud-colored CAMOUFLAGE TARP.

MAL
Here we go...

INT. INARA'S SHUTTLE - DAY

Fess is sitting down in the shuttle. Inara is cleaning up tea stuff.

INARA
A criminal hearing?

FESS
My father's ordered me to attend. See, there was this man... It happened when I was growing up here. He stole a ton of money from my dad, and gave it to the poor, to my father's workers. And he's become kind of a folk hero in Canton.

INARA
Go on.

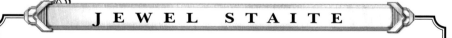

JEWEL STAITE

I remember the most riding of the Mule that we had to do was in 'Jaynestown'. It was in this dusty desert part of California, and was just gross. There was sand everywhere, in my mouth and in my eyes and it was just so unbelievably hot, we were all just drenched and trying to hang onto the Mule with sweaty hands. It was always pretty precarious. It was like a dirt bike, but much larger. Alan was always behind the wheel, which made me totally nervous, because he'd decide to slam on the gas and take us for a spin. It was difficult to hang on — I was so paranoid of falling off that thing. I'd broken my collarbone about a year before, falling off something else, and my doctor had told me that it would only take the slightest fall for it to re-break. That was the worst pain ever. I was hanging onto the back going, 'I'm going to wipe out and break my collarbone again, I just know it...' Gina said, 'Just grab onto me.' So I'm hanging on in the back, and Joss says, 'Why are you clutching Gina's can? It's weird — we can see it in the shot. Don't do that!'

THE MULE

Production designer Carey Meyer: "We had a little ATV, an all-terrain vehicle, a four-wheel job, and really, it was just the cheapest thing that we could come up with [laughs] that we could actually have an actor drive. We created a little wagon that could connect to it and drag stuff around, and then of course we tried to art-direct it and make it feel like Serenity; but there wasn't a big process in the design to that end, it was very much an ATV that we could get quite inexpensively and then dress up and it actually worked. However, everybody felt cheated that we went with that concept and that's why, in 'Heart of Gold', we created the floating car for the main character."

❖ Above: The Mule's license plate.

FESS
Well, he's back. Apparently he landed here yesterday.

INARA
Yesterday.
(sighs, to herself)
Oh, no.
(to Fess)
I know this man. He's — he just has this idiotic sense of nobility, you know? He can never just let things be — He thinks he's this hard-hearted criminal, and he can be unrelenting... but there's a side to him that is so...

FESS
You mean you actually know Jayne?

You could knock her over with a feather.

INARA
Jayne? Jayne Cobb? You're talking about Jayne Cobb.

FESS
Yes. Jayne Cobb, the Hero of Canton. The only person I ever saw who stood up to my father.

INARA
I — wha — nnn?

FESS
My dad traced him back to his ship. He had Port Control put a land-lock on it. Jayne'll get back and find out he's grounded. I sort of hate the idea of his getting caught.

INARA
(still thrown)
Yes. That would be bad.

INT. CANTON TAVERN - DAY

Simon picks through a plate of MUDDER FOOD, nose wrinkling at every greasy item on it.

SIMON
Uh... Ahem, could I just get the — the check, please?

Then he sees that the bartender is gone. The door SLAMS open. Stitch Hessian stands in the doorway, backlit.

STITCH
Heard tell you run with Jayne Cobb...

Simon, squinting into the daylight, with Stitch's shadow falling over him.

SIMON
Excuse me?

STITCH
You're gonna take me to that dirty low-down shingle of a man...

Stitch strides toward Simon, who bristles, somewhere between affronted and afraid.

SIMON
Listen, "sir", I don't know who you think you —

Stitch backhands Simon across the face with vicious force, slapping him to the floor.

STITCH
Sir!? Look at me, ya' pantywaist idjit!

He kicks Simon in the guts, hard.

STITCH (cont'd)
I just spent the last four years steamin' in a hot-box and you're sirrin' me?

He kicks him again, then reaches down and lifts him up with one hand. Simon reaches desperately for a clay beer bottle off a table as Stitch talks.

STITCH (cont'd)
Folks say you're part a' Jayne's team. So —

Stitch pulls a SWITCHBLADE from his belt and flicks it open alongside Simon's face.

STITCH (cont'd)
Where is that no-good reptile hidin' hisself? You tell me, boy, or I'm a' cut off every last bit a' your good looks.

Simon brings the bottle up and smashes it against the side of Stitch's head. Stitch SLASHES THE KNIFE ACROSS THE BACK OF SIMON'S FOREARM! Simon drops the jagged bottle neck.

SIMON
Aaagh!

Stitch slams his fist into Simon's face, dropping him.

STITCH
(low chuckle)
Not done yet, youngin'... That's gonna cost you an eye.

Stitch whips his head around as he hears an O.S. chanting, down the street:

CROWD (O.S.)
Jayne! Jayne! Jayne!

He hauls Simon toward the door.

STITCH
Come on.

EXT. CANTON STREET - DAY

The Mule drives by, as its riders witness the MASS OF MUDDERS thronging in the distance.

EXT. CANTON SQUARE - DAY

Jayne stands before his statue, arms upraised, amid a throng of MUDDERS, who chant his name.

CROWD
Jayne! Jayne! Jayne!

The Foreman and his PRODS stand in a tight snarl of hip-boots and truncheons. The Prod turns to the Foreman.

PROD
Come on, sir, let's just get in there and —

FOREMAN
No. Magistrate says no, so we hold position. Understand me?

The Prod and his ilk are chomping at the bit.

INT. SERENITY - CARGO BAY - DAY

THE MUDDERS

Costume designer Shawna Trpcic says that the biggest costume challenge in all of *Firefly* were the 'Jaynestown' Mudders. "We had to cover about 350 extras in mud each day and then collect those clothes at the end. We couldn't really wash them; we were able to anti-bacterialize the inside, so they could at least put clean clothes against the body. But it was pretty gross and muddy and really dirty. The mud is what we call 'clean mud' — it's a mixture that we made ourselves from a lot of different materials — and we splattered the clothes before the people came in. I had an ager, Julia Gombert, and she aged all the clothes and came out with us to the set and finished the job while people were wearing them so it looked more natural. We tried to use as much cotton as possible, mainly because a lot of it was rented, so we wanted to use something we could shake off and throw into the washing machine to save on the dry cleaning costs; also, to make sure we didn't destroy any fabrics, because we really had to respect our renters. So the costumes were cotton and wools — wools are pretty easy to clean, although they're not as easy to throw in a washing machine — and rubber, of course. Some of the stuff was from the movie *Waterworld*, which was supposed to be wet and gooey, so that was perfect, because it was already aged and it was rubber or plastic or something that could handle it."

Mal, Zoe, and Wash haul crates of STOLEN PROP up the ramp (off the Mule?) sweating from the honest labor of lifting. Mal slaps the top of the last crate with finality, breathing easy for the first time in a day.

MAL
Zoe, pack down this cargo. Wash, you heat up Serenity. We're blowin' this mess inside a' half an hour.

Wash heads off for the bridge.

WASH
Already there.

MAL
(to Kaylee)
Let's go get our wayward babes.

He turns and starts heading back out the door. Kaylee follows.

EXT. CANTON SQUARE - DAY

Meadows finally manages to quiet the townfolk. Meadows cries out.

MEADOWS
Speech!

CROWD
Speech! Speech!

A wave of public-speaking anxiety sweeps over Jayne, but he succumbs to the will of the people.

JAYNE
I'm no good with words. Don't use 'em much, myself...
(crowd chuckles)
But I want to thank y'all, for bein' here, and for thinking so much of me... Far as I see it, you people have been given the shortest end of a stick ever offered a human soul in this crap-heel 'verse... But you took that end, and you, you know... Well... You took it. And that's... I guess that's... somethin'.

Jayne nods. The crowd APPLAUDS. Kaylee and Mal have just arrived.

KAYLEE
Wow... That didn't sound half bad...

MAL
I'm shocked, my own self.

The applause halts as A SHOTGUN BLAST EXPLODES.

Stitch stands there, shotgun pointed skyward and smoking, Simon, bloody, held up by the scruff. He hurls Simon forward, he pitches into the dirt, barely conscious.

JAYNE
(moment of disbelief)
Stitch Hessian...

STITCH
Hey there, Jayne. Thought I'd make ya watch

while I butcher me one a' your boys.

Jayne looks down at Simon. He covers for him.

JAYNE
Ain't one'a mine, Stitch...

Stitch looks at Simon, then at Jayne, skeptical.

JAYNE (cont'd)
(mirthless chuckle)
Where you been hidin'? You gone and got yourself
lookin' mighty hideous...

STITCH
(laughs at it)
Yeah...

Stitch walks past Simon, squaring off with Jayne,
about twenty feet between them.

The Prods and the Foreman look on. The Prods are
jumpy, but they see that the Foreman is smiling.

FOREMAN
Yep. Now Jayne gets his...

Kaylee gets to Simon and gathers him up into her
arms.

SIMON
Kaylee —?

KAYLEE
Aw honey...

STITCH
So what's this 'bout the "Hero a' Canton"? Was I
hearin' that right? Four years' lock-down can play
tricks on the ears...

Jayne looks around at the crowd, their scared
eyes, remembering suddenly he has an audience.

JAYNE
Ain't no hero, Stitch. Just a workin' stiff like yourself...

STITCH
(fit of cackling)
Whoo! Yessir! Now that is funny...
(to the crowd)
Yep. He's right, Jayne is. Fact, we used to work
together, he an' I.

The crowd looks to Jayne, who seems to redden a
bit. Mal gets to the front of the crowd, about ten
paces from Stitch; he's too tuned in. He swings his
shotgun at Mal, covering him.

STITCH (cont'd)
Now you let ol' Stitch speak his piece.

Mal raises his hands slightly. Instinctively, Mal
knows he's dealing with a cold and deadly son-of-
a-bitch.

MAL
(slight nod)
Go on, then.

STITCH
Whole lotta money inna Magistrate's safe,
weren't there, Jayne?
(to crowd)
Got away clean too. But then our plane took a hit,
an' we were goin' down. Dumped the fuel reserve,
dumped the life support, hell we even dumped
the seats. Then there was Jayne, the money and
me. And there was no way he was gonna drop that
money...

MEADOWS
He did! He dropped it on the Mudders!

STITCH
By accident, you inbred dunghead! He tossed me
out first. We run together six months and he
turned on me 'fore I could scream.

JAYNE
You'd'a done the same.

STITCH
Not ever! You protect the man you're with — you
watch his back! Everybody knows that — 'cept the
"Hero of Canton".

JAYNE
You gonna talk me to death, buddy? That the plan?

Meadows turns to Jayne, eyes imploring him.
Jayne looks away. Jayne's hand is sliding up his
side, reaching for the hilt of his knife.

STITCH
This is the plan.

Stitch lifts up the shotgun, cocking it in the same
motion, and fires, square at Jayne.

Meadows hurls his body in the way, taking the
blast full in the chest.

END OF ACT THREE

ACT FOUR

EXT. CANTON SQUARE - DAY

Meadows falls, dead. Jayne throws his knife.

Knife whizzes through the air and catches Stitch
dead center in the chest. He staggers back, and
throws the spent gun to the side. He and Jayne
charge each other, ROARIN' LIKE BULLS.

Jayne catches him, they struggle. Jayne spins
Stitch, shoving him (he's beginning to flag from
the knife) back.

Jayne gets to his statue and starts smashing the
back of Stitch's head against it. Over and over. As
much as is showable, he Peckinpahs Stitch's sorry
ass.

The crowd, Mal, our crew, the Prods, everyone is
silent. Jayne rears up from the O.S. bloody mess of
his ex-partner, and turns to Meadows' body,
which lies in the mud near him. He starts to pick
him up, but the man flops, lifeless.

JAYNE
Get up you stupid piece-a — Get up!

Jayne looks down into Meadows' open, dead eyes.

The YOUNG BOY (thirteen, from the end of Act
One) stands over Stitch's body. He reaches for the
knife...

JAYNE (cont'd)
(still to Meadows)
What'd you do that for? What's wrong with you?
Didn't you hear a word he said? I'm a mean, dumb
sommbitch!

(drops the body)
An' you don't take no bullets for a dumb somm-bitch, you dumb sommbitch!

Jayne turns back to the crowd.

JAYNE (cont'd)
All of you! You think someone's just gonna drop money on ya, money they could use? There ain't people like that! There's just people like me.

Jayne turns to the boy, who holds his bloody knife out to him. Jayne takes it, seeing the unabated reverence in his eyes.

Jayne's eyes go wild for a beat. He walks past the boy, to his statue.

With a MIGHTY HEAVE he pushes it back, top-pling it, continuing on out, the others following.

INT. SERENITY - CARGO RAMP - DAY

They jog up the ramp, Kaylee helping Simon. Jayne stalks in after them, head down, silent. He just keeps walking. Mal hits the ship's comm.

MAL
Wash, we're in. Get us the hell offa this mud-ball.

WASH (O.S.)
(over intercom)
Uh... yeah... I'm — uh — workin' on that.

INT. SERENITY - BRIDGE - DAY

Wash's screens all flash: "LAND-LOCK"!

WASH
(to himself)
<Goo yang jong duh goo yang.> [Motherless goats of all motherless goats.]

He hits switches all over, trying to override it. Inara walks into the bridge.

INARA
Hello, Wash. Has there been any problem with take-off — ?

WASH
Is there a problem? Is there a problem?!

The "LAND-LOCK" message changes to "LAND-LOCK RELEASED". Wash sits up, calms down.

WASH (cont'd)
Uh, no. We're fine.

Inara just smiles as we hear the ENGINES START TO WARM UP.

EXT. HIGGINS' MOON - LANDING AREA - DAY

Serenity takes off, leaving this ugly-ass moon behind.

INT. HIGGINS' HACIENDA - DAY

Fess sits at the dining room table. His red-faced, furious father looms over him, barking. Fess smiles, relaxed.

HIGGINS
You did WHAT!?

FESS
I sent an override to Port Control. Lifted the land-lock on Serenity.

HIGGINS
I ought to tear that smile off your head! How dare you defy me! You — You —

FESS
You wanted to make a man of me, Dad. I guess it worked.

INT. SERENITY - PASSENGER DORM

River sits, reading intently — and ripping a page out, setting it beside her. Book passes, coming from his room with his taped together bible. He moves to speak —

RIVER
(not looking up)
Just keep walking, Preacher-man.

He does.

KAYLEE (O.S.)
You got to be steely.

INT. SERENITY - SIMON'S ROOM

It's darkish in here — intimate, as it's near bed time. Simon sits on his bed, a bandage on his cut forehead, a bit of a bloody eye. Kaylee touches his face, gently, as she talks.

KAYLEE
Can't be letting men stomp on you so much.

SIMON
Wasn't exactly a plan...

KAYLEE
You ain't weak — You couldn't beat him back? Or would that not be "appropriate"?

SIMON
You're never letting go of that, are you?

KAYLEE
Well you confound me some, is all. You like me well enough, we get along, and then you go all stiff.

SIMON
(misunderstanding)
I'm not — I didn't —

KAYLEE
See? You're doing it right now! What's so damn important about bein' proper? Don't mean noth-in' out here in the black.

SIMON
It means more out here. It's all I have. My way of being, polite or however — it's the only way I have of showing you that I like you. Of showing respect.

A beat as she takes this in.

KAYLEE
So when we made love last night —

SIMON
(ack!)
When we what?

KAYLEE
(laughing)
You really are such an easy mark.

INT. SERENITY - CARGO BAY - NIGHT

Jayne stands looking at his knife on the catwalk above the bay. Mal walks in, Jayne sees him, sheathes the knife. Mal rests his hands on the rail by him. Then, after a long beat.

JAYNE
Don't make no sense.
(beat)
Why the hell'd that Mudder go an' do that, Mal? Jumpin' in front a' that shotgun blast. Weren't a one of them understood what happened out there — hell, they're probably stickin' that statue right back up.

MAL
Most like.

JAYNE
Don't know why that eats at me so...

MAL
It's my estimation that every man ever got a' stat-ue made of him was one kind of sommbitch or another. Ain't about you, Jayne. 'Bout what they need.

Beat as Jayne takes this in. Neither man moves.

JAYNE
Don't make no sense.

END OF SHOW

THE BALLAD OF SERENITY

The Firefly Theme Song

JOSS WHEDON

I think you can sum up the compromise we made with the network in terms of the theme song, which has kind of a pumped-up orchestration for what it is. It's a very downbeat song. It should have been one guy and a twangy acoustic guitar, really dampened, and instead, it's almost like the theme for an action show. It's got all these instruments and all this momentum; it's a little bigger than that song actually should be. It's well-done, it's well-produced, it's not a dig. Quite frankly, I thought they were going to make me throw it out [laughs] — I was amazed they let me do it at all. But we were worried and there was some talk about, 'Well, we want to make sure that it's peppy.' Because it was written as a very downbeat number, before the pilot. The day I sold the idea of the show to the network, I came home and wrote that song, then started work on the pilot. It's a song of life in defeat, and that's kind of what the show is about. It's about people who have been either economically or politically or emotionally beaten down in one way or another and how they cling to each other and how they fail each other and how they rebuild themselves. I wrote it so that it could be sung as a Civil War lament, and yet — 'Take me out in the black' could be space, could be death. It's basically a way of saying, 'We've lost.' Which is not usually what you come in humming in most of your shows.

GREG EDMONSON

Composer Greg Edmonson: "I did the arrangement and called all the players and got them in and we just worked it out as best we could. The vocalist was Joss's pick. He found this really interesting guy, Sonny Rhodes. Very famous people wanted to sing this, but Joss found Sonny and stuck with him. We had Charlie Bischerod on fiddle; Lee Sklar, who's very famous, on bass, John Goux and Craig Stull played guitar, and Brad Dutz played percussion. There are no drums, per se — it's a guy beating on found percussion — a hubcap, a can. We were trying to make music with what we had. We did cheat on the guitars, because we needed to tune them up a little bit, but that was the approach, not some big bombastic pop song.

"I think Joss always saw this as a lone black man sitting on the front porch, kind of like Leadbelly, singing this post-apocalyptic song. However, the network envisioned this as an action series and so they wanted a theme song [he imitates driving action music], 'Tonight on *Firefly*!' And so the final theme song was as much of a compromise as could be done and Joss still be able to live with it. And you can hear that if you listen. You can hear it in the way it flows and in the way it could have been one single black man with an acoustic guitar singing this song." Although, there are some swirling fiddles in there. "Well, there are *now*," Edmonson laughs. "That was the compromise."

The Ballad of Serenity
By Joss Whedon

Take my love
Take my land
Take me where I cannot stand
I don't care
I'm still free
You can't take the sky from me

Take me out
To the black
Tell 'em I ain't coming back
Burn the land
And boil the sea
You can't take the sky from me

Have no place
I can be
Since I found Serenity
But you can't take the sky from me

PRODUCTION DESIGN

An interview with Carey Meyer

THANKS LONI!

❖ Above: A photo of the original concept model of Serenity, which Carey Meyer gave to Loni Peristere.

❖ Opposite: This model of Serenity was formed using a rapid-prototyping method, by computer-guided laser from layers of laminated paper. It has the apparent density of wood and is finished in grey primer spraypaint. It was used to envision scenes involving the ship during the planning stages of an episode.

Production designer Carey Meyer was no stranger to Joss Whedon when he was tapped to work on *Firefly*. "I had been designing *Buffy the Vampire Slayer* for about five years," Meyer explains. "I'd come on as the art director in the first season and stayed on as the designer for the subsequent seasons after that. Joss asked me if I would like to work on *Firefly* and if I could put forward some concept art in terms of the design of the spaceship. He gave me a couple of pointers on what he was thinking, and so we started doing some concept boards. From that I was able to convince him that I could do it. This was in mid-December and we really needed to get a jump on it, because our shoot date was early February."

The design of Serenity was the chief concern, Meyer says. "Joss wanted it to have an insect feel, an ugly duckling feeling, a really battered, run-through-the-wringer feel. Also, he had very strong ideas about how the ship was constructed and put together spatially. He wanted the spaceship to be another character in the show."

There were a lot of discussions between Meyer, Whedon and Loni Peristere of CGI firm Zoic, Meyer relates. "We created illustrations from the concept model. From that, it went directly into somebody working on a computer, and going back and forth between myself and Loni and Joss, and that started to dictate how the exterior looked. We did build some of the exterior, mainly the landing gear and the faces of the two large jet engines, and so once they

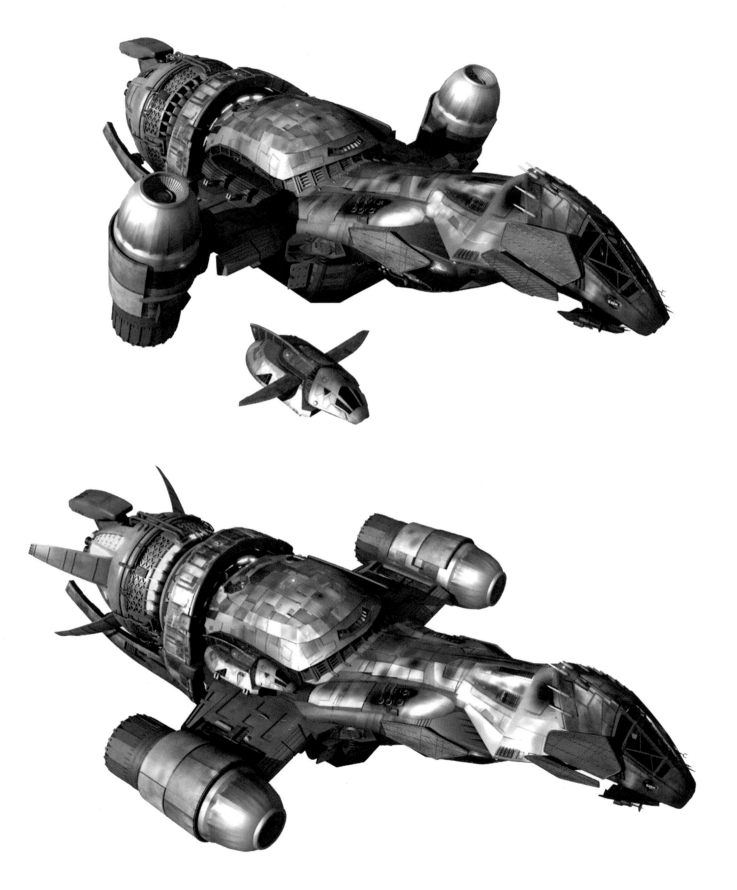

were actually finished in the design process in the CG environment, we were able to reverse-engineer that and construct a match to it on the exterior of the ship — where you had to have the cargo bay door that comes down and lands on the ground, the two large engines and the two feet that land in front.

"We ended up taking some very large pieces of landing gear and two arms that were extremely heavy from an airplane junkyard. Once we had located that large piece of landing gear, we were able to go back to the CG guys and say, 'Well, this is what we're going to use and we can add this, based on the design that you guys are working with, but this has to change a little bit to match what we've got...' It just went back and forth until we all locked in on something. So what did actually exist on the set were those two large arms that came out of the side of the ship and then came down to two large feet that were on the ground. We mostly hid them underneath set dressing, bushes or snow, wherever we were, because they didn't really look anything like what the feet of the landing gear looked like in the CG environment.

"We ended up filming pretty much only the interior," Meyer continues, "although we did build the exterior of what we coined 'the tortoiseshell', the very middle top of the ship, which was the dome over the galley. We built that, and the windows that looked into that room, for an episode ['Objects in Space'] where we really needed to isolate in-camera photography, where you had a lot of actors on the exterior of the ship."

"We completely built the interior and it mostly had breakaway walls, although, because it's such a very tight and complicated space, there were several areas where it didn't break away; it was not like an ordinary set, where you just have four walls and each wall can be removed."

It was Whedon's idea, Meyer says, to build one contiguous set for Serenity's lower deck and another for the upper deck. "Joss always said he wanted to try to go from point A to point B, from the front of the ship all the way to the back. I think even in the pilot, we tried to go from the upstairs all the way to the cargo bay in one shot.

❖ Opposite: A 3D mesh render of Serenity.

❖ Above: The Serenity exterior on the *Firefly* set.

❖ Left: The design for the exterior of the ship.

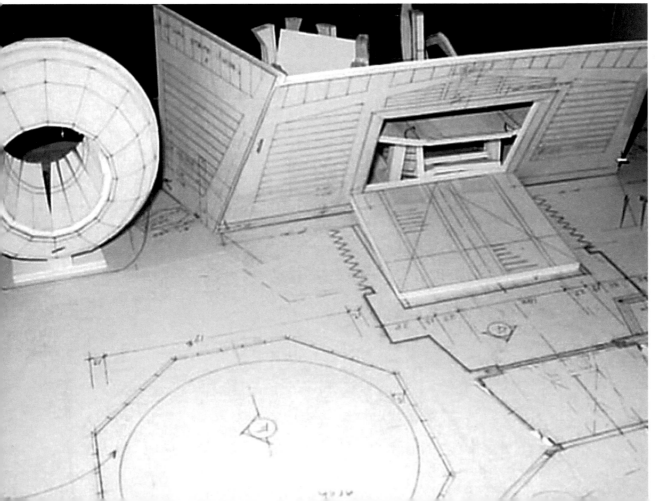

FIREFLY MODEL 01
REFURBISHED THROUGH HANG CHI YARDS

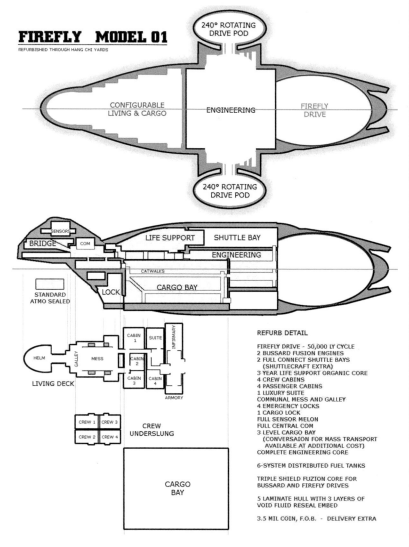

240° ROTATING DRIVE POD

CONFIGURABLE LIVING & CARGO — ENGINEERING — FIREFLY DRIVE

240° ROTATING DRIVE POD

SENSORS
BRIDGE   COM   LIFE SUPPORT   SHUTTLE BAY
ENGINEERING
CATWALKS
LOCK   CARGO BAY
STANDARD ATMO SEALED

HELM   GALLEY   MESS   CABIN 1   SUITE   INFIRMARY
CABIN 2
CABIN 3   CABIN 4
LIVING DECK   ARMORY

CREW 1   CREW 3
CREW 2   CREW 4   CREW UNDERSLUNG

CARGO BAY

REFURB DETAIL

FIREFLY DRIVE - 50,000 LY CYCLE
2 BUSSARD FUSION ENGINES
2 FULL CONNECT SHUTTLE BAYS
   (SHUTTLECRAFT EXTRA)
3 YEAR LIFE SUPPORT ORGANIC CORE
4 CREW CABINS
4 PASSENGER CABINS
1 LUXURY SUITE
COMMUNAL MESS AND GALLEY
4 EMERGENCY LOCKS
1 CARGO LOCK
FULL SENSOR MELON
FULL CENTRAL COM
3 LEVEL CARGO BAY
   (CONVERSAION FOR MASS TRANSPORT
    AVAILABLE AT ADDITIONAL COST)
COMPLETE ENGINEERING CORE

6-SYSTEM DISTRIBUTED FUEL TANKS

TRIPLE SHIELD FUZION CORE FOR
BUSSARD AND FIREFLY DRIVES

5 LAMINATE HULL WITH 3 LAYERS OF
VOID FLUID RESEAL EMBED

3.5 MIL COIN, F.O.B. - DELIVERY EXTRA

❖ This page clockwise from the top: A diagram of the interior of a Model 01 Firefly; part of the exterior of Serenity; the corridor leading from the bridge to the galley; the infirmary looking towards the door.

❖ Opposite page top: The design for Inara's shuttle.

❖ Opposite page below: The design for the Reaver ship.

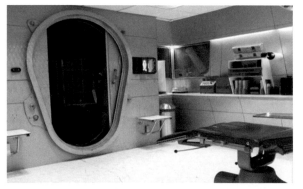

Obviously there was a cut, because we had to go from the upper-floor stage to the lower, but we tried to make it a seamless cut and make it feel like it was all one continuous set. That went along with the whole concept of trying to feel the space and not to break walls away, to try to light from within the existing space. It became an overall approach for everybody."

It was certainly the approach adopted by *Firefly* director of photography David Boyd, Meyer notes. "David was very interested in trying to shoot the space as it was and trying not to break the walls away for camera and/or lighting. David and I had a very similar approach in that sense. We both wanted to not only see but also light and shoot the space as it was. He went out of his way to work within the confines of the space, and to let the camera feel that. He went with Arriflex cameras, which are smaller, and he did a lot of handheld, so they weren't on a dolly — which takes up a lot more room and requires a lot more mechanics to move the camera around. So when you see scenes inside Serenity, a lot of it is handheld. That was a conscious choice, not only because it helped give it a more visceral feel and a documentary feel, but also because it really enabled you to feel the space a little bit more realistically."

Asked to sum up his *Firefly* design experience, Meyer concludes, "It was *the* most challenging project I've ever worked on and to that extent, the most fun I've ever had designing anything, and certainly the most fun TV show that I've ever worked on." ◉

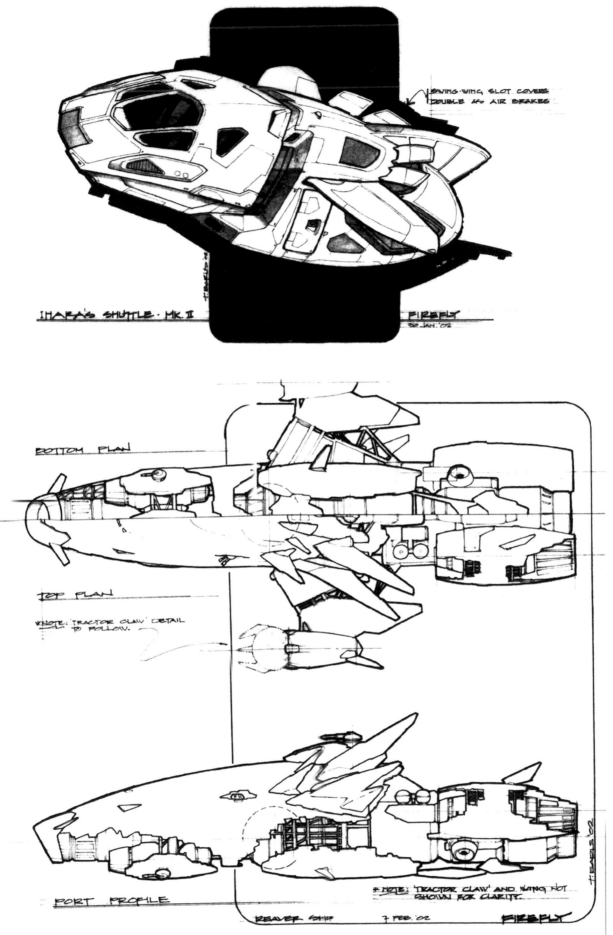

INARA'S SHUTTLE · MK. II

UPPER-WING SLOT COVERS
DOUBLE AS AIR BRAKES

FIREFLY
30 JAN. '02

BOTTOM PLAN

TOP PLAN

NOTE: 'TRACTOR CLAW' DETAIL TO FOLLOW.

PORT PROFILE

*NOTE: 'TRACTOR CLAW' AND WING NOT SHOWN FOR CLARITY.

REAVER SHIP   7 FEB. '02   FIREFLY

OUT OF GAS

Written by Tim Minear
Directed by David Solomon

TIM MINEAR

"It's my favorite," Minear reveals. "It was a really hard episode to break. I remember it took us days to figure out what it was. Joss had this notion of them running out of gas. He wanted to do an episode where they just got stuck in the middle of nothing. I remember initially his idea was that they would come across another ship that could be them, not literally, but another ship of possibly pirates. And to show what makes our people different from your average ship of pirates: that was what the story was going to be. I was having a lot of trouble with it. I thought it wouldn't go anywhere and it would turn into a play and I wasn't that interested. I remember we were having dinner, which we often did when we couldn't figure stuff out. We would go eat! Joss said, 'Can it start with Mal being gut-shot?' I'm like, 'Cool! Now, I'm interested... How did that happen?' We started talking about flashbacks and how it would be flashbacks to the core crew and how they came on board. It was that simple, and once we figured that out, it was pretty easy to figure out what the beats were."

The episode also reflected Mal's deep connection with and love of his ship. "His love affair with Serenity was in other episodes, so it's not like it was a new thing in that episode, but it's the way it starts and the way it ends. He is shot, and he's remembering the first time he brought Zoe onto the ship and talking about what it means: freedom, a life, tomorrow — it's everything. The fact that he won't abandon the ship,

Inara mistakes it for some kind of old sea captain chivalry, but that really wasn't what it was. It was, 'If the ship goes down, then I go down anyway. I'm not leaving it, not when there is a chance of saving it.'

"I've heard people say 'Out of Gas' should have come sooner, but I disagree. I don't think it would have resonated because you didn't know the crew yet.

"It's not that thick on plot. If you think about it, the story is really simple. As far as the flashbacks go, again they feel like they are moving the story forward, but it's in a very elliptical, poetic way. I do remember when we sent it to the network they didn't like it. They wanted it in chronological order and I had to try to explain to them: 'If you think you are confused, wait until you try to put this in chronological order. There is no chronological order! It's jumping around all over the place and it makes sense the way it's structured.' Basically, what I told Joss was that if they force us to do this thing, 'I quit. I'm done.' He said, 'I support you.' And then they didn't ask us to change it; I think at that point they didn't care enough about the show to fight it. My feeling was that if they don't get this, they'll never get it. We weren't canceled yet, but we were seeing the writing on the wall. We made a web commercial of Mal sending out a mayday for people to watch the show. We made that when making 'Out of Gas'. It gave us the idea to do the mayday actually."

TEASER

EXT. SPACE

Serenity in the Big Black of space. She might seem a bit cock-eyed to us at the moment. No engine movement. She's less floating and more just kind of hanging there. Either near dead — or hurt real bad. Reserve emergency power gives it just a flicker of life. As we nose closer, we peer into the bridge. No sign of anyone...

INT. SERENITY - UPPER DECKS

Various shots of the ship. Quietly holding silent images.

The cockpit: empty.

Looking down the body of the upper decks — no one in sight.

The dining area — evidence of recent habitation. A dinner party was in progress, but seemingly cut short. The table is askew. Dishes and an uncut cake have all crashed to the floor. But not a soul here.

The engine room. The entrance and walls are

scorched. The big turbine sits silent. No movement.

INT. SERENITY - BELOW DECKS

It looks like a tornado blew through here. In the common area: debris is everywhere, furniture is upturned, caught up against walls. But no sign of anyone anywhere. The ship seems eerily abandoned. Until finally we go to —

INT. SERENITY - CARGO BAY

More debris. More strewn cargo. And then —

MAL

falls INTO FRAME, landing hard on the floor of the cargo bay. Sweating, pale, somewhat delirious. And alone.

(We may or may not notice a piece of an engine part lying nearby.)

He struggles to stay conscious; it's a struggle he's not winning at the moment. As we PUSH IN closer to his feverish face, we start to HEAR what HE HEARS... VOICES IN HIS HEAD:

SALESMAN (V.O.)
Yep. A real beauty, ain't she? Yessir. A right smart purchase, this vessel. Tell you what, you buy this ship, treat her proper, she'll be with ya for the rest of your life.

Mal smiles weakly at the memory — or possibly the irony. Now the SOUND of the AIRLOCK DOORS, KER-CHUNK! A sliver of DAYLIGHT hits him in the face. The light UNFOLDS, growing, blinding him. He squints against it, as —

INT. SERENITY - CARGO BAY

THE AIRLOCK DOORS open, revealing two FIGURES, SILHOUETTED by sunlight, BLUE SKY behind them. (The ramp is down, and it seems we're planetside someplace.)

The figures step onto the ship — and now we see that it's Mal and ZOE. They enter the cargo bay. They might look slightly different than we're used to, because it's now a few years earlier.

Zoe steps deeper into the ship, takes it all in, as if for the first time. In fact, this is the first time she's set foot on Serenity. Mal watches for her reaction.

They are the only two here. The cargo bay itself is

now TOTALLY EMPTY. Big, empty and echoey. And everything's covered with a thick layer of dust.

MAL
Well?

ZOE
(after a good long look)
You paid money for this... On purpose?

MAL
Come on, Zoe. Serious. Whaddya think?

ZOE
Honestly, sir. I think you were robbed.

MAL
Robbed? What, no! What do you mean?

ZOE
Sir, it's a piece of <fei-oo.> [junk.]

MAL
<Fei-oo?> [Junk?] Okay. So she won't win any beauty contests, that's true enough. But she's solid. Ship like this, be with ya til the day you die.

ZOE
Yessir. Because it's a deathtrap.

MAL
That's not... You are very much lacking in imagination.

ZOE
I imagine that's so, sir.

MAL
C'mon. You ain't even seen most of it. I'll show you the rest.
(as they go)
Try to see past what she is, on to what she can be.

ZOE
What's that, sir?

MAL
Freedom, is what.

ZOE
(pointing)
No, I meant — what's that?

He looks down, sees something we don't need to see, something he was about to step in.

MAL
Oh. Just step around it. I think something must've been living in here.

As they move off:

MAL (cont'd)
I tell ya, Zoe, we find ourselves a mechanic, get her running again. Hire on a good pilot. Maybe even a cook. Live like people. Small crew, them as feel the need to be free. Take jobs as they come — and we'll never be under the heel of nobody ever again. No matter how long the arm of the Alliance might get... we'll just get us a little further.

ZOE
Get her running "again"?

MAL
Yeah.

ZOE
Sooo... not running now?

MAL
Not so much.
(then)
But she will.

He moves deeper into the ship, back toward the common area/infirmary. She follows. We don't, we stay in the cargo bay and let them move off.

MAL (cont'd)
I even know what I'm gonna call her.
(they're OFF SCREEN by now, fainter)
Got a name all picked out...

That last bit trailing off as their footsteps recede. We assume he's telling her the chosen name, but now they're too far away for us to make it out. We do, however, hear a BURST of LAUGHTER from off-screen Zoe.

As the LAUGHTER echoes and fades, CAMERA BOOMS DOWN to a TIGHT FACE in the FORE-GROUND...

...Mal, back in the present day, curled up on the cargo bay floor, wincing in his pain... CAMERA MOVES down his body, and now WE SEE the wound... gut-shot. Blood, almost black, bubbles at his abdomen.

A thick drop of Mal's blood drips through the grating on the cargo bay floor...

...and falls into —

BLACKNESS

END OF TEASER

ACT ONE

INT. SERENITY - CARGO BAY

Where Mal's breathing is coming in sharp, painful gasps. He reaches for the fallen engine part that lies nearby. Grabs it and starts dragging himself back toward the infirmary. Above him, echoey GROUP LAUGHTER from somewhere in the ship.

CAMERA moves off the crawling Mal, RISES, passing through darkness, moving toward the sounds of joviality, the LAUGHTER becoming more present, until we are:

INT. SERENITY - DINING AREA

Mid LAUGHTER BURST from the assembled. A communal dinner. Or what's left of it. Gathered are: Mal, Zoe, JAYNE, KAYLEE, SIMON, RIVER, INARA and BOOK. Book has been telling them a story and they're all in stitches.

ZOE
(laughing so hard it hurts)
No, no, no. That is not true.

BOOK
I swear it is!

INARA
(catching her breath)
Surely one of you must have told him!

RON GLASS

The scene was that we were all supposed to be sitting around the table where we ate. It was supposed to open with everybody responding to a joke I had told, so they were supposed to be laughing really, really hard. The first time we did it, they said, 'action' and I started this laugh and I started to look around and get everybody to join in and they were all looking at me like I was nuts. So, of course, it takes a moment to hit that it's a practical joke. It became clear that Nathan has told everybody, 'Let's not laugh!' That was really fun and funny. It helped keep a certain kind of camaraderie and good spirits on the set. It's not in my nature. I'm not a practical joker. I can appreciate them but I don't do them.

BOOK
No! There wasn't one among the brethren had the heart to say anything. He was so proud of it!

LAUGHTER. WASH enters from the bridge, the guy who missed the joke. He smiles/laughs clueless along with them.

WASH
What? What was he proud of? Who he?

BOOK
(tears from the laughing)
Looked rather natty, truth be told!

Another explosion of laughter. It's contagious. Even for Wash, who's still anxious to be let in on the joke.

WASH
(as he sits)
I want to hear about the natty thing.
(reaches for serving bowl)
What was natty?

Book gets his laughter under control, takes a drink, waves Wash away with a "nothing, nothing" gesture.

KAYLEE
Shepherd Book was just tellin' funny stories about his days at the monastery.

WASH
Monastic humor. I miss out on all the fun.
(sees serving bowl is empty)
And all the food, too, apparently...

ZOE
Now just who do you think you're married to?

Zoe lifts a napkin off a plate piled with food.

WASH
I love my wife.

He kisses her. They sit close, a couple, easy and relaxed. He digs in.

MAL
So we got a course set?

WASH
We do. Took a little creative navigating, but we should make it all the way to Greenleaf without running afoul of any Alliance patrols. Or a single living soul, for that matter.

MAL
Good. Way it should be.

WASH
'Course, what should be an eighteen hour trip's gonna take the better part of a week by this route.

MAL
We're in no rush. I like an easy, languorous journey.

Kaylee rises, picks up some plates.

KAYLEE
What would that be like, I wonder?

SIMON
(moves to assist)
Let me help you with that —

KAYLEE
Not a bit. In fact, it's your turn.

SIMON
(clueless)
My turn...?

KAYLEE
Shepherd told a funny story 'bout bein' a preacher. Now you tell a funny story about being a doctor.

SIMON
Funny story...

JAYNE
Yeah, 'cos sick people are high-larious.

SIMON
Well, they can be...
(chuckles)
In fact, I remember there was this one time I was working the E.R. and this fellow, very upright sort of citizen, comes in complaining of...

JAYNE
(interrupts)
Now Inara — she's gotta have some real funny whorin' stories, I'd wager.

INARA
Oh! Do I ever! Funny and sexy! You have no idea!
(then, deadpanny)
And you never will.

Zoe SNORTS with laughter. She likes the dissing of Jayne.

INARA (cont'd)
I don't discuss my clients.

JAYNE
Aww, come on 'Nara. Who'd know?

INARA
You.
(then)
Anyway, a Companion doesn't kiss and tell.

MAL
So there is kissing?

She shoots him a look — and a half smile. He smiles back.

ZOE
Hey, Doc?

He looks at her. She's nestled nice and close to her hubby.

ZOE (cont'd)
(nods behind Simon toward:)
I think maybe our Kaylee could use your help after all —

He turns and is surprised to see her carrying aloft a sweetly pathetic ship-made birthday cake with miss-matched candles ablaze.

KAYLEE
Care to make the first incision, Doctor Tam?
(then)
Happy birthday, Simon.

EVERYONE
(variously)
Happy birthday! Yeah, many more. Happy birthday, son.

Simon reacts, taken aback. It's clear they all knew.

SIMON
Well this is... I didn't... How did you know?
(glances to:)
River, did you — ?

RIVER
"Day" is a vestigial mode of time measurement. Based on solar cycles. Not applicable.
(then)
I didn't get you anything.

WASH
I'm afraid it was me who ratted you out, Doctor.

SIMON
You?

MAL
Seems a fresh warrant for your arrest come up on the Cortex. Had your birth date attached right to it.

SIMON
Oh. I see. Well. That's...
(worried)
Really?

KAYLEE
(re: the cake)
Hope you like it. Couldn't get a hold of no flour, so it's mostly protein. In fact, it's pretty much what we just had for supper. But I tried to make the

frosting as chocolatey tasting as possible.

He looks at Kaylee. It's very warm and wonderful.

SIMON
Thank you. I'm really very deeply moved.

Kaylee beams her Kaylee-ness right back at him.

JAYNE
Well deeply move yourself over there and blow out them candles so we can try a slice.

SIMON
Right...

KAYLEE
Come on, Doc. Give a good blow.

He does a slight take. She's sort of poker-faced. He smiles, nods, leans forward, is about to blow out the candles, when... something makes a ghastly noise deep inside the ship. A GRINDING back near the engine. The power DIMS and FLICKERS, the engine stops...

A beat. They all pause at this pregnant moment. Then the familiar HUM of the engines again.

JAYNE
What the hell was that?

KAYLEE
Maybe just a hiccup. I'll check it out.

She sets down the cake on the counter. Starts to move off.

WASH
(rising)
I'll take a look at the helm.

Now he heads off toward the bridge. River is staring at the cake.

RIVER
Fire...

Simon glances at her, then back to the cake. The candles.

SIMON
Right. Okay, okay...

He leans in to blow out the candles and —

Kaylee is stepping up to the door that leads to the aftdeck hall —

BOOOOM! A horrific EXPLOSION from the back of the ship, at the engine room.

Zoe is on her feet in an instant. She lunges for Kaylee as —

— a giant BALL OF FIRE roils from the back of the ship, filling the aft corridor. Zoe shoves Kaylee clear of the doorway, but the big ass FIREBALL bursts at the doorway. Zoe is knocked back hard by the concussion of the blast, her body glancing off the dinner table, then hitting a wall — goddamn hard. Wash comes running back from the

foredeck hall —

WASH
Zoe!

Everyone's a bit disoriented. Wash flies to his wife's side. Inara and Book move to Kaylee, who was shoved out of the way pretty damn hard.

Mal has run over to the aftdeck doorway. Feels another ERUPTION coming —

ANOTHER FIRE BALL growing down there, exploding toward us. Mal forces the big metal door shut, latches it just before it hits. He's knocked back by the blast that impacts on the other side of the closed door.

RIVER
Fire... fire...

Mal turns, sees that Simon is already with Wash at the downed Zoe.

WASH
Zoe, honey, talk to me — you gotta talk to me, baby...

Mal passes Jayne as he hoofs it toward the bridge, pausing only long enough to say:

MAL
Seal off everything that leads below decks. Do it now.

Jayne moves to do that. Mal runs to the bridge —

INT. SERENITY - BRIDGE

Mal works some controls on the console —

EXT. SPACE

As the ramp lowers into space, while —

INT. SERENITY - ENGINE ROOM

The fire rages —

INT. SERENITY - DINING AREA

Wash is beside himself, has his wife's limp hand pressed between his. Simon's feeling for a pulse.

WASH
She gonna be okay?

SIMON
I need my med kit.

Simon rises, turns toward the aftdeck, sees that the door is shut.

KAYLEE
(shakes her head)
We got fire.

He turns, moves to the foredeck, steps up to —

FOREDECK DOOR

Jayne is just coming up from around the corner where he's sealed off that exit.

JAYNE
Where you think you're going?

SIMON
Zoe's badly hurt. I need my medical supplies.

JAYNE
Sorry, Doc. Nobody leaves.

SIMON
If you don't let me through, she could die.

JAYNE
I let you through — and we all die.

Off this stand off —

INT. SERENITY - BRIDGE

Mal continues to work the ship's controls, as —

INT. SERENITY - CARGO BAY

The AIRLOCK DOORS open, revealing the black of space and now —

INT. SERENITY - ENGINE ROOM/ AFTDECK/ STAIRS

The fire becomes a SNAKE as it is sucked down toward the lower deck, toward the vacuum of space, making sharp, violent turns —

INT. SERENITY - COMMON AREA/INFIRMARY

As the SNAKE OF FIRE races down the stairs, whips past the infirmary, furniture and not-nailed-down items getting sucked along with it, and into —

INT. SERENITY - CARGO BAY

The pillar of fire goes ROARING through the cargo bay and, along with some loose cargo, is spit out into space —

EXT. SPACE

As the snake of fire shoots out of the cargo bay, dissipating in cold space.

INT. SERENITY - BRIDGE

Mal watches through the bridge window as the fire shoots out, extinguishing itself in the void. He sighs.

INT. SERENITY - CARGO BAY

As the ramp closes and the airlock doors close. The storm is over.

CUT TO:

INT. SERENITY

Mal ENTERS from the cargo bay, staggering down the steps, every step more laborious than the last. CAMERA LEADS HIM as he reaches the bottom of the steps, turns towards the infirmary.

CAMERA ANGLES DOWN past Mal's face, down his chest to his midsection, where his bloody hand clutches at his stomach wound. Blood seeps through his fingers. He holds the catalyzer in his other hand.

He struggles to make it to the closed infirmary doors. He reaches to open the doors, and as they start to slide open —

CUT TO:

INT. SERENITY - COMMON AREA/INFIRMARY

BAM! The infirmary door is shoved open and Mal, Wash and Jayne carry in the unconscious Zoe, place her on the examination table. Simon gets right to work.

Everyone else is close at hand, variously in the infirmary and lingering outside in the common area.

SIMON
No sign of burning. Must be internal. I'll have to do a scan.

He starts hooking her up to his equipment. Wash at his side, concern etched on his face. Mal fades back, away from the activity there, to...

COMMON AREA

Kaylee is hovering just outside the door of the infirmary in the common area. Mal approaches her.

MAL
Kaylee. Kaylee.

She's in shock. Staring.

MAL (cont'd)
Look at me.

She does.

MAL (cont'd)
I need you up in the engine room, figuring out what caused this.

KAYLEE
(feeling it)
She ain't movin' —

Mal glances from spacey Kaylee to Zoe through the glass. His attention is drawn back to Kaylee by:

KAYLEE (cont'd)
Serenity's not movin'.

Mal realizes she meant the ship, not Zoe. Nods, keeping cool.

MAL
I know it. Which is why we gotta suss out what it was happened so we can get her going again, right?

She nods. Tries not to cry.

MAL (cont'd)
Think you can do that?

KAYLEE
Yes, Cap'n.

MAL
That's a good girl.

Kaylee gathers herself, heads off. Mal turns his attention back to:

INFIRMARY

Simon works on Zoe. Wash is at his wife's side, inches from out-of-his-mind with distress.

WASH
Come on, baby. Stay with me. You're strong. Strongest person I've ever met. You can do this.

JAYNE
She gonna make it?

SIMON
Please. I need to work.

Mal appears at the door.

MAL
Wash.

Wash won't look away from his wife.

MAL (cont'd)
Wash, I need you on the bridge.

WASH
Zoe's hurt.

MAL
And the Doctor's gonna do everything he can. Meantime, I gotta have you on that bridge. We need to know how bad it is.

Wash laughs grimly to himself, under his breath.

WASH
(turning on him)
How bad? It's bad, okay, "sir"? My wife may be dying, here. So my feeling is it's pretty damn bad.

MAL
Wash...

WASH
I'm not leaving her, Mal. Don't ask me again.

MAL
(no joy in this)
I wasn't askin'. I was tellin'.

WASH
(without looking back)
<Chur ni-duh.> [Screw you.]

Mal sighs. Reaches in, grabs Wash by the shirt, swings him around, shoves him up against a wall.

For all the physicality of that, Mal is calm, cool.

MAL
You're gonna get to the bridge and get us on our feet, because if we can't do for Zoe here, you're gonna have to be the one that saves her.

Well, yeah there's tension right about now. Simon continues to minister to Zoe. No one else says a word. Mal eases off. Wash's back is now to the infirmary door. A beat.

He goes, just totally fucking torn up inside. Mal looks back to the faces looking back at him, then he exits, too.

INT. SERENITY - BRIDGE

We're looking at Wash's pilot's chair. Empty at the moment. CAMERA moves off that to find... Wash on his back, examining the cockpit innards. His face is somewhat obscured from us.

He's speaking to someone who is O.S., also he seems much calmer than he did moments before.

WASH
Oh, yeah. This is all very do-able.

Wash slides out — and the first thing we notice is the big, bushy moustache. He stands and now WE SEE, outside the cockpit windows, BLUE SKY. We're parked someplace in the day again.

WASH (cont'd)
Shouldn't be a problem at all. A few modifications, get some real maneuverability out of this boat. You'd be surprised.

Mal and Zoe stand at the cockpit door as Wash looks the vessel over.

MAL
So you'll take the job, then?

As Wash sits into the pilot's chair, gives it a little swivel.

WASH
Might do, might do. Think I'm startin' to get a feel here.

MAL
Good. Well, take all the time you need. Make yourself at home. Fiddle with them dials. We'll be nearby.

Wash swivels away from them. Fiddles with dials.

MAL AND ZOE

moving away from the cockpit, down the foredeck, toward the dining area as they confer —

MAL (cont'd)
He's great, ain't he?

ZOE
I don't like him.

MAL
(taken aback)

CINEMATOGRAPHY

Director of photography David Boyd: "For the flashback sequences, we shot color reversal film, Fuji Velvia, to give it that very contrasty, old look, almost like our own kind of 'flashbacks'. If we look at our old home movies in Kodachrome, it would give it that idea. It's a white-white and a black-black, and the colors are very saturated, very vibrant and colorful."

What?

ZOE
Something about him bothers me.

MAL
(losing patience)
What? What about him bothers you?

ZOE
Not sure. Just... something.

MAL
Well, your "somethin'" comes up against a list of recommendations long as my leg. Tanaka raved about the guy. Renshaw's been trying to get him on his crew for a month. And we need us a pilot.

ZOE
I understand, sir. He bothers me.

MAL
Look, we finally got ourselves a genius mechanic, now it's about time we hired someone to fly the damn thing.

A BUFFED, SURFER-ISH DUDE, BESTER, passes through frame.

BESTER
(nodding "excellent!")
"Genius". No one's ever called me that before. Shiny.

Zoe doesn't even register that Bester passed by. She's musing on Wash in the distance.

ZOE
(musing on Wash)

Just bothers me.

INT. SERENITY - INFIRMARY - HEART MONITOR

Starts to BEEP AN ALERT. Zoe's hooked up to the equipment now. Simon reacts.

SIMON
Her heart's stopped...

INARA, BOOK AND JAYNE

looking on, helpless. Nervous.

BOOK
Maybe someone should get her husband down here...

MAL
No.

They see Mal has appeared. He moves into the infirmary. Simon's racing around the infirmary, grabbing things.

MAL (cont'd)
What do you need, Doc?

As Simon chooses a vial of something from several —

SIMON
(pointing)
Top cabinet —

Mal pulls it open. Sees a large hypo. Big needle.

SIMON (cont'd)
That's the one.

He hands it to Simon who doses it up.

INARA
What is it?

SIMON
Pure adrenaline —

Simon readies himself, poises the needle right

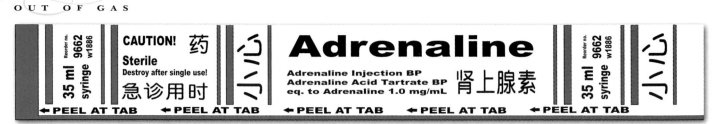

❖ Above: The label on the adrenaline hypodermic needle packaging.

over Zoe's heart. Ready for the *Pulp Fiction* moment? 'Cause that's always funny.

Inara turns away.

Simon plunges the needle in. Zoe's body JOLTS and we

HARD CUT TO:

INT. SERENITY - INFIRMARY

MAL HOWLS in pain. He's alone in the infirmary, sitting on the edge of the examination table, wrapping a bandage around his midsection, it's quickly filling with blood. He breathes hard, then tries to rise. He nearly passes out merely from that.

He manages to steady himself, moves to the counter, rummages around in some of Simon's supplies — comes up with the big ass needle that we saw Simon shoot up Zoe with. He injects himself. Has violent reaction.

CLOSE — MAL

His eyes wide, wide awake. He blinks, fueled with the stuff. Now he moves to the engine part that we saw him dragging. It's near the door. He picks it up, but looks toward the infirmary door, as:

KAYLEE (O.S.)
Cap?

INT. SERENITY - INFIRMARY/COMMON AREA

Earlier that day. Mal turns away from the table where Zoe lies. Now the medical monitor beeps a constant, steady rhythm. The crisis seems past. Mal moves to Kaylee at the infirmary door. She looks pale, worried. Bad news a'comin'. They step into —

COMMON AREA

KAYLEE
Zoe gonna be okay?

MAL
You let the Doctor worry about Zoe. Tell me what you know.

KAYLEE
Catalyzer on the port compression coil blew. That's where the trouble started.

MAL
I need that in Captain Dummy talk, Kaylee.

KAYLEE
We're dead in the water.

MAL
Can you fix it?

KAYLEE
I could try...

MAL
Just get us to limpin'. That's all I need.

She looks at him. Nearly staring. Nods. He senses more...

MAL (cont'd)
What? What is it?

KAYLEE
Well. It's worse'n just the coil.

MAL
How can it be worse?

KAYLEE
Main life-support's down on account of the engine being dead.

MAL
Right. But we got auxiliary —

KAYLEE
No. We don't. It ain't even on. Explosion musta knocked it out.

MAL
So what are we breathin'?

KAYLEE
Whatever got pumped into the atmo before the explosion shut it all down.

Jayne has overheard part of this, joins them.

JAYNE
Mosta that oxygen got ate up by the fire when it went out the door.

KAYLEE
Whatever's left is what we got.

Mal takes a beat, weighing his very slim options —

MAL
How long?

KAYLEE
Couplea hours, maybe.

Now Simon appears, emerging from the infirmary.

SIMON
She's stabilized. I think she's out of the woods.

Off Mal, Kaylee and Jayne, not quite ready to celebrate —

BLACK OUT.

END OF ACT ONE

ACT TWO

INT. SERENITY - AFTDECK/ENGINE ROOM

Stillness for a beat, then... the ENGINE PART (which we will soon come to know as the catalyzer) is slammed down before Mal.

He's forcing himself up the stairs and around the corner into the aftdeck corridor.

INJURED MAL moves into the engine room, PAST LENS. We HOLD FRAME, looking (from the engine room POV) down the empty aftdeck. A beat, then...

...MAL APPEARS advancing from the dining area,

coming down the aftdeck toward the engine room. He's uninjured Mal.

MAL
Bester!

And WE ARE:

INT. SERENITY - ENGINE ROOM

— in a different time. Mal's looking for his mechanic (the handsome mechanic we saw earlier).

MAL
What's this I been hearin' 'bout yet another delay?

As Mal moves closer to the engine room, we can make out BESTER'S ARMY BOOTS sticking out from under the engine. Presumably doing his grease monkey thing.

MAL (cont'd)
You were supposed to have that engine fixed and us up and...
(as he sees:)
What in the name of <suo-yo duh doh shr-dang...?> [all that's proper...?]

Bester's shorts are... well, down around his army boots. He's having the sex with an unseen FEMALE. There is energetic humpage. Mal's a bit scandalized. Casts his glance away from the action. Might clear his throat.

MAL (cont'd)
Bester.

Much with the dirty humping. Mal gives it a beat.

MAL (cont'd)
Bester.

They seem to be, uh, finishing.

MAL (cont'd)
BESTER!

Bester climbs out, mostly still naked, yanking up his shorts.

BESTER
What?

Bester just looks to Mal. Innocently inquisitive. There is some deadpan staring on Mal's part. Oh, yes there is. Then:

MAL
You do realize we been parked on this rock near a week longer'n we planned?

BESTER
Yeah, but... there's stuff to do.

MAL
As for example that job we got waitin' for us on Paquin. When we landed here you said you just needed a few days before we were space worthy again and is there somethin' wrong with your bunk?

BESTER
What?

More impatient staring, then Bester gets it finally: right. The naked girl behind the engine. Bester laughs.

BESTER (cont'd)
Oh! No. Cap!
(leans forward "confidentially")
She likes engines. They make her hot.

MAL
Bester. Get your prairie harpy off my boat and put us back in the air.

BESTER
'Kay. But... can't.

MAL
Whaddya mean "can't".

BESTER
No can do, Cap. Secondary grav boot's shot.

KAYLEE (O.S.)
No it ain't.

Kaylee pops up, getting dressed. The men look at her.

KAYLEE
Ain't nothing wrong with your grav boot. Grav boot's just fine.
(to Mal)
Hello.

She drops down again, out of view. Mal glances at Bester. Bester's a bit flustered.

BESTER
(to Mal)
She don't... That's not...
(to Kaylee)
No it ain't!

KAYLEE
(reappearing)
Sure it is. Grav boot ain't your trouble. I seen the trouble plain as day when I's down there on my back. Your reg couple's bad.

BESTER
(clueless)
The... the what?

KAYLEE
Reg couple. Right here. See?

BESTER
No.

KAYLEE
This.
(Bester is still of the blank expression)
I'm pointin' right at it.

She rolls her eyes, sighs, reaches in, breaks off a part of the engine.

BESTER
Hey!

KAYLEE
Here.

She plunks the part in Bester's hand. She reaches back in, tinkers.

KAYLEE (cont'd)
Don't really serve much of a purpose anyway. Just tends to gum up the works when it gets tacked.
(re: a nearby wrench)
Hand me that, will ya?

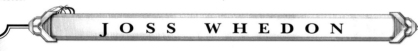

JOSS WHEDON

Did Joss Whedon and/or Tim Minear always know what the characters' back-stories were going to be, or did they come up with the various histories when 'Out of Gas' was being created? "Pretty much came up with them," Whedon says. "I had a vague idea that Wash is the kind of guy who would just be hired, who wouldn't have an adventure; and we'd made jokes about the idea that Jayne had been trying to rob them when they hired him. I worked on this — not to take away from Tim — he wrote; David Solomon directed, did an amazing job — but the two of us worked out the back-stories together. Kaylee's — I don't know if I'd thought of that before and had it in my pocket, but it just seemed like such a delightful thing. Although, a lot of people were very upset: 'Why did they make Kaylee a whore?' they said. And I was like, 'I don't recall her being *paid* at any point.' She's just havin' sex. She's Kaylee. But, you know, a television audience is very... interesting. The Inara one was pure Tim. I wasn't really sure how to make that work at all and, god, I love that scene so much. The ironic thing is, I watched the second season première of *The West Wing* and they did the flashbacks, the origins, and I was like, 'It's a little early in the show to be doing this.' And then I ended up doing it in episode seven of season one. But we didn't start with the flashbacks. The idea was simply, what happens if we run out of gas? And the idea of doing the three-tiered structure, that was really Tim, of Mal trying to get the thing in and then save himself and then everything falling apart and everybody coming on board — we felt like in order for the emotion of the thing to be as great as we felt it was, we wanted to show what drove all of these people. It is my favorite episode — and that includes the ones that I directed — because I just think it's so beautiful, and it just *kills* me. And, of course, Mal's introduction to the ship, starting with 'The ship will stay with you for life' and then finding out it's not the ship that's being pitched to him. Which some people didn't get. But no, no, no, you don't go to a salesman and have him point out a ship. You see it across a crowded room, like Tony and Maria [from *West Side Story*]. And that's probably the most romantic introduction of them all."

(he does)
So I figure, why even have it? Better to just plug your g-line straight into the port pin-lock and that should...

She's done. WHIRRR the turbine starts to turn.

KAYLEE (cont'd)
There.

She shoves it in Bester's hand. Fiddles with the engine.

BESTER
What'd you do?

MAL
She fixed it.

KAYLEE
Well, it wasn't really broke.

Bester looks at the part in his hand.

MAL
Where'd you learn to do that, Miss?

KAYLEE
(shrugs)
Just do it, that's all. My daddy says I got a natural talent.

MAL
I'd say you do at that.

BESTER
(re: the part)
We don't need this?

KAYLEE
Not 'specially.

MAL
You work for your daddy, do you?

KAYLEE
When he's got work. Which lately ain't been too often.

MAL
And have you had much experience on a vessel like this?

KAYLEE
Never even been up in one before.

MAL
You never been... How'd you like to?

KAYLEE
(points skyward)
You mean...?

MAL
Sure.

KAYLEE
For how long?

MAL
Long as you like. Long as you can keep her in the sky.

KAYLEE
(getting it now)
You offering me a job?

BESTER
What?

MAL
Believe I just did.

KAYLEE
Just gotta ask my folks!

She pulls her hastily assembled wardrobe about

THE ENGINE ROOM

Prop master Randy Eriksen: "On the ship, Serenity, we pretty much got away with murder. I'd say, 'Okay, we need a box and some wires.' You know, Kaylee's up there fixing it, so we'd get some crummy hinged-lid metal box and some electrical wires. We used the same stuff over and over. I had these little blinky lights which were actually earrings, I guess. For the first couple of episodes there was blinky stuff all over the place; then, by episode ten, as the batteries ran down and the budget ran down, we'd look around and say, 'Look, there's one, over there', if we happened to spot one still working! David the DP [director of photography] was really great. He was hand-holding stuff and lighting stuff real loose. He liked the blinky things. If you had it, he'd use it."

her, pushes past Mal and a stunned Bester.

KAYLEE (cont'd)
Don't leave without me!

Mal watches Kaylee go, tickled. Bester just blinks, stunned.

BESTER
Mal. Whaddya need two mechanics for?

MAL
I really don't. Pack your things.
(then)
She got a name?

INT. SERENITY - ENGINE ROOM

MAL
Kaylee!

Mal has entered the engine room. He looks off screen, a little annoyed to see —

Kaylee is just sitting there. Forlorn. She's holding the same piece of equipment that Mal was dragging in here. But the one she's got is twisted and melted and screwed up. She stares at it.

MAL (cont'd)
Kaylee, what are you doing?

KAYLEE
I'm sorry, Captain. I'm real sorry. I shoulda kept better care of her.

KAYLEE (cont'd)
Usually she lets me know when something's wrong. Maybe she did and I wasn't paying attention.

MAL
(patiently)
I cannot be having this from you right now. We got work to do. <Dong-ma?> [Understand?]

KAYLEE
(re: the warped engine part)
Catalyzer's broke. Gonna need a new one.

MAL
There is no new one. You gotta make do with what you got.

KAYLEE
It's broke.

She just sits there. He gently makes her stand up.

MAL
Come on. This the part?
(she nods)
Well that don't hardly seem like nothing at all. Where does it go?

She shows him the spot in the engine.

KAYLEE
Here. But it won't fit no more.

He tries to install it, no go.

MAL
Then you gotta figure a way to make it fit.

KAYLEE
Tried. Sometimes a thing gets broke, can't be fixed.

MAL
Engine don't turn without this?

She shakes her head "no".

MAL (cont'd)
Engine don't turn, life support won't function, we don't breathe. You want to keep breathin', don't you?

She nods.

MAL (cont'd)
So do I.
(then)
Will you try again?

She looks at him. Doesn't want to disappoint. Nods. He smiles. Puts his hand on the back of her neck. Off this moment —

INT. SERENITY - COMMON AREA/INFIRMARY

Simon checks the still unconscious Zoe's vitals. Inara appears at the infirmary door.

INARA
How is she?

SIMON
Still unconscious. But her vitals are strong. She won't know it, but as long as her condition remains like this... she'll outlive us all.
(then)
She's using less oxygen.

He moves into the common area. Sits. She joins him.

SIMON (cont'd)
I always thought the name "Serenity" had a vaguely funereal sound to it.

INARA
I love this ship. I have from the first moment I saw it.

SIMON
I just don't want to die on it.

INARA
I don't want to die at all.

SIMON
Suffocation's not exactly the most dignified way to go. The human body will involuntarily —

INARA
Please, I don't really require a clinical description right now.

SIMON
I'm sorry. I just...
(after a beat)
It was my birthday.

He smiles wistfully. She smiles back. Puts her hand over his. Off this moment...

INT. SERENITY - BOOK'S QUARTERS

Book sits at his little table. We can see he's scared. Reading from the Psalms. Trying to find comfort in those ancient words.

RIVER (O.S.)
Don't be afraid.

He looks up, a bit startled to see River haunting his doorway.

RIVER
(re: his bible)
That's what it says. Don't be afraid.

BOOK
Yes.

RIVER
But you are afraid.

BOOK
Yes.

RIVER
You're afraid we're going to run out of air. That we'll die gasping.
(then)
But we won't. That's not going to happen.

He looks at her. Taken by her utter certainty. He finds a kind of comfort there. Well, that is until:

RIVER (cont'd)
(flatly)
We'll freeze to death first.

CUT TO:

INT. SERENITY - BRIDGE

Wash is at the helm. He's torn up with worry and anger. He's seething a bit. Mal enters. Wash doesn't even turn.

MAL
You get that beacon sent?

WASH
(much with the resentment)
Yeah, it's sent.

MAL
Good.

WASH
(under his breath)
Pointless.

MAL
What was that?

WASH
Nothing, sir. It's a brilliant plan, I'm sure we'll all be saved.

MAL
Getting a little weary of this attitude, Wash.

WASH
Are you? Well I'm very sorry about that, sir. I guess the news that we're all gonna be purple and bloated and fetal in a few hours has made me a little snippy.

MAL
It's possible someone might pick up the signal.

WASH
(pissed)
No, Mal. It's not possible. Nobody's gonna pick up the damn signal. You wanted us "flying under the radar", remember? Well, that's where we are: out of range of anyone or anything.

MAL
Then make it go further.

WASH
What?

MAL
Make the signal go further.

WASH
Can't make it go further.

MAL
Not if all you're gonna do is sit here and whine about it, no.

WASH
What do you expect me to do, Mal?

MAL
(building)
Whatever you have to. And if you can't do it from here, then you put on a suit and get out on the side of the boat and...

WASH
(voice rising)
And what? Wave my arms around?

MAL
Wave your arms around, jump up and down. Divert the nav sats to the transmitter. Whatever.

WASH
Divert the...? Right. Because teenage pranks are fun when you're about to die!

MAL
Give the beacon a boost, wouldn't it?

WASH
Yes, Mal. It'd boost the signal, but even if some passerby did happen to receive, all it'd do is muck up their navigation!

MAL
Could be that's true.

WASH
Damn right it's true! They'd be forced to stop and dig out our signal before they could go anyplace!

A beat as Wash let's what he just said sink in. He snaps:

ZOE

"Okay people, if it moves, shoot it."

At the heart of all the bickering and capers that take place on *Firefly*'s ship, Serenity, are the captivating characters and their dysfunctional family dynamic. One such character is warrior and second-in-command, Zoe Washburne. As one half of the only married couple on board the ship, Zoe and her husband, Wash, frequently draw emotional strength from one another while providing a fresh perspective.

"I have to say that I consider their marriage a very healthy one," offers Gina Torres. "At its core you have two people that really love each other and are getting to work jobs they both love and excel at. And Zoe can be vulnerable and silly with Wash. Their marriage is a part of the show that allows the audience to relax because they are so completely themselves with each other."

Nonetheless, that doesn't mean there aren't disagreements or jealousy. During 'War Stories' Wash looses his cool over his wife's professional history with Malcolm Reynolds, and her tendency to follow his orders blindly. Torres explains, "Finding that kind of unconditional love, support and understanding with someone is very rare. Zoe managed to find it twice [in both Mal and Wash]. I guess you can't blame Wash for wanting to be the only one."

At the beginning of the episode 'The Message' the characters briefly revisit their Unification War days. Torres remarks, "I suppose we could have gone on talking about the war, but actually seeing it was far more effective. "

That episode features a figure from Zoe and Mal's military past. When former ally, Tracey, betrays them and goes to shoot Wash, Zoe doesn't hesitate to take him down. "She loves her husband and will not stand for her family being threatened," states Torres. "That part is not at all complicated. I promise you Zoe slept great that night. Her former 'comrade' was always a screw-up with a gift for 'self-preservation', if you will."

Another key moment for Zoe came in 'War Stories' when Mal and Wash are taken prisoner by the sadistic Niska, and Zoe has to rescue the two most important men in her life. "At the risk of repeating myself, she loves her husband!" declares Torres. "And the rescue was great, mostly because we got to enlist the help of the other crewmembers, and not all of them were very comfortable with weaponry."

Despite the drama and intense emotions of 'War Stories', it is 'Out of Gas' that Torres pinpoints as her favorite episode. The story finds the ship in crisis mode, while flashbacks detail Mal amassing together his crew. "It's all that back-story interwoven with Mal's fight for life," Torres explains. "It gives us an insight into him, how he cares about and needs us. And it also contains some of the funniest writing we had on the show."

While playing Zoe, Torres had to endure much physical hardship fighting the enemy but as she recalls, it was her sweltering costumes that caused her the most discomfort. "The toughest challenge I met was shooting in the desert in 110 degree weather wearing our costume of boots, trench coats, leather and wool. Not fun. The space suit created its own claustrophobic set of challenges as well."

There's no doubt the talented cast gave 100 percent to *Firefly* yet they knew how to laugh too. Torres smiles, "At the end of every week, around six p.m., no matter what we were shooting, and particularly if it involved Ron, Jewel and Sean, a case of the giggles would overwhelm us. Finishing a sentence would become damn near impossible because anything and everything could set us off."

Dedicated viewers were devastated when their beloved *Firefly* was canceled so prematurely, and they weren't the only ones. Torres remembers that day well: "I was on the set like everyone else, putting in my day's work, when Joss came down to deliver the news. Of course there was the immediate anger and sadness but I also felt relief. We had been working for a few weeks not knowing whether we were going to live or die. I didn't realize how stressed I was feeling about it until the axe finally fell. I could breathe again. Unfortunately it was a mournful breath."

Thankfully, *Firefly*'s cult status continued to grow when its DVD sales rocketed. The sci-fi series proved to be a memorable experience that really resonated with fans. "I like to think that people connected to other people, not entirely unlike themselves, who were able to step up and sometimes achieve great things, and other times just survive in what were pretty impossible situations," concludes Torres. "That can be inspiring for some." ◀

WASH (cont'd)
Well, maybe I should do that, then!

MAL
(snapping back)
Maybe you should!

WASH
Okay!

MAL
Good!

WASH
Fine!

JAYNE
HEY!

Jayne has appeared, forces himself between the two of them.

JAYNE (cont'd)
What the <guay> [hell] do you two think you're doing?! Fightin' at a time like this.

A moral lecture from Jayne. They both ease off. Cool down.

JAYNE (cont'd)
(as he turns and goes)
You'll use up all the air!

WAAA! WAAA! WAAA! A KLAXON SOUNDS and WE ARE:

INT. SERENITY - ENGINE ROOM

Where the ALARM originated. Mal, gut-shot, listens to the ship warning him that:

SERENITY (V.O.)
Life support failure. Check oxygen levels at once.

Then the same ALERT repeats IN CHINESE.

SERENITY (cont'd; V.O.)
<Jeo-shung yong-jur goo-jang. Jien-cha yong-chi gong yin.> [Life support failure. Check oxygen levels at once.]

Mal's bleary-eyed, fumbling with the ship part, trying to install the catalyzer into the failed compression coil. But he's having a fuck of a time.

He wipes sweat from his brow with the back of his hand — leaving an ugly smear of blood. He blinks it back. It's in his eyes. Shit.

The KLAXON continues to sound. The ship's message repeats in English again.

Mal nearly has the part installed... but it slips from his bloody fingers and drops into the engine. Lost to him.

He can't believe that just happened. And the alert continues to sound —

BLACK OUT.

END OF ACT TWO

ACT THREE

EXT. SPACE

Dead Serenity just hanging there.

INT. SERENITY - COMMON AREA/INFIRMARY

Everyone sits huddled together. They're wearing coats and blankets. It's cold. Mal stands before the assembled, grim. He's a bit distracted, tries to keep focused. A combination of the situation and the thinning of the air.

MAL
Well. As you're all keenly aware... seems we, uh, run into a... bit of a situation. Engine's down. Life support's on the fritz. And I got nine people here all wanting to breathe.
(tries to be light)
Could take turns, I suppose.
(thud)
But that doesn't really appear to be an option. Truth is... ain't got a whole lot of options at this juncture.

A beat. They all look back at him. Watch him as he casts a glance up at Serenity. Runs his hand along a bulkhead or wall. Then gives it an affectionate pat. Continues —

MAL (cont'd)
So now instead of focusing on what we don't got — time to talk about what it is we do. And what we got are two shuttles. Short range. Won't go far. But they each got heat, and they each got air. Last longer than what's left in Serenity.

SIMON
Long enough to reach someplace?

MAL
No.

BOOK
So... where will we go, then?

MAL
Far as you can get. We send both shuttles off in exact opposite directions — betters the chance of somebody being seen, maybe getting picked up.
(then)
Shepherd Book, Kaylee and Jayne'll ride with Inara in her shuttle. Doc, you and your sister will go with Wash and Zoe — seein' as Zoe still needs some doctorin'.

KAYLEE
What about you?

MAL
Four people to a shuttle. That's the arrangement. Even's the odds.
(then)
I'm staying with Serenity.

KAYLEE
Cap'n —

MAL
We sent out a beacon. Even managed to boost it a little. Now, if by some chance we do get a response, there's gotta be someone here to answer.

That hangs there for a moment. Nobody believes that's going to happen.

MAL (cont'd)
Let's get those shuttles prepped.

Wash stands, starts moving to the stairs near the infirmary.

MAL (cont'd)
Wash — shuttles are that way.

WASH
I know. But like you said — someone might answer the beacon. And when they do, I want to make sure you're able to call us all back. Won't take me a minute.

Mal nods. Wash moves off.

MAL
Jayne, get shuttle II ready. I'll see to Inara's.
(to everyone else)
Let's get moving.
(as he goes)
Take only what you need.

Mal moves off. Everyone's a bit stunned. Inara moves to follow Mal.

INT. SERENITY - CARGO BAY/CATWALKS

Mal heads up to the catwalks, moving toward Inara's shuttle. She appears, following.

INARA
Mal...

MAL
You fly smart, don't push too hard, shuttle life support should last you a good long while.

INARA
Mal, this isn't the ancient sea. You don't have to

go down with your ship.

MAL
She ain't going down. She ain't going anywhere.
(then)
Jayne'll be worth something if you run into trouble. But don't trust him, and don't let him take
over. You're paid up through the month. It's still
your ship.

INARA
Mal...

MAL
But so far as your security deposit goes... that I
think I might have to owe you.

He enters her shuttle. She follows —

INT. INARA'S SHUTTLE

Inara steps through first. She's wearing different
clothing. Mal steps in behind her. The shuttle is
either empty or dressed differently. Mal's showing
her the "property".

MAL
Well, here she is.

She glides in, takes in the space for the first time.

MAL (cont'd)
Nice, ain't she?

INARA
Smallish...

MAL
Not overly. How much space you really need for
what you do, anyway?

She ignores that, still considering the shuttle. She
moves into the cockpit. Blue sky outside the windows. Mal follows.

MAL (cont'd)
Got a surveyor and his wife interested in renting
it. They're just waiting to hear back.

INARA
What's her range?

MAL
Standard short. She'll break atmo from a wide
orbit. Get you where you need to go, bring you
back home again.

INARA
This shuttle — it seems newer than the rest of the
ship.

MAL
My understanding is this airlock was added some
years back. Certain modifications and improve-
ments been made over the course of the years.

INARA
Mmmm.

MAL
But she's space worthy. Like the rest of Serenity.

INARA
No need to sound so defensive, Captain.
(sliding past him)
I prefer something with a few miles on it.

He watches her as she moves into the main chamber, looking it over. Looking her over...

INARA (cont'd)
Were we to enter into this arrangement, Captain
Reynolds, there are a few things I would require
from you. The foremost being complete auto-
nomy. This shuttle would be my home. No crew
member, including yourself, would be allowed
entrance without my express invitation.

MAL
You'd get your privacy.

INARA
Good. And just so we're clear, under no circum-
stances will I be servicing you or anyone who is
under your employ.

MAL
I'll post a sign.

INARA
That won't be necessary. The other thing I would
insist upon is some measure of assurance that
when I make an appointment with a client I'm in
a position to keep that appointment. So far as
such assurances are possible on a vessel of this
type.

Mal blinks at all that for a beat, letting it register,
then:

MAL
That's an awful lot of caveats and addendums
there, Miss.

INARA
As I stated, I just want to be clear.

MAL
Well. I'll be sure and take all of that into consideration when I review the applications.

INARA
Don't be ridiculous. You're going to rent this
shuttle to me.

MAL
Am I?

INARA
Yes. And for one quarter less than your asking
price.

MAL
(like hell)
That a fact?

INARA
It is.

MAL
And you figure you'll be getting this discount...
why exactly?

INARA
You want me. You want me on your ship.

MAL
Do I?

INARA
Yes. Because I can bring something that your "surveyor" or any of the other fish you might have on
a line can't — a certain respectability.

MAL
Respecta —

INARA
And based on what little I've seen of your... operation... I suspect that's something you could use.

MAL
Fine. Let me ask you this: if you're so
"respectable", why are you even here? I mean, I
heard tell of fancy ladies such as yourself shipping
out with the big luxury liners and the like. But a
registered Companion on a boat like this? What
are you running from?

INARA
I'm not "running" from anything.

He looks at her. Doesn't believe her.

MAL
If it's Alliance trouble you got, you might want to
consider another ship. Some on board here fought
for the Independents.

INARA
The Alliance has no quarrel with me. In fact I supported Unification.

MAL
Didja? Well, I don't suppose you're the only whore that did.

She looks at him. Smiles, won't let this guy rankle her.

INARA
Oh — one further addendum. That's the last time you get to call me a "whore".

She walks past him.

MAL
Absolutely. Never again.

INT. INARA'S SHUTTLE

Mal moves about the cockpit, checking gages, dials, etc.

MAL
Keep everything set as low as possible. Don't waste what you got.

She pushes him out of the way, takes over.

INARA
Let me do that. You never could operate this thing.

He lets her take over. Gazes down at her. Now she looks at him. So much to say. He sees that. Feels similarly.

MAL
And try not to talk. Talkin' uses up air. There ain't no need for it.

INARA
Mal... come with us.

MAL
Can't. Four to a shuttle, Inara. Four.

INARA
One more person. You know it can't make a difference. Not now.

MAL
I'm not leaving Serenity.

INARA
Mal — you don't have to die alone.

MAL
Everybody dies alone.

NATHAN FILLION

I have one moment that not a lot of people mention, but the people that do, it gets them teary-eyed. It was a scene in 'Out of Gas', at the end, when I am with Inara in her shuttle. She says, 'Mal, you don't have to die alone.' And I say, 'Everybody dies alone.' That moment for me... and there's a beautiful shot at the very end that our director, David Solomon, came up with. To me, it strikes something in my heart. I know I am watching me up there and I know I am watching Morena, but in moments like that in can only see Malcolm Reynolds and Inara. I feel so much for them. I feel for them so badly. It's a favorite.

ALAN TUDYK

"On the last day of shooting *Firefly*, we were doing the final scene on the bridge and it was really depressing. The red button had been put on after the bridge was built because it comes into the episode, 'Out of Gas'. It was only stuck on with this tacky, gum stuff that you hang pictures on the wall with. So I was like, 'I'll be damned if I'm not taking something!' I tried to pull a couple of things off but they were screwed on too tight. I grabbed a hold of that button and it came off and was mine! We then had to come back onto the bridge to shoot one last time — and so the button wasn't there. I held onto it for a few days going, 'I got this thing,' and then Joss had given all those speeches and I thought it was such a perfect thing for him to have." Alan then sent the button to Joss Whedon when the show was canceled with a note saying: "When your miracle gets here, call us back."

WE hold on their look to each other, we PRE-LAP the horrible SOUND of the KLAXON SOUNDING —

CUT TO:

INT. SERENITY - AFTDECK/ENGINE ROOM

Gut-shot Mal fishes out the part to the compression coil. Works to fit it into the damaged engine. It takes some work, but he does it.

He fires it all up — the turbines start to spin. It works. The BLARING ALERT stops. Power restored. Life support functioning again. He starts dragging himself toward the bridge —

INT. SERENITY - BRIDGE

We're in Mal's POV, moving toward the seemingly empty bridge — but Wash appears in the doorway.

WASH
Everything's set and ready.

REVEAL — MAL (uninjured-Mal) moving toward the bridge.

MAL
Good.

WASH
I linked the nav systems of both shuttles into the helm, here.

Wash points out a LARGE, DISTINCTIVE BUTTON on the navigation control panels.

WASH (cont'd)
When your miracle gets here, you just pound this button once. It'll call back both shuttles.

Mal nods. Wash wants to say something. Everything's all fucked up. He's about to speak, but before he can:

MAL
Go see to your wife.

Wash takes a beat. Then exits.

INT. SERENITY - CARGO BAY

Mal walks with Jayne. Jayne has a duffle and some guns slung over his shoulder.

JAYNE
I went ahead and closed off all below deck vents. Diverted what there is to the bridge. It ain't much. So my advice, seal off everything tight behind you when you go back up. Might buy you some time.

Mal nods. He's looking up to —

MAL'S POV

Of the upper catwalks. To the left, Wash and Simon carry a stretcher with unconscious Zoe into the second shuttle. River follows.

Mal looks to his right —

Book and Kaylee enter Inara's shuttle. Inara stands at the doorway, looking down at him.

JAYNE (cont'd)
And I prepped a suit for you. It's hanging in the foredeck. When the time comes, you can just...

MAL
(cuts him off, though not angrily)
I won't be needing it, but thanks.

JAYNE
Okay. Well.

Jayne takes a beat. Then he moves off, heading up the catwalk stairs.

WASH at the door to shuttle II. He slides the door shut.

JAYNE reaches the top of the catwalk. Motions for Inara to go inside. A beat. Her eyes on Mal. Then she disappears inside. Jayne follows, shuts the door. Mal stands alone in the big, empty cargo bay, as...

EXT. SPACE

The two shuttles detach from Serenity, go their separate ways, off into space.

INT. SERENITY - CARGO BAY

Mal moves through the door leading to the infirmary, shuts up the door behind him.

INT. SERENITY - UPPER DECK

Mal closes off the door to the aftdeck. Moves through the dining area, moves into the foredeck, slides that door shut behind him.

INT. SERENITY - BRIDGE

Mal closes off the bridge. He sits into the pilot's seat. Sighs. And WE SEE his FROZEN BREATH misting. He sits alone. Staring out into the empty vastness of space.

The air is thin and he starts to get drowsy. Each breath is COLD MIST. The MIST getting thinner and thinner. He shivers. His eyes start to close —

EXT. SPACE

Serenity. Silent. Alone. Not moving.

INT. SERENITY - BRIDGE

Some time has passed. Mal looking half frozen and unconscious in the pilot's chair. He doesn't react

to the SOUND of a SIGNAL as it starts to come through on the console...

CLOSE — MONITOR (INSERT)

THE SIGNAL on the console. A FUZZY IMAGE. A MAN'S FACE through the mostly STATIC. Barely discernible.

CAPTAIN (V.O.)
(filtered)
Firefly Serenity... This is the private salvage S.S. Walden. Receiving your distress beacon, do you read?

We're only getting about a third of that as it's trying to break in on Serenity's wounded half-powered system. It continues to repeat and CRACKLE.

Mal sits motionless. Not hearing it. Maybe dead.

More STATICKY SIGNAL. More CRACKLING. But now Mal starts to stir slightly. A few more WORDS of the DISTRESS REPLY crackle through...

Mal forces his heavy-lidded eyes open just as... The transmission ends. No more signal.

Mal tries to orient himself. Did he hear something? His head lolls as he looks to the now silent monitors. Could have been a dream. His bleary eyes shift up to the window —

ANOTHER SHIP

TWICE THE SIZE OF SERENITY rises up there, right the fuck in front of the window. Which is as good a place as any for —

BLACK OUT.

END OF ACT THREE

MUSIC

Composer Greg Edmonson: "That was a terribly emotional episode. The main thing I remember about the music is that even during the opening scene everything is still and everything is quiet, because the ship's dead at that point. And so the music needed to convey that feeling. There were lots of scenes, once everyone left, of Mal walking through the ship. There's a scene when he does everything he can do, nothing works, and he finally goes to his cabin to prepare to die. He is prepared to die — he's going down with his ship. So the music wasn't meant to do anything but just be part of that."

ACT FOUR

EXT. SPACE

The S.S. Walden nose-to-nose with the smaller Serenity.

INT. SERENITY - BRIDGE

Mal on the bridge. WE SEE the IMAGE of the CAPTAIN of the Walden on the vid monitor. A serious sort; Mal without the funny. Mal does his best to keep up, but lack of oxygen and the extreme cold aren't helping.

CAPTAIN
I'm sorry for your troubles, Captain. They sound many. But you do understand I can't invite you on board my vessel. I got folks here to consider. They depend on me to make the right choices. And I don't know you.

MAL
I'd do the same myself, were the situation reversed. 'Course, one of my idiot crew'd probably talk me into changing my mind... You got idiots?

CAPTAIN
No.

MAL
Well I'm not looking for a ride, Captain. Just a little push is all.

CAPTAIN
Right. Your mechanical trouble. Compression coil, you say?

MAL
It was the catalyzer.

J E W E L   S T A I T E

I thought that was one of our strongest episodes. Joss came up with some amazing philosophical ideas for that one. I think it's really poignant, especially the scene where Mal tells us to get into the two different shuttles and split up and there's that shot of the ship alone and the two shuttles flying away in opposite directions. I cry every time I watch that episode. I love it.

CAPTAIN
Not even the coil? Catalyzer's a nothing part, Captain.

MAL
It's nothing til you don't got one. Then it appears to be everything.

CAPTAIN
It is possible we might have something that'd do you. We just come from a big salvage job off Ita Moon. Picked the bones'a half a dozen junk heaps not unlike the one you're sittin' in.

MAL
Mmmm.

CAPTAIN
I suppose we could dock, take a look around, see if there ain't some way we might come to terms. That's if we have the part —

Captain looks off screen, presumably at some unseen person speaking to him.

CAPTAIN (cont'd)
I'm told we do.

MAL
I would appreciate it.

CAPTAIN
Trouble is... how can I know for certain your story's true? Ambush could be waiting for me and my people on the other side.

MAL
You can plainly see both my shuttles been launched, just like I said. And I'm sure by now you scanned me. You know I got no life support.

CAPTAIN
(muses, then)
I don't expect to see any weapons when we board.

MAL
And I do expect to see that engine part before I open the door.

CAPTAIN
(smiles)

I feel like maybe we can do business.

FZZZT. The Captain's face disappears from the monitor.

EXT. SPACE

As the S.S. Walden's airlock attaches to that of Serenity...

INT. SERENITY - CARGO BAY

Mal, breathing very shallow, waits near the standing airlock door controls.

The Captain appears at the airlock doors. He holds up the catalyzer at the window. Mal activates the airlock doors.

As the doors open, there is a tremendous RUSH OF AIR from the other side — blessed oxygen. Mal nearly passes out from the drinking in of it. He closes his eyes for a beat, just sucking down as much as he can. When he opens his eyes again —

The Captain and his FOUR PEEPS have their guns raised and aimed at him. Mal's hands go up instinctively.

CAPTAIN
Check him.

One of the Captain's crew moves in, frisks Mal as —

CAPTAIN (cont'd)
(to another flunky)
Search the ship. Start in the cockpit, work your way down.

MAL
This what you meant by "ambush"?

CAPTAIN
(smiles)
We're just verifying your story.
(to flunkies)
You find anyone on board not supposed to be — you shoot 'em.

The Captain was hoping that last bit would elicit a reaction from Mal. It doesn't. As the lackeys go —

MAL
Thought we were gonna be reasonable about this?

MARCO
Reason?

No, that wasn't a typo, because suddenly we are:

EXT. SERENITY - RAMP/CARGO BAY - DAY

On the open ramp of Serenity and it's Mal and Zoe in an armed stand off with another gang — THREE PRICKLY BANDITOS, a grizzly fellow called MARCO their leader.

MARCO
(to his partner)
He's gonna talk to us about "reason", now.

JAYNE
Yeah. That's a joke.

Oh, yeah — Jayne's one of the members of the rival gang.

MAL AND ZOE — a brief, sotto exchange:

MAL
Which one you figure tracked us?

ZOE
The ugly one, sir.

MAL
(long beat)
Could you be more specific?

THE OTHER GANG

MARCO
Do we look "reasonable" to you?

MAL
Well. Looks can be deceiving.

JAYNE
Not as deceiving as a low down dirty... deceiver!

MAL
Well said. Wasn't that well said, Zoe?

ZOE
Had a kind of poetry to it, sir.

JAYNE
You want I should shoot 'em now, Marco?

MARCO
Wait until they tell us where they put the stuff.

JAYNE
That's a good idea. A good idea. Tell us where the stuff's at so I can shoot ya.

MAL
Point of interest? Offering to shoot us, don't work so well as an incentive as you might imagine. Anyway, we've hidden it. So if you kill us, you'll never find it.

JAYNE
Found you easy enough.

ZOE'S COSTUMES

Costume designer Shawna Trpcic: "Zoe wore the same straight pants as Mal toward the beginning of the series and then we tightened them up and made them a little bit sexier as we got a little more freedom. But same idea — she's a warrior. She's not Xena, but we wanted to highlight her figure and her strength and her poise with really clean lines. So the leather vest fit tight and could resemble a bulletproof vest and actually acted as one in the pilot, 'Serenity'. So she was from the same background as Mal, but obviously different."

MAL
Yeah. Yeah you did, actually.
(then)
How much they paying you?

JAYNE
Wubba — huh?

MAL
I mean, let's say you did kill us. Or didn't. There could be torture. Whatever. But somehow you found the goods. What would your cut be?

JAYNE
Seven percent, straight off the top.

MAL
Seven? Huh.

Mal makes a "wow, that's pathetic" grimace. Jayne squints.

JAYNE
What?

MAL
Mmm? Nothing. Not a thing. Just…
(to Zoe)
That seem low to you?

ZOE
It does, sir.

JAYNE
It ain't low…

MARCO
Stop it.

JAYNE
Seven percent, that's standard.

MAL
Who told you that?
(re: Marco)
Him?
(then)
Okay. Zoe, I'm paying you too much.

JAYNE
Why? What does she get?

MARCO
Knock it off.

MAL
Look, forget I said anything. I'm sure you're treated very well. You get the perks. Got your own room…
(off Jayne's reaction)
No? You share a bunk?

JAYNE
(re: the other guy)
With that one.

MAL
Really.

MARCO
Jayne, this ain't funny.

JAYNE
Yeah, I ain't laughin'.

MAL
You move on over to this side, we'll not only show you where the stuff's at — we'll see you get the share you deserve. Not no sad "seven".

JAYNE
Private room?

MARCO
Jayne!

MAL
Your own room. Full run of the kitchen. Whole shot.

MARCO
Jayne. I ain't askin' —

POW! Jayne shoots Marco in the leg and instantly drops the other bandito (who was just barely starting to turn on Jayne) without really looking.

JAYNE
Shut up.
(to Mal)
How big a room?

Off that —

INT. SERENITY - CARGO BAY

The Captain with his gun trained on Mal. Now the others start to return to the cargo bay.

LACKEY #1
Ship's clear, Captain.

CAPTAIN
You check the engine room?

LACKEY #1
(nods)
It's like he said. Catalyzer's blown. That's all he needs.

MAL
Now anything that's worth anything's really right

here in this cargo bay. You take a look around, decide what you think's fair.

CAPTAIN
Already decided.

BOOM. The Captain shoots Mal in the gut. It happens suddenly and without passion.

CAPTAIN (cont'd)
We're taking your ship.

Mal's eyes go wide and he sinks to his knees. Topples onto his back. The Captain coolly instructs his crew. Tosses the catalyzer to one of his men.

CAPTAIN (cont'd)
Billy, get this plugged in. Jesse, call Stern over here. You and him'll pilot this pile of <go se> [crap] out of here.

MAL'S POV

Looking up under Jayne's workout bench where there is a gun taped to the underbelly.

RESUME

CAPTAIN (cont'd)
We'll get it as far as —

He stops short as he hears the sound of a GUN being COCKED —

CAPTAIN'S POV

Looking down the barrel of Mal's gun.

MAL
(eyes on Captain)
Jesse, don't call Stern. Billy, leave the catalyzer.

CAPTAIN
(nervous, nods)
Do as he says.

The lackey with the catalyzer sets it on the cargo bay floor.

MAL
(to Captain)
Take your people and go.

CAPTAIN
You would have done the same.

MAL
We can already see I haven't.
(then)
Now get the hell off my ship.

And now the Captain and all his men back away to the airlock doors. Mal, through sheer force of will, rises to his feet, keeping the gun on them, moves to the airlock door controls. Hits the button as they step through. The doors shut.

And Mal collapses on the cargo bay floor. Exactly where we first found him.

EXT. SPACE

As the larger salvage ship detaches from Serenity and heads off.

INT. SERENITY - VARIOUS

The cargo bay floor, blood there.

The common area, infirmary, and the trail of blood left behind by the wounded Mal.

The engine room, the turbines turning with the restored part.

The aft and foredeck corridors, the trappings of the interrupted party... and the tell-tale trail of blood.

INT. SERENITY - BRIDGE

We find Mal. He's dragging himself to the bridge. He reaches for the button to call back the shuttles. But before he can touch it... he passes out.

BLACKNESS.

UP FROM BLACKNESS

VOICES. Familiar voices. Growing more present as Mal wakes in —

INT. SERENITY - INFIRMARY

Mal blinks as he sees —

Simon, Book, Inara, Jayne... then River, then Wash, and finally even Zoe, who's sitting up nearby. No

one (save maybe Zoe) is directly facing him. Various backs to him. They're in conversation, though since we're in Mal's POV we can't quite make out what they're saying. Zoe's the first to notice that Mal's come into consciousness.

ZOE
Welcome back, sir.

The others follow her look, see he's waking up.

MAL
(disoriented)
I go someplace?

BOOK
Very nearly.

INARA
We thought we'd lost you.

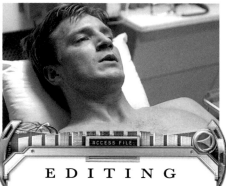

EDITING

Film editor/associate producer Lisa Lassek: "The order of the flashbacks and the transitions between them were really well thought out. It was just like a puzzle, and all the pieces only fitted together as it was written. People always say, 'Oh, the editing is so great in that episode,' and I have to reply, 'Well, it was actually written perfectly to begin with.' David Solomon directed that episode, so not only was it really well conceived in the script form, it was beautifully directed; so that when it came to the editing, it was completely easy. In post we discovered how far to push the color in those flashbacks. We started with what we thought was a little too much and then we kept going," Lassek laughs, "until the color was really stylized.

"Sometimes Joss would see something in the footage, at the editing stage, that you would never expect, that you'd never got a glimpse of in the script. He said on 'Out of Gas', 'Why don't we have a sound montage before Mal wakes up?' It was a brilliant idea and so fun for an editor. I went through the whole show and grabbed little sound bites that could have many meanings, and interwove them over black after Mal passes out, and then he wakes up in the infirmary. I did try to represent everybody, I really did. And I was also thinking — again, this is the joy of working for Joss, you can think, 'Oh, what would Mal care about?' or 'What would he be recalling?' Although you want it to be a dream, where it's just random and it's not meaningful, because that's how dreams really are," Lassek laughs, "but I did get a chance to think about bigger things."

SUMMER GLAU

I loved 'Out of Gas'. It's really sentimental for all of us. A lot of people in the cast and crew, even Joss and Tim, consider it their favorite episode, because it's the story of where everybody came from and how we all ended up on the ship — and how we stick together and come back. It still makes me cry every time I watch it. It's really important to all of us and I think it's our best episode.

I remember the night we were shooting the scene where Mal wakes up and we were all there, we were so tired and were getting really punchy and laughing so hard we were crying. It was probably one of my very favorite days we ever had shooting. We were picking on each other and laughing and crying and it's how I feel about us — we are a family. It's the story of who we are, I think.

MAL
(disconnected)
Been right here.

Mal notes Wash hooked up to an IV — he's giving Mal a transfusion. Mal, in his out-of-it-ness doesn't quite understand that.

MAL (cont'd)
Wash, you okay?

WASH
(amused)
Yeah, Mal. I'm fine.

MAL
Got a thing in ya.

WASH
Yeah.

SIMON
(to Mal)
Try not to speak. You're heavily medicated and you've lost a lot of blood.

MAL
Oh.
(then, realizing)
Thought I ordered ya'll off the ship?

The others exchange looks. Jayne glares at Inara.

JAYNE
(under his breath, accusatory)
Told ya.
(points to Wash)
It was them! They come back first! Their shuttle was already here when we docked.

MAL
(to Wash, trying to remember)
I call you back?

WASH
No, Mal. You didn't.

ZOE
I take full responsibility, Captain.

SIMON
That decision saved your life.

ZOE
It'll never happen again, sir.

MAL
(to Zoe)
Good. And thank you. I'm grateful.

JAYNE
(huh?)
You are?

Zoe smiles, nods.

ZOE
My pleasure, sir.

They hold the look between them. The original two. A special connection. Jayne observes that exchange.

JAYNE
Hey! That ain't... We'da been here first! But there's something wrong with 'Nara's shuttle! She done somethin' to it, Mal. Smells funny.

INARA
(heard this all day)
I've told you — that's incense.

JAYNE
Whatever.

Kaylee enters. Sees Mal's awake.

KAYLEE
(brightly)
Captain! You fixed the ship!
(then, a serious professional assessment)
Good work.

MAL
Thanks.

SIMON
All right. I have to insist. The Captain needs to rest.

MAL
(nodding off)
Yeah. I think maybe Doc's not wrong about that. Just for a few...
(forces himself not to drift)
You're all gonna be here when I wake up?

BOOK
We'll be here.

Mal allows himself to close his eyes.

MAL
(eyes closed, smiles)
Good. That's good...

As we PUSH IN closer to his face, which, if I can say, exhibits a kind of serenity. We start to HEAR what HE HEARS... VOICES IN HIS HEAD:

SALESMAN (V.O.)
Yep. A real beauty, ain't she? Yessir. A right smart purchase, this vessel.

EXT. USED SPACESHIP LOT - DAY

SALESMAN
Tell you what, you buy this ship, treat her proper, she'll be with ya for the rest of your life.

The Used Ship SALESMAN giving Mal the hard sell.

Now WE SEE that they're standing in front of a totally different ship. Not Serenity at all.

SALESMAN (cont'd)
Son? Hey, son?

The Salesman notices that Mal doesn't seem to be paying a bit of attention.

SALESMAN (cont'd)
You hear a word I been sayin'?

He hasn't, really. Because he's looking across the lot at something else...

MAL'S POV

Across the lot sits Serenity, dirty, a bit broken down... and silently speaking to Mal. Off that —

BLACK OUT.

END OF SHOW

YOU CAN'T STOP THE SIGNAL

Firefly Fans

F*irefly* fans tend to feel they have a lot in common with the Browncoats — in fact, that's what most of the fans call themselves. Like Joss Whedon's creations, the fan Browncoats have fought against impossible odds in the face of a dream-squelching bureaucracy. However, in the fans' case, the outcome has been lot better. First (and most important), nobody actually died. Second, fans helped raise *Firefly* from the ashes of cancellation into the feature film *Serenity*, arguably through Internet visibility and a letter-writing campaign and inarguably through purchasing the *Firefly* DVD box set in quantities that caused the project to be taken seriously.

There is even a fan-made documentary, *Done the Impossible*, narrated by Adam Baldwin and featuring interviews with many *Firefly* personnel, chronicling the history of *Firefly* fandom and the support for the nascent *Serenity*.

Jeremy Neish, one of *Done the Impossible*'s producers/directors, reckons that organized *Firefly* fandom may have begun with the *Firefly* Immediate Assistance program. "A couple of months before the show was canceled, they organized write-in campaigns to both the network [Fox] and its advertisers, raised funds for an ad in [the show business publication] *Variety*, organized fan viewing parties and invited the local press to them. From that point on, the fandom has grown. Though I wouldn't go so far as to call the cancellation of a TV show a tragedy, I would say that the sense of mourning created a powerful bond between complete strangers, who in turn directed their energy to not letting such a wonderful work of art die. Considering how shockingly good *Firefly* was in so few episodes, can you imagine how stunning it would have been by season three or four? I don't think any of us wanted to give up that dream — most of us still don't."

One example of what makes *Firefly* fans distinctive is an event known as the Backup Bash. It's not that something like this *couldn't* happen in other fandoms, but so far, it hasn't: a sold-out *Firefly* convention in December 2006 in Burbank, California, is canceled the day before it was it was scheduled to begin. Rather than stay home, the California Browncoats — spearheaded by Adam and Karla Levermore-Rich, Arielle Kesweder, Louise Du Cray and James Riley — organize within hours, find a new venue and the result is a three-day celebration with about three hundred attendees, many of whom have flown in from out of state or overseas for the original event, despite rumors of cancellation, having a great time. At various points throughout the weekend, Nathan Fillion, Adam Baldwin, Alan Tudyk, Morena

SUMMER GLAU

I have one little fan that I see when I go to England. She is just so special to me. She has been my loyal pen pal and tries to make it to everything that I do in the U.K. The last time I was there, she dressed in River's dress, when she fights the Reavers, and she had her sword and her axe. There was a costume contest and everybody walked across the stage. When she got to the middle, she knelt down in River's pose from the European poster. It was the most precious thing, and I was thinking, 'Oh my gosh! People are practicing that pose!' It is really amazing that she loves River and wants to dress up like her.

ADAM BALDWIN

Funny, what I found in my initial delving into the message boards is the intellect level of the fans of the show was inspiring. Their kindness flowed through it as well and that fascinated me. I have nothing but the highest appreciation for all of those people who participated in it and have taken the time to build up fan sites, fanzines, and everything that went along with it. It is really interesting stuff.

❖ Clockwise from opposite page: Summer Glau, Jewel Staite, Joss Whedon, Nathan Fillion and Ron Glass at the 2005 Flanvention; Christina Hendricks at the Backup Bash; Adam Baldwin at the Backup Bash; Nathan and Joss answering questions from fans at the 2005 Flanvention; Alan Tudyk, Mark A. Sheppard and Nathan Fillion enjoying the Backup Bash.

Baccarin, Ron Glass, Christina Hendricks, Michael Fairman, Mark A. Sheppard and Jonathan M. Woodward variously sign autographs, pose for pictures and just hang out with fans, as does *Firefly* executive producer (with Joss Whedon) Tim Minear, 'Trash' episode and *Firefly* comics writer Brett Matthews, composer Greg Edmonson, costume designer Shawna Trpcic, *Serenity* actors Yan Feldman and Rob Lee and *Serenity* graphics designer Geoffrey Mandel. Even actors from *Buffy* are on hand, including Clare Kramer — whose husband Brian Keathley opened his La Cantina Restaurant on Hollywood Boulevard to the Bash's Saturday night shindig — Camden Toy, James Leary and Robia LaMorte; while Corey Bridges talked about *Firefly*'s future as a licensed Massively Multiplayer Online game from Multiverse.net, beta-launching in 2008.

Amy Mayrhofer, one of the fans who traveled cross-country even after learning of the original event's cancellation, says, "We still wanted to come because the fans are such a great family and we heard that the California Browncoats were going to throw a great party no matter what, and it's so kind of the actors to come and donate their time."

Mark A. Sheppard says, "We love to have a good time, and the idea of canceling something is not a good time, so we'll do everything that we can to make it a good time."

Jonathan M. Woodward says he enjoys the vibe the fans create in each other's company. "I did a four-day shoot in 2002. I had no idea that it was going to become such a family, such a group, such a commitment and such a blessing. I just like being around people who are so excited to see each other."

"It was so amazing to see the sheer joy on people's faces when [the actors and creative personnel] showed up," says Backup Bash organizer Adam Levermore-Rich.

NATHAN FILLION

When we got canceled I wrote in a blog to say, 'Hey, if you ever see me on the street I know you want to come up to me and say, "Why did your show get canceled, it shouldn't have gotten canceled, I think this and blah blah blah."' And I said, 'You know what, it's a little close to my heart. You don't have to say all that. If you see me on the street, all you have to do' — and one guy did it, it was awesome — I said, 'is nod and say, "Captain".'

"The fact that there are so many people willing to step up within twenty-four hours, just the outpouring of support and a willingness to look out for each other is just inspiring."

"*Firefly* attracts people like this," says *Done the Impossible*'s Tony Headlock. "It took somebody like Joss Whedon and something like *Firefly* to bring us out of the woodwork. And it turns out that [*Firefly* fans] are not just good people, they're some of the best people I've ever met."

A R I E L

Written by Jose Molina
Directed by Allan Kroeker

JOSE MOLINA

Writer Jose Molina says, "Joss wanted to do a story where Simon hired the crew to rob a hospital so that he can get River onto a machine and look at her brain. Ben Edlund was waist-deep in 'Jaynestown', so Brett Matthews, Cheryl Cain and I holed up in my office to break 'Ariel', and every few days, Joss would come around and hear what we had."

In the sequence where Mal, Zoe and Jayne are trying to memorize the spiel Simon gives them, Molina says, "A good chunk of that was the actors, especially Nathan, just being completely in character. A couple of times, he ad-libbed — he screws up at one point and goes, 'shiny'. But most of the screw-ups were carefully scripted. It's a testament to how good those guys are that they made it look as natural as they did."

Showing Simon saving the dying patient, Molina explains, "was to show how proud River was of Simon and to play out the tragedy that he was not being what he could have and should have been, because of her."

How was it decided that Jayne would try to sell out Simon and River? "What we didn't have in the original premise was a huge personal stake. We kept going back to the drawing board and trying to figure out what was missing. Then one day we came up with this brilliant idea. I called Tim and said, 'Jayne betrays Simon and River'. Joss was in the middle of directing 'Spin the Bottle' for *Angel*, so we pitched him what we had on the big hotel stage at *Angel* between takes. Joss being Joss, he had more good ideas in an hour than we had come up with in a couple of weeks. So after about two hours of that, we were done. Ben and I went and put the outline together on a Thursday night, so I had from Thursday night to Monday morning to hand in a draft.

"The idea of Mal punching Jayne because he realized what had happened was either me or Brett, but on the beat sheet was the idea that Mal just hits him over the head and knocks him unconscious. Ben said, 'What if, instead of tying Jayne up and forcing him to confess, Mal throws him into the airlock, and opens the ramp so Jayne's got thirty seconds before he's going to die.'

"It evolved out of Jayne's betrayal in 'Serenity'. There's a moment between Mal and Jayne where they talk about the fact that Jayne's loyalty lies with no person but with the payday. Mal asks what's going to happen when the money is too good, and Jayne says, 'Well, that'll be an interesting day.' So the idea of the interesting day was something that we talked about constantly in the writers' room and this was the interesting day.

"By making Mal so definitive, I painted the guys into a corner where Jayne has to say something really valid to save his own life. Being typical Jayne and offering money and trying to bribe him, trying to lie, wasn't going to work. But actually showing that he is a human being, that he realizes he messed up and that maybe he does deserve to die for his mistake and that he is truly, honestly sorry at the moment where he believes he's going to die, was the only way to get Mal to close the ramp. So it came from the characters just being themselves and not out of any master plan, just out of wanting to show Jayne's humanity."

TEASER

EXT. SPACE

Serenity in space.

INT. SERENITY - DINING AREA

JAYNE sits at the table, in his Blue Sun shirt, cleaning a pistol. At the coffee table, KAYLEE and INARA play a kind of two-person mah jong. In the kitchen area, SIMON takes a pot from a burner and spoons a sludgy gumbo into one bowl for himself and one for RIVER. She wrinkles her nose at it.

RIVER
I don't want it.

SIMON
River, you have to eat. It's good, it tastes like —
(tries it, it's awful)
It's good.

JAYNE
Smells like crotch.

KAYLEE
Jayne!

JAYNE
Well, it does.

They sit across from Jayne to eat, River mostly stirring her food around, her eyes often drifting to Jayne. WASH and ZOE enter, mid conversation —

WASH
We don't even have to do anything fancy. We'll just go to a park or something, feed the pigeons.

ZOE
Sure. We'll feed the pigeons... probably get the firing squad for littering.

WASH
Come on, it's not that bad.

ZOE
Yes, it is. It's a Core planet. It's spotless, there's sensors everywhere, and where there ain't sensors, there's feds. All the central planets are the same.

WASH
(to Inara)
Could you please tell my wife the fun she's missing out on.

INARA
Ariel's quite nice, actually. They have some beautiful museums, not to mention some of the finest restaurants in the Core.

WASH
But not all boring like she made it sound. There's, uh...

He kicks at Simon's chair: help.

SIMON
There's... there's... hiking. You can go swimming in a bioluminescent lake.

ZOE
I don't care if it has sunsets twenty-four hours a day, I ain't setting foot on that place.

MAL
(entering)
No one's setting foot on that fancy rock. I don't want anyone leaving the ship. Come to

❖ Above: Jayne's gun-cleaning kit.

think of it, I don't want anyone looking out the windows. Or talking loud. We're here to drop Inara off, that's it.

JAYNE
What's the point of coming to the Core if I can't even get off the boat?

MAL
Could've gotten off with Shepherd Book at the Bathgate Abbey. You could be meditating over the wonders of your rock garden right about now.

JAYNE
Better'n just sittin'.

WASH
(you idiot)
It is just sittin'.

Jayne grumbles, puts away the pistol, starts cleaning his knife.

ZOE
(to Inara)
How long you going to be planetside?

INARA
Shouldn't be more than a day or two.

WASH
Big stop just to renew your license to Companion... Can I use "Companion" as a verb?

INARA
It's Guild law. All Companions are required to undergo a physical exam once a year.

Jayne spits a large glob of saliva on his blade, wipes it on his shirt, shining it.

SIMON
Could you not do that while...
(beat)
...ever.

Jayne looks him square in the eye, then does it again. Simon moves down the table. River gets up and goes to the kitchen. Wash resumes his train of thought —

WASH
So, two days in a hospital, huh?
(Inara nods)
That's awful. Don't you just hate doctors?

SIMON
Hey!

WASH
I mean, present company excluded.

JAYNE
Don't be excluding people, that's just rude.

A blur. Suddenly something's coming at Jayne. It's River with a kitchen knife. She attacks, slashing at his Blue Sun t-shirt. Jayne barks, he's cut. SMACK! He reflexively backhands her

THE GALLEY LOCKERS

Prop master Skip Crank: "In the galley there were these aircraft lockers. Often a character had to open them and take stuff out. I'd always put severed heads and hands in them to freak them out. Gina would want to make tea, so I'd tell her the tea was in this locker — but I'd put a head in there too. Pretty soon they'd be like, 'What's in there today?'"

across the room. Bedlam ensues, and all of this happens in an instant: Simon and Inara rush to River's side, Mal, Zoe and Kaylee to Jayne's; mah jong tiles spill, food falls from the table, as the following overlaps —

MAL SIMON
Jesu — River, no — !

ZOE INARA
It's deep — Oh, god, honey...

KAYLEE
He's bleedin'.

SIMON
(shocked)
River...

RIVER
(matter-of-fact)
He looks better in red.

INT. SERENITY - INFIRMARY

Mal and Jayne talk as Simon stitches up the shirtless Jayne. Jayne is rightfully irate.

JAYNE
Gorramn freak's completely off her axel.

SIMON
I'm sorry about this. I don't know what she —

JAYNE
Shut it. I ain't talking to you.

(to Mal)
She's gotta go. Both of them's gotta go. Ariel's as good a place to leave them as any. Might even pick us up a reward for our troubles.

Simon shoots Jayne a nasty look. Jayne couldn't care less. Simon continues what he's doing.

MAL
No one's getting left.

JAYNE
She belongs in a bughouse. You don't pitch her off this boat right now, I swear to you...

MAL
What? What do you swear, Jayne?

JAYNE
They don't get gone... you better start locking up your room at night. Next time lil' sister gets in a murderin' mood, might be you she comes calling on.
(beat)
Maybe Kaylee. Or Inara. You let 'em stay... we're gonna find out.

Simon glances to Mal, wants to say something. Mal doesn't even look at him, his eyes on Jayne.

MAL
Finish your work, Doctor.
(to Jayne)
This is my boat, and they're part of my crew. No one's getting left. Best you get used to that.

Jayne steps off the table, not happy. He moves for the infirmary door, addressing Simon without turning —

JAYNE
You owe me a shirt.

Simon's about to speak, but Mal beats him to the punch.

MAL
She's to stay confined in her room at all times, no exceptions. You want to take her to the kitchen, the infirmary, whatever — you ask me first. You understand?

SIMON
I do.

MAL
When I took you and your sister in, the deal was you keep her in check. You can't hold up your end, we're gonna have to revisit that deal.
(after a silent beat)
She's getting worse, isn't she?

SIMON
Yes.

Off Simon, the admission killing him...

EXT. ARIEL - DAY

Serenity flies over the cityscape of the obviously wealthy Core city of Ariel, sweeps past, lands on a tarmac in the FG.

INT. SERENITY - CARGO BAY

Kaylee walks with Inara towards her shuttle. Below, Mal, Zoe, Wash and Jayne toss horseshoes.

KAYLEE
Look at the bright side, maybe you'll meet a young, handsome doctor and he'll ask you out and —
(beat)
What's Companion policy on dating?

INARA
It's... complicated.

KAYLEE
Figures.

Inara smiles, kisses Kaylee on the cheek —

INARA
Stay out of trouble.

— and heads into her shuttle.

KAYLEE
You too.

THE HORSESHOE TOSS

JAYNE
How're we gonna find a job if we don't leave the ship?

MAL
Alliance territory. Ain't any jobs worth havin'.

WASH
Nor the last three places we been.

JAYNE
My pop always said anyone who can't find work ain't looking hard enough. We ain't even looking at all.

SIMON
You can stop looking.

Actually, they all stop and look at him. Kaylee has drifted down here by now.

SIMON (cont'd)
There is a client. Me.
(then, to Mal)
I have a job for you.

Off everyone's reactions —

END OF TEASER

ACT ONE

INT. SERENITY - CARGO BAY

Right where we left off. Mal and the others looking at Simon.

MAL
You got a job for us?

SIMON
One that'll pay for itself ten times over.

JAYNE
Forget it. We ain't that desperate.

Simon pulls a vial out of his pocket.

SIMON
Do you know what this is? It's a common immunobooster called isoprovalyn. Street value for a dosage this size, fifty platinum, maybe twenty credits.
(another vial)
Propoxin, maybe eighty.
(another)
Hydrozapam, two hundred. And these are just from the med kit I had with me when I came on board. At a hospital like the one in Ariel City, they'd have shelves of this stuff. Whatever the take, more than enough payment for what I have in mind.

WASH
So the medvault's not the job?

SIMON
That's the payment. I tell you how to get in, get out, and what's worth taking. If you help me get River into the hospital's diagnostic ward.

MAL
What's in the diagnostic ward?

SIMON
A 3-D neuroimager. If I can get River in there, I

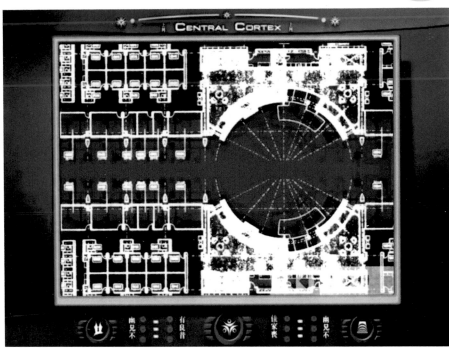

might be able to figure out what they did to her at the Academy.

MAL
So we get you and your sister into the whatchathing, you tell us how to clean out the hospital?

SIMON
Yes.

KAYLEE
Not to be negative — but don't the hospital need that medicine?

ZOE
Government run facility. They'd have it restocked in a matter of hours.

SIMON
She's right. They'll never miss it.

MAL
And folks on the rim could use it.

WASH
You know, it's very sweet — stealing from the rich and selling to the poor. But we are talking about breaking into a highly secure Alliance facility. How do you plan on getting around security?

SIMON
It's not easy, but it can be done.

Simon starts to pace, laying it all out...

SIMON (cont'd)
Like all Core hospitals, St. Lucy's has its own dedicated security force...

INT. SERENITY - DINING AREA

Continuing the movement. SIMON paces into FRAME...

GRAPHICS

Prop master Randy Eriksen: "I did a lot of the graphics, like weird colored maps and layouts on acetate, which we used on light boxes or TV screens. When they're planning the heist in 'Ariel', they had a hand-held light box, which I'd retro-fitted with batteries, to show the layout of the hospital. It probably would have made my life easier on the show if I hadn't done the graphics, but I love doing it, it's my thing."

❖ Above: The Cortex display screen showing the hospital schematics.

SIMON
...A small battery of local Alliance federals, sub-stationed here.

The dining area has been turned into a war room, with a portable Cortex screen on the kitchen table, and assorted diagrams and schematics scattered around. Simon pauses occasionally to indicate on the Cortex —

SIMON (cont'd)
Every floor, every doorway, every room is equipped with sensors. And at all points of entry: patient ident scans. However, once clear of those checkpoints, movement within the facility itself should be relatively unhindered. The standard layout should put the medvault somewhere...

MAL
Back up to the ident scans. You and your sister are tagged fugitives. How you figure we're gonna get you in the building?

SIMON
Through the front door.

(off their looks)
Believe me, Captain — getting the two of us in is going to be easy. The rest of you... that's going to be the real trick...

More pacing.

SIMON (cont'd)
We'll have to procure a few items off ship. I've made a list. Given my status as a fugitive, someone else will have to...

Kaylee, Wash and Jayne all instantly thrust their hands in the air. Mal and Zoe just look at them.

SIMON (cont'd)
We have some volunteers... good. Before we ever make it to the front door, we're going to have to breach the perimeter. Only official vehicles are allowed in. So, we'll need one.

EXT. JUNKYARD - DAY

BIG SHINY CITYSCAPE. Tilting down to find, on the edge of the city —

SIMON (V.O.)
Obviously, we can't steal what we need. Any illegal activity in the planning stages could end this thing before it starts.

DECREPIT SANDLOT. Kaylee and Wash in the junkyard — every corner is littered with engines, carburetors, rusted out shuttles, carts, etc.

SIMON (cont'd; V.O.)
Ariel City Hospital contracts with a local municipal dumpyard for its large disposals.

KAYLEE
Figures... first time on the Core, what do I get to do? — dig through trash. Why couldn't he send me shopping at the triplex, or —
(sees something)
Ooh, synchronizers!

As Wash starts looking around...

SIMON (V.O.)
Big hospitals mean big waste. We shouldn't have any trouble.

Wash waves Kaylee over to where he is — he's found something. He points to —

— a highly crappy, broken down and discarded body of an old AMBULANCE SHUTTLE.

INT. SERENITY - DINING AREA

Simon's still pacing...

SIMON
We'll have to look like we belong.

EXT. CITY STREET - DAY

Jayne loiters at a PUBLIC VIDPHONE. He sees a PARTICULARLY DRESSED MAN moving his way. He's carrying a PAIR OF BUNDLES under his arm. As he passes the vidphone "booth", he reaches out and picks up an ENVELOPE that is sitting on a lip near Jayne.

SIMON (V.O.)
That means uniforms, ID badges...

He keeps walking. A few steps, and he drops the bundles, never losing stride. Jayne walks over and sweeps up the bundles, heads off.

INT. SERENITY - COMMON AREA

Jayne dumps the bundles from the street onto the common area table. He picks out a PHOTO ID from amidst the stash — which includes EMT uniforms — looks at the ID. An Asian man is pictured. Jayne starts cutting out the picture.

SIMON (V.O.)
All of these items are easy to obtain.

INT. SERENITY - DINING AREA

Simon stops pacing. Looks to the group.

SIMON
They'll get us up to the door. Now in order to get in...

CUT TO:

INT. SERENITY - INFIRMARY

Simon sits on the examination table, Mal, Zoe and Jayne gathered around him. Mal is mid-spiel —

MAL
The patients were cynical and not-responding and we couldn't bring 'em back.

SIMON
So they were cyanotic and non-responsive and you were unable to resuscitate. Good. Which methods did you use?

ZOE
We tried the, uh, pulmonary stimulators and the cardiac, um...

SIMON
Infusers. Right. What about the cortical electrodes?

This asked of Jayne. He hesitates.

JAYNE
Um... we forgot 'em?

SIMON
Let's try that again.

INT. SERENITY - CARGO BAY

Wash screws open a plastic panel, pulls out a motherboard, starts fussing with the parts. A CLICK and a WHOOSH and he turns to see Kaylee brandishing a lit blowtorch.

INT. SERENITY - INFIRMARY

As before —

MAL
Pupils were fixed and dilapidated —

SIMON
Dilated.

MAL
Dilated, dilated — <ching-wah TSAO duh liou mahng.> [frog-humping sonofabitch.]

INT. SERENITY - CARGO BAY

VARIOUS SHOTS

— Wash untangling a mess of wiring, straightening them out and connecting one part to another.

— Kaylee welding two metal plates together, a rain of sparks around her.

— Wash manning a paint gun, spraying white paint over a smooth metal surface.

INT. SERENITY - INFIRMARY

And one more time —

MAL
By the time we got there, the patients were cyanotic and, uh... non-responsive. We tried, but we couldn't revive them — resuscitate them — despite our best efforts.
(beat)
They kicked.

SIMON
Yes. Which methods did you use?

ZOE
We used the pulmonary stimulators and cardiac infusers.
(beat)
Or is it cardiac stimulators and pulmonary infusers?

SIMON
You had it right the first time. What about cortical electrodes?

This, once again, asked of Jayne —

JAYNE
We, uh, used them electro... magnetic... Hell, I don't know, if I wanted schooling, I'da gone to school!

Simon reacts — it'll have to do.

INT. SERENITY - CARGO BAY

TRACKING WITH SIMON as he enters the cargo bay, a pleased expression on his face.

SIMON
That's amazing.

We don't yet see what he's looking at as he's joined by Kaylee and Wash.

SIMON (cont'd)
You two did an incredible job.

Now we see what they're looking at — the broken down shuttle has been retro-fitted to look just like a shiny new Ariel City Hospital ambulance.

KAYLEE
And the finishing touch —

Out of the ambulance emerge Mal, Zoe, and Jayne dressed in EMT uniforms, complete with clipped-on IDs and keycards, looking very much the part.

SIMON
If I didn't know better, I'd say you're ready to save

❖ Above (clockwise): False IDs for Wash, Jayne, Mal and Zoe.

some lives.

MAL
Now all we need's a couple of patients.

SIMON
Corpses, actually. For this to work, River and I will have to be dead.

JAYNE
I'm startin' to like this plan.

PRELAP —

SIMON (V.O.)
We're going to be asleep.

INT. SERENITY - RIVER'S ROOM

River sits on her bed, Simon at her side, explaining.

SIMON
Captain Reynolds and the others will have to pretend that we're dead to sneak us into the hospital, but once we're inside we'll wake up and everything will be fine. You understand?

RIVER
You're going to suspend cerebral, cardiac and pulmonary activity in order to induce a proto-comatose state.

Simon reacts — of course she'd get the science.

ACCESS FILE:

THE ARIEL AMBULANCE RESCUE GROUP

The ambulance began life as a mock-up of a helicopter fuselage, which was used in Hollywood films. Carey Meyer rented the fuselage from Mark Thompson's Aviation Warehouse and the *Firefly* crew modified and repainted it to become the ambulance. After 'Ariel' was filmed, the ambulance was returned to the Warehouse, which later sold it to the El Dorado Aircraft Supply Co. Ltd, who kept it in their scrap yard in Mojave, California. Scott S. Atkins discovered it in Spring 2005, and reported the find in his LiveJournal. After a phenomenal online fan response, the Ariel Ambulance Rescue Group was formed by Adam Whiting, and they purchased the ambulance on 6 May 2006 (dubbed 'Ariel Ambulance Day'). The ambulance is being gradually restored and has been outfitted with props from the movie *Serenity* donated by The Prop Store of London, including: an Alliance Lab Assistant costume, an Alliance medkit prop, and a bank heist money display. The intention is for the ambulance to travel around to conventions, stopping off at museums in between. Its first highly successful visit was to WorldCon64 in August 2006 where Loni Peristere, Jane Espenson and Tim Minear signed it!

❖ Clockwise from the top: The Ariel ambulance backstage; signatures on the inside of the restored ambulance; Jane Espenson with the ambulance; Adam Whiting, Tim Minear, Loni Peristere and Scott S. Atkins with the ambulance; Scott S. Atkins having his 'Wash moment'.

SIMON
That's right.

RIVER
I don't want to do it.

SIMON
I know.

RIVER
I don't want to go to that place. I don't want to die.

SIMON
No one's going to die. It's okay. The others will take care of us while we're asleep and when we get back —

RIVER
(on and on)
No, no, no —

SIMON
Shhh... it's okay. River. River.
(she calms)
This could be what we've been hoping for. When this is over... I'll be able to help you. I'll be able to make the nightmares go away. Okay?

Very much not okay, River nods.

SIMON (cont'd)
Okay. Lie back.

She does. Simon preps his syringe.

SIMON (cont'd)
It's time to go to sleep.

He injects her.

INT. AMBULANCE - NIGHT

Jayne, Mal and Zoe all huddled in the M.A.S.H.-like medi-shuttle. We're IN FLIGHT but it's all tight and interior.

MAL
We speak only when spoken to, we avoid any unnecessary contact and we stay together until we reach the morgue. Understood?

ZOE
Yes, sir.

Jayne doesn't reply — he's mouthing his lines. Trying to get them right.

JAYNE
(really just muttering)
Applied the cortical electrodes. Unable to get a neural reaction...

MAL
Jayne?

JAYNE
Yeah, yeah I got it.

MAL
Are we gonna have a problem?

JAYNE
I know what I gotta do.

MAL
That's not what I'm talking about. Am I gonna have a problem with you and Simon?

JAYNE
That's up to him.

MAL
Look. You got a little stabbed the other day, that's bound to make anyone a mite ornery. So I figure...

JAYNE
(cuts him off)
It's a good plan.

MAL
What?

JAYNE
Doc did good, coming up with this job. Don't mean I like him any better... but nothing buys bygones quicker'n cash.
(then)
Maybe I'll give him a tattoo while he's out.

MAL
You let him do his thing, then you get them out. No messing with him for a laugh.

JAYNE
Don't worry about me. Long as I get paid, I'm happy.

As Jayne goes back to muttering his script...

EXT. HOSPITAL - E.R. LANDING STRIP - NIGHT

The ambulance lands in front of the hospital, a pair of body bags attached nacelle-like to the side of the ambulance. [NOTE: the body bags are hard, silver shells without a discernible zipper.]

Mal, Zoe, Jayne and Wash (in his EMT uniform) spill out of the ambulance, unhook the bodybags.

ANGLE: THE PAVEMENT

as the wheels of a retractable gurney hit the ground.

WIDER — The casket-like body "bags" are now on wheels. As Mal, Zoe and Jayne start to move off with them —

WASH
We got just a few hours before the morning shift.

MAL
Won't be an hour.

And they're moving —

EXT. HOSPITAL - GANGWAY - NIGHT

Mal, Zoe and Jayne wheel the gurneys towards the door.

A R I E L

Production designer Carey Meyer: "I think we shot the junkyard on stage and pretty much the entire environment, short of a couple of foreground pieces, was practical. We brought in several pieces of junk and created essentially a foreground area for Wash and Kaylee to walk into, and then the heaps and piles of junk beyond it were a matte painting or a CG front.

"We created the ambulance for that sequence as well, where it comes in and lands at the end of that long gangway outside the hospital. We rented a fake fiberglass helicopter body and added parts to it to make it look like the CG version. We completely mocked up the interior as well, for the interior set. All the movement was CG — although it was moved from the exterior to the stage and was filmed inside the cargo bay. So it moved, but not on camera.

"The hospital interior was a white building out in Valencia that used to be called Skunkworks, where they created a lot of jet engines and military engineering. I think we used the exterior to some extent as well. It was a location that we had known during *Buffy* and relied on a lot. You often go back to places you know, because you already know the practical details and what's already there and what you're able to create. I can't stress enough how in television production, just to get to the end of the day and still be alive is a huge challenge [laughs] — and you really need to be creative. That location played perfectly. We did a lot of built-in scenery to tie into scenery that we created on the stage, namely a long hallway that led up to the operating room. The lab and the hallway that led up to it were on stage, but as the characters came out of an elevator into that hallway, the interior of the elevator and the hallway on the other side of the elevator were at Skunkworks."

CINEMATOGRAPHY

Director of photography David Boyd: "'Ariel' is one of the times when I began to put motion picture lights into the frame. In other words, we would photograph [the lights]. There's a scene in the hospital lobby and the lighting that's seen outside those windows is actually our own lighting, which played as kind of a klieg light out of the windows there, which I thought was tremendously effective. There were times when we'd get flared out by them, where the frame just gets obliterated by the light, but by hiding them behind things and seeing them occasionally at oblique angles, we got away with that pretty well."

INT. HOSPITAL - RECEIVING CHECKPOINT - NIGHT

Mal, Zoe and Jayne wheel in the body containers toward a NURSE and a RECEIVING DOCTOR.

RECEIVING DOCTOR
What have you got?

MAL
Couple DOAs. By the time we got —

RECEIVING DOCTOR
(abruptly)
Take them down to the morgue.

The doctor waves a beeper-like device over the body bags and the bags go from silver to black —

Mal, Zoe and Jayne just sort of blink. Receiving Doctor goes back to whatever it was she was doing. Jayne isn't about to go without blurting:

JAYNE
We applied the cortical electrodes but were unable to get a neural reaction from either patient!

The Receiving Doctor just looks up blankly. She didn't ask. A beat and our people move off. And they're in.

INT. HOSPITAL - MORGUE - NIGHT

Mal, Zoe and Jayne wheel in the gurneys. Jayne takes in the many blue-tinged bodies on slabs and examination tables, many of them in various stages of post-mortems. He'd rather be anywhere but here.

MAL
Let's get 'em out.

Jayne and Zoe pull a tab on each body bag and they slide open neatly, parting down the middle. They pick up Simon and River and lift them onto a pair of nearby examination tables. Another pull on the tab and the body bags close, retaining their shape.

Mal pulls a hypo out of his med bag, injects Simon and River.

MAL (cont'd)
That should bring them out of it in a few minutes. As soon as they're up, get them to the imaging suite, let Simon do his thing, then haul it back to the roof. Fifty minutes.

JAYNE
Got it.

Mal and Zoe wheel their gurneys back out.

JAYNE (cont'd)
I'll just... sit here.

And he does. For a beat. Creeped out by all the dead people. Another beat, then Jayne peeks out the door before moving out into —

INT. HOSPITAL - RECOVERY WARD - NIGHT

Jayne walks down a corridor, stops at a Cortex terminal. He swipes a card on the terminal, and in a moment a face appears on the Cortex screen — this is AGENT McGINNIS.

JAYNE
I'm in.

AGENT McGINNIS
Do you have the fugitives?

JAYNE
You got my reward?

AGENT McGINNIS
Yes. Just like we talked about.

JAYNE
Then I got your fugitives.

AGENT McGINNIS
Good. We'll see you shortly. Congratulations. You're about to become a very rich man.

Off Jayne —

END OF ACT ONE

ACT TWO

INT. HOSPITAL - MORGUE - NIGHT

Jayne slips back into the morgue, where Simon and River still lie unconscious. Now that he's alone, Jayne is even more spooked by this place. Especially the quiet.

Behind Jayne (and unseen by him) River SITS UP INTO FRAME. She's just woken up and is a bit dazed, disoriented. She's inches behind him as she says —

RIVER
A copper for a kiss.

Jayne jumps — she startled the hell out of him.

JAYNE
Jesu — ! What — what did you say?

River falters — even she's not sure what just came out of her mouth.

In the BG, Simon now bolts awake with a CHOKED GASP. Jayne jumps again. Simon goes into a coughing jag, every cough causing him noticeable pain.

JAYNE (cont'd)
What's the matter with you?

SIMON
Nothing, just after-effects from the drugs.
(coughs, it hurts)
I'll be fine, just give me a second.

JAYNE
(you weenie)
Your sister seems okay.

From behind Jayne comes the sound of River throwing up. Jayne looks behind him, sees the mess — yuck. He turns back to Simon and tosses him a bundle of clothes.

JAYNE (cont'd)
Get dressed. We gotta move.

INT. HOSPITAL - CORRIDOR - NIGHT

A pair of elevator doors open and Mal and Zoe push their gurneys down a quiet corridor.

MAL
Two rights, two lefts and we're there. You see

anyone, smile.

ZOE
I don't think people smile in hospitals.

MAL
'Course they do. It's the Core, everybody's rich and happy here. Why wouldn't they smile?

From O.S., a voice calls to them —

OFFICIOUS DOCTOR (O.S.)
'Scuse me —

Mal turns, sees an OFFICIOUS DOCTOR.

MAL
(big smile)
Hi!

OFFICIOUS DOCTOR
(unsmiling)
Where are you taking those bodies?

MAL
Just downstairs to the morgue.

OFFICIOUS DOCTOR
(pointing behind them)
Downstairs is that way.

MAL
Right. Must've got turned around.

OFFICIOUS DOCTOR
Let me see your badge.

Mal hands it over.

INT. HOSPITAL - RECOVERY WARD - NIGHT

Simon and Jayne wheel River down a corridor in a wheelchair. She's in a hospital gown, Simon is in scrubs, Jayne still wears his EMT uniform.

RIVER
We're doing it backwards. Walking up the down slide.

JAYNE
Keep her quiet.

Simon leans in close to River as he walks, as soothing as ever —

SIMON
This is the recovery ward. This is where patients come to get better.

RIVER
They're going to die.

SIMON
No one's going to die.

RIVER
(indicates a patient)
He is.

Simon looks where River's indicating. A fortysomething PATIENT lies in bed, a cocky YOUNG INTERN tending to him.

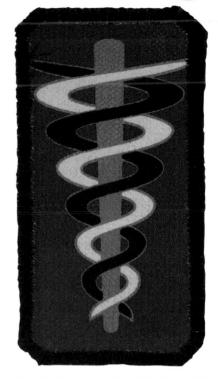

❖ Above: A patch from one of the EMT uniforms worn by the crew.

SIMON
No, he's not. That man standing next to him is his doctor, he's going to help him.

RIVER
He's not going to help him right.

SIMON
River, the doctors here are the best in the system. This is one of the top hospitals in the Core or anywhere else.

RIVER
Where you should be.

Simon does his best to not react to that. River grabs the wheels on the wheelchair, effectively slamming on the brakes. She starts to get up; Jayne won't let her.

JAYNE
Uh-uh. No wandering off.

RIVER
(to Simon)
You have to help him.

SIMON
River, we don't have time to —

RIVER
(loud)
He's killing him!

The monitors by the patient start BEEPING, alarms going off. And now River is struggling against Jayne, trying to get up out of her chair.

YOUNG INTERN
Code blue!

NURSES converge on the trauma area. Simon sees them working frantically, knows he can help —

SIMON
(to River)
Stay here. Don't move.

With a look to Jayne that says "watch her", Simon jumps into the fray. This is FAST —

SIMON (cont'd)
What do we have?

YOUNG INTERN
Forty-two-year-old, double bypass post-op. Prognosis was positive —

CRASH TEAM NURSE
BP sixty over twenty, pulse is thready.

Simon rips the patient's gown open, listens to his heart.

YOUNG INTERN
(to Simon)
Who are you?

CRASH TEAM NURSE
He's crashing —

SIMON
(to Nurse)
Get the cart.

She moves to get the crash cart; that's when a long, constant BEEEEEP starts coming from the EKG —

CRASH TEAM NURSE
We have flatline —

YOUNG INTERN
We gotta crack him —

SIMON
(stern, to Intern)
We're not cracking a post-op.
(to the Nurse)
Get the infusers and point-four of atropine.
(to Intern)
What did you give him?

YOUNG INTERN
Just twenty of alprazaline push.

Simon gives him a look — whatever that means, it means the Intern fucked up.

The Nurse hands Simon a hypo and a pair of pen-like devices. (These are cardiac infusers, and they look not unlike a pair of tire pressure gauges.) Simon puts the hypo between his teeth, applies the infusers to the patient's chest —

SIMON
Clear —

PHUMP! A blip on the EKG, then back to flat-line —

SIMON (cont'd)
Clear —

PHUMP! A blip on the EKG, this time it keeps blipping, but another ALARM SOUNDS. Simon gives the infusers to the Nurse.

YOUNG INTERN
(an accusation)
He's going tachy.

Simon takes the hypo from his teeth —

SIMON
(dismissive)
But his heart's beating.

— plugs it into the IV, pushes in the atropine. Instantly, the alarms stop. A beat, then the EKG blips become slower and more regular.

Everyone breathes a sigh of relief, especially the Intern.

YOUNG INTERN
(willing it)
He's okay...

Simon gets in his face, genuinely pissed —

SIMON
Explain to me how you justify administering a vasoconstrictor to this patient?

YOUNG INTERN
Alprazaline's a painkiller, not a —

SIMON
Unless you combine it with dilavtin, which any first year should know is the standard prep medicine your patient was taking before his surgery. Your patient should be dead. And you'd be standing here scratching your head as to why.

YOUNG INTERN
I — I'm... sorry, Doctor.

SIMON
Good.

Simon moves back to River and Jayne. River's practically beaming. Jayne's not unimpressed.

SIMON (cont'd)
Let's go.

INT. HOSPITAL - CORRIDOR - NIGHT

Mal and Zoe and the Officious Doctor, moments after we left them. The Doctor examines Mal's ident badge carefully.

OFFICIOUS DOCTOR
(moving towards a vidphone)
Walk with me a minute.

Mal gives Zoe a look — better do something. She sidles over to a crash cart.

MAL
Where we going?

The Doctor stops, actually seems offended at the question. He holds up his ident card.

OFFICIOUS DOCTOR
You see this badge? It says "Doctor". I say walk with me, you walk with me.

Mal stays put — he already hates this guy.

MAL
Yeah, but... Where we going?

Now the Doctor is pissed —

OFFICIOUS DOCTOR
You must be new.
(Mal doesn't deny it)
Don't get comfortable; your type doesn't last long here. When your supervisor hears about the rude and disrespectful attitude you just —

PHUMP! The Doctor collapses to the ground. Zoe stands behind him, a pair of cardiac infusers in hand.

ZOE
Clear.

INT. HOSPITAL - IMAGING SUITE - NIGHT

Simon and Jayne push River into the suite, Jayne hanging back and looking both ways out the door before shutting it.

Simon crouches next to River, as soothing as he can be —

SIMON
Ready?

Although clearly apprehensive, River nods.

INT. HOSPITAL - ANOTHER CORRIDOR - NIGHT

Mal and Zoe push their gurneys down the corridor, stop at a door.

MAL
Twelve-oh-five. This is it.

He looks around, makes sure the coast is clear, then swipes his keycard through the scanner. A RED LIGHT flashes on the scanner — the door won't open. He tries again. Again, red light.

BEN EDLUND

I think the show is actually at its strongest when it discusses the tension between the frontier and the Core worlds. That's why 'Ariel' strikes me as one of the strongest episodes, because you get both. You get the dirty, unwashed real people coming back to this plastic utopia. That mix — not that it should be in every episode — was something very important.

MAL (cont'd)
Zoe.

Zoe tries her keycard. Twice. Same thing: the light blinks red.

ZOE
They must've been de-mag'd.

Mal pulls the tab on one of the bodybags — it opens to reveal the Officious Doctor, who is MOANING but unconscious. He snatches his keycard, slides it through the scanner. The door opens.

MAL
His works.

INT. HOSPITAL - IMAGING SUITE - NIGHT

Simon helps River onto the steel table and she leans back, her eyes staring straight up. This place clearly scares her.

Simon moves to a podium-like control column, wheels it over close to River. He inserts a PLASTIC TAB into the column, then presses a few buttons, turns on the machine. The entire room starts to make a WHIRRING SOUND.

River closes her eyes. Jayne simply watches.

INT. SUPPLY VAULT - NIGHT

This is thief heaven. Simon was right — the shelves are lined with vial upon vial of medicine. Mal dumps the Officious Doctor on the floor, and he and Zoe start filling the body bags with drugs.

In a series of JUMP CUTS, they quickly, efficiently clean out the room, cramming as many vials as they can into the body bags, reading labels and tossing away the worthless ones before sealing the jammed packed body bags again.

INT. IMAGING SUITE - NIGHT

The WHIRRING is a little louder now. Simon works for a moment longer before —

SIMON
River... I'm going to start the scan now. You okay?

River is trying very hard to keep her shit together; she's on the brink of freaking. Her lips are moving fast, but no words are coming out.

SIMON (cont'd)
River?

RIVER
(snapping)
Just do it.

Simon works the controls and a HOLOGRAPHIC IMAGE APPEARS, a three-dimensional scan of her brain floating above her like a bizarre rain cloud. Numbers and wave-graphs flank the central image of her brain.

INT. HOSPITAL - CORRIDOR - NIGHT

Just outside the supply vault. Mal and Zoe push the gurneys back out into the corridor. Mal shuts the vault door with the Doctor still inside.

INT. IMAGING SUITE - NIGHT

Jayne sits in a corner, watching Simon work at the control column. (An LCD window on the column reads DOWNLOADING DATA.) Simon mans the controls like the professional he is — rotating the image, punching up new numbers and scans. He's riveted by the flood of information, stares at the images before him in disbelief.

SIMON
<Yen guo duh hwai dan.> [Castrated bastards.] How anyone could do this to another person... She's seventeen...

Jayne remains impassive, not wanting to be drawn into this. Nonetheless, Simon turns to him —

SIMON (cont'd)
They opened up her skull. Look —

NATHAN FILLION

'Ariel' I loved! Adam Baldwin did a great job as Jayne, this big, blundering, not-too-bright but extremely excellent warrior. If you are gonna fight, you are gonna want Zoe and Jayne on your side. I loved that the audience was like, 'Oh that Jayne! He's such a big lovable lug!' But he's a flawed character. He will sell you out if the price is right. He said in the pilot, 'Money wasn't good enough.' It's not profitable enough. That says a lot about Jayne, but Jayne proved it. They could have let him be lovable and loyal all the time, like a big Chewbacca, but Jayne's not Chewbacca. Jayne is a flawed character and when the right price came along, he sold them out. I thought it was a great episode and important to show people that he is not to be trusted.

Using the controls, he highlights (Madden-like, but slicker) a straight line drawn across River's frontal and temporal lobes — an incision line.

SIMON (cont'd)
That's a scalpel scar. They opened up her skull... and then they cut into her brain.

Curiosity gets the best of Jayne —

JAYNE
Why?

SIMON
The only reason to make an incision in someone's brain is to lobotomize them — you go in to remove damaged tissue. Why someone would cut into a healthy brain...

He lets it hang there — the answer is beyond him.

SIMON (cont'd)
They did it over and over.

The downloading window switches to DOWNLOAD COMPLETE. Simon absently takes the plastic tab out of the machine, pockets it. A moment, as Simon looks at something else.

SIMON (cont'd)
They stripped her amygdala...

JAYNE
(growing discomfort)
Her what?

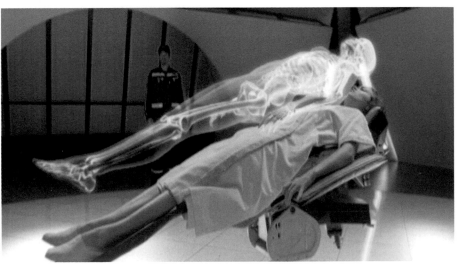

WASH

"I can be terse. Once, in flight school, I was laconic."

Many have theorized that *Firefly* fell victim to being too far ahead of its time, and maybe just a little too smart for what television was ready for. Shedding the conventional trappings of what science fiction on film looks like, and using the Western metaphor literally, made the show externally unique, but at its heart, the series was always about the dynamic personalities that lived together on Serenity. Alan Tudyk thinks that's the key to what attracted so many diehard fans to the show — the common threads humanity will always exhibit through space and time. "My description of *Firefly* is this: it is set in space, but the great thing about it is that it brings the human condition to space. People argue, people get hungry and don't like the food they are eating. It's not like other shows, which I'm not going to mention, where they can just order up their food in a little processor and go 'beef sirloin' and they have it. We have these protein cakes, which are kind of moldy. We don't have much cash. Sometimes I make mistakes flying, like you do when you're driving

and you miss an exit. I can miss a whole planet if I'm not paying attention!"

No one can argue that the rapport between characters and amongst the actors also infused the series with an intimacy that was a great attraction for viewers. Tudyk says that connection was real and it made the show live. "The cast all bonded over the material. I think we knew going in that Fox was already having problems with the vision of the show and the minute any kind of noise like that happens, you look to the person beside you, grab hold and say, 'We're in this together. We are going to fight this out!' Very quickly, we became a tight knit family. It's really fortunate when it works out that you enjoy working with the people that you are spending fourteen hours of the day with."

Like his fellow cast, Tudyk is the first to say that a lot of that bonding stemmed from Nathan Fillion. "Nathan is so perfect as the Captain because he really is a leader himself. When things were screwing up like they do on any TV show, like the lighting was wrong or you can't get something, there was never a complaint from him. Actually when I first read the script, the Captain was a very important role and I was like, 'Who did they get to play the Captain?' They told me the name and I didn't recognize it. I was like, 'I hope this works; I hope they got a good guy.' The first day I walked in, I was like, 'God dangit, he's so not right! He's not right for the role, just by looking at him, they screwed up, god this is going to tank!' So I was like, 'Hi, hi' and we introduced ourselves and I said, 'Wow, so you're the Captain?' and he replied, 'No, no! I'm the Doctor.' It was Sean," he laughs. "It's true! And then I met Nathan and I was like, 'Oh good, that's going to work out fine.'"

Tudyk's other favorite connection was with actress Gina Torres, who played his better half, Zoe. "I love Gina," the actor enthuses genuinely. "She's the greatest. We got to have a post-coital scene in the series. We did some making out, which was fun. We did some fighting together and she saved me. I don't think I ever saved her — that would be fun! For me to save her and be the bad ass for once would have been fun." ⏴

SIMON
You know how... you get scared. Or worried, or nervous. And you don't want to be scared or worried or nervous, so you push it to the back of your mind. You try not to think about it. The amygdala is what lets you do that — it's like a filter in your brain that keeps your feelings in check.
(beat, disturbed by this)
They took that filter out of River. She feels everything. She can't not.

That's as perturbing to Jayne as it is to Simon, but he's not going to get drawn into River's problems.

JAYNE
That's fascinating.
(grabs the tab, puts it in Simon's coat pocket)
We should get moving.

SIMON
(looks at a wall clock)
We still have twenty minutes.

JAYNE
Wrong. Plan changed when you were out. We're meeting out the back way in five.

RIVER

Her eyes snap open.

THE HOLOGRAM

Images begin to change furiously as River's brain starts firing, going berserk. Greens go to red, levels spike, warning lights flash. Simon has his back momentarily turned, addressing Jayne.

SIMON
I could use another couple of minutes. I'm sure if we contact Captain Reynolds —

JAYNE
Captain gave his orders. We play it by the book.

River lets out an ear-splitting SCREAM OF TERROR.

Simon turns, sees the hyperactive hologram. He shuts off the machine and rushes to River's side. She's in full freak-out mode now; her dialogue overlaps with everyone else's.

SIMON
River — it's okay, you're okay.

JAYNE
Get her in the chair and let's go.

RIVER
No, no, no — they come out of the black. They come when you call.

SIMON
It's okay, it's over.
(looks at Jayne)
We're leaving.

River fixes Jayne with a look — like she sees right into him. It's wigging him a bit.

RIVER
Your toes are in the sand.

JAYNE
(defensive)
And your head's up your —

SIMON
Hey! Back off.

JAYNE
Just make sure she keeps her mouth shut. We don't need her screeching while we're trying to make a quiet getaway.

Jayne goes to the door, looks around outside, then looks back at Simon and River. She's in hysterical tears, her hands clutching his shirt. He's stroking her hair, cooing, trying to calm her. Off Jayne... is he starting to feel guilty?

CUT TO:

INT. HOSPITAL - RECOVERY WARD - NIGHT

Jayne leads the way as Simon pushes River in her wheelchair. Her lips are again moving soundlessly.

SIMON
(quietly, to Jayne)
You should've let me know when the plan changed.

JAYNE
I told you when you needed to know.
(off Simon's look)
What are you griping about, you got what you came for.

They turn a corner into —

INT. HOSPITAL - ANOTHER CORRIDOR - CONTINUOUS

The reach the back exit doors, are about to push through when River puts the brakes on the chair.

RIVER
No... can't go back, don't want to go back...

SIMON
Shh, it's okay. We're just going back to the ship. We're almost home.

River reluctantly allows herself to be pushed through the doors to —

EXT. HOSPITAL - BACK EXIT - CONTINUOUS

The doors aren't even shut behind them when SPOTLIGHTS spark to life, pinning Simon, River and Jayne in their crosshairs.

AGENT McGINNIS (filtered)
Federal Marshals — don't move.

They shield their eyes... just enough to see that they're surrounded by armed feds. Lots of them, and moving cautiously towards them, rifles raised.

AGENT McGINNIS
River and Simon Tam. By the authority of the Union of Allied Planets, you are hereby bound by law.

Off their reactions —

BLACK OUT.

END OF ACT TWO

ACT THREE

EXT. HOSPITAL - BACK EXIT - NIGHT

As we left them. The feds come up to Simon and River, who offer no resistance as they're patted down and cuffed, their hands behind their backs.

AGENT McGINNIS
Take them to processing.

The officers start ushering Simon and River away, another comes to cuff Jayne, who plays along, takes a slow step towards McGinnis —

JAYNE
(sotto)
So... you gonna take me away for questioning now, or how d'ya wanna play it?

AGENT McGINNIS
You're under arrest for aiding and abetting federal fugitives. Better get a lawyer.

Jayne almost laughs. McGinnis doesn't.

JAYNE
You're kidding, right?

McGinnis says nothing.

JAYNE (cont'd)
(through his teeth)
Where's my rutting money?

AGENT McGINNIS
You mean my money? For apprehending the three fugitives? I expect I'll be getting it soon.

With that, McGinnis walks away. Jayne realizes he's been double-crossed. He yanks free of the fed

ADAM BALDWIN

On Jayne's good intentions for turning Simon and River over to the Alliance: "Well, he wasn't betraying anyone; he was doing it for the crew. Jayne came at it from the angle that he was helping them out, and if he makes a little money along the way, great. It wasn't like he was betraying the crew. They had some weird passengers on their heads, too. I like the scene where they describe the blue hands, and those little wands that make people's heads explode from the inside."

❖ Above: The Sonic prepaint, this is the Alliance sonic rifle master model.

cuffing him (one cuff on, one off), he starts to lunge at McGinnis, when —

A FED

swings around with his SONIC RIFLE. We're LOOK-ING DOWN THE BUSINESS END as a wave of compressed sound DISTORTS THE AIR and slams into Jayne like a wrecking ball, sending him FLYING hard into a wall.

EXT. HOSPITAL - E.R. LANDING STRIP - NIGHT

Mal and Zoe trot the gurneys out towards the ambulance shuttle. Wash hops out and helps them strap the body bags to the outside of the shuttle. He reacts to the weight of the bags. (They're essentially filled to the brim with liquid.)

WASH
How much did we get?

Zoe smiles at Wash — it's a lot. Mal downplays it.

MAL
Enough to keep us flying.

ZOE
(psyched)
Can we fly somewhere with a beach?

WASH
Maybe a naked beach.

Wash and Zoe kiss.

MAL
Cut it out. Job ain't done til we're back on Serenity.

ZOE
Sorry, sir. Didn't mean to enjoy the moment.

MAL
(to Wash)
Where are the others?

INT. HOSPITAL - SECURITY SUBSTATION - RECEPTION - NIGHT

FED #1 escorts Jayne, Simon and River into the reception area. Simon whispers to the defeated-looking Jayne:

SIMON
I appreciate what you tried to do out there.

JAYNE
(defensive)
I didn't do nothing.

SIMON
More than I did.

They are herded over to a bench, shoved onto it. Jayne is in between Simon and River.

They eyeball McGinnis in the near distance, talking to FED #2, prepping paperwork.

SIMON (cont'd)
If those officers hadn't been armed, I think you'd have had a chance.

JAYNE
Guy shoved me, I shoved back. Not like I was trying to mount a rescue.

SIMON
Still. I appreciate you trying.

JAYNE
You know what I'd appreciate? If you'd stop flapping your pretty mouth at me. I'm trying to think of a way out of here and I can't do it with you yammering.

RIVER
They took Christmas away.

JAYNE
What the hell now?

RIVER
Came down the stairs for the shiny presents, but they took the tree and the stockings. Nothing left but coal.

JAYNE
(to Simon)
Shut her up.

RIVER
(to Jayne)
And don't look in the closet, either. That's greedy. It's not in the spirit of the holiday.

JAYNE
(very harsh)
Shut. The hell. Up. Right now. Or so help me I will shut you up.

INT./EXT. AMBULANCE SHUTTLE - NIGHT

Mal, Zoe and Wash.

MAL
Time.

ZOE
Ten minutes past rendezvous.

MAL
Something happened.

Wash opens a communication channel with Serenity.

WASH
Kaylee, are you linked?

INTERCUT:

SUMMER GLAU

'Ariel' was, for me, the hardest episode to shoot. The scenes in it were very emotional and I had to say a lot of things that I didn't understand. I found it very complicated, emotionally. However, I am really proud of the way it turned out. I love that episode. We were up in this old apartment building; it was really creepy and such a challenging shoot. Sean and I were working so much, that whenever I sat down in my chair I would just fall asleep.

INT. SERENITY - BRIDGE - NIGHT

Kaylee's on the bridge, in the pilot's seat. She taps a few buttons and the Cortex pops up on the helm screen.

KAYLEE
I am now. What do you need?

WASH
Find out if there's been any kind of security alert in the hospital.

KAYLEE
Hang on...

As Kaylee works —

ZOE
Could be they're just late.

MAL
Not this late. Jayne would've sent up a flag.

Kaylee gets what she's looking for.

KAYLEE
Nothing from hospital security. Nothing on local pipeline, either. Although I'm getting some weird chatter on the official two-six-two. Sounds like they're talking about... ducks?

ZOE
(to Mal)
Code?

MAL
(nods)
Feds got 'em.
(to Wash)
Have her bring up the hospital schematics on the Cortex. Find me a way into the security substation.

Zoe ducks into the ambulance, tosses Mal his gun. He tucks it in his vest; she lifts up her pantleg and straps her shotgun to her calf with bandage tape.

WASH
Wait a minute, you don't even know for sure they're in there —

Now Zoe places an earwig in her ear, hands one to Mal, who does the same.

MAL
Gonna find out.
(presses the earwig into his ear)
Check.

ZOE
(re: her earwig)
Coming in clear.

WASH
So you're just gonna walk in through the front door?

MAL
No. You're gonna find me a way round the back.

They shut the ambulance doors and move off.

INT. HOSPITAL - SECURITY SUBSTATION - RECEPTION - NIGHT

McGinnis approaches the bench where Simon, Jayne and River sit (armed feds in evidence).

AGENT McGINNIS
(to Simon)
Get up.

SIMON
What's going to happen to us?

AGENT McGINNIS
I said get up.

McGinnis grabs Simon by the arm; he yanks himself free.

SIMON
Agent McGinnis, I'm certain you're working under a superior who's keeping close tabs on this case. I'm certain of that because important people don't do field work. I'm also quite certain your superior wants me and my sister alive. I'm not going to move from this spot until one of two things happen: you answer my very simple question, or you shoot me.

McGinnis bristles, but has little choice but to answer.

AGENT McGINNIS
We're transferring you to a holding area until you can be retrieved.

SIMON
Retrieved... by whom?

AGENT McGINNIS
By people who want you alive. People not me.
(to the feds)
Take 'em.

PRELAP the sound of a BUZZER and —

CUT TO:

INT. HOSPITAL - SECURITY SUBSTATION -

HOLDING AREA - NIGHT

A security door opens and two feds escort Jayne, Simon and River through the holding area. The feds usher the prisoners around a corner and towards a cell.

River and Simon file in, as does Jayne. As Fed #2 goes to shut the door, Jayne springs — SLAMMING HIS HEAD into Fed #2's nose and shattering it, knocking him out.

Fed #1 raises his rifle, but Jayne rams into him shoulder first, practically lifting him off the ground and CRUSHING him against a wall. The impact is such that both men go down, the rifle skittering away. Jayne quickly wriggles his cuffs past his feet. His hands are in front of him now. He grabs Fed #1 with both hands, one hand on his mouth, the other on his throat.

The following is dirty, ugly and almost completely silent:

Jayne squeezes hard, crushing his windpipe. The fed tries to pry Jayne's hands off him, but Jayne's too strong. So the fed bites down on Jayne's hand; blood streams down, but Jayne keeps his hold on both mouth and throat.

Simon goes to help Jayne, but hears Fed #2 stir — he's coming to. Simon moves to him, kneels on his throat. He won't make a sound.

Still wrestling on the ground, Fed #1 gouges at Jayne's eyes, gets him pretty good, causing Jayne to look away and allowing the fed to flip Jayne on his back. Fed #1 straddles him, proceeds to SLAM Jayne's head repeatedly on the marble floor. (Jayne should get a forehead welt in all of this that we carry to the end of the show.)

River watches the violence.

INT. HOSPITAL - RECOVERY WARD - NIGHT

Mal and Zoe.

MAL
Wash, a little direction, please.

INTERCUT AS NEEDED:

INT. AMBULANCE SHUTTLE - NIGHT

Wash talks into his transmitter —

WASH
Working on it...

Then into the com —

WASH (cont'd)
Kaylee, whaddya got?

INT. SERENITY - BRIDGE

Kaylee's looking at the hospital blueprints on the Cortex.

KAYLEE
Tell them to make a left when they get to cryo. They'll see a door —

INT. HOSPITAL - RECOVERY WARD - NIGHT

Mal and Zoe, moving fast —

WASH
Go through that door and down to green level.

Mal and Zoe go through the door and into —

INT. HOSPITAL - PURPLE STAIRCASE - NIGHT

They descend the steps, taking them two and three at a time. As they do —

MAL
This is exactly what I didn't want. I wanted simple, I wanted in-and-out, I wanted easy money.

ZOE
Things always get a little more complicated, don't they, sir?

MAL
Once, just once, I want things to go according to the gorramn plan!

They reach the bottom of the steps, head for the door, when —

WASH (V.O.)
Um, guys... you might want to hurry.

MAL
Is there a problem?

INT. AMBULANCE SHUTTLE - NIGHT

Wash looks out the window, sees an ominous-looking shuttle descending towards City Hospital and landing on its roof.

WASH
I think the reinforcements are here.

Off Wash's dread...

INT. HOSPITAL - SECURITY SUBSTATION - HOLDING AREA - NIGHT

Back to the ugly, quiet fight at the substation.

Simon continues to put pressure on Fed #2's throat.

Jayne knees the fed in the nuts — it's enough to try to flip on top of him. They roll around, Jayne repeatedly taking punches as he tries to squeeze the life out of this bastard.

Finally the fed goes limp. Jayne gives him a few squeezes and shakes for good measure. Lets the body drop. He takes the keys off the dead fed. Moves to Simon, who is expressionless, standing over the unconscious body of Fed #2. No remorse from Simon at what Jayne has just done. Maybe even a bit impressed. Jayne uncuffs him, then moves to do the same for River.

Simon picks up the fed's sonic rifle. Jayne turns back to him just as Simon tosses the rifle to Jayne.

SIMON
Come on.

Simon starts to move to an intersecting corridor. Jayne is going back toward the front door. Simon turns to him —

SIMON (cont'd)
What are you doing?

JAYNE
Going out the way we came in.

SIMON
There's at least four armed feds out there.

JAYNE
Six.
(holds up the rifle)
I know.

SIMON
(re: a corridor)
We run.

JAYNE
You got no idea where that goes.

SIMON
We'll find our way.

JAYNE
I ain't chancing that. I can handle the feds.

RIVER
Doesn't matter.

Jayne and Simon turn to her. She's hugging her arms to her body as if cold... actually, she's just terrified.

RIVER (cont'd)
They're here.

INT. HOSPITAL - SECURITY SUBSTATION - RECEPTION - NIGHT

McGinnis can be seen with his back toward reception, talking to one of his men who is doing paperwork. Another of his men approaches him, whispers something to him. Something like, "they're here". McGinnis turns, registers recognition as he spots someone over at reception that we DON'T YET SEE. As McGinnis crosses toward the unseen newcomers:

AGENT McGINNIS
Gentlemen. That was prompt. We're almost finished here. Prisoners'll be out in a minute. Let me get the paperwork together for you.
(to one of his men, re: paperwork)
Bobby, bring all that over here.
(looks to unseen men)
Not that it's gonna mean much. The men were tight lipped. And the girl was just spewing gibberish. We got it all down, for the good it'll do.

REVERSE — TO INCLUDE TWO MEN

Relatively non-descript, except for the blue gloves they wear. (They will henceforth be known as the BLUE GLOVES.)

JEFF RICKETTS

Jeff Ricketts, along with Carlos Jacott, Andy Umberger and Jonathan Woodward, is one of Joss Whedon's four 'hat-trick' actors, who have appeared on all three Whedon series: *Buffy* (Ricketts played one of the Watchers chasing Faith in 'Who Are You?'), *Angel* (same Watcher in 'Sanctuary', plus the sewer monster in 'Sacrifice') and *Firefly*, as one of the sinister Blue-Gloved Men in 'The Train Job' and 'Ariel'.

What was Ricketts initially told about the Blue-Gloved Men? "I think the words were, 'Futuristic CIA'. It was a teaser at the end of 'The Train Job', the Colonel comes in and says, 'Yes, sir, we've been expecting you,' and my line is, 'We didn't fly eighty-six million miles to open a box of band-aids, Colonel.' How much better can you tantalize someone? I was ready to do it arch, taste every word, and Joss, who directed that episode, said, 'Just say it. Less acting.' Which is great fun.

"In the beginning, I didn't know what to expect. He seemed like a suit and tie, office-type character, a little bit self-consciously bureaucratic, but of course in 'Ariel', we're making people bleed from their orifices," Ricketts laughs, "so I think I'm a little bit more than one of Kafka's bureaucrats.

"It felt like, this is a new universe. I can't even describe it, other than obviously the design felt more open, a new squeaky-clean feel to it, and yet there was a little more anxiety in the *Firefly* world. Maybe it was because the characters we were playing were so squeaky-clean, but horrible, horrible people, too.

"I took the bureaucrat thing very seriously. When they're holding River for us, Federal Agent McGinnis is instructed not to speak to the prisoners. From the Blue-Gloved Man's point of view, you just have a few orders: 'Get the prisoner, don't speak to her, hold her for us.' And McGinnis violates this one thing. Since I'm a very nit-picky bureaucrat, if you do one little thing that I told you not to do, then we have to take out this instrument which makes you bleed from your eyes. So I'm very fastidious about the rules. It was Dennis Cochran, Blue-Gloved Man Number Two, who had to handle that instrument. Somehow, he managed to endow it with a supernatural property.

"The blue gloves were the subject of some debate," Ricketts recalls. "By 'Ariel', the exact shade of blue was being debated offstage." This was partly because blue screens are used in special effects. "'The Chromakey won't deal with this shade of blue.' Also, they didn't want them to look like we were about to go do dishes," Ricketts laughs.

FIRST BLUE GLOVE
You spoke to the prisoners?

AGENT McGINNIS
Well, yeah. Had to process 'em. There was no kind of interrogation, if that's what you mean.
(lightly)
Didn't do your job for you.

The SECOND BLUE GLOVE reaches in his suit pocket, pulls out a thick rod-like device. He squeezes it and a thin spicule extends from each end.

SECOND BLUE GLOVE
Did your men also speak with them?

AGENT McGINNIS
Much as they had to.

A trickle of blood drips from McGinnis' nose. He feels it, dabs at it with his hand, sees it's blood.

ANGLE: HIS HAND

as he turns it over... revealing his fingernails. Blood is seeping from under them. He brings his hand up closer to his face... We FOLLOW his HAND to his FACE, revealing —

His eyes have gone red, bloodshot through. And blood is already streaming down his cheeks as he BLEEDS OUT.

He SCREAMS... Whatever is happening to him is excruciating...

THE BLUE GLOVES

watch. Impassive. McGinnis's SCREAMING takes us to —

BLACK OUT.

END OF ACT THREE

ACT FOUR

OVER BLACK.

The SOUND OF SCREAMING.

INT. HOSPITAL - SECURITY SUBSTATION - HOLDING AREA

Jayne, Simon and River react to the SCREAMS. First it's just the one. Then more — all in the same agony as McGinnis when he died.

JAYNE
What the hell is that?

Simon shakes his head, doesn't venture a guess. River's breathing is coming quicker now. She knows what's out there and it fills her with terror. She's backing away, moving away... Simon sees this.

RIVER
(muttery)
Two by two, hands of blue. Two by two, hands of blue.

She keeps moving backward, stumbles, is nearly running now. Simon starts after her.

Jayne is left listening to the nearby carnage. A beat. He follows the others.

INT. HOSPITAL - SECURITY SUBSTATION - RECEPTION

ON McGINNIS

as we left him, very much dead. Then, CAMERA DRIFTS through the reception area... FINDING another fed. Also dead, also bleeding out of many orifices. CAMERA CONTINUES TO DRIFT... finding another fed. Same thing. And another. And another. Every fed we've seen lies dead in a pool of blood.

CAMERA CONTINUES TO DRIFT... finding the Blue-Gloved Men walking through the carnage, completely unaffected. They walk up to the separator door, walk through.

INT. HOSPITAL - STEEL ROOM - NIGHT

River leads Jayne and Simon into the guts of the hospital. This space is more industrial, less pristine. She keeps moving fast, Simon and Jayne following.

JAYNE
Where the hell's she goin' —

SIMON
There must be some sort of an exit this way.

INT. HOSPITAL - SECURITY SUBSTATION -

❖ Left: The prototype rod weapon for the Blue-Gloved Men.

HOLDING AREA - CONTINUOUS

The Blue-Gloved Men walk in, past the separator door and into the cell area. There, they find the two laid out feds Jayne took out. First Blue Glove takes the pulse of one, Second Blue Glove the pulse of the other.

FIRST BLUE GLOVE
Dead.

First Blue Glove looks in the direction Jayne and the others went.

SECOND BLUE GLOVE
This one's alive.

Second Blue Glove takes out The Device from his pocket.

INT. HOSPITAL - STEEL ROOM - NIGHT

JAYNE
I don't see any exit, and I got no intention of running around like a rat in a maze til we're dead. We're going back.

Jayne starts to go. He pauses at SCREAMING from somewhere above. Maybe best not to go back thataway...

INT. HOSPITAL - SECURITY SUBSTATION - HOLDING AREA - NIGHT

The Blue-Gloved Men step over or past the now BLED-OUT fed, moving ever forward, as...

INT. HOSPITAL - HUM ROOM - NIGHT

River runs down the steps, Jayne and Simon following.

RIVER
Almost there. Almost there.

She reaches the bottom of the steps, keeps running, Simon and Jayne gaining... then she finally stops at a large steel door.

RIVER (cont'd)
There.

Jayne tries the door — locked. A faint TAP-TAP-TAPPING can be heard in the distance. Jayne looks in its direction — fear starting to become evident in his face.

JAYNE
Stand back.

He takes aim at the door with the sonic rifle, BLASTS IT! In these echoey halls, it makes an ENORMOUS REVERBERATING BOOM! But it does nothing to the door. When the sound subsides, the TAP-TAP-TAPPING starts to get closer.

JAYNE (cont'd)
(under his breath)
<Shee-niou> [Cow sucking] high-tech Alliance crap.

Jayne looks towards the tapping sound... about to

freak... turns the rifle around, starts wailing on the lock with the rifle butt. WHAM! WHAM! Nothing. WHAM! WHAM! Nothing.

Simon looks back the way they came. If possible, maybe the SHADOWS of the APPROACHING BLUE-GLOVED MEN nearing the doorway.

Jayne continues to POUND on the locked door with the butt of the rifle.

RIVER
(under her breath)
Hurry...

Then — BLAM! That's the sound of a shotgun blast ripping through the lock from the other side.

The blasted door drifts open... and there stand Mal and Zoe, guns in hand, Zoe's shotgun pluming a bit of smoke.

Jayne reacts, never so relieved to see anyone, as...

REVERSE

HUM ROOM ENTRANCE

As the Blue-Gloved Men appear. They react to —

THEIR POV — of only a little smoke hanging at the empty door. Off that —

INT. SERENITY - CARGO BAY

The ramp is in the process of opening as Kaylee comes down the stairs from the bridge, runs into Inara coming out of her shuttle. She peers out the ramp as she addresses Inara —

KAYLEE
Hey, 'Nara. How was your checkup?

INARA
(dismissing it)
Same as last year.
(re: her peering)
What's going on here?

KAYLEE
Well, let's see. We killed Simon and River, stole a bunch of medicine, and now the Captain and Zoe are off springing the others got snatched by the feds.

Inara's jaw drops. Before she can ask any questions —

KAYLEE (cont'd)
And here they are now!

The ambulance shuttle flies in. As soon as it touches down, Mal, Zoe, Wash, Jayne, Simon and River spill out. Kaylee and Inara join them on the floor, Kaylee moving to the control panel to close the ramp.

MAL
Tell me we weren't followed.

WASH
Nothing in the rearview the whole way back.

MAL
(to Wash)
Take us out of the world. The quicker, the better.

WASH
We'll be out of atmo in five minutes.

Wash books towards the bridge, Zoe in tow.

MAL
Hey. How was your thing?

INARA
As advertised. Lots of needles and cold exam tables. I heard you had some excitement.

MAL
Nothing much. Lots of running around. A little gunplay.
(beat)
Couple of needles.

JAYNE
Next time we come to the Core, I'm staying with the Preacher.

MAL
(nonsense!)
You hadn't come, you wouldn't be getting your big pay day.

Jayne looks to Mal — is there something behind that seemingly innocuous statement? Mal just turns to Simon.

MAL (cont'd)
Did you get what you needed?

SIMON
I think I did. I have the information I downloaded from the imager. I just have to go over it and...
(pauses, hint of a smile)
I'm hopeful.

Kaylee notes the injuries to Jayne's face.

KAYLEE
What happened to your face?

JAYNE
Nothin'.

SIMON
He was amazing. I can't begin to tell you... We wouldn't be standing here if it weren't for him.
(to Jayne, means it)
Thank you.

JAYNE
Hey. You're part of my crew.

MAL
I think I might cry.
(then —)
Jayne, help me with the cargo. Everyone else... make yourselves useful. You got jobs, go do 'em.

Everyone disperses but Mal and Jayne, who unload the body bags from the ambulance, haul them over to the smuggling hold. As they work —

JAYNE
Gotta be one of our best takes ever.

MAL
Doc had a good notion. Boy's got a decent criminal mind.

Jayne kneels by the hold, stowing the goods.

JAYNE
What're you buying with your cut?

WHAM! Without warning, a WRENCH WHIPS Jayne across the temple, knocking him out. Mal drops the wrench by his inert form.

EXT. SERENITY - DAWN

As she takes off and shoots towards the atmosphere.

INT. SERENITY - CARGO BAY/AIRLOCK - DAY

Jayne comes to in the airlock. Trapped between the closed ramp and the double airlock doors. He stands, sees Mal through one of the windows.

JAYNE
The hell are you doin'?!

MAL
(via intercom)
Job's done. Figured it was a good time for a chat.

MUSIC

Composer Greg Edmonson: "I don't remember too much about the music during the airlock scene. I was doing piano. What I thought was amazing about that scene was this was when you begin to see the humanity of these characters, because Jayne really doesn't want them to know what he did. There's a part of him that's ashamed. It's a human moment. I can only tell you how I saw the scene. I just watched it and did music that I thought worked. In other words, I didn't have to lead anybody, I didn't have to punch it up — it was all on screen. It would have worked had I done no music to it. That's the anomaly of this show — it worked because the writing and the acting were so magnificent. I got to be part of the fabric without having to think that the music made something work."

He works the controls, cracks the ramp open. The airlock area fills with WIND. Jayne reacts to that...

MAL (cont'd)
Seems to me we had a solid plan. Smooth, you might say. What I can't figure is what you were doing 'round the back exit.

JAYNE
What? I couldn't make it out the front, I had to improvise. Open the damn door!

MAL
You called the feds.

JAYNE
(indignant)
What — I got pinched!

MAL
Kind of thing that happens when you call the feds.

JAYNE
(selling it well)
I would never do that. My hand to God, may He strike me down where I stand.

MAL
You won't be standing there long. Minute we break atmo, you'll be a lot thinner, you get sucked out that hole.

A loud KLAXON BLARES, a RED ALARM LIGHT goes on — Jayne SLAMS his fists against the airlock doors —

JAYNE
Mal! C'mon! This ain't no way for a man to die. You wanna kill me, shoot me! Just let me in!

MAL
Heard tell they used to keelhaul traitors back in the day. I don't got a keel to haul you on, so...

JAYNE
Okay! I'm sorry, all right?!

MAL
Sorry? What for, Jayne? Thought you'd never do such a thing?

JAYNE
The money was real good — I got stupid. I'm sorry.

Mal says nothing.

JAYNE (cont'd)
Be reasonable. Why you taking this so personal? It's not like I ratted you to the feds.

MAL
But you did. You turn on any of my crew, you turn on me. And since that's a concept you can't seem to wrap your head around, means you got no place here.
(then)
You did it to me, Jayne. And that's a fact.

The fight goes out of Jayne. Jayne takes a long moment, looking at the ramp. He really thinks he's going to die here. Mal starts to go, when —

JAYNE
What are you gonna tell the others?

MAL
About what?

JAYNE
'Bout why I'm dead.

MAL
Hadn't thought about it.

JAYNE
Do me a favor...

❖ Above: Mal and Jayne's coms. These are found items made from obsolete firefighter's distress signal units.

(beat, genuine)
Make something up. Don't tell them what I did.

A long beat.

Then Mal hits the controls and the ramp starts to close.

MAL
Next time you decide to stab me in the back... have the guts to do it to my face.

With that, Mal goes, leaving Jayne between the ramp and the airlock doors. Jayne doesn't bother calling after Mal; he knows he's lucky to be alive. He simply sits. Someone will come let him out... eventually.

INT. SERENITY - RIVER'S ROOM

River sits at a table, scribbling on a pad. Simon enters, a hypo kit in hand.

SIMON
Hi.
(sees her scribbling)
What are you doing?

RIVER
Drawing.

Simon looks at her pad — she's drawn a very well-rendered sketch of a matryoshka (a nesting doll), each layered doll lined up from big to small.

SIMON
That's really good.

RIVER
(re: the hypo kit)
What are you doing?

SIMON
Oh, I... brought some medicine. You remember why we went to the hospital?

River nods.

RIVER
Is it time to go to sleep again?

SIMON
No, mei mei. It's time to wake up.

Off Simon, hopeful...

BLACK OUT.

END OF SHOW

JOSS WHEDON

When we got to episode eight, we had something totally wrong, and I remember thinking, 'Simon. We've got to make Simon cooler. He's got to hire them to do a job,' and Jose worked out all that beautiful hospital stuff. And it seemed like a good time for Mal and Jayne to have a confrontation. At first, I was kind of like, 'Wow, that's a lot of plot.' I was worried about it. And then Tim and I started talking about what we refer to as 'the Jesus Corleone speech', where he says, 'You do it to any of my people, you do it to me!' and that, we knew, was such an essential piece of who Mal had become and was so hard, but at the same time so extremely decent, that we knew it was necessary. And it was Nathan who said, 'Let's use these little intercoms so I don't have to yell through the window and then we can have some blocking,' and it was Adam who said [meek voice], 'Can I come in now?' while we were rolling, both of which helped the scene enormously. We could have held out for it [to have happened later in the season], but again, we were going, 'Okay, let's make sure we are primal. This guy has a lot of threat to him. Let's make good on our threat, because we want people to be galvanized by what they're seeing and not just vaguely intrigued, because we don't have time for vaguely intrigued [laughs].'

CINEMATOGRAPHY

An interview with David Boyd

❖ Left: Scenes from 'Objects in Space'.

❖ Below: Lighting the bridge.

❖ Opposite page top: Lighting the galley.

❖ Opposite page below: Wash steers the ship during 'The Message'.

D avid Boyd started his college education majoring in physics before falling in love with film, changing universities and becoming a cinematographer (recent credits include TV shows *Deadwood* and *Friday Night Lights*). He believes his passion for Westerns helped him get the *Firefly* gig.

Meeting Joss Whedon for the first time at the job interview for *Firefly* director of photography, Boyd says, "For some reason, we had a fantastically great study of the John Ford film *The Searchers*. We ended up just saying the dialogue to each other, because we'd memorized the scenes," he laughs. "When I said, 'As sure as the turnin' of the Earth,' I think I had that job. My enduring remembrance of *Firefly* was working with Joss Whedon. He's just plain great."

While it is common for television series to build sets with removable walls, Boyd was against this for *Firefly*. "When we play tricks on audiences, they know it. If we use a lens that's a little too long a focal length for the space that the audience knows we're in, I think they sense it. So I was adamant that we would never pull a wall. We would always stuff ourselves in a corner with some camera and get what we could. And what we couldn't see in that frame, we would just cover in some other way. So it would truly be as if we were way out in the universe somewhere. And outside was so dangerous."

There were some unique aspects to *Firefly*'s filming style, Boyd adds. "I love [light] flare. I started off *Firefly* with a lens that was very expensive and very well designed. It had tremendously good coding on it, but this thing would not take a flare. So I quickly got rid of it," Boyd laughs, "and found the cheapest lenses out there I could, which gave us the best flares."

Boyd and production designer Carey Meyer were in constant communication with one another. "I think the hardest task for me probably was having lighting concepts incorporated into the design of the ship that would allow it to be believable," Boyd notes. "That took an awful lot of care and time in the pre-production process as the set was being built. Carey Meyer was so helpful in designing recesses or corners or headers around which I could put lights, or something that would be behind a grid-like material that could mask what it was, but making sure that it would put light in the right places and could be flexible, so that when a character walked one way or another, I'd be able to illuminate that person. In the bridge, Carey put in these wacky goose-neck lights that came across the console. I

knew we couldn't point those things at the actors' faces, so I stole some square aluminum heat pads from the galley set, took them up to the bridge and taped them to the console. We would shine these goose-neck lights into these square aluminum pieces of metal. You'd see the pads in shot. You don't really question what they are, but the light from the lamps bouncing off the heat pads is actually illuminating their faces.

"Strictly from a cinematographer's point of view, *Firefly* was huge," Boyd continues. "In terms of the distance that light was thrown, in terms of the spaces on a stage that needed to be lit appropriately, and the size and weight of the things that got moved around. Before and after, I haven't done anything that big. If we did flying shots outside the bridge, we'd move a big crane around much faster than it was ever intended to be moved around because it had a light on it and this would approximate the roll and yaw of the ship. With a camera on the bridge, and the moving around of this very big light outside the bridge so quickly, you could get a fast bank or a big turn going. To make that stuff happen takes an awful lot of planning ahead of time and also takes a lot of skill on the part of the grips and electricians and camera people to pull it off."

The work has paid off in people's memories, Boyd points out. "People that I've run into since then have said, 'My god, you shot *Firefly*!' Here on *Friday Night Lights*, people want to know about it and they want to learn about it — they want to know how it was done. There's still tremendous interest for that project. Other shows go and never come back. No one wants to know about them. This one endures." ◔

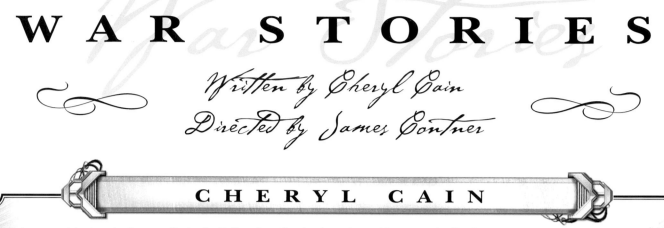

WAR STORIES

Written by Cheryl Cain
Directed by James Contner

CHERYL CAIN

A former assistant production coordinator for *Buffy*, writer Cheryl Cain returned to Whedon's universe as a staff writer for *Firefly* in 2002. 'War Stories' was her first credited episode for the series. Talking about the episode's origins, Cain remembers, "The idea was, what would happen if Zoe had to choose who to save — her husband, Wash, or Mal. I remember Joss and I talking about it in my initial interview. I went, 'Well, she'd have to save Mal.' And he said, 'No, she'd have to save Wash! Because she knows that Mal can save himself and she doesn't trust that Wash would be able to save himself.' It was such a brilliant way to deal with the characters, because there is so much more conflict.

"By the time we got to my episode, it had gotten pretty crazy because Fox wanted the episodes fun and lighthearted. So Brett [Matthews], Ben [Edlund] and I would be working on that and then they would say they wanted it dark instead, and we'd have to scrap ideas. So we started the first day of prep going, 'Crap, we don't have anything!' Joss, being brilliant, came in with, 'Hey, remember we were talking about that triangle idea? Let's do this and this and go back to Niska and see what happens from that.' He gave us a lot of material and we sat down and broke it. Since we had such a collapsed time schedule, we all had our hands in it, just to get it done. I did the initial work on the outline and the rough, rough draft and then we all went in to deepen it. I feel really blessed I have my sole name on something that really had everybody's hands in it. It kept the essence of these people, who were a family and were willing to

do anything to save family. The core was about family.

"The violence was quite a crank up, as was the many ways that we killed people. This was probably the most violent episode. We just mowed through people to save Mal. Fox came back to us and there was one comment about when the guy is melting — to turn away from him. Otherwise, their big thing was that we couldn't have two women kissing on screen. We were like, 'We can kill people in multitudes of ways on screen, but heaven forbid we have two women kissing?' Joss, god love that man, just said, 'Forget it.' And he could say that. We probably cut back on it a little bit, but we were able to keep it.

"I love the moment where Zoe has to go back to that triangle and choose who she is taking out."

Cain reveals Jayne's now trademark line, "I'll be in my bunk", wasn't from her pen. "It either had to be Joss or Ben. Jayne was always the fun guy to write for.

"I loved Inara and Mal. One of the things when I interviewed with Joss that we were both really interested in was, what if Mal and Inara sleep together? He said, 'Would that ruin it?' I'm like, 'No! Then you know that Mal would never be able to be with her because he could never get over his own demon.' How cool would it be for them to sleep together? They have that beautiful moment together and then he fucks it up. I would have loved to see that. They had such chemistry on screen."

TEASER

ANGLE: A reading of River's brain — shown on a screen in the infirmary. Information runs past it — information gathered in 'Ariel'.

BOOK (O.S.)
Have you ever read the works of Shan Yu?

INT. SERENITY - INFIRMARY/COMMON AREA - DAY

SIMON is studying the data. BOOK is as well, though not as close or intently.

SIMON
Shan Yu, the psychotic dictator?

BOOK
Yep. Fancied himself quite the warrior poet. Wrote volumes on war, torture... the limits of human endurance.

SIMON
(absorbed in the screen)
That's nice...

BOOK
He said, "Live with a man forty years, share his house, his meals, speak on every subject. Then tie him up and hold him over the volcano's edge.

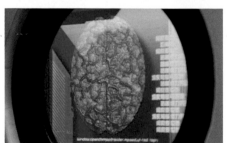

And on that day you will finally meet the man."

SIMON
(looking at his notes now)
What if you don't live near a volcano?

BOOK
I expect he was being poetical.

SIMON
Sadistic crap legitimized by florid prose. Tell me you're not a fan.

BOOK
I'm just wondering if they were. The people who did this to River.

Simon actually looks up at that.

SIMON
The government did this to her.

BOOK
A government is a body of people, usually notably ungoverned.

SIMON
Now you're quoting the Captain.

BOOK
I'm just wondering if they put her through this just to see how much she could take. To "truly meet her", as Shan Yu would have said.

SIMON
No. The more I see, the more I think their purpose was very specific.
(he shows a readout)
Look at that. The pattern. Besides, if all they cared about was hurting River, they wouldn't still be after her. This isn't my specialty, but whatever they were doing, I gotta figure they were close to succeeding.

BOOK
But she's doing better?

SIMON
I've tried a couple of different medications. She's sleeping better, but nothing really stable.

We see a shelf full with pills and liquids.

SIMON (cont'd)
I'll keep trying — certainly got enough drugs on hand...

BOOK
Yes, I'd forgotten you're moonlighting as a criminal mastermind now. Got your next heist planned?

SIMON
No, but I'm thinking of growing a big black moustache. I'm a traditionalist.

On that last line, RIVER and KAYLEE run through the background, from the passenger rooms toward the cargo bay. They are laughing, having kid fun as River flees from Kaylee, holding an apple aloft.

KAYLEE
You give that back! I mean it!

INT. SERENITY - CARGO BAY - CONTINUOUS

The girls rush in and start dodging about the crates.

MAL and INARA are up at the catwalk, in mid-conversation. They look down, but continue on topic:

MAL
I said yes already. Where's the outstanding issue?

INARA
The Councilor is an important political figure and a very private person. I wouldn't —

MAL
So he visits you here instead of you going to his place. Fine. Is the ship not clean enough?

INARA
I just want the Councilor to feel comfortable. And when I say comfortable I mean totally alone.

The cries of "that is mine" and "you gotta get it" and the like that have been accompanying the

running about downstairs finally get Mal's attention.

MAL
(smiling)
Ah, the pitter patter of tiny feet in huge combat boots.
(to the girls)
SHADDAP!
(to Inara)
There's nobody sets foot on my boat that I don't meet 'em. Don't worry, I won't start any sword-fights. I'm over that phase.

INARA
Well, I'd appreciate it if you would keep the others from ogling.

The girls, who have failed to shut up in any way, have come up the stairs, headed for the bridge. Mal stops them with:

MAL
One of you is gonna fall and die, and I'm not cleaning it up.

They are breathless, laughing:

KAYLEE
She took my apple!

INARA
Jayne bought a crate of them.

KAYLEE
And that one's mine!

RIVER
Not anymore —

And they're off again, up the stairs —

INT. SERENITY - FOREDECK HALL/DINING ROOM - CONTINUOUS

Into the foredeck hall and then to the dining room. ZOE and WASH sit at the table, Wash eating an apple and Zoe picking one out of a bowl as the girls pass and pitch into the couch area, where they wrassle until Kaylee gets her apple back, holding it victoriously aloft.

KAYLEE
No power in the 'verse can stop me!

She takes a big ol' bite as River goes over to the table to get her own. Wash looks at River affectionately.

WASH
How you doin'?

She smirks, curtsies, takes a bite. Zoe has a knife out, begins methodically cutting her apple into wedges before eating them.

ZOE
These really are the genuine article. I could get used to being rich.

WASH
It's Jayne being so generous with his cut that

confuses and frightens me.

ZOE
It does kind of freeze the blood.

KAYLEE
Zoe, how come you always cut up your apples?

WASH
You do?

KAYLEE
Her an' the Captain both, whenever we get fresh fruit you never just munch on 'em.

ZOE
Do you know what a Grizwald is?

JAYNE
(entering)
It's a grenade.

ZOE
(shows with fingers)
'Bout the size of a battery. Responds to pressure. Our platoon was stuck in a trench outside New Kasmir during the winter campaign... More'n'a week, completely cut off, and the Alliance entrenched not ten yards away. We even got to talking with 'em, yelling across insults and jokes and such, 'cause no ammo to speak of, no orders, what are you gonna do? We mentioned we were out of rations and ten minutes later a bunch 'a apples rained into the trench.

WASH
And they grew into a big tree and they climbed up the tree into a magical land with unicorns and a harp. Honey, there are children present.

RIVER
Tiny helpless children...

KAYLEE
Blew off their heads, huh?

ZOE
Captain said wait, but they were so hungry. Don't make much noise, just little pops and there's three guys kinda just end at the ribcage.

Mal enters over:

WASH
But these apples are good and healthsome.

JAYNE
(dryly)
Yeah, grenades cost extra.

As Mal speaks, he takes an apple, unthinkingly cuts it up.

MAL
We're about 20,000 miles from our last drop, people. Then we can take a break, think about spending some of this money.

A smattering of yays and applause. River looks queasy a moment, shakes it off.

WASH
Could've made more...

MAL
It wasn't a bad idea, Wash, but eliminating the middleman is never as simple as it sounds.

Wash looks surprised — looks to Zoe, who looks busted.

WASH
So you heard about my —

MAL
'Bout fifty percent of the human race is middlemen, and they don't take kindly to being eliminated. This quadrant, we play nice. Got enemies enough as it is.

EXT. SKYPLEX

To establish.

INT. NISKA'S TORTURE ROOM - DAY

NISKA casually watches his TORTURER, a creepy, lethal-looking man, whip what looks like rusted barbed wire into the chest of an almost unconscious hanging victim.

NISKA
(to the Torturer)
Hold, please.
(to the man)
So. Now we are past the... uh... the preliminaries. The little questions — why you skim from the

protection fund, how you could betray my trust — this we are past.

The Torturer hands him a horrible looking knife. A beefy minion, DALIN, enters.

NISKA (cont'd)
Now we get to the real questions. About you. About who you truly —

DALIN
I'm sorry, sir.

NISKA
Ach! I get to the heart of the matter and always interruptions.

DALIN
One of our long ranges picked up a read on the other side of the world. Might be Serenity. Malcolm Reynolds' boat.

NISKA
Oh! Oh, this is exciting news! Malcolm Reynolds, I must see him again!
(to the man)
If it's any consolation, what I'm going to do to Captain Reynolds will make this seem like a bris.
(to Dalin)
Send a team. Bring him here to me. Very exciting.

DALIN
Yes, sir.

Dalin exits, Niska turns back to his man. Comes closer to him.

NISKA
Now. We get to spend some time finding out about your true self, yes. Tell me —

He digs in the knife offscreen — the man gasps in pain, unable to scream...

NISKA (cont'd)
Are you familiar with the works of Shan Yu?

END OF TEASER

ACT ONE

EXT. SERENITY - EZRA - DAY

Serenity coming to land on an arid-looking desert planet.

INT. SERENITY - BRIDGE - DAY

As Wash brings her in and shuts her down, he continues a conversation with Zoe that she doesn't much wanna have. Wash's tone is dryly humorous, but he is not actually amused.

WASH
So when you said you didn't get a chance to tell the Captain my idea...

ZOE
(little voice)
Yeah-huh?

WASH
What you actually meant was that you told him my idea, he rejected it out of hand, and you didn't argue the point or even give it another thought.

ZOE
I gave! Honey, I...

WASH
And then came the lying to me about it, which for me is sort of the highlight of this little adventure.

ZOE
Is there any way I can get out of this with honor and dignity?

WASH
You're pretty much down to ritual suicide, lambie-toes.

ZOE
I didn't want to upset you.

WASH
What did you think of it?

ZOE
Of what?

WASH
My idea. Call the local MDs, forget the fence and go to the source. Better prices, and we know the drugs get to the right people.

ZOE
Captain thinks it'll get back to someone, just

cause trouble.

WASH
<TAI-kong SUO-yo duh shing-chiou doh SAI-JIN wuh duh PEE-goo> [All the planets in space flushed into my butt] was I ever not asking what the Captain thought.

ZOE
Well, I tend to agree with him.

WASH
Tend to? Or have to? I love that you two are old army buddies and have wacky stories with ribcages in them but could you have an opinion of your own please?

ZOE
(a bit pissed)
You're losing the high ground here, sweet-cakes.

WASH
I'm sure you and Mal will take that hill and fortify it with the bodies of —

ZOE
I thought your plan was too risky. I. Thought.

WASH
Then tell me! I'm a large, semi-muscular man, I can take it. Don't hide behind Mal 'cause you know he'll shoot it down for you. Tell me.

ZOE
Right, 'cause what this marriage needs is one more shouting match.

WASH
No, what this marriage needs is one less husband.
(beat)
Right now it's kind of crowded.

He exits, leaving her to stew.

INT. SERENITY - RIVER'S ROOM - DAY

Simon enters to find River shaking, very sweaty, sitting on the bed.

SIMON
Whoah! Mei mei, how are you doing?

RIVER
I threw up.

SIMON
I'm sorry, it's a side effect... We just have to find the right treatment for you. How do you feel now?

RIVER
Going. Going back, like the apple bits coming back up. Chaos.

SIMON
But you felt okay this morning...

RIVER
(smiles)
Played with Kaylee, the sun came out and I walked on my feet, heard with my ears...
(crumbling)
I hate the bits, the bits that stay down and I work,

I function like I'm a girl. I hate it because I know it'll go away, the sun goes dark and chaos is come again. Bits. Fluids.
(really crying now)
What am I?

He takes her in his arms, calms her shaking.

SIMON
You're my beautiful sister.

A beat.

RIVER
I threw up on your bed.

SIMON
Yep. Definitely my sister.

She smiles a little.

INT. SERENITY - CARGO BAY/PASSENGER DORM - DAY

Mal and Inara wait near the airlock. Kaylee and Jayne are peeking out the doorway to the passenger dorm. Book sits with a book (not the bible) on the couch.

BOOK
Didn't Inara express a wish for privacy?

KAYLEE
Oh, we gotta see who she's got! I bet he's handsome.

JAYNE
You gonna give him a lecture on the evils of fornicating?

BOOK
Astonishingly enough, I have other things on my mind.

KAYLEE
Do you think he'll bring her flowers?

Inara shoots a very disapproving look at Kaylee, who shoots her a big grin and a thumbs up.

INARA
Honestly, Mal —

She stops as a tall, handsome MAN in a suit, wearing sunglasses, comes up the ramp.

MAL
Seems a respectable sort.

ANGLE: KAYLEE

KAYLEE
Ooh! There he is!

Book pops up, cranes to look from the bottom of the stairs.

The man walks around the cargo bay, checking everything. Mal holds his hand out to the man.

MAL
Welcome aboard. I'm Capt —

The man turns away, depresses a mike in his ear.

MAN
We're all clear here, Councilor.

ANGLE ON the ramp as a beautiful, composed woman, the COUNCILOR, thirties, comes up the ramp. Inara walks over to her smiling, takes the woman's hands in her own in greeting. Mal doesn't move.

MAL
Huh.

Inara links her arm through the Councilor's, leads her toward the stairs.

ANGLE: THE OTHERS

are surprised.

BOOK
Oh my.

KAYLEE
Well, gosh, I knew she took female clients but... They look so glamorous together...

A beat, as they all watch.

JAYNE
I'll be in my bunk.

Jayne turns, goes back toward the aft stairs.

❖ Left: Shawna Trpcic's costume designs for the Councilor.

official

@ home w/ family (dinner)

Front

Councilor

BACK

Step 3

Shawna Trpcic-02
= Fixing =

INT. SHUTTLE II - DAY

Zoe and Mal are getting her ready to go. Zoe is having trouble working the controls. Mal is securing the crate o' drugs.

MAL
Bolles is ready and waiting. Lucrative as this stuff is, I'll be glad to see the last of it. Kinda makes us a target —

ZOE
(interrupting)
Did River get in here, start playing around? Ignition sequence is completely turned about. I can't even —

WASH
(entering)
I can.

MAL
Get it set, okay? We got to be moving.

WASH
Here's a funny twist: no.

MAL
No what?

WASH
No sir.

ZOE
You changed the sequence?

WASH
(to Zoe)
Didn't want you taking off without me. In fact, didn't want you taking off at all. Thought maybe I'd take this run instead. Me and the Captain.

MAL
The Captain who's standing right here telling you that's not gonna happen?

WASH
Well, it's a dangerous mission, sir, and I can't stand the thought of something happening that might cause you two to come back with another thrilling tale of bonding and adventure. I just can't take that right now.

MAL
Okay, I'm lost, I'm angry, and I'm armed. If you two have something to work out —

ZOE
It's all right. We've dealt with Bolles before, shouldn't be a problem. I wouldn't mind sitting this one out, sir.

Beat, Mal looking at both of them.

MAL
This is a <FANG-tzang FONG-kwong duh jie> [knot of self indulgent lunacy] but I don't have time to unwind it. Wash, get her started. Zoe, the ship is yours.

Wash and Zoe pass each other. She's pissed, but not overly so. They're about on a par, actually, but

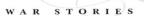

he smiles at her.

WASH
Bye hon. We promise not to stop for beers with the fellas.

She shuts the door behind her. Mal moves into the copilot seat as Wash whirrs her up for lift off.

WASH (cont'd)
So. You wanna sing army songs, or something?

EXT. SERENITY - DAY

As the shuttle lifts off, it crosses over Serenity, taking the camera to the first shuttle, on which we zoom...

INT. INARA'S SHUTTLE - DAY

Inara massages oil onto the naked back of the Councilor, who's lying on her stomach on Inara's bed, eyes closed with pleasure. Filmy sheets cover what needs to be covered. Inara's in an off-the-shoulder silky dress, tied at the shoulder with a ribbon.

COUNCILOR
That feels amazing. Oh, right there. Perfect.
(sighs)
I should've done this weeks ago.

INARA
(flirty)
I wouldn't have been here weeks ago.

COUNCILOR
And that would've been a shame.

INARA
For me as well... You have such beautiful skin...

The Councilor turns on her side, looks at Inara.

COUNCILOR
There's no need for the show, Inara. I just need to relax with someone who's making no demands on me.

The Councilor starts to lay back down again. Inara stops her with a hand on her shoulder. The Councilor sits up, facing Inara, curious.

INARA
Most of my clientele is male, do you know that?

COUNCILOR
No...

INARA
If I choose a woman, she tends to be extraordinary in some way. And the fact is, I occasionally have the exact same need you do. One cannot always be one's self in the company of men.

COUNCILOR
Never, actually.

INARA
So no show. Let's just enjoy ourselves.

Beat. The Councilor raises her hand, caresses Inara's face.

COUNCILOR
(hushed)
You are so lovely...

Inara smiles, leans into her. The Councilor kisses her; a soft, sexy kiss. Inara deepens it by placing her hand behind the Councilor's head.

The Councilor reaches up to the ribbon on Inara's shoulder, unties it. We see from the back as

Inara's dress slithers down...

EXT. EZRA - DAY

Shuttle II soars over the barren terrain. Cool desertscape passing by below them.

INT. SHUTTLE II - CONTINUOUS

Wash flies. Mal in the seat next to him.

WASH
So, not a man?

MAL
Not so much.

A beat.

WASH
Damn.

MAL
I mean, I knew her clientele was... varied...

WASH
Yeah, but, I mean, you know... damn.

MAL
Yeah.

Beat.

MAL (cont'd)
Look, this thing with you and Zoe —

WASH
Really not looking to talk on that topic.

MAL
Hey, I let that <NIOU-se> [cow dung] trick of yours slide 'cause this is a milk run. But I go on a mission, I'm taking Zoe and that's the drill. You know that. Suppose we get into a situation here.

WASH
Hey, I've been in a firefight before. Well, I was in a fire. Actually, I was fired, from a frycook opportunity — I can handle myself.

MAL
And you understand what Zoe's job entails.

WASH
I'll learn as I go.

TIME CUT TO:

EXT. EZRA - RIDGE - DAY

The ship behind them, Mal and Wash are walking down the ridge, Wash carrying the crate of drugs.

WASH
So, now I'm learning about carrying.

EXT. EZRA - MOMENTS LATER

At the bottom of the ridge, Mal and Wash meet up with a large man, BOLLES, their contact. He has two men flanking him.

BOLLES
That it?

MAL
As described. The money?

BOLLES
Open it first.

Wash pries open the box. Bolles looks in, sees the medicine.

BOLLES (cont'd)
Nice to know you're still trustworthy.

MAL
Not so trustworthy that I don't want to see that money you promised me.

Bolles reaches into his jacket, pulls out a pouch. Tosses it to Mal.

BOLLES
(shaking his head)
Can't believe you knocked over an Alliance hospital. The pair you have.

MAL
Stuff legends are —

Mal stops because there's a red laser dot on Bolles forehead.

MAL (cont'd)
<Tzao-gao!> [Damn it!]

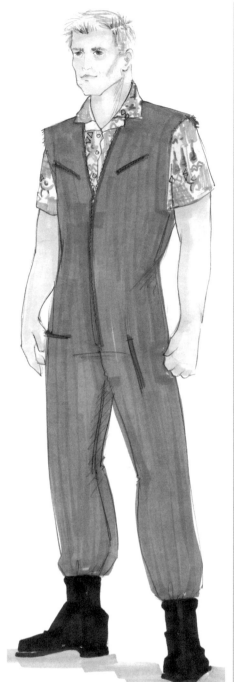

WASH'S COSTUMES

Costume designer Shawna Trpcic: "Wash's look was taken from Harry Dean Stanton's character in *Alien*. That was one thing that Joss threw out there. We created our own variation with the flight clothes, but the Hawaiian shirts, that's very Harry Dean Stanton. Wash's character is more lyrical and he's a lighthearted guy, and so we tried to use colors, oranges and greens, that weren't as intense or earthy as Zoe and Mal."

A SHOT rings out, and Bolles drops, dead. Just as Mal drags Wash to the ground, two more dots appear on Bolles' men's foreheads. BANG. BANG. They drop, also dead.

Mal and Wash lying on the ground. Their bodies covered in laser sights as several men in desert camouflage, holding rifles, approach. Wash looks over at Mal, a bit freaked.

WASH
Now I'm learning about scary.

Off Mal's look.

END OF ACT ONE

ACT TWO

INT. SERENITY - CARGO BAY - DAY

Book works out at the bench press. Jayne stands over him, spots him. Jayne's attention wanders at the sound of GIGGLING. He glances over to see —

INARA AND THE COUNCILOR

have emerged from Inara's shuttle. They look like bestest buddies, laughing and giggling together as they descend the stairs. Inara's showing her out. Jayne can't take his eyes off this, his imagination fueled.

Book's struggling a bit with a heavy loaded dumbbell. Jayne's looking off as —

Inara kisses the Councilor sweetly on the cheek. The women embrace. The Councilor exits.

Inara turns back, catches Jayne's eye, then moves off.

Book struggles with the weights. Without looking, Jayne easily grabs the bar, deposits it in the holder.

JAYNE
I'll be in my bunk.

He turns to go. But now Zoe appears.

ZOE
Jayne — grab your weapon.

Book gives a raised-eyebrow look that says, "Funny you should put it that way." The double entendre goes right past Jayne.

JAYNE
Why? What's going on?

ZOE
Maybe nothing. Maybe trouble.

JAYNE
The drop?

ZOE
(she nods)
They're late. Shoulda been back more'n an hour ago.

BOOK
You try to radio them?

ZOE
(shakes her head "no")
Errand such as this, Captain always orders radio silence until the deal's made. If there was trouble... he shoulda been the one to break it.

JAYNE
That's if he could...

That hangs there.

ZOE
(to Jayne)
We go by ground. We'll take the Mule.

Jayne nods, starts to go, but pauses as Book says to Zoe:

BOOK
I'll go with you.

ZOE
No offense, Shepherd — but I sure as hell hope they don't need a preacher.

BOOK
Three sets of eyes'll be better'n two. Might see something you don't.

Zoe and Book hold a look. Finally, Zoe nods.

ZOE
Let's move.

CUT TO:

EXT. EZRA - DROP SPOT - DAY

Shuttle II can be seen sitting up on the ridge. We PULL BACK... the Mule is parked down here. Now, in the foreground, Zoe turns over a DEAD BODY. It is:

ZOE
Bolles.

Jayne turns over another body.

JAYNE
None of 'ems ours.

Book examines one of the dead men.

BOOK
This is precision work. Sharpshooters. From the look of these wounds, I'd say a 54R sniper rifle. Laser sights.

Jayne looks at Book, suspicious/curious.

JAYNE
You do a lot of shootin' at the abbey, Shepherd?

BOOK
Rabbits.

JAYNE
For stew. Sure.

ZOE
Whoever did this... they weren't after the goods.

She knows this because she's indicating the spilled box of stolen meds.

BOOK
No. They were after our people.

JAYNE
(indicates terrain)
Laid in wait. Patient under this sun. Triangular formation. Probably trenched in — there. Maybe...
(sees something)
— there.
(then)
We ain't gonna find 'em here. They're off planet already.

Book and Zoe join him — look where he's looking: down a ridge to a BLACKENED SCORCH MARK in

the distance.

JAYNE (cont'd)
Only one kinda transport I know leaves that kinda mark.

ZOE
Fast burn rocket shuttle.

BOOK
Craft like that wouldn't commonly be part of a ship. More likely we're looking at —

ZOE
A space station.
(then)
I know who's got them...

CUT TO:

EXT. NISKA'S SKYPLEX

Shuttles dock, ships fly around this busy skyplex.

INT. NISKA'S TORTURE ROOM - DAY

BAM! Mal and Wash, blindfolded and hands tied, are shoved with force into the torture room by some GOONS. The GOONS exit, shutting the heavy door behind them. After a beat.

MAL
You okay?

WASH
I think I've been kidnapped.

MAL
Yeah.

WASH
You see where we are?

MAL
No.

Wash listens, tries to get a bead.

WASH
It's not a ship. I don't think we're traveling.

MAL
Good to know...

WASH
What in the name of god is that smell?

MAL
(lies)
Could be anything. Try not to think about it.

WASH
Okay. I'll just... I'll stop breathing. Mal, what the hell is going on?

MAL
Not sure exactly.

WASH
But you've got some theories.

CINEMATOGRAPHY

Director of photography David Boyd: "Again, Carey Meyer put together a set that was eminently shootable. Through the slits in the walls, I could put lights in a ring and have the flare that makes, I think, those scenes believable. Also, the vast majority of it was done with two hand-held cameras, using very lightweight zoom lenses made out of plastic that actually picked up the flare of those lights more than a glass lens would. Then we hung our strong overhead lights over their faces, straight down, as if in the old movies where someone's being interrogated by the Nazis, and then played the rest in shadow. We introduced smoke to that environment to pick up the very bright lights from outside."

MAL
Still working it through.

WASH
I don't want you to spare me, Mal. If you think you know what's happening, then you tell me. You wouldn't spare Zoe if she were here with you, would you?

MAL
Well...

WASH
That's right. You'd be conferring and planning and plotting and possibly scheming. So whatever Zoe would do in this instance is what I want to do. And you know why?
(before Mal can speak)
Because no matter how ugly it gets, you two always come back. With the stories. So I'm Zoe. Now. What do I do?

MAL
Probably not talk quite so much.

WASH
Right. Less talking. She's terse. I can be terse.

Once, in flight school, I was laconic.
(beat, nothin')
If I'm not gonna talk, then you have to. What else?

MAL
Just gotta keep our heads.

WASH
Right. Keep our heads. That way we'll be able to, you know, keep our heads. You and Zoe been in plenty of situations like this before, right?

MAL
Many a time.

WASH
Many a time. You and Zoe...

MAL
Once we know who it was took us...

WASH
Zoe and you. Together in a tricky... Mal, she's my wife.

MAL
Huh?

WASH
What gives you the right to put her in a dangerous situation like this?

MAL
I didn't.

WASH
You did!

MAL
She ain't here, Wash.

WASH
No, but she would have been!

MAL
Okay, but...

WASH
It never really hit me until... Well until I got hit. And blindfolded and kidnapped and this smell is burning my nostrils...

MAL
Wash...

WASH
I mean, I'm the one she swore to love, honor and obey!

Mal's about to fire back, but does a take with:

MAL
She swore to obey?

WASH
Well, no. Not... But that's my point! You she obeys! She obeys you! There's obeying happening right under my nose!

MAL
Zoe and I have a history. She trusts me.

WASH
What's that supposed to mean?

MAL
Don't mean a thing. You're making out like Zoe just blindly follows my every word, and that ain't true.

WASH
Sure it is.

MAL
Not so. There've been plenty of orders of mine she didn't obey.

WASH
Name one!

MAL
She married you.

Wash does a take, looks over at Mal. Well, turns his head at any rate, what with the blindfold thing.

They both react now as the door opens. They hear someone entering. Mal's blindfold is ripped off — he reacts to the sight of —

NISKA

standing there. Grinning. It's your basic "oh, shit" moment.

MAL (cont'd)
<TAH-mah-duh hwun-DAN.> [Mother humping son of a bitch.]

WASH
(still blindfolded)
What?

INT. SERENITY - DINING ROOM - DAY

Money of varying denominations being dumped on the table. Book, Simon and Inara are there, all pitching in. Zoe is gathering it up, shoving it all into a canvas bag. Kaylee appears, adds her share to the kitty.

KAYLEE
Here's all I got left.

ZOE
Thanks.
(calling)
Jayne!

BOOK
How do you know he won't just grab you, as well?

ZOE
Don't think that's like to happen, I walk in there unarmed, make the offer. Niska has his own code, twisted as it may be. Very excited about "reputation". He'll see reason.

INARA
Reason? He's a gangster. The money he paid you for that other job, it was already returned to him.

ADAM BALDWIN

'War Stories' was probably my favorite to shoot and watch, or at least in my top three. I always loved the scene with Mal, Wash and Niska. I always loved Niska. There is something cool about the way we charged down that hallway in a good action scene, and the stray bullets that will get you. That episode also had one of my favorite lines: 'Could be he's harboring some resentment at us for putting his man through our engine.'

JAYNE
(appearing)
Could be he's harboring some resentment at us for putting his man through our engine.

Jayne tosses some money onto the table. Zoe glances at it, grabs it up, then looks to the others.

ZOE
Wait a reasonable amount of time... But if you don't hear back, you take Serenity and you get out of this quadrant. This don't play out right, there's no guarantee he wouldn't come looking for the rest of you.

INT. NISKA'S TORTURE ROOM - DAY

Mal and Wash are both strapped to semi-vertical torture boards, their shirts ripped open and electrodes attached to their skin. The Torturer presides. Niska is there.

As we come into the scene, Mal's body seizes in pain as ELECTRICITY surges through him. Niska nods to the Torturer who turns down the dial. Once the latest surge subsides:

MAL
(with some difficulty)
I'm not... gonna say it...
(turns to Wash)
...again. Shipboard romance complicates things.

WASH
For who? For you?

MAL
For everyone.

WASH
Yeah? Well, what about lo —
(electric surge)
...VEAAAAHH!

MAL
(fighting the pain)
Ain't against it as a rule. But in a situation such as ours, tends to cause problems. Splits loyalties.

WASH
(hmmmph)
Know what I think?

MAL
What?

NISKA
I hire you to do job...

Niska nods. Another jolt for the both of them.

NISKA (cont'd)
Job does not get done...

Wash is totally dazed by the pain. Mal strains to see him, get him to focus. Ignores Niska totally.

MAL
(prodding)
What? What do you think, Wash? 'Cause I'm interested.

WASH
Huh?

NISKA
You make lie of my reputation...

MAL
(to Wash)
You were gonna say something to me. What was it?

WASH
(woozily)
Wha — ? Oh. This "policy" you got against shipboard relationships... that's just you projecting your own intimacy issues onto everyone else.

NISKA
I show you my reputation is no lie. Is truth —

MAL
Yeah? Well that's just downright insightful. It surely is.

Niska nods to Torturer — big ZAP. Wash coughs (maybe some blood?). Looks for a second like he doesn't know where he is.

MAL (cont'd)
Or, could be it's a mite simpler than that. Could be I just don't think you're good enough for Zoe.

WASH
(finally registers)
I don't give a good gorramn what you think.

MAL
Don't you?

WASH
No.

MAL
See, I think you do care. Think you care quite a lot.

WASH
You're wrong.

Niska nods. Pains ensues. Wash blinks helplessly and confusedly at Niska and Torturer. Mal presses on:

MAL
You know me and Zoe got a history — and I figure you gotta be asking yourself some fairly fundamental questions about the nature of that history...

Wash laughs weakly to himself, isn't buying it.

WASH
You never slept with my wife.

MAL
You know that for a fact, do you? You ever ask her?

More electricity. Mal rebounds. Wash not so much.

MAL (cont'd)
We were together a good long time before you come around, Wash. And she is a damn fine lookin' woman.

Wash rallies enough sass to respond, despite his weakening condition:

INARA

"Every well-bred petty crook knows — the small concealable weapons always go to the far left of the place setting."

While Inara's position as the beautiful, refined Companion who entertained an elite clientele (while providing a certain air of legitimacy to the ship) often kept her inside her shuttle, she nevertheless played an essential role in the dynamic of the Serenity crew. "Inara was sort of the heart of the ship," says Morena Baccarin. "Kaylee could also lay claim to that title because she had feelings for everyone, but Inara bridged the gap between them all. In a sick and twisted way, Mal and Inara were like the momma and papa of the ship. They were the parents who don't really want to be parents but they can't help but take care of people. She cared a lot about everyone on Serenity and she offered a level of experience and intelligence they weren't quite familiar with. Everybody had their function but she tied them together. She's very selfless. Inara doesn't let anyone worry about her feelings. She sees what is happening and does her best to keep the harmony.

"I think the reason everyone was cast the way they were is because none of us had to struggle to create those characters. It sort of just fitted. I imagined Inara in my head from what Joss had given me, and we never had arguments about how she would say this or that. A couple of times I would say, 'This line is a little too Western, a little too like the guys' talk, Inara would keep herself removed from that,' and he would agree and change it."

The relationship between Mal and Inara was one of the most intriguing aspects of the show; although they bickered constantly, the chemistry between the two characters was unmistakable. "It is funny," laughs Baccarin, "we would have these little jokes on set where any time I got to do a scene with Nathan during rehearsals and Joss was there, I would just turn to Nathan and say, 'I love you. I hate you. I love you.' That was basically their relationship. They have this intense connection and this love for each other but so many things get in their way — pride being the number one thing. Who knows what would happen if they actually got together? I don't know if they could sustain a relationship. They have such strong ideas and are so pig-headed about them.

"I have several favorite moments between them. I really loved in 'Our Mrs. Reynolds' where I wake up, everyone is in the room, and I'm worried that Mal is going to figure out I kissed him. And then at the very end of the episode, he says, I get it. I know what happened. 'I knew you let her kiss you.' Inara thinks he knows she kissed *him*. I love that they are constantly not getting it."

Firefly was Baccarin's inauguration into television, and naturally she learned a lot from all the talent that surrounded her. "From Nathan, I learned you don't have to memorize anything until you get to the make-up room," she explains. "I was always amazed. He would have pages and pages of dialogue, just read it once, and would know the whole thing. He is a really hard worker and so am I. I was trained classically in theater where you are taught to be really disciplined. He did it with such pleasure, so I learned how to have fun with Nathan. Do your work to the best of your ability but don't take it too seriously. It was all a lesson to me just in terms of the technical stuff and dealing with a camera in your face."

The series has left an everlasting impression on Baccarin. "I believe the last thing we shot was the group of us walking towards the weird aluminum house in 'Heart of Gold'," she recalls. "Or was it? It is so hard to remember because there were so many goodbyes. It was very tearful and really sad. We felt cheated and robbed and were just trying to make the best of it. Everybody felt it was very special and I know, for me, it was a huge lesson in how I want my career to go. I don't want to settle for anything less than that."

WASH
Never happened... Know how I know?

MAL
How. Tell me, Wash.

WASH
The whole "captain" thing isn't Zoe's trouble. It's the guy-she-never-slept-with thing. Hell, Mal — I wish you had slept with her! Then at least she'd be over it!

MAL
You want me to sleep with her? That make you feel better?

WASH
It might!

MAL
Imagine it'd do wonders for her, too.

WASH
Screw you!

MAL
Get in line.

ZAAAAP! Wash starts to go. He's cracking, starts to pass out, maybe never to come back.

MAL (cont'd)
Okay. Gonna do it, then. Wash? Wash! First thing, we get back — I'm taking your wife into my bed. Gonna get me a piece 'a —

Wash's eyes SNAP OPEN he lets out a PRIMAL YELL. Mal relaxes — then Mal is screaming too as the VOLTAGE SURGES. Off their screams —

EXT. NISKA'S SKYPLEX

Shuttle II pulls into the skyplex, begins to dock.

INT. SHUTTLE II

Zoe pilots the shuttle as it lurches, indicating that it has latched onto the skyplex.

Zoe steels herself, rises, moves to the door/airlock. Pushes open the door revealing —

INT. SKYPLEX - CORRIDOR

Goons and guns. Lots of them. Zoe's already got her hands in the air, one of them holding the canvas bag. Even as Goons rush her —

ZOE
I'm unarmed.

They frisk her. Take the bag, look at it.

ZOE (cont'd)
I want to talk to Niska.

Off that —

INT. NISKA'S TORTURE ROOM

SCREAMS. Niska watches with pleasure. Mal and Wash both breathing hard from the pain of the last bit of torture. It's a pause in the action. Dalin appears, whispers something to Niska. Niska listens, motions for the Torturer to hold. Nods to Dalin, who exits.

NISKA
(to Mal)
You will not mind if I pause to do a little business?

MAL
Knock yourself out. No, really.

INT. SKYPLEX - CORRIDORS

The armed henchmen escort Zoe through the skyplex. Zoe paying close attention to every detail of her surroundings. The corridor has large windows along the side that look out onto the factory.

They arrive at Niska's door, where a couple more armed henchmen await. A henchman slides A KEYCARD near the door, opening it. WE MOVE INTO —

INT. NISKA'S TORTURE ROOM

We're in Zoe's POV as the full horror of it is revealed. She sees Mal and Wash both there, restrained and in pain. She tries to stifle her reaction. They don't notice her yet: Mal is whispering something to the droopy-eyed Wash.

Dalin has given the bag of money over to Niska, who looks at it. Takes in the amount. Now Wash blinks through his haze, seeing Zoe there. Mal follows his look to her —

WASH
(muttering)
No, no, no... run... run...

She ignores him, looks away, to Niska.

ZOE
It's five times what you paid us for the train job.

NISKA
Yes. You have had, you say it, good times... I see that.

ZOE
Should be more than enough to buy back my men.

NISKA
This is your opinion, is it?

ZOE
It is.

NISKA
They are perhaps damaged now. Are they worth so much to you?

ZOE
Yes.

NISKA
And to me... they are worth more. I think it is not enough.

Zoe clenches her jaw muscles. Fucker's not going for it.

NISKA (cont'd)
Not enough for two. But sufficient, perhaps, for one.

She looks at him. Sees where this is going.

NISKA (cont'd)
So you now have a question to make an answer. It is for you, pretty lady, and only you, now to ch —

ZOE
(cuts him off)
Him.

She points at Wash. Niska's a bit thrown.

ZOE (cont'd)
I'm sorry. You were going to ask me to choose, right? Didja wanna finish?

Off Niska, open-mouthed, still back at the not-being-able-to-get-his-sentence-out moment —

END OF ACT TWO

ACT THREE

INT. NISKA'S TORTURE ROOM

WASH FALLS INTO FRAME, dropping hard onto his knees in front of Zoe. She helps him shakily to his feet. Niska eyes the money. Waves a dismissive hand at them.

NISKA
He is yours. We are ended now.

WASH
(whispers, desperate)
Mal...

He tries to look over at Mal. Zoe takes him gently by the chin, turns his head back to her.

ZOE
(in his eyes)
Shhh. Start walkin'.

INT. NISKA'S OFFICE - CONTINUOUS

Zoe and Wash move through Niska's office, away from the sound of Mal's continued HOWLING. The door to the torture room slides shut, only slightly muffling the sound. They exit.

INT. SHUTTLE II

Zoe and Wash enter. The moment the door closes, Wash basically collapses. Zoe manages to guide him down to his knees. And she sinks right along with him. He's stunned, staggered, his mind still back in that room. She looks at him with a mixture of relief, worry and, goddamn it — love.

WASH
He's insane.

ZOE
I know it.

WASH
I mean... you've told the damn stories. Saved you in the war. But I... I didn't know...

ZOE
You mean Mal?

Wash nods.

WASH
He's crazy.

She looks at him, not sure if he's in shock or making any sense at all.

WASH (cont'd)
He wouldn't break, Zoe. And he kept me from... I wouldn't have made it.

She tries to hold it together. Touches his face.

WASH (cont'd)
Niska's gonna kill him.

ZOE
He'll make it last as long as possible. Days, if he can.

A look of stoic resolve crosses Wash's face. He rises shakily but surely to his feet —

WASH
Bastard's not gonna get days.

— and moves to the pilot's seat of the shuttle. Off Zoe, watching her pilot husband fire up the shuttle —

INT. SERENITY - CARGO BAY

Zoe and Wash emerge from the shuttle. Wash in the lead.

BOOK
Thank God you're safe.

SIMON
(to Wash)
Let me take a look. How bad is it?

He obeys. She turns to go, leading Wash.

NISKA
A moment, please. This money...

Zoe stops, turns — are they going to have a problem now?

NISKA (cont'd)
There is too much. You should have some small refund.

ZOE AND WASH

Film editor/associate producer Lisa Lassek: "The relationship of Wash and Zoe is one of my favorite things in the show. And that was something that was really important to Joss. In fact, the entire episode of 'War Stories' comes from the moment where Zoe decides to choose Wash; that decision being so instantaneous is something that tells you so much about their marriage. That moment to me is a signature of *Firefly*, but, more importantly, a signature of the larger questions that are in *Firefly*. It shows that the relationship between Zoe and her husband is so different to the relationship between Zoe and Mal. It's what Joss loves to do: switch things on your expectations. It's a big dramatic moment where somebody has to make a decision, and Joss takes that completely away. And it makes perfect sense. You see Zoe's decision comes from a place of love. I mean that's just where you are when you're in that relationship."

ZOE
(tries to move)
Keep it.

NISKA
No, no, no. I insist.
(to Torturer, in Czech)
They have enough for a slice.
(to Zoe, in English)
I wouldn't want the talk to be that Adelai Niska is a cheat.

The Torturer has picked up a knife, moved to Mal — and SLICES Mal's ear clean off. Mal SCREAMS in agony. Niska produces a handkerchief from his pocket. The Torturer places Mal's ear in the handkerchief. Niska then hands it to Zoe, who remains impassive, despite Mal's ROARS OF PAIN.

NISKA (cont'd)
Now we are ended.

Dismissed, Zoe and Wash move for the door, their backs turned to Mal, as his SCREAMS REVERBERATE in the small room.

MICHAEL FAIRMAN

"In 'War Stories'," Niska's alter ego Michael Fairman recalls with a laugh, "I spend the entire episode torturing the Captain." His reaction on first reading the script was, "'Oh my god, this man is being tortured for an hour.' I wondered how that would play, since the only reason Niska is torturing Mal is because he messed up the job. Well, the other reason is to send a message, but there's no real active reason; I'm not trying to get information or make him do something — it's just retribution for him having crossed me. So I had to find different reactions, different approaches to it. The choice I made was sexual. I mean, Niska is psychotic. I was trying to communicate a perverse sexual pleasure — not so that it would hit people over the head, but so that it was just sort of delicious for me. Even though I mention in 'The Train Job' I have a wife, I didn't make too many choices about what went on with her — but I do know that when I had to torture Mal, it was a sexual delight."

Unlike the *Firefly* regulars, Fairman didn't have to speak Chinese — instead, he had a line in Czech: "There was a woman on the set, one of the people behind the camera, and she was Czech. She wrote it out phonetically for me — 'Cut off his ear'. I pretty well butchered it; as I recall, I made a motion with my hand."

At the end of the episode Niska is still alive. Fairman reminds us, "I scurry away like the rat I am. Which was very good. My heart sang when that happened because I thought, 'Oh, I'm going to come back and do this again!' I couldn't believe it when they canceled the show."

KAYLEE
You okay? What happened?

WASH
(pulling away from Simon)
I'm fine.

INARA
Where's Mal?

ZOE
Niska wouldn't let him go.

Wash pushes past everyone, still steely-resolve guy, heads for the stairs.

INARA
Is he alive?

ZOE
For now.

She moves to follow Wash. As she goes, she hands Simon the handkerchief with the ear.

ZOE (cont'd)
Take that to the infirmary, put it on ice.

KAYLEE
What is it?

SIMON
It's his ear.

Inara, Kaylee and Book recoil, noticeably sickened. Simon looks at it, his head tilted.

BOOK
(pissed)
<Huh CHOO-sheng tza-jiao duh tzang-HUO!>
[Filthy fornicators of livestock!]

ZOE
We're getting him back.

JAYNE
What are we gonna do, clone 'im?

SIMON
(re: the ear; clinically)
It's a clean cut. With the right equipment, I should be able to reattach it.
(looks at them, also clinically)
That's assuming there's a head.

But Wash and Zoe aren't there anymore to answer that. Off the perplexed and worried looks, with emphasis on Inara, whose mind is racing —

INT. NISKA'S TORTURE ROOM

Mal grits and bears the pain. The Torturer is near him, working at his body somewhere BELOW CAMERA. What he's doing is left to our imagination.

NISKA
Do you know the writings of Shan Yu?

MAL
We're starting a book club? What? Are you trying to torture me?

The Torturer reapplies his torment sporadically as they speak.

NISKA
Yes, today I meet you... and you are quite a man.
(Mal cries out again)
An extraordinary man. Yes. But these are not times for extraordinary men. Business is not war. Heroics, they are unseemly. They complicate.

Niska walks across the room to a standing cart, starts wheeling it towards the Torturer.

NISKA (cont'd)
For you I have special machine. Very precious.

The Torturer reaches in, pulls out a thick mechanical hose with an opening like a lamprey's mouth at the end.

The Torturer hands the device to Niska, who holds it close to Mal's face so that he can see its many sharp metal teeth. It's a rather nasty, ugly-looking device. Niska practically strokes it.

MAL
And they say people don't look like their pets...

Niska hands the device to the Torturer, who moves to attach the mouth to Mal's chest.

NISKA
Let's see if we can't learn more about you.

The device WHIRS TO LIFE. The mouth attaches itself to Mal, writhing metallic tendrils shooting out from its jagged teeth, burrowing under his flesh, creeping outwards from the skin on his chest down to his nether regions and up to his head. As Mal SCREAMS —

CUT TO:

EXT. COUNCILOR'S HOUSE - NIGHT

A country house, to establish.

INT. COUNCILOR'S HOUSE - NIGHT

Inara waits in the foyer of this opulent home, uncomfortable about being here. The Councilor is sitting, a bit blindsided by Inara's presence. Imperious — but also a bit nervous.

COUNCILOR
This is an unwarranted imposition. You are in my home. It belittles both our stations to —

INARA
A man will die, horribly, if I do not act. I apologize for my conduct, but as a member of the World Council you cannot be unaware of what Adelai Niska is.

COUNCILOR
His skyplex is beyond our jurisdiction. I really must ask that —

HUSBAND (O.S.)
Sweetie, we're looking for Maynard's elephant...

The Councilor's very vanilla HUSBAND enters with a young boy, their son. The husband sees Inara as he kisses the Councilor on the head. He regards Inara with benign irritation.

HUSBAND
We're taking solicitors at the house? I thought you promised...

The Councilor blanches, moves to speak —

INARA
Forgive me. I imposed on a mutual acquaintance

for the audience. I appreciate your position, Councilor. Goodnight.

Inara, now getting the Councilor's coldness, exits.

EXT. COUNCILOR'S HOUSE - NIGHT

Inara descends the steps to the house.

COUNCILOR (O.S.)
Inara —

Inara stops as the Councilor approaches.

COUNCILOR
You had me in an awkward situation, you didn't press your advantage.

INARA
I'd never take advantage of a client's confidence.

COUNCILOR
I... I appreciate it. I'm just sorry I can't do more to help you.

INARA
(temper rising)
Then do more — help me. The Council can claim jurisdiction over Niska's skyplex —

NISKA'S TORTURE SPIDER

Chris Calquhoun of Applied Effects explains the origins of the Torture Spider. "I got a basic sketch. They wanted it tripod-like but kind of 'nurnified'. I designed it in Solidworks, a 3D CAD program, then printed out the files on our 3D wax printer. The printer is a rapid proto-typing machine which will produce a 3D model in wax. Then I made silicone rubber molds of the pieces and poured urethane resin parts." The flexible, lightweight tubing coming from the back of the device is what Applied's crew calls 'Ridley-Flex', after Ridley Scott's *Alien*.

Chris made a fully functional, spring-loaded hero prop. "I made up some little bronze pins to act as catches and hold the sprung legs in the closed position. The hexagonal section on top is spring-loaded in the up position and the catches click into little recesses in the top. When the spider is pushed against someone's body, the hexagonal cap is depressed, the catches pop out of the recesses and the legs spring out. The resin was gray in color, so I sprayed the finished prop black and added silver dry-brush on the surface to pick out the detail and make it look old and used.

"We made a really light foam version of the spider with pin-backs, like earring-retainers, on the feet. This was clipped to the henchman's shirt for the sequence where Mal attacks him with his own device and he runs around screaming. There was a really detailed hero version too, where you could see the detail on the inside, and another which they glued to Nathan."

❖ Above: Niska's Torture Spider.

COUNCILOR
A year ago, maybe, but Niska's become... He's bought off most of the Council. I'd be in the minority and on my way to the grave. I wish —

INARA
(leaving)
I haven't time to wish.

COUNCILOR
I thought Companions weren't allowed to take lovers.

Inara stops one last time.

INARA
He's not my lover.

COUNCILOR
He must be an extraordinary Captain, then.

INT. SERENITY - DINING AREA

A stash of weapons — guns, knives, grenades — is laid out on the dining room table. Zoe and Wash are strapping on as many as they can. Jayne leans against the doorway, watching this lunacy.

ZOE
Here. Six shots, then just drop it. Keep moving.

He nods, adds it to his arsenal. Wash is still recovering, but ignoring any lingering shakiness — he's all about the resolve still.

JAYNE
This here's suicide. You do know that, right?

Wash picks up a knife —

WASH
Worth taking?

ZOE
(chooses a different one)
I'd go with something like this.

He takes her choice. Sheaths it.

JAYNE
You really think you can mount a two-man frontal assault on Niska's skyplex and live?

WASH
Technically it's a one-man/one-woman assault. A unisex.
(to Zoe)
Grenades?

ZOE
Oh, yes. Thank you, dear.

He hands her some flash grenades. She puts them in her belt.

ZOE (cont'd)
(to Jayne)
They won't be expecting it.

JAYNE
Right. 'Cause they ain't insane!

Kaylee enters from the bridge —

KAYLEE
Just got a wave from Inara. No luck with the... Councilor...
(to Jayne)
What're they doing?

JAYNE
Fixin' to get themselves killed.

ZOE
We're goin' to get the Captain.

KAYLEE
Oh. Good!
(then, aside to Jayne)
Can they do that?

JAYNE
No.

WASH
There's a certain motto Jayne. A creed among folk like us, you may have heard it: "Leave no man behind."

JAYNE
Suicide.

INT. SERENITY - SIMON'S ROOM

Simon sits on his bunk. River appears at the door.

RIVER
You're not responsible. It's not your fault.

SIMON
What?

RIVER
You think because it was your idea to steal that medicine, and because it happened when he was out there trying to sell it, that's why he got took.
(confused beat, trying again)
Taken.
(no, beat)
Abducted. The Captain was abducted.

There, she got the grammar right. She smiles at him, looking for his approval. He smiles back.

CUT TO:

INT. SERENITY - CARGO BAY

Zoe leads Wash into the cargo bay.

ZOE
Got a good look at the layout on my way in last time. You let me lead, cover my... back.

Zoe trails off when she sees Kaylee, Simon and Book at the already open weapons locker. All of them arming themselves.

ZOE (cont'd)
What's this?

SIMON
We're going with you.

KAYLEE
If it were any one of us, Captain wouldn't hesitate.

Book holds up a large rifle.

BOOK
This should do.

ZOE
Preacher, don't the bible got some pretty specific things to say about killing?

BOOK
Quite specific. It is, however, somewhat fuzzier on the subject of kneecaps.

Zoe shakes her head, but she's touched.

ZOE
All right, then. If you're looking for me to talk you out of it...

CHUK-CHUK. From above, the sound of a large gun being cocked.

The gang looks up in unison — on the catwalk stands Jayne, Vera in hand, an assortment of guns and knives tucked into every available nook and cranny in his clothing. He's like Space Rambo. They all stare. He's a bit self-conscious.

JAYNE
What?

Zoe smiles.

ZOE
Let's go get the Captain.

Off this triumphant moment:

INT. NISKA'S TORTURE ROOM

The screams have stopped. The Torturer pokes limp Mal twice. Poke, poke. No response. He turns to Niska.

TORTURER
Yep. He's dead.

BLACK OUT.

END OF ACT THREE

ACT FOUR

INT. SKYPLEX - NISKA'S TORTURE ROOM

CLOSE UP ON two CARDIAC INFUSERS as they press into human flesh and fire with buzzing voltage — QUICK TILT UP to Mal's face as his body bucks, convulsing back to life.

Eyes still closed, Mal's head lolls as consciousness returns. He's been taken down from the steel plank he was shackled to, and lies out on a table. The Torturer puts the infusers down and touches two fingers against Mal's neck, checking his pulse.

Niska stands nearby, sipping whiskey from a glass. The Torturer turns to him and nods.

NISKA
Good, good...

The tendril device has been removed from Mal's chest. The Torturer gives its toothed nozzle a

shake, and Mal's blood spatters off it. He goes to the array of TORTURE DEVICES, looking them over.

Niska steps up to Mal, dips his fingers into his whiskey and flicks the alcohol at the flat hell of Mal's severed ear.

NISKA (cont'd)
Mr. Reynolds.

Mal stirs at the pain, coming-to a little bit more, though his eyes stay closed through all the following dialogue:

MAL
[weak groan]

NISKA
You died, Mr. Reynolds.

MAL
(groggy)
Seemed like the thing to do.

The Torturer holds up a DEVICE. Niska shakes his head.

NISKA
When you die, I can't hurt you anymore. And I want two days at least. Minimum.

The Torturer holds up another WICKED IMPLEMENT, and Niska shakes his head.

NISKA (cont'd)
I think many people know the name Malcolm Reynolds. Many know he crossed Niska. They must know what happened after that.

The Torturer holds up another IMPLEMENT, and Niska nods.

NISKA (cont'd)
They must know that business is still running.

Mal looks up, sees the implement, and closes his

eyes again, turning away slightly. He's losing his fight, bit by bit.

EXT. NISKA'S SKYPLEX

Serenity cruises into frame, a black silhouette heading for the skyplex. The ship's lights are out, and its engines are dead.

INT. SERENITY - BRIDGE

Wash sits in the pilot chair, his arms crossed. Jayne and Zoe stand behind him. It's dark in the bridge too. The only light comes from the skyplex, which grows larger in their windows.

JAYNE
Think this'll work?

WASH
Well, except for the com static I'm piping out on all frequencies, we've been completely powered

❖ Above: The cardiac infusers or defibrillator paddles used by the Torturer to revive Mal.

down since I fired our attitude thrusters half an hour ago — We should come up on their screens as a radar glitch, if they aren't looking too close...

JAYNE
And what if they're lookin' too close?

WASH
(shrugs)
Hell, I'm just glad we're on course.

JAYNE
(unsatisfied grunt)

ZOE
It's like throwing a dart, Jayne — and hitting a bull's eye six thousand miles away.
(smiles at Wash, puts a hand on his shoulder)
That's my man.

WASH
You guys should get down to the bay. We'll be at their front door in less than a minute.

Wash starts hitting switches, getting ready to power up. Jayne exits. Zoe leans in and kisses Wash on the cheek.

WASH (cont'd)
I'll be right behind you, baby.

INT. SERENITY - CARGO BAY

Powered down; dark. By the light of a lantern, Book finishes affixing some kind of gas tank to the front of the MULE, which is positioned in the middle of the cargo bay, facing the door. Zoe and Jayne enter the bay from above.

ZOE
Book, you good?

BOOK
Yes ma'am. Ready when you are.

ZOE
Kaylee, how we doing on that over-ride sequence?

Kaylee is by the ramp door, working on a BAT-TERY-POWERED KEYBOARD wired into a control pad on the wall. Simon holds a flashlight on her.

KAYLEE
Pretty sure this will pop their airlock doors, if Wash can make a seal on his first try...

JAYNE
You know, I'm smellin' a lot of "if" comin' offa this plan.

Zoe smiles at Jayne — she knows he's in this for the whole haul.

ZOE
Coulda stayed in your bunk.

JAYNE
(smiles back)
Coulda, woulda, shoulda...

He cocks a shell into Vera's chamber, as the LIGHTS COME ON and we hear Serenity POWER-ING UP.

Wash comes running down into the bay, carrying his gun.

WASH
We're set —

Simon and Kaylee lift up SMOKE CANISTERS, ready to pull their pins.

ZOE
Okay, people —
(cocks her gun)
If it moves, shoot it.

KAYLEE
Unless it's the Captain.

ZOE
(nods, all business)
Unless it's the Captain.

INT. SKYPLEX - ENTRY ROOM

It's the same spot where Zoe entered earlier. Niska's radar operator reads a magazine, feet up on his counter. His MONITOR SCREEN flashes with static, until it doesn't, and we see the front of Serenity filling the screen, hurtling forward.

A PROXIMITY ALERT buzzes, and he sits for-

❖ Right: The small lantern used by Book to work by.

ward, just as his booth rocks with the impact of Serenity. On his screen we see the first set of air-lock doors slide open. PAN OFF HIM to the air-lock, through his windows. The cargo ramp begins to fall open, as SMOKE BELCHES OUT of it, into the airlock, obscuring his view. He hits an ALARM.

INT. SKYPLEX - NISKA'S TORTURE ROOM

Niska looks up at the ALARM. Mal, in pain, looks up too.

MAL
Listen, if you got guests, I can come back later —

INT. SKYPLEX - AIRLOCK/ENTRY ROOM

The ALARM still blares. THREE OF NISKA'S MEN arrive, guns out, just as the airlock door opens. The smoke has settled somewhat, and rolls out in a hip-high blanket. An O.S. MOTOR REVS and the Mule ROARS down the hazy ramp toward them. Niska's men OPEN FIRE on the Mule, their bullets hitting the tank strapped to its front, which EXPLODES, taking out the men.

Zoe, Jayne, and Wash come out from either side of the cargo door and march down the ramp. Wash is wincing, walking stiffly, still pained by his tor-ture session.

Inside his booth, the radar man pulls a gun out from under his counter. Jayne swings Vera at him and fires. The GLASS separating the radar man

JOSS WHEDON

I think the torture device was inspired by the machine that goes 'Ping!' in *Monty Python's The Meaning of Life*. You use electricity because it makes big sparks and people can scream and you don't actually have to do anything and there's no blood.

from the airlock SHATTERS and he sails back, caught by Jayne's shot.

More of NISKA'S MEN pile through the lefthand door leading out of the entry room. Zoe levels her rifle and fires. The lead guy drops and the other three back into the cover offered by the doorway. Zoe pulls a GRENADE from her belt, arms and tosses it.

It bounces off the doorway's edge into the corridor beyond and EXPLODES. One of the two men hiding there falls out into the entry room, CHARRED and SMOKING.

Zoe hits the wall next to the doorway, Jayne rolls to its far edge, covering the curved corridor with Vera.

ZOE
Second team!

Book, Simon, and Kaylee come down the ramp, weapons out.

ZOE (cont'd)
Hold this position. We lose this ground, we lose it all.

She nods to Wash and Jayne, who move into the corridor, taking cover behind struts.

She's about to go, but turns and eyes Kaylee, Simon, and Book for a quick beat. They sure as hell ain't soldiers.

ZOE (cont'd)
You're going to hold this ground, understand me? That's an order.

The far door opens and one of NISKA'S MEN storms for them, gun raised. In a flash, before even Zoe gets a bead on him, Book fires from the hip, hitting the guy in the KNEECAP.

He pitches forward with a SCREAM, his face smashing into the side of the Mule — out cold.

Book turns to Zoe, calm and ready.

BOOK
Understood.

ZOE
(nodding)
Okay then.

INT. SKYPLEX - CURVING CORRIDOR

Zoe strides forward, past Wash and Jayne, who cover her from either side. A group of GUNMEN run around the curving corridor towards them, the front two blasted back by Zoe's rifle. Zoe dashes to the side as the rest return fire.

INT. SKYPLEX - NISKA'S TORTURE ROOM

Mal looks unconscious again. Niska and the Torturer turn from him, looking toward the office, listening to the O.S. FIREFIGHT. Niska hits an intercom.

NISKA
Dalin — What is this? Dalin —

Mal opens his eyes, seeing their backs.

The Torturer, looking on as Niska hits the intercom button again, suddenly arches his back, SCREAMING. We hear the SOUND OF THE TENDRIL DEVICE firing its tendrils out. He claws at his back — turning to show us that the tendril device has sunk its teeth into him, through his jacket (so we don't need any prosthetics).

He drops out of frame, revealing Mal, on his feet. Niska shrinks back in surprise.

Mal BACKHANDS him across the face. The old man crumples onto the steps up to his office, mouth bloody, arm up, defending feebly. Mal shuffles toward him, in pretty bad shape, but standing.

MAL
(low, burning rage)
Looks like business ain't running so much as crawling away...
(deadly)
You wanna meet the "real me" now...?

INT. SKYPLEX - CORRIDOR

Zoe, Jayne and Wash continue their firefight, pressing forward down the corridor. A bullet GRAZES Jayne's side.

JAYNE
(just pissed)
Ow, gorramn it —

Zoe (who is BLEEDING from a few FLESH WOUNDS herself) empties a rifle into the guy who shot Jayne. She drops it, and rolls behind the cover of a corridor strut. She pulls twin HANDGUNS from cross-strapped shoulder holsters and pivots back into the fray, firing.

INT. SKYPLEX - ENTRY ROOM

Book covers the door to the entry room; he's got A GUNMAN pinned down with his fire, a distance down the corridor. He peers out and Book shoots, hitting the guy's hand. He screams, dropping his gun.

SIMON
Book — We, uh —

Simon and Kaylee cover the opposite door, and Simon starts firing as GUNMEN head down it toward them. Book rushes over and shoots too.

Kaylee, however, holds her gun shakily, unable to fire. She backs away, wincing as gunmen pitch to the floor under the hail of Simon and Book's fire.

She can't do it.

More GUNMEN come, through the door Book was covering before he went to Simon's aid. They fire at Book and Simon, who manage to dodge into the corridor, using the return of the doorway as cover, but are now pinned between two groups of men.

Kaylee lowers her gun, backing towards the ramp, terrified, paralyzed.

Simon and Book have their hands full, firing down the corridor at two remaining GUNMEN.

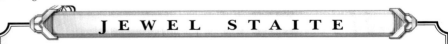

JEWEL STAITE

On Kaylee using a gun: "I don't think Kaylee had seen much violence, other than the stuff she'd seen on the ship. It was probably an incredibly terrifying thing to face. I imagined it as the scariest moment in her life, and she felt like she was going to die until River came in and grabbed the gun and saved her."

Staite had no gun training for the episode. "They made sure I didn't," she laughs. "So it looked like I had absolutely no idea what I was doing. The sweet part is, Kaylee's willing to do whatever she can to be a part of it, save her ship and help save the crew. In the movie, it was nice to see her get a little gutsy and fight along with the rest of them, but I like that innocence in her."

JAYNE'S KNIFE

Prop master Randy Eriksen: "Adam is a prop actor, he likes props. He always wanted more and different ones and was always adding his own touches. His character needed the knives and the guns. He had this whole arsenal in his room. Jayne's knife is a found item, it's a coffin-handled Bowie [a model 225, 'Patrick Henry Liberty Bowie' made by Roughrider]. I think we molded it and made some rubber ones. The leather sheath with the star was also found."

❖ Left and below: Jayne's stunt knife and leather sheath, used throughout the series.

Others slink in through the opposite door. Book fires on them, and they scatter, firing back. Book has to take cover.

THREE OF THEM see Kaylee on the ramp and fire on her, moving in towards Serenity. She darts behind the cover of the cargo bay doorway, as bullets SPARK off its metal hull.

INT. SERENITY - CARGO BAY

Kaylee stifles sobs, clutching the gun to her chest as the gunmen stalk cagily toward the ramp in the background.

And then suddenly River is there, standing before her, with a slight, compassionate smile on her lips. Kaylee startles. River reaches out and takes her gun, Kaylee too surprised to stop her.

River peeks out from behind the cargo bay doorway. The men are on the ramp. They fire as River swings back behind the cover.

RIVER
(flat, unreadable)
Can't look. Can't look.

She closes her eyes, and spins out into the doorway firing three shots, eyes closed, pop pop pop — machine-like. This is from Kaylee's POV.

Kaylee looks out onto the ramp, where the three men lie dead. River, holding the smoking gun, turns to her.

RIVER (cont'd)
No power in the 'verse can stop me.

Off Kaylee's horrified look —

INT. SKYPLEX - NISKA'S OFFICE

Mal backhands Niska again (they've moved up into Niska's office) and Niska hits the floor, scrabbling backward. Mal slowly shuffles after him.

The Torturer enters behind Mal, brandishing the barbed-wire whip from the teaser. Mal is too focused on Niska to notice.

The Torturer jumps him from behind, brings

the whip around, clotheslining Mal and pulling him backwards.

As they struggle, Niska staggers away.

INT. SKYPLEX - ENTRY ROOM

Book and Simon stop firing; the coast is clear, except for the piles of thug BODIES that surround them. They exchange a look.

INT. SKYPLEX - NISKA'S OFFICE

Mal and the Torturer struggle. Mal bends forward, lifting the strangling Torturer onto his back, then hurls them both backward, smashing through one of Niska's windows —

NISKA'S SKYPLEX

Production designer Carey Meyer: "The spaceship, Serenity, was definitely the most challenging piece of the whole show. But outside that, I would probably say it was Niska's world, which was a very large spaceship. We had to have Serenity dock and connect to that ship and then have a shootout that took place in a roundabout, or donut, hallway that led up to Niska's office. That also had to connect with somebody falling out of a window in Niska's office into a void or a central cylinder of endless mechanical machinery. Getting that built on a schedule of four or five days, and actually having it connect to the spaceship physically, and make it work so that we could light it and shoot it in such a way that we could connect the CG environment to it, and get all those pieces actually there — along with the actual torture room, which was down just a little bit past his office — getting that whole process done was probably the most physically challenging piece, because it was very large and complicated to put together."

Visual effects supervisor Loni Peristere: "I loved the character of Niska and setting up his domain, that really creepy, spindly space station. I loved designing that space station."

INT. SKYPLEX - FACTORY SHAFT

Mal lands on the Torturer, slamming into a steel balcony that overlooks the abyss of the factory shaft. The Torturer releases his grip on the whip, and Mal pulls it from his throat — the Torturer ain't out though; he starts getting up, and they square off again. Mal's strength is all but gone.

MAL
(spent sigh)
Haven't you killed me enough for one day?

INT. SKYPLEX - CORRIDOR

Dalin's body rocks as he takes several bullets and falls back. Zoe pushes forward, trailed by Jayne and Wash.

She drops to one knee, frisks Dalin's corpse

quickly and comes up with a KEYCARD.

INT. NISKA'S OFFICE

Zoe, Jayne and Wash come in. They rush to the open window, see Mal fighting the Torturer on the edge of the factory shaft precipice. Jayne lifts his gun, takes aim... about to plug the Torturer. Zoe grabs his arm.

ZOE
This is something the Captain needs to do himself.

Jayne lowers his gun.

MAL
(calling back to them)
No, it's not —

ZOE
Oh.

As one, Zoe, Jayne and Wash raise their weapons and OPEN FIRE on the Torturer, filling him with as many holes as standards and practices will allow. The Torturer's bullet-ridden body falls into the blackness below.

EXT. DESERT PLANET

Serenity is parked amongst the dunes, much as it was in Act One.

INT. SERENITY - CARGO BAY - DAY

Inside, Simon repacks some high-tech MEDICAL DEVICE into a METAL CASE. Book and Inara stand nearby. Mal enters.

Kaylee sits on one of the stairways, a distance from them, arms hugged across her body.

Mal gingerly touches at his ear, which has been re-attached. A faint line of fresh scar circles it.

MAL
Sure this thing's gonna stay on?

SIMON
This dermal mender creates an excellent tissue bond. It should be fine... Just don't fiddle with it.

MAL
(to Inara)
Be sure to thank the Councilor for me. Awful nice of her to pull strings and lend us this equipment.

INARA
It was the very least she could do. I just wish you'd killed the old bastard.

MAL
I got regrets on that score my own self.
(to Book and Simon)
I'm told ya'll took up arms in that little piece of action back there.

Book nods. Simon looks uncomfortable.

SIMON
Yes, I — Yes.

MAL
How you farin' with that, Doctor?

SIMON
I don't know... I never shot anyone before.

Book smiles and claps Simon on the shoulder.

BOOK
I was there, son. I'm fair sure you haven't shot anyone yet.

Mal chuckles, heading for the stairs. As he passes by Kaylee, he rests his hand on her hand tenderly. She smiles up at him. He exits up the stairs.

Kaylee turns back and catches sight of River standing at the far end of the bay, on an upper catwalk. She goes cold.

River looks down at her, face blank. After a beat she turns, and disappears into a dark doorway.

INT. SERENITY - DINING AREA

Zoe has just finished making soup for her husband, who sits at the table. She puts it down in front of him. We see that her wounds from the firefight are bandaged.

WASH
Mmmm. Wife soup. I must have done good.

ZOE
(kisses the top of his head)
Yes, dear. You done good. But this is a one time thing, so I suggest you savor it.

Mal enters.

MAL
Did you tell her?

WASH
Tell her what?

MAL
(to Zoe)
Your husband has demanded that we sleep together.

ZOE
(looking at Wash)
Really.

WASH
What? Mal, come on —

MAL
He seems to think it would get all this burning sexual tension out in the open. You know, make it a fair fight for your womanly affections —

WASH
No — That was just the torture talking...
(looking at Zoe)
Remember? The torture?

Mal steps over to Zoe and holds her hips.

Wash pushes his chair back, and winces to his feet.

She puts her hands on his shoulders, and they stare into each other's eyes, play-acting. Jayne enters, also bandaged. He catches this display.

MAL
Sergeant, it's a difficult mission — but you and I have to get it on.

ZOE
I understand. We have no choice. Take me, sir. Take me hard.

Jayne looks at them for a beat.

JAYNE
Now somethin' about that is just downright unsettlin'.

Wash cuts in, takes Zoe by the hand and pulls her away.

WASH
We'll be in our bunk.

They exit. Jayne looks down at the table.

JAYNE
Hey. Free soup.

BLACK OUT.

END OF SHOW

EDITING FIREFLY

An interview with Lisa Lassek

If you ask film editor Lisa Lassek if there was anything different about working on *Firefly* compared to other TV shows she replies, "Everything. First off, *Firefly* was a special case because I've never been so involved in a show. I was an a.p. [associate producer], so I supervised all the editing, and then mixed all the episodes and supervised the visual effects on all the shows besides the ones that I was personally editing."

Firefly had two other editors, J.P. Bernardo and Sunny Hodge, in addition to Lassek. Lassek cut 'Serenity', 'Our Mrs. Reynolds', 'Out of Gas' and 'Objects in Space'. "That's how the rotation fell, but I worked on all the episodes. I would oversee the first versions of everything and then pass them on to Joss; and then I did all the mixes, the sound effects, the music and things that we put in at the last minute. So I was living and breathing *Firefly*. I feel like *Firefly* is by far the most ambitious show I've ever worked on, because not only is it tackling the politics of a whole new universe, and the social commentary on our own world, but the characters were much richer and there are more stories to tell with them than we ever got a chance to tell, unfortunately. I remember being on the set one day and Joss and Tim running up to me, like they couldn't contain themselves, to tell me the story that was eventually going to be 'Out of Gas'. Not only are the creators engaging in dialogue with everybody all the time, but they were so excited about this episode they had just been breaking that they couldn't wait to tell me about it."

Firefly was edited on three Avid computer systems, though Lassek feels her film school training, physically handling film, helped teach her the importance of the individual frame. For her, editing is a very organic process. "When you're in the act of editing, it's so intuitive. You can go back [in hindsight] and say, 'Oh, the effect of this was to achieve this.' But when I'm doing it, it's whatever feels right."

Lassek experienced many challenges in creating a new universe, not least when it came to soundeffects: "We had a heck of a time coming up with beeps that weren't beeps, so we called them 'chones' — somewhere between a chime and a tone. The guns couldn't sound like regular guns — they had to have a little bit of something extra. We had an amazing sound team [at post-production facility] Todd-AO. The harder things were when we were creating sounds for the first time, like, what does the airlock sound like, and what sound does every single ship make?

"There will be nothing like *Firefly* again in my life," says Lassek, who went on to edit *Serenity*. "After it was canceled, we finished those last three episodes with the same amount of love that we did the other episodes, but we knew that that was it. We were in denial and then eventually we got around to acceptance, but we really were grieving. Except for Joss, who I feel never got past the denial phase," Lassek laughs. "Our grief hit us in the heart, we felt like we were slain, and we tried to pick up the pieces. The end, the finality of the end and that grief that you have never happened for Joss, so he never gave up and in his mind, he was like, 'This show has got to go on.' He never lost that passion to make it happen. That's how *Serenity* the movie got made, Joss's inability to accept that *Firefly* was over. The day they finally announced that Universal would green-light it was the greatest joy, because it was so unexpected. It's hilarious that one of the catch-phrases for the show is, 'done the impossible', because it couldn't fit more perfectly." ◁

❖ Left: Jayne's flashback scene from 'Out of Gas'.

❖ Below: Mal, Zoe and Wash on the bridge during 'Objects in Space'.

"I CALL IT VERA"

Jayne's Weapons

❖ Above: Profiles of the Hero prop.

"Callahan fullbore autolock, customized trigger and double cartridge thorough-gauge." She really does sum up Jayne's character very nicely: big, awkward, entertaining, clunky and very, very dangerous.

This prop has become one of the icons of the show. If you talk to Browncoats anywhere and mention Jayne, it isn't long before Vera pops up. Vera was made in Mike Gibbons of Gibbons Ltd's shop and is based on a Saiga 12 automatic shotgun, made in Russia and designed on the Kalashnikov assault rifle.

"Randy Eriksen would call from time to time asking for something different for an episode. You know, different looks or something completely new. I forget exactly how it was scripted but he wanted a world-beater — a big, nasty weapon for Jayne. They didn't have a huge budget for it. I remembered I had this bad guy weapon from the De Niro/Murphy movie *Showtime*. Randy, Larry, my gunsmith Jim Bolland and myself all sat round and put our heads together to come up with the modifications Randy wanted. You know, the cartridges in the buttstock, the different types of scopes, the flash-hider on the muzzle. We put it together basically from what was already here. I think the only pieces we actually custom-made for Vera were the flash-hider, the scope mounting rail and the cartridge holder in the stock. Of course, this is on top of what we'd already done for *Showtime*."

Although Vera never actually fired in *Firefly*, she was seen to 'shoot' at the energy web in 'Our Mrs. Reynolds'. Mike admits, "She never really fired. That was a gag that Special Effects came up with." The script called for Vera to be inside a space suit. There was a second flash-hider made which was attached to a gas-gun rig in the suit. A gas gun is a tube, a reservoir of gas and a solenoid valve which allows the gas to be released through the tube in controlled bursts. A pilot light on the side of the flash-hider ignited the gas as it came out of the tube. The result is a gas flare which looks very much like a large muzzle flash but without the noise and percussion of a blank. "We decided that using shotgun blanks and actually firing Vera would have destroyed the space suit. On the *Showtime* gun Vera is based on, the actual barrel length is around six inches. To make the gun work properly the blanks were pretty horrendous. They were very powerful

in order to develop the pressure required to cycle the action. Close range work with those things was out of the question. The noise, the flash and the concussion were too much. In fact, the director of *Showtime* described them as 'evil'."

Vera's construction is unusual. The Saiga 12 has been chopped down to a simple receiver block and short barrel with all the other machined parts bolting on. In the original *Showtime* configuration, the guns were designed to operate either folded or unfolded. Folded meant the buttstock and barrel both hinged up and collapsed onto the top of the gun. Vera's additional parts mean she can no longer be folded without removing the scopes, the scope mounting rail, the flash-hider, the cartridges and cartridge holder in the buttstock. In *Showtime*, the guns were firing live shotgun blanks, and Vera has a magazine and adapter which will accomodate these. She also has a

VERA'S VITALS:

Length: 90cm
Height, top of scope to bottom of mag: 45 cm
Width: 7 cm at widest point
Capacity: 12 rounds
Caliber: 12 gauge
Construction: CNC machined aluminum alloy components anodized in lilac, blue and gold. Some steel parts and phenolic-impregnated, laminated wood grips.
Weight: Around 12.69 kg (28 lbs) depending on the configuration

second magazine which carries the huge, brass-cased dummy rounds used in *Firefly*.

In the hands, Vera has a tendency to feel a little top-heavy and there isn't a great deal of room for your hand on the forward grip. However, she's an extremely charismatic prop and an iconic piece of television history. Vera represents an ideal pairing of character and hand prop. You really can't imagine Jayne without her, or vice versa. Vera also pays tribute to the creative people behind *Firefly*, proving you can do great work on a limited budget. As Jayne himself says, "This is the best gun made by man... I call it Vera."

❖ Above: Profiles of the Hero prop and Jayne's big bullets.

❖ Below: Jayne's belt and holster, including his leather knife sheath.

The man they call Jayne is a bit of a character. It's only fitting that his weapon of choice would be too. Jayne's sidearm was made at Gibbons Ltd's Burbank workshop (Gibbons supplied all the weapons on *Firefly* with the exceptions of the Alliance sonic rifles and Mal's pistol). Mike Gibbons remembers the prop well: "When Randy Eriksen first came in and we were looking at stuff for the show, we had some replica, but live-firing, Civil War Le Mat revolvers. These are unusual in that they are a nine-shot revolver and they have a short shotgun barrel in the middle of the cylinder, under the main barrel. Randy had seen some of the guns we'd done for the Jet Li movie *The One* and thought something like that might be good, so some of the influences for the Jayne pistol came from there. The *Firefly* production loved that Le Mat. They designed lots of stuff to go on it. It's a big, ugly Western-style revolver, but they fell in love with it. We made two Hero guns for Jayne."

The base gun is a live-firing reproduction of a Civil War Le Mat Cavalry model. Very few changes were made to convert the Le Mat into Jayne's gun. A crenellated top-rib was machined out of steel to fit along the top of the barrel. The front sight was removed and a small, flat, steel piece made to fit in the now-empty dovetail in front of the new rib. The shotgun barrel was removed and an assembly of machined parts made to replace it. The cylindrical assembly comprises three parts — inner barrel, outer barrel and end cap — all held firmly in place with recessed socket head Allen screws. The retainer ring for the original shotgun barrel was left in place and the machined parts are assembled around it. All in all, a very strong arrangement. The only other addition was a turned steel stem, with a sphere at the end. This replaces the original loading ramrod — an essential tool for the black powder shooter but not required in the future.

There's a scoop-shaped fairing slung under and in front of the cylinder. Its purpose is to change the lines of the Le Mat and make it look a little more sci-fi. The scoop is

retained in place by a spring-loaded press stud. To disassemble the piece the stud is depressed allowing the scoop to swing down into the open position. The whole section forward of the cylinder will now unscrew. The barrel and the machined section move as one piece. The pistol can be seen disassembled for cleaning on the mess table in 'Ariel'. If you look closely at the disassembled gun on the table, you can see that there are nine brass cartridges in a line next to it. As supplied, the Le Mat is a black powder weapon requiring each cylinder to be loaded with powder, wad and ball — like a miniature cannon. Mike says, "The base gun was a black powder weapon converted to fire cartridges. There are several reasons for doing the conversion: it's safer, no horsing around with loose black powder; you don't have to worry about chain-fires (several cylinders firing at once); you don't have all the grease and the goo and the wads flying out the front; it's much safer and it saves the production money because reload time is much shorter and reliability is much better. Since the Le Mats were converted to cartridge long before *Firefly* came along, we sleeved down the existing shotgun barrel in the middle of the cylinder to .38 caliber so we could fire it on screen with a blank, should the need arise."

In the hand, Jayne's pistol dives, nose first, toward the deck at an alarming rate. The total lack of balance is a little worrying until you put your second finger onto the trigger guard spur. It all suddenly makes sense. The base weapon was designed for a cavalry officer and, on horseback, a steadying influence is required for a sure aim. The second finger provides this, and the gun settles into balance quite nicely. It's still very hefty, at 1.96 kg (4.32 lbs) unloaded, but it doesn't feel ungainly. Jayne's gun fits snugly into Joss Whedon's *Firefly* universe. It's a fusion of the old and new, past and future. Initially it seems rather contradictory and a bit of an oddball. But it grows on you. ◁

TRASH

Written by Ben Edlund & Jose Molina
Directed by Vern Gillum

BEN EDLUND

Ben Edlund reflects: "'Trash' to me, because it was more, say, sci-fi ambitious, didn't have quite the focus as a story that the others [Edlund's 'Jaynestown', Molina's 'Ariel'] did. It wasn't as much a story about *Firefly* and about those people as it was telling more about Saffron and building her up as a romantic foil in the series. It was more a puzzle piece for a larger puzzle than it was a fully formed episode, in my opinion. If that had been allowed to go its way over a couple of seasons, my guess is that Saffron would constantly come back, always fuck them over, but almost affectionately. Saffron and Mal would appreciate each other for their bombastic, crazy misdeeds, and there would be a relationship that would tease itself along through the episodes, so that there could be moments where Inara would be actually jealous of Mal and Saffron. I think primarily the drive behind 'Trash' was to reintroduce Saffron and find a way for her to fuck them over. Perhaps Mal and Inara together are a better team and Inara is in fact a better person to have at your back than you suspected at the beginning of the show. Really, it was about trying to find a story that would highlight the dynamics between those three characters."

There's also some resolution between Jayne and Simon and River. "I think that there were some things that had to be addressed a couple of times in terms of the crap that Jayne pulled in 'Ariel'. You want to feel like everything has its impact, that there were feelings that would be festering and had to be dealt with over time. This was organic to where those characters would be and gave them something to go through in the course of that story."

TEASER

EXT. WASTELAND - DAY

SLOW CAMERA PAN across a flat vista of shattered rock. Barren. Lunar. PAN ONTO a MAN, seated a short distance away on the ground. His side is to us, and he is BUCK NAKED. It's MAL REYNOLDS. He lifts his head, nodding to himself as he takes in his surroundings.

MAL
(flatly)
Yep... That went well.

CUT TO BLACK:

TITLE APPEARS: "SEVENTY-TWO HOURS EARLIER..."

EXT. DUST PLANET - NIGHT

A LARGE CRATE slams down onto the ground, hard. The two SMUGGLERS who were hefting it straighten, turning to go. WIDEN to see that Mal stands close by, arms crossed.

A PILE OF SIMILAR CRATES lies in the dust around Mal. Other SMUGGLERS carry more crates, adding to the pile. (All smugglers sport holstered firearms.) They are ferrying them from the lowered FREIGHT PLATFORM of a SPACESHIP, which looms overhead.

MONTY (O.S.)
Malcolm Reynolds!

A VERY LARGE MAN steps off a ladder that goes up from the platform to the belly of the ship,

beaming at Mal.

He's a big, gut-toting bear of a man. Not pretty. Not in the least. Think of a greasy Brad Garrett with bad teeth.

MONTY
Y'old son-of-a — Com'ere!

MAL
Oh hey Monty —

He sweeps a mildly protesting Mal up into a bearhug, lifting him off his feet for a beat.

MAL (cont'd)
(wheezes)
How — you — do — in'?

Monty releases him, one mitt still clapped on Mal's shoulder, shaking it with rough welcome.

MONTY
They didn't tell me you were picking up this leg of the run.

MAL
Yeah, things were a little slow. Figured to do a little honest smuggling 'tween jobs.

MONTY
(scans desert)
Where's that sorry-ass ship a' yours?

As they speak, Monty's ND CREW continues offloading the crates, passing in and out of frame.

MAL
Monty, two boats like ours meeting on an empty

JOSE MOLINA

Due to an ever-more-demanding schedule, Jose Molina says the *Firefly* writing process became an increasingly joint effort. "When 'Ariel' was done, Cheryl Cain did a full draft of 'War Stories'. After that, everything was a lot more collaborative in the scripting stage. 'Trash' and 'The Message' were the two additional episodes that the network ordered, so when people were sent off to script, we had caught our breath a little bit, but not enough that one person could go off and crank out a script at a fast enough pace. So on 'Trash', Ben Edlund and I were sent off together to write two acts each.

"The Macguffin came to be what it was after 18,411 things were eliminated," Molina semi-quips. "For a while, the Macguffin was going to be *Sgt. Pepper's*, but we couldn't get the rights. I had the idea that

it would be a globe of Earth-That-Was, which is something that had been referred to a lot of times, but we'd never seen it. I called Ben and he thought that was very cool. By the time we got into work on Monday, Joss had already had the idea that he wanted it to be the first laser gun. The ultimate argument was that a big fat ball wouldn't fit down the trash chute and it would look a little ridiculous if Mal was trying to hide a big globe. He'd look like pregnant Mal!"

Who came up with the idea of the opening? "Joss," Molina laughs. "The idea of starting with naked Nathan in the middle of the desert at five in the morning, when it's freezing cold in the middle of Lancaster [California], I think just appealed to Joss too much to not figure out a story to go with it."

---

rock like this, it just screams contraband to the fed. Or have you forgotten that time you got pinched on Beylix?

MONTY
(points to his own temple, nodding)
Always thinking, ain't ya. Smarts. That's what you got. Smarts.

MAL
(shrugs)
Okay.
(looks closer at Monty)
Something's different.

MONTY
(smiles proudly)
Yup.

MAL
You look — there's something —
(Monty strokes his chin)
The beard! You shaved off the soup-catcher!

MONTY
Yup.

MAL
I thought you were gonna take that ugly chin-wig to the grave —

MONTY
(chuckles)
So did I. But she didn't much like my whiskers...

MAL
She — ?

MONTY
(calls out)
Bridgit!
(to Mal)
What the hell am I thinking, I got to introduce you to the missus!

MAL
Monty! You've fallen from our noble bachelor ranks?

MONTY
Wasn't looking to, but she kinda swept me off my feet. Bridgit!

A woman hurries to them obscured by the smuggly bustle.

MAL
Well she must be a rare specimen indeed.

MONTY
That don't begin to cover it. Mal, I want you to meet my Bridgit.

And she steps out from behind Monty, smiling — until she recognizes Mal. A beat as he and SAFFRON look at each other.

Saffron sweeps a foot under a smuggler's leg, tripping him forward, pulling his gun from its holster as he falls, and pirouetting over his body as he hits the dirt, coming out of the spin with the gun locked on Mal's head, just as Mal's gun is flashing from his holster, locked on hers — a Woo-off. They are frozen, Monty right in the middle, nonplussed.

MONTY (cont'd)
So... you guys have met.

BLACK OUT.

END OF TEASER

ACT ONE

EXT. DUST PLANET - NIGHT

Right where we left off. Mal and Saffron sidestep, guns trained, slowly circling, very intense. Monty stands nearby, brow knitted with confusion.

MONTY
Mal — why you got a piece trained on my wife?

MAL
She ain't your wife, Monty —

MONTY
Huh? I married 'er, didn't I?

MAL
Yeah, so did —

Mal's cut off before he can finish, because in the

instant Mal's eyes flick toward Monty, Saffron scissors up a high kick, knocks the gun out of Mal's hand. She has the drop on Mal for an instant, but doesn't fire. Mal lunges, sweeping her arm to the side, catching her wrist in his grip and squeezing hard. She drops the gun. Saffron throws her head forward, smashing into Mal's nose painfully.

MAL (cont'd)
Gaaah!

MONTY
Bridgit!

Mal staggers back, buffeted by a series of punches from Saffron. Mal fires one punch back, catching her on the chin and knocking her to the ground.

MONTY (cont'd)
Mal!

She lands on her back, mostly unfazed, and instantly rolls for the gun a short distance away. Just as she almost reaches it, Mal sails in on top of her, tackling her flat.

SAFFRON
Get OFF!

She swings an elbow back, hits the side of Mal's head hard. He reels, she rolls on top of him, hands around his throat. He does the same, and now they're strangling each other. They do this for a vicious beat, until —

MONTY (O.S.)
(roars)
Gorramnit! That's enough!

Monty's big hands drop into frame, lifting them both off the ground and pulling them apart. They're both breathless, Mal's got a BLOODY NOSE.

MONTY
Now what the hell is goin' on here? Whaddya mean she ain't my wife?

MAL
She ain't your wife... 'cause she's married to me.

SAFFRON
(also huffing)
Don't listen to him!

MAL
It's true. Half-a-year back, out at the Triumph Settlement. Didn't call herself "Bridgit" then. It was "Saffron". Hitched me by surprise, got on my ship, and tried to steal it out from under me... She's as cold as ice and dead crazy on top of it.

SAFFRON
You're a liar, Malcolm Reynolds!

MONTY
Oh, he's a lot of things. But a liar he ain't. All the terrible thick we been through, he ain't never lied to me, not even once.
(pointed to Saffron)
And I never got to telling you his name.

MAL'S COSTUME

Costume designer Shawna Trpcic: "The direction from Joss was American, go back to the frontier and pioneer of the land. We researched World War One and Two pilots and Civil War and frontier characters and, out of all those different images, we came up with five or six different types of sketches and Joss picked them out. It was pretty much Civil War pants and a Civil War jacket, but made out of leather like a frontiersman. It was a mishmash of a bunch of different things and a little Han Solo thrown in — because we like him [laughs]! The Han Solo influence is in the holster and the gun belt, which isn't a copy at all, that's where the design came from — slung over the side like a cowboy."

NATHAN FILLION

Fillion says finding Mal was a challenge, since his own life is so different from the character's, but Whedon's attention to detail, even down to costuming, helped him assume Mal's skin. "Joss was very specific in his vision. I didn't look at my Mal Reynolds costume and say, 'You know what this needs?' or 'You know what sucks about this?' No, I was very happy about it. I looked like a mean Charles Ingalls [Pa on *Little House on the Prairie*]. I really liked that — the frontierism of what we were doing. I loved that we weren't wearing silver jumpsuits or jumpsuits of any kind. I was very excited about that."

Saffron drops all pretense — the jig is up.

SAFFRON
Oh, hell. Fine. Be like that.

She pulls away from Monty and starts neatening herself up, brushing back her hair, wiping the dirt from her face.

MONTY
(hurt)
You said you loved me for me...

Mal looks at Monty, saying with tender frankness:

MAL
Believe me, Monty, she says that to all the boys.

Off of Monty's crestfallen face we CUT TO:

EXT. DUST PLANET - NIGHT

MONTY'S SHIP as its engines FIRE UP, whipping a small cloud of dust around the tiny figures of Saffron and Mal. [Note: the design of this ship must be such that it can take off without its engines incinerating what is directly beneath it.]

SAFFRON stands with her arms crossed, looking up irritably, lit by the O.S. glare of the ship's lights. Mal is in the BG, with the crates. He dabs at his bloody nose with a white kerchief. Monty's voice echoes down over the SHIP'S

LOUDSPEAKER, choked with hurt.

MONTY (O.S.)
Damn you, Bridgit! Damn you ta Hades! You broke my heart in a million pieces! You made me love you, and then y — I SHAVED MY BEARD FOR YOU, DEVIL WOMAN!

SAFFRON
Whatever.

After a beat, a DUFFEL BAG drops into frame from above, SLAMMING into the ground. The O.S. ship pulls away with a burst of engine thrust, the light from it fading.

SAFFRON (cont'd)
<BUN tyen-shung duh ee-DWAY-RO.> [Stupid inbred stack of meat.]

She moves to the duffel bag, crouches, unzips it, and roots around inside. The barrel of Mal's pistol enters frame, pressing against her temple.

MAL
You're goin' to wanna pull your claw out of that bag, nice and slow.

SAFFRON
Relax. I'm not going for a gun or anything.

She slowly pulls a small cylinder out of the bag, and shows it to him, cranking it. It's lipstick.

SAFFRON (cont'd)
Just freshening up.

She's about to apply it when Mal snatches it and hucks it out into the O.S. desert.

MAL
You and lipstick is a dangerous combination, as I recall.
(gestures with gun)
Now get up and turn around.

She does so, with some impatience. Mal moves in and frisks her, trying to be businesslike, but she responds in a way that crackles with sexual tension.

SAFFRON
Oh... Yeah... Just like old times.

MAL
We don't have any old times. I just don't want you pullin' a pistol out of... of anywhere...

She writhes into him a little as he finishes frisking her.

SAFFRON
(super sexy)
Mmmm. You missed a spot...

Mal gives her a rough shove and she stumbles forward a step.

MAL
Can't miss a place you never been.

She am freaky — turns to him not with anger, but with practiced emotion — playing to Mal as if they have a troubled, but real marriage.

SAFFRON
Marriage is hard work, Mal. I know it... But that doesn't mean we have to give up...
(moves closer to him)
Sure, we've had our spats. Maybe I made some bad decisions along the way.

MAL
Oh, you're a tweaked one, you are.

SAFFRON
(smiles)
But face it, hubby. I'm really hot.

MAL
Uh huh.
(waves gun at her)
Start walkin'.

SAFFRON
Walking? Walking where?

MAL
Pick a direction. Just don't turn around.

SAFFRON
Come on. Mal.

MAL
This is my scrap of nowhere. You go on and find your own.

SAFFRON
You can't just leave me here, on this lifeless piece-of-crap moon...

MAL
Sure I can.

SAFFRON
I'll die.

MAL
Well, as a courtesy, you might start getting busy on that, 'cause all this chatter ain't doin' me any kindness.

Saffron sits down on her duffel bag with a defiant pout. But she seems done with the full court press, more herself now.

SAFFRON
Why don't you just go ahead and shoot me, then?

MAL
I dunno.
(thinks on this)
Why didn't you shoot me? Back there, when I took my eyes off you for a split? Shamed to say it, but I gave you the window.

SAFFRON
(condescending sigh)
You and Monty, you fought in the war together, right?
(he nods)
I could smell that. The war buddy bond is a tough one to crack. I knew if I shot you I'd lose Monty anyway. You just had a better hand of cards this time.

MAL
It ain't a hand of cards. It's called a life. I've got a better life than you. And that's just barely, and just 'cause I don't spend my every waking hour pissing all over it, like some folks I'm holdin' a gun on...

Saffron flashes a tight, insincere smile.

SAFFRON
Touché, mon amour.
(as she stands)
Seriously, Mal. You have to give me a ride.

MAL
(bitter laugh)
Woman, you are completely off your nut.

SAFFRON
I won't make trouble. You can stick me in one of those crates if you like. Just don't leave me he —

Mal SHOOTS. A bullet kicks up the dust about three feet from her. A beat. She sticks out her tongue. ANOTHER BULLET kicks up dust, two feet away. Another beat. She bends, lifting one strap of her heavy bag. She starts dragging it off, struggling. Then she stops and turns again.

SAFFRON (cont'd)
This was all your fault, you know. I had a perfect crime lined up.

MAL
Sure. You were stealing a man's beard.

SAFFRON
No, you <HOE-tze duh PEE-goo!> [monkey's ass!] A million-square job. The big time. I was going to cut Monty and his crew in, but you screwed that royal.

MAL
(raises gun again)
Odd, but I don't think I'll be losing sleep over it.

SAFFRON
I've got the layout, entrance codes, believe me, this thing practically robs itself.

MAL
Bye now.

SAFFRON
I'm handing you a fortune on a gold platter, sweetheart! Don't you even want to hear the details?

Mal considers that for a beat, then looks at the kerchief, BLOODIED from his nose. He raises his gun again.

INT. SERENITY - CARGO BAY - NIGHT

JAYNE stands by the cargo bay door, pulling on leather work-gloves. Behind him, BOOK, SIMON, KAYLEE, and ZOE stand at the ready.

JAYNE
Sure you're up to liftin' this stuff? Crates are fair heavy, I gather.

The engines are HUMMING, and the bay ROCKS a bit as Serenity sets down. Kaylee nods, enthusiastic.

KAYLEE
I can handle it.

JAYNE
Wasn't talkin' to you.

Jayne smiles at Simon, who mocks a pained expression. Jayne hits a button — the airlock opens, and the ramp beyond it starts to lower.

The lowering ramp reveals Mal, standing in front of the pile of crates, alone. He doesn't look too happy. He has a wadded up TWIST OF TORN KERCHIEF in each nostril, to stem the blood.

JAYNE (cont'd)
Woah there, Cap... Tell me you didn't get into a fight with Monty.

KAYLEE
Really? But I thought we loved Monty!
(to Zoe, sincere question)
Don't we love Monty?

ZOE
Sweetie, if he had a tussle with that sasquatch, we'd be in the dirt right about now, scoopin' up the Captain's teeth.

Mal stomps up the ramp, holding them all in an even glare.

ZOE (cont'd)
Ain't that so, sir?

MAL
You know what? I don't particular want to talk about it. Now we got work. Let's shut up and do it.

Zoe looks from the Captain to the others, then back, eyebrows raised. WASH comes down the cargo bay stairs closest to the bridge, stops by Mal.

WASH
Inara was asking for you. Wanted to —

Mal walks away.

WASH (cont'd)
So later with the talking then.

Wash walks down toward camera, mouthing words to Zoe and Book, who carry one of the crates up the ramp.

WASH (cont'd)
(mouthed silently)
"What happened?"

EXT. SPACE

Just a stock shot of Serenity for transition please.

INT. SERENITY - INARA'S SHUTTLE

Mal enters INARA's chamber —

MAL
Heard you were looking for me?

— to find her seated, preparing tea. Her whole attitude is formal, yet inviting...

INARA
I was. Care to sit?

He does, slowly.

INARA (cont'd)
I was hoping to talk a little business. Would you like some tea?

He stands again, less slowly.

MAL
Okay, what's the game?

INARA
I offered you tea.

MAL
After inviting me into your shuttle of your own free will, which makes two events without precedent and which makes me more'n a little skittish.

INARA
Honestly, Mal, if we can't be civilized and talk like —

❖ Below: Inara's teapot.

MAL
I'm plenty civilized. You're using wiles on me.

INARA
I'm using what?

MAL
Your feminine wiles. Your Companion training, your some-might-say uncanny ability to make a man sweaty and/or compliant, of which I have had just about enough today.

INARA
Maybe this isn't the best time.

MAL
(sitting again)
It's a fine time. Just talk plain, is all.

INARA
I'm not sleeping with you, Mal.

Beat.

MAL
Uh, no, I think I would have noticed if you were. My keenly trained... senses would have...

INARA
You're not my lover. Neither are you my mother my house mistress or anyone who has the slightest say in how I conduct my affairs.

MAL
Well enough. So?

INARA
So let me conduct my affairs!

MAL
Who's keeping you from —

INARA
I haven't had a client in three weeks. Backwater moons, slums, frontier planets without so much as a temple built —

MAL
We go where the work is!

INARA
There's all kinds of work, Mal.

MAL
And ours is the kind the Alliance shuts you down for. I opt to stay off the radar —

INARA
There's plenty of worlds where both of us could work. We used to visit them, remember?

MAL
<EE-chee shung-hoo-shee.> [Let's take a deep breath.] Are you saying I'm doing this deliberate on account of you? There's some reason I don't want you on the job?

INARA
Is there?

MAL
(sighing, pacing)
Well this is one of the crazier things I've heard today and when I tell you about the rest of my day, you'll appreciate —

INARA
Mal, I'm not accusing you of anything, it's just —

MAL
Hey, no, we'll set course for Planet of the Lonely Rich and Appropriately Hygienic Man. I'll just tell Wash, we can park there for a month.

INARA
(rises as well)
Not all of your work is illegal. And the —

MAL
What, you're trying to get me off the job now?

INARA
And the best job you ever pulled was on a central planet!

MAL
How about I stay out of your whoring —

INARA
That didn't take long —

They're right in each other's faces now, goin' at it.

MAL
And you stay out of my thieving. I know my business plenty well, thank you.

INARA
Right. You're a criminal mastermind. What was the last cargo we snuck past the Alliance to transport?

MAL
We made a perfectly good piece —

INARA
What was the cargo?

MAL
They were dolls!

INARA
They were little geisha dolls with big heads that wobbled!

MAL
People love those!

INARA
And what exactly was our net profit on the famous wobbly-headed doll caper?

MAL
"Our" cut? You're in the gang now?

INARA
Well, since I can't seem to find work as a Companion, I might as well become a petty thief like you!

Beat. Oops. The air goes out of both of them.

MAL
Petty.

INARA
(backtracking)

I didn't mean petty.

MAL
What did you mean?

INARA
(meekly)
<Suo-SHEE?> [Petty?]

MAL
That's Chinese for petty.

INARA
No, that's a narrow... there's nuances of meaning that...

MAL
Maybe you shoulda stuck with your wiles.

INARA
Don't put this all on me, Mal. You know you haven't been after serious work in a —

MAL
Serious work? You wanna know what I —

He stops himself.

INARA
What?

MAL
Nothing.

INT. SERENITY - CARGO BAY - SOON AFTER

Mal, alone, descends the stairs into the cargo bay. He goes to the crates, scanning over them for a moment, finding one that has TWO BULLET HOLES in its lid. He pries it open, pulls the lid away and looks in.

MAL
All right. Tell me more about this job a' yours.

OVER HIS SHOULDER INTO CRATE

Where, frowning with discomfort, wedged kinda sexily into a shipment of PROTEIN PACKETS, lies Our Mrs. Reynolds...

CUT TO BLACK.

END OF ACT ONE

ACT TWO

INT. SERENITY - DINING AREA

Jayne, Zoe, Wash and Kaylee are all gathered at the dining room table. Presently they're staring a bit open-mouthed at — MAL AND SAFFRON standing variously before them as Saffron makes her pitch. She's sort of in the middle of it:

SAFFRON
The mark's name is Durran Haymer. Maybe one of the biggest collectors of Earth-That-Was artifacts in the 'verse. Guy's got warehouses full of stuff. But his prize piece is sitting in his parlor — an antiquity of unspeakable value: the Lassiter. The original hand-held laser pistol. One of only two known to still exist. The forerunner of all modern laser technology. Haymer got lucky, picked it up during the war for nothing.

MAL
But it wasn't just luck.
(then)
Tell them.

SAFFRON
Haymer's Alliance. Bio-weapons expert during the war. He'd target neighborhoods with valuables, wipe out every living soul without ever damaging the goods. Go in, take whatever he wanted.

MAL
He's living fat on a private estate on Bellerophon.

Saffron tosses some future computer disks onto the table.

SAFFRON
I managed to get ahold of his schedule for the next eighteen months — the layout of the estate grounds... and every security code for the place.

No one moves to touch them.

MAL
Saffron's got a notion we can just walk in — take the Lassiter right off his shelf.

More with the staring. Finally Wash speaks:

WASH
I'm confused...

SAFFRON
(ahead of him)
You're asking yourself if I've got the security codes, why don't I just go in and grab it for myself — why cut you in?

WASH
No. Actually... I was wondering...
(to Mal, suddenly)
What's she doing on the ship!? Didn't she try to kill us?

SAFFRON
(rolls her eyes)
Please. Nobody died the last time.
(suddenly unsure)
Right? Where's the old guy with the hair?

WASH
We're in space. How'd she get here?

MAL
She hitched.

WASH
I don't recall pulling over...

MAL
Look. Point is, there's more'n one of us here wouldn't mind sticking it to a <Chiang-BAO HOE-tze duh> [monkey raping] Alliance bastard. Besides that, this could be a very lucrative venture for all of us. This ain't no wobbly-headed doll caper. This here's history.

Jayne's been thinking hard. Raises his hand.

JAYNE
Okay. I got a question. If she's got the security codes, why don't she just go in and grab it for herself — why cut us in?

A beat as they stare. Then:

SAFFRON
Good point. Getting through the door and putting our hands on the Lassiter is easy. Getting out with it... that's the tricky part.

MAL
It's tagged and coded. Second it passes through the door — alarms, security, feds.

SAFFRON
This isn't a one-woman operation. To do this right, I need...

INARA (O.S.)
Idiots.

They turn. Inara has entered the room.

SAFFRON
Partners.

INARA
Dupes. And that's what you'll all be if you trust her.

MAL
Could be that's so. Lord knows ain't none of us "criminal masterminds". So if you got something better, Inara — something not "petty" — we'd sure be willing to hear it.

A beat as Inara and Mal hold the look between them. Saffron doesn't hate the tension that's evident there. Finally:

INARA
(turns and goes)
<Nee-mun DOH shr sagwa.> [Idiots. All of you.]

MAL
(looks back to gang)
Okay. So the question remains — how do we get the artifact out without setting off the alarms?

KAYLEE
You don't. Not through the door, anyway.
(reaches for the disk)
This the layout?

SAFFRON
Full blueprints of the entire grounds.

KAYLEE
Could be we look hard enough, we find a way.

Mal smiles, that's what he likes to hear.

MAL
You dig into that, little Kaylee.

(looks to Zoe)
Zoe. You ain't said a word. Time to weigh in.

ZOE
Take sounds ripe enough. That's assuming we can fence it.

SAFFRON
I know a guy on Persephone. He's already got half a dozen buyers on the bid. The split is gonna be sweet.

ZOE
But Inara's not wrong —
(eyes on Saffron)
— she can't be trusted.

MAL
I ain't asking you to trust her. I'll be with her on the inside the whole time.

SAFFRON
See there? Only one thing you gotta do if you want to be a rich woman, hon — and that's get over it.

ZOE
Mmmm. Okay.

POW — Zoe hauls off and slugs Saffron in the mouth. She goes down on her tush. Everyone's a little astonished.

ZOE (cont'd)
You, too. Hon.
(then, to Mal)
I'm in.

Off nobody offering to help Saffron up —

INT. SIMON'S ROOM - DAY

Jayne is dumping off a bunch of food and water packets, talking to Simon and RIVER.

JAYNE
Captain says you're to stay put. Doesn't want you runnin' afoul of his blushin' psychotic bride. She figures out who you are, she'll turn you in 'fore you can... say... "Don't turn me in, lady".

SIMON
The bounty on us just keeps getting more exciting.

JAYNE
(busying himself)
Well, I wouldn't know.

RIVER
(looking at Jayne)
She's a liar.

JAYNE
That don't exactly set her apart from the rest of us. And the plunder sounds fun enough.

RIVER
She's a liar and no good will come of her.

JAYNE
Well, I say as a rule that girlfolk ain't to be trusted.

R A S H

RIVER
Jayne is a girl's name.

JAYNE
Well Jayne ain't a girl.
(to Simon)
She starts on that "girl's name" thing, I'm a show her good an' all I got man parts.

SIMON
I'm trying to think of a way for you to be cruder. It's just not coming.

JAYNE
I just heard enough ab —

SIMON
(wearily dismissive)
<KWAI chur hun-rien duh di fahng.> [Go far away very fast.]

JAYNE
And I WAS gonna leave you a deck of cards...

He goes, shutting the door behind him.

SIMON
Great. Another exciting adventure in sitting.

RIVER
Afraid.

SIMON
We'll be okay. Why the Captain is trusting that <BOO hway-HUN duh PUO-foo> [remorseless harridan] is beyond —

RIVER
Not her. Jayne.

SIMON
(amused)
Afraid? Since when?

RIVER
Since Ariel.

Simon is no longer amused.

RIVER (cont'd)
Afraid we'll know.

INT. SERENITY - CARGO BAY - CATWALKS

Zoe is headed up the catwalks from the cargo bay, Inara comes down the stairs leading from the bridge, heading to her shuttle.

ZOE
We should be on Bellerophon by oh-six. I figure the job should be —

INARA
Please. I really don't wanna know.

ZOE
Least it's your kind of world. You got appointments made?

INARA
The minute we hit atmo, I'm gone. I've booked a few choice clients, should help me get my mind

off Mal's descent into lunacy —

ZOE
(curious)
What happens if you got an appointment coming and you ain't finished the one you're at?

INARA
Overbooking is a cardinal sin. Clients must feel the experience is timeless. Only thing worse is a badly faked fall.

ZOE
See, that's where me and Companionship part ways. I never could work the notion of pretending a man was gettin' it done when he wasn't.

INARA
So you've never pretended to fall.

ZOE
Well, never is a strong word... sometimes it's easier.

INARA
What about with Wash?

ZOE
One time. Poor boy was bone-tired...

INARA
And?

ZOE
He knew. Son of a bitch called me on it.

INARA
That's the one you marry.

ZOE
Damn right.

Zoe starts to leave.

INARA
Zoe. Don't let Mal trust her.

ZOE
Thought you didn't care about the job.

INARA
I really don't. I just want there to be someone around to pick me up when I'm done.

ZOE
<FAHNG-sheen.> [Don't worry.] I got his back.

Captain starts thinking with his <JAN-doh duh ee-KWAI-ro,> [dangly piece of flesh,] I'll step in.

INARA
The man's a moron. Everything Saffron is, is a lie. She'll get the drop on him — which as far as I'm concerned is what he richly deserves.

ZOE
Ain't sayin' it ain't risky. Don't count Mal out, though. He just knows the estate is —

Inara holds up her hands.

INARA
No details. I meant that. Just be careful.

ZOE
See you when we're wealthy...

They split up, Zoe heading up toward the bridge, Inara going into her shuttle.

ANGLE: SAFFRON — has been eavesdropping from above, near the second shuttle. Mal steps out —

MAL
You give me a hand in here. No wandering about, remember? Or I'll stick you back in your crate.

WASH (V.O.)
(from the com)
Cap'n?

Mal keeps his eye on Saffron as he hits a nearby button.

MAL
Yeah?

WASH (V.O.)
We think we got something...

INT. SERENITY - DINING AREA

Mal, Zoe, Jayne, Wash, Kaylee and Saffron are gathered around the table. Kaylee has the portable display (seen in 'Ariel') with the estate schematics. It gets passed around as she and Wash speak:

WASH
Bellerophon Estates... Home to the rich and para-noid... gracious living... ocean views...

"I think basically we wanted to do another caper show," Whedon says, "and Saffron always was charming and sexy and kept you off-balance and we could have another 'This is how the rich live and we're going to have a caper on a floating island and garbage,' and have a lot of fun with that, but still turn things around, still play Mal and Inara's tension. It was an idea of having a good time and not being bottled up in the ship, opening it up a little bit. The idea that the first laser pistol is an antique helps with the timeline, too, it helps tell you how these people live."

Was it also desirable to show Inara doing something useful as a member of the team? "Always a good thing and difficult to do," Whedon notes, "because she's not a bank robber." But she can get down and dirty when she needs to? "Well, she wasn't that dirty," Whedon points out. "She was sitting on a high wall."

EXT. BELLEROPHON - DAY

Ocean as far as the eye can see. Floating above the blue expanse are enormous manors — estates hovering a mile above the water, complete with greenery, landscaping, etc.

WASH (V.O.)
...and state-of-the-art security, including local patrols, and multi-code-keys needed at all entrances and exits...

INT. SERENITY - DINING AREA - CONTINUOUS

SAFFRON
Which we have —

WASH
Right. You and Mal will split off in Shuttle II as we make our approach...

EXT. BELLEROPHON - DAY

SERENITY zooms into the shot (continuing CGI shot from before). Shuttle II splits off from Serenity, veering slightly up. CAMERA STAYS WITH SHUTTLE II as it approaches the floating estate, other flying vehicles coming and going.

WASH (V.O.)
There's a landing port just south of the main house.

INT. SHUTTLE II - DAY

Mal at the helm.

MAL
Prepped for landing. You ready?

Saffron appears from the back, two ENORMOUS FLOWER ARRANGEMENTS in her arms.

SAFFRON
Ready.

EXT. FLOATING ESTATE - DAY

The well manicured grounds. SHUTTLE II lands in the distance. CAMERA PANS to find various DOMESTICS bustling about who carry covered trays, carts loaded with fine china, a BARTENDER setting up an outdoor bar, etc.

WASH (V.O.)
Haymer's throwing a big party this weekend, so you should have no trouble blending with the hired help who'll be there setting up.

CAMERA FINDS Mal and Saffron carrying the flower arrangements, now moving through all of this.

WASH (cont'd; V.O.)
All you gotta do is get through the back door.

EXT. FLOATING ESTATE - BACK ENTRANCE - DAY

Mal and Saffron arrive at the back door. Saffron pulls out a punch-pad and small round "enabler". Attaches the small cylinder to the door, taps in

her code, the cylinder LIGHTS —

MAL (V.O.)
Shouldn't be a problem, unless someone's been less than truthful —

The DOOR CLICKS open, Saffron looks to Mal, smiles...

INT. SERENITY - DINING AREA

Saffron's looking to Mal, here, too.

KAYLEE
The parlor with the Lassiter's on the ninth floor. You'll have to disable the display. Won't be any trouble. 'Course, once you got your hands on the goods, you can't take it out the front door, nor the back door, nor any door. Every piece of pretty is tagged for the scanners.

SAFFRON
Right. So what do we do?

KAYLEE
(to Wash)
You wanna tell them?

WASH
(waves it to her)
It was your genius idea.

KAYLEE
(proud)
You chuck it in the garbage.

Saffron stares at her, unimpressed.

INT. FLOATING ESTATE - CORRIDORS - DAY

Mal and Saffron move through the interior estate still carrying their flower arrangements. They pass a YOUNG HOUSEKEEPER as she moves past with a garbage bag.

KAYLEE (V.O.)
All the estates on Bellerophon use an automated garbage drone system.

Mal and Saffron exit further into the estate. WE STAY WITH the Housekeeper who moves to a chute opening. She dumps the bag down, then moves to a panel on the opposite wall.

KAYLEE (cont'd; V.O.)
You hit one little button, and the drone whooshes off with the trash.

The Housekeeper touches the panel. Words appear ONSCREEN: "READY FOR DISPOSAL. YES. NO." She touches "Yes".

INT. SERENITY - DINING AREA - CONTINUOUS

SAFFRON
(not really)
Brilliant.

KAYLEE
Thanks.

SAFFRON
Oh, except it's idiotic. Those drones take the disposal bins straight to reclamation. Thirty seconds after we hit the button, the booty'll get incinerated.

KAYLEE
Not if we reprogram the bin. Give it new coordinates.

EXT. UNDERNEATH THE FLOATING ESTATE - DAY

Underneath the floating estate, a futuristic dumpster (lined with computer panels) is latched onto the body of the estate. We hear the low THUD of the bag landing inside.

KAYLEE (V.O.)
Once I override the standard guidance protocol, I can tell the disposal bin to go wherever we want.

A flying GARBAGE DRONE GLIDES INTO FRAME, flies towards the dumpster, and its forklift-like claws clamp onto the dumpster with a loud METALLIC KLANG.

JAYNE

"I'll be in my bunk."

Firefly featured an eclectic rag tag crew of survivors ranging from two fugitives to a space prostitute and a holy man, yet the grumpiest of the lot was Jayne Cobb, a man who often only had his own welfare in mind. Nonetheless, somehow Jayne emerged as one of the series' fan favorites. "Jayne is the handsomest and strongest," laughs Adam Baldwin. "You have to ask people why they like him. I think it goes back to the fact that, at first glance, you see him as this ugly duckling bad guy with a gruff exterior — who turns out to be saying what is really on your mind. 'We don't have to do that. We can do this. It's quicker.' He's the poseable action figure. You make him run, jump, scream, yell, shoot, holler, get into fights, and leer at girls. It's all the stuff you don't get to do in real life."

Jayne had an attitude that didn't always make him a team player. He often came into conflict with other crewmembers, most notably River and Simon. "Well, River's crazy!" exclaims Baldwin. "Jayne felt Simon wasn't fit for the job; that he wasn't tough enough to be out there; that he was raised in too cushy of an existence to belong. He felt they were excess baggage. And I remember Simon's line describing Jayne as 'man ape gone wrong thing'. Yeah, Simon felt like he needed to lash out and call me names. Maybe there was some sort of underlying homo erotica or subtext Joss was trying to build there..." he laughs.

Though Serenity had no shortage of beautiful females on board, Jayne never managed to hook up with any of them. "I had an ongoing battle with Joss Whedon because

I always felt the perfect woman for Jayne would have been Inara, because she wouldn't be there in the morning," recalls Baldwin. "The perfect relationship for Jayne — but Joss never let me get that far. It is so hard to speculate on what could have been... but that's one of Jayne's little secrets I came up with, to keep things interesting.

"For me, the oddest relationship Jayne had was with Zoe, because they were portrayed as physical equals, although I could have kicked her ass," he continues. "She was tough, so that was a respectful relationship. Obviously, she didn't respect me because she thought Jayne was dumb, but she wanted me around in a fight. That was the toughest one to figure out. River was just crazy, and Kaylee was more of the little sister who I'd try to protect."

Jayne always seemed to be throwing a punch or getting into trouble. "I had a really great fight scene in 'Ariel' with the guard, who was played by our stunt coordinator," recalls Baldwin. "It was fun to try and fight with handcuffs on behind your back! And I liked dangling on the wire and going down to the train through the hole [in 'The Train Job']. I love doing that stuff. As far as I'm concerned, movies and television are entertainment, so you jump in there and get some action going, and have some popcorn! I think some people take themselves too seriously when they are doing this stuff. It is hard work and you are trying to tell a story, but don't tell it by pretending to be more important than you are."

If clothes maketh the man, then Jayne's tight t-shirts, baggy army pants and outrageous hats certainly make a loud statement. Baldwin comments that his Firefly threads were "Brave. Daring. Dirty. Practical. Functional. And had a lot of pockets." He continues, "The hat originally was for jumping into the train and not getting blown away in the wind. Then it just became a running joke. Whenever we could, we'd grab a hat. The last episode we shot was 'The Message', and it had a knitted hat with a pompom on it. It's become this nice souvenir that folks have knitted quite a few of, and you see them frequently at conventions. I still have that hat. I am getting my eBay sale ready..."

With credits such as Predator 2, Independence Day, The X-Files and Angel, Baldwin has become a sci-fi staple. However, he maintains Firefly was his dream role. "I've been fortunate to have had a few 'gigs of a lifetime', but this is my favorite so far," he says. "I realized it right away. I knew that this guy and group of people was something special. And I had learned from Full Metal Jacket, which I did when I was twenty-three, that you need to appreciate what you are doing while you are doing it, and not look back ten years later and wish you had appreciated it then. I actually did come to work every day looking to keep it special, positive, and fun. We were under the gun pretty much from the get go and I think we all appreciated how fleeting it can be and how much of a risk you are taking with making television. That is why the work came out so well and at such a high level."

The dumpster shudders with the impact, then detaches from the structure and the drone whisks it away. Another dumpster drops into place where the other one was.

INT. SERENITY - DINING AREA

SAFFRON
And where would that be?

WASH
The loneliest piece of desert we can find. Here. Isis Canyon. Drone dumps the bin, we claim the goods when we're all together again.

SAFFRON
How do you plan on getting to the bin to re-program it?

KAYLEE
You get to the loot — we'll get to the bin.

EXT. SERENITY/UNDERNEATH THE FLOAT-ING ESTATE - DAY

WIDE — CGI. Serenity RISES INTO FRAME, hovering steadily a few feet below the dumpster. Bright sunlight and wind whipping up here.

CLOSER — THE HATCH opens and Jayne emerges. He's wearing goggles, his thrilling heroics hat and a harness with cable (which dangles at the moment).

He pulls himself out of the hatch and crawls carefully up the hull and attaches the safety latch of his cable to a rung on the ship.

Now from the hatch, Kaylee emerges, also wearing goggles and protection from the wind and cold. She hands up the end of her safety harness to Jayne. He clips it. She hands him out a tool kit. He takes it, then helps her up onto the top of the ship. She crawls toward him on her belly. They're under the bin now.

He makes her lie flat, one arm over her protecting her as he pulls out his com, speaks into it, yelling over the ROARING WIND —

JAYNE
Okay! We're planted!

INT. SERENITY - BRIDGE - DAY

JAYNE (V.O., FILTERED)
Take us up —

Wash white knuckling it. Zoe at his shoulder. He pulls back on the controls, as...

EXT. SERENITY/UNDERNEATH THE FLOAT-ING ESTATE - DAY

Jayne and Kaylee still lying flat. Serenity rises up. Jayne and Kaylee look up as the bottom of the estate looms closer.

JAYNE
(into com)
That's good! Hold 'er there.

Kaylee, still face down, pops open her mobile tool kit, hands an electric (space age?) screwdriver to Jayne. Jayne gets to his feet with great care — reaches up to the control panel side of the trash bin. It's all very precarious now as he sets to work on the panel, removing

the face of it...

INT. FLOATING ESTATE - CORRIDOR - DAY

Mal sneaks down a corridor, Saffron standing watch at the other end of the hall. She's keeping an eye on Mal — specifically, on his ass. Mal turns to her —

MAL
Clear.

She trots down to him, looks at a Palm-like device which displays the house's blueprints.

MAL (cont'd)
Which way?

SAFFRON
Left.

They continue on.

EXT. UNDERNEATH THE FLOATING ESTATE - DAY

Jayne pulls off the front panel of the control mechanism, sets about removing the innards, hands the motherboard down to Kaylee, who begins work on it.

INT. FLOATING ESTATE - CORRIDOR - DAY

Mal and Saffron move down another corridor — one that opens into a larger room. Saffron peeks at her Palm as Mal peers into the room,

addresses him in a whisper —

SAFFRON
This should be it.

Mal holds up a finger. The sound of VOICES in the other room slowly drifts away. Then he nods and they walk into —

INT. FLOATING ESTATE - PARLOR - DAY

They ENTER into a room that defines opulence. Beautiful furnishings, expensive art on the walls. Memorabilia of Earth-That-Was fills the room. This room alone cost millions to decorate.

MAL
<Shun-SHENG duh gao-WAHN.> [Holy testicle Tuesday.]

And, on the mantel, in the proper place of honor: a Buck Rogers lookin' laser gun. It is to phasers what those huge old clunky cell phones were to modern ones.

Mal and Saffron set down their flower displays, move to it. She reaches out. He stays her hand. Holds up a small aerosol-looking can, sprays and a FORCE FIELD becomes visible for a moment. Mal reaches into his flowers, pulls out a mini-tool kit.

MAL (cont'd)
Let's get to work...

EXT. SERENITY/UNDERNEATH THE FLOATING ESTATE - DAY

Kaylee hands the jerry-rigged motherboard back to Jayne.

KAYLEE
Okay! She's set!
(yelling over roar of wind)
Careful! It's hot!

Jayne nods, starts to replace the innards. Serenity rises up a few inches, closing the distance between the bottom of the estate and Jayne's head.

JAYNE
(sharply into com)
Gorramn it, Wash! Hold it steady!

INT. SERENITY - BRIDGE

Wash and more with the white knuckles.

WASH
Sorry...

Wash eases off...

EXT. SERENITY/UNDERNEATH THE FLOATING ESTATE - DAY

As Serenity dips ever so slightly, Jayne gets a bit more "head room". Continues to work. Kaylee reacts as she watches:

❖ Above: Kaylee's reprogrammer

KAYLEE
Jayne! No! The dyna-ram's live!

He can't hear what she's saying over the ROAR. Glances at her, annoyed —

JAYNE
What?

KAYLEE
(worried)
Don't touch the dyna —

ZAP! A BLUE BOLT of energy jumps out of the bin control innards, zapping Jayne and knocking him out. He falls and lands hard on the top of Serenity and starts sliding, out like a light. Kaylee instinctively grasps for the tether as Jayne's body slides and rolls, the tether taught. This all happens very fast and off Kaylee's SCREAM!

INT. FLOATING ESTATE - PARLOR - DAY

Mal uses a space-aged allen wrench as he digs into an open panel under the Lassiter.

MAL
Where's the trash chute?

SAFFRON
We passed it in the vestibule.

FOOTSTEPS...

SAFFRON (cont'd)
Someone's coming...

Mal quickly shuts the panel, moves away just as — DURRAN HAYMER, the master of the house, enters the room, freezing both Mal and Saffron. He looks from one to the other, in shock.

DURRAN
(to Mal)
You...

Mal waits.

DURRAN (cont'd)
You found her...

He takes Saffron in his arms.

DURRAN (cont'd)
Oh, god, you've brought back my wife!

Off Mal, in jaded awe...

BLACK OUT.

END OF ACT TWO

ACT THREE

INT. FLOATING ESTATE - PARLOR - DAY

Durran holds Saffron close to him... His face is away from Mal's, hers toward Mal. She looks vexed, though she hugs him back.

DURRAN
Oh, my dear...

Mal mimes hitting the guy. Saffron shakes her head slightly, no.

DURRAN (cont'd)
Oh, my own sweet Yolanda...

Mal mouths "Yolanda?" amused. Durran holds her at arm's length.

DURRAN (cont'd)
I thought I would never see you again.

He's fighting welling emotion. To Mal:

DURRAN (cont'd)
Forgive me... I don't mean to make a show...

MAL
Please. I'm the one intruding.

DURRAN
Not at all. I owe you a great debt of thanks.

MAL
Just gave the lady a lift.

CHRISTINA HENDRICKS

"I had so much fun doing 'Trash'," says Christina Hendricks. "When I came back, I really already felt like a friend and I felt very solid about what the character was. For a while I liked the second episode better than 'Our Mrs. Reynolds', although most people disagreed with me, because you see the big switch with the character in the first episode. But I had a blast on 'Trash'. I loved it. There are some great scenes in it. I loved the scene where Mal and Saffron are inside stealing the Lassiter and get caught, and Saffron has a chain reaction of lies and cover-ups. That's probably one of my favorite scenes. Plus we filmed out in these beautiful Japanese gardens in the San Fernando Valley and it was just really cool to be out there and see what props and costumes had done with everybody."

What about the canyon where Saffron dumps Mal? "That stuff was out near Palmdale — it was a bit of a trek out there to the desert."

Hendricks has enjoyed discovering the world of being on trading cards and appearing at conventions, too. "Who knew that this was going to happen?" she laughs. "It's been wonderful. I get to travel around and meet all these people, who are excited about this one special thing. I had absolutely no idea about fandom."

Has Hendricks learned anything else from her *Firefly* experience? "I learned things about my range as an actress that were exciting; and I think I learned a lot about what I expect and how I think most people deserve to be treated on set, as I found on *Firefly* a group of people who respect and work together in a healthy way, which I think is really important. It was great."

DURRAN
You did much more than that. You returned to me the only thing I truly treasure.

MAL
Well, then, this is a day I'll feel good to be me.

DURRAN
Do I owe you any —

MAL
No. Trip weren't even out of our way.

SAFFRON
I promised him 800 square.

MAL
But, no, I never agreed to —

DURRAN
Please. I'd be embarrassed not to make some recompense... In my study, I... Are you hungry? You both look so tired, there's food, or... Yolanda, I'm babbling like a moon brain...

SAFFRON
Hush. We'll both have plenty to say by daybreak.

DURRAN
Six years...

SAFFRON
Is that all?

DURRAN
From the day we found your shuttle —

SAFFRON
They set on me at Parth, these awful men...

MAL
That wasn't me, though. I don't know those men.

SAFFRON
They said they wanted ransom, but they... they sold me... to slavers...

MAL
Also unknown to me...

DURRAN
(ashamed)
At first I thought — well, you disappeared the same day as Heinrich —

SAFFRON
Heinrich?

DURRAN
The security programmer. And he was young, and I'd seen you two talking, and I thought — but after they found his body...

MAL
They killed Heinrich. Guess he wasn't useful anymore.

DURRAN
(to Saffron)
I never stopped looking.

SAFFRON
I knew you wouldn't.
(tears and all)
That's the thought that kept me alive.

They kiss passionately. Mal looks around, at his nails, at the wall...

SAFFRON (cont'd)
(seductively)
We have so much time to make up...

MAL
Well, that's my cue to skedaddle...

DURRAN
Let me get your money.
(to Saffron)
You won't disappear again?

SAFFRON
Never.

He goes. A beat, as her loving look hardens.

SAFFRON (cont'd)
We gotta move fast.

As Mal returns to the dismantling of the force field with his space-aged allen wrench...

MAL
Yeah, he might come back and hug us in the act.

INT. SERENITY - FOREDECK HALL - BELOW HATCH, LOWERING

Zoe (who's wearing goggles and anti-wind-clothing) and Book struggle to lower the dead weight of an unconscious Jayne into the ship. Zoe is halfway up the ladder, using Jayne's tether to guide him down to Book. She wears a tether harness vest now.

KAYLEE (O.S.)
Zoe?

ZOE
(calls out of hatch)
I'm comin', Kaylee —
(down to Book)
Book — You got him?

BOOK
I got him — I got hi —

Zoe unhitches his tether line and Jayne's full weight topples toward Book. He staggers back, pinned against the wall of the corridor by Jayne's bulk.

BOOK (cont'd)
(wheezes)
Lord — this boy weighs — a solid ton —

He lowers Jayne to the floor. Simon appears, having been summoned. Zoe hitches the tether line to her vest.

ZOE
Doctor, you got yourself a patient to see to.

Simon nods, face clouded with subtle darkness.

SIMON
Yes. I'll take care of it.

Simon moves to assist Book. Zoe hauls herself up out of the hatch.

INT. FLOATING ESTATE - PARLOR - DAY

As Mal continues his dismantling...

TRASH

SAFFRON
You don't know him. He's everything I said he was.

MAL
Oh, he's a killer of men. Why I'll bet he eats up babies.

SAFFRON
You're wasting time.

He's actually being very efficient while continuing.

MAL
But let's take a breath here, Yolanda. You're sneaking into a place you could walk into as welcome as glad news. What's the math on that?

SAFFRON
The math is you not adding up that Durran Haymer would as soon cut your throat as —

MAL
You would?

SAFFRON
If possible.

MAL
No. That ain't it at all. You'da knocked him on the brain, were that the case. You don't want him knowing the truth. Unlike all the — I'm gonna go with hundreds — of men you've married, you actually want this one to think well of you after you've gone.

A FLASH and WE SEE the FORCE FIELD appear then DISAPPEAR. Mal reaches in easily, grabs the Lassiter.

MAL (cont'd)
My god... Could it be that I've just met your real husband?

She has backed up to her flower arrangement, whips out a small gun at him, furious.

SAFFRON
Congratulations, anything else you want on your tombstone, you piece of crap?

DURRAN
Now I'm intruding.

She puts the gun down, genuinely upset that Durran has busted her.

SAFFRON
Durran... This isn't what it looks like...

MAL
Unless it looks like we're stealing your priceless Lassiter, 'cause that's what we're doing. Don't ask me about the gun, 'cause that's new.

As he says this, Mal has elegantly moved past Durran, dropped the Lassiter into the trash chute just outside the door, hit the button.

DURRAN
Well. I appreciate your honesty. Not, you know, a lot, but —

SAFFRON
Durran, you don't know what he's forced me to —

DURRAN
Stop. Yolanda, please just stop.

There is terrible sadness in his voice. And a frantic misery in hers:

SAFFRON
Durran... Don't look at me like that...

A beat. She whips the gun at him.

SAFFRON (cont'd)
I said don't look at me like that!

She might just shoot him as we GO TO:

EXT. UNDERSIDE OF FLOATING ESTATE - DAY

Kaylee teeters on precarious tippy-toe, straining to plug a piece of HARDWARE into the top part of the control panel on the dumpster. Zoe steadies her, heels dug in, one hand gripping Kaylee's tether.

KAYLEE
Almost... done... Just have to plug the interface strike-plate back... in...

There's a CLACKING of machinery from the dumpster, and a BEACON LIGHT begins flashing.

ZOE
That's the pick-up call — they must have dropped the Star... How we doing?

Kaylee strains but can't quite reach.

KAYLEE
(growls)
Can't reach it —

Zoe looks to —

ZOE'S POV — of A [CGI] GARBAGE DRONE in the distance, taking a hard turn towards them, like a shark nosing toward its prey.

Zoe speaks into her com.

ZOE
Wash — we need a little more altitude — now —

WASH (O.S.)
Working on it, dear —

ZOE
Kaylee —

Kaylee fumbles with the plate as Serenity lurches up another foot or two.

ZOE (cont'd)
KayleeKayleeKaylee —

Kaylee snaps the strike-plate into place.

KAYLEE
Got it!

Zoe pulls hard on Kaylee's tether —

GARBAGE BIN

as Kaylee is yanked hard down OUT OF FRAME, just as the drone SLAMS into place, right where Kaylee had been a micro-second before. It attaches to the dumpster with a DEAFENING BONG.

ZOE AND KAYLEE

lay prone on the top of the ship, exchange a look. Start to scurry forward out of frame and we GO TO:

N A T H A N   F I L L I O N

It was no secret that Christina Hendricks was extremely talented and super-attractive. She has a real way about her. She played two characters in this episode exceedingly well. It's another case of how other people do my job for me. I don't have to worry about how I react to Saffron's seductions because all I'm doing is standing there getting some love from Christina Hendricks. I loved it!

INT. SERENITY - BRIDGE - DAY

Wash pilots hard as Zoe's voice crackles in over the com.

ZOE (O.S.)
We're in! Go! Go!

WASH
Copy that —

Wash pulls back on his controls.

EXT. UNDERSIDE OF FLOATING ESTATE - DAY

Serenity drops away from the underbelly, peeling into a dive and sailing off, as the drone detaches the dumpster and flies off in the opposite direction.

INT. FLOATING ESTATE - PARLOR - DAY

Mal inching his way around from the door; Saffron staring down Durran, gun pointed at him...

MAL
Whoa, whoa, let's not get worked up here —

SAFFRON
(to Durran)
Are you really so naive? Do you really think your life is anything to me?

Mal is next to his flower arrangement — whip-quick he pulls his own gun from it, is drawn and pointed at her in a heartbeat.

MAL
Okay, we're not killing folk today, on account of our very tight schedule. So why don't you drop that pistola, Yo-Saf-Bridge, and we'll be about our —
(suddenly as fierce as a cop)
DROP IT NOW.

He comes at her as he shouts it, his whole attitude wrought with controlled fury, putting the gun to her head. She drops hers to the floor, knowing he means business, but never takes her eyes off Durran. They play everything to each other, even when talking to Mal. (Mal retrieves her gun, pockets it.)

SAFFRON
Did you think I was a princess? That I would stay locked up here in the tower? With you?

DURRAN
I hoped.

SAFFRON
You're a rutting fool.

MAL
Saffron, you wanna finish the damn job? We're short on minutes here. I'm sorry mister —

DURRAN
How long have you been with him?

MAL
Oh we're not together.

SAFFRON
He's my husband.

MAL
Well who in the damn galaxy isn't?

She starts working.

DURRAN
I feel so bad for you.

SAFFRON
Bad for me? I'm not the patsy getting stole from. You had half a brain you'da called the feds the minute you saw me.

DURRAN
Oh, I did.

They stop. He points to his ring. It's modern, with a stone like a button. That is a button.

DURRAN (cont'd)
Emergency signal. For kidnappings and the like. I love you, Yolanda, but I couldn't think for a second you were actually here for me.

The sound of approaching cops, etc.

DURRAN (cont'd)
That would be them now.

A beat, as Mal and Saffron fume.

SAFFRON
Men.

EXT. FLOATING ESTATE GROUNDS - CONTINUING

As a trio of POLICE CRUISER-SHIPS descend on the estate, sirens blaring, lights flashing.

END OF ACT THREE

ACT FOUR

INT. FLOATING ESTATE - DAY

We hear the SIRENS and POLICE ANNOUNCING their arrival. Saffron sidles desperately up to Durran...

SAFFRON
Durran, peaches, just call them off. Tell 'em it was a mistake.

DURRAN
You need help, Yolanda.

SAFFRON
I'll do whatever you want... You know how I can make you feel...

DURRAN
Please. You're embarrassing yourself.

She punches him into unconsciousness.

SAFFRON
I'm embarrassing? Who's the dupe on the floor?

She spits on him as Mal comes up, grabs her arm.

MAL
I hate to bring up our imminent arrest during your crazy time, but we gotta move.

He tugs at her and they take off.

EXT. FLOATING ESTATE - GROUNDS - DAY

COPS (armed with those SONIC RIFLES we saw in 'Ariel') at the doors, speaking into a COM.

POLICE SERGEANT
...Police. Responding to emergency call code. Request entry, all points.

A BEAT, then the doors BUZZ as the locks give. The cops race inside...

INT. FLOATING ESTATE - CORRIDOR - DAY

Mal and Saffron hoofing it out of here. A COP comes around the corner, heading right at them. The cop is more surprised than they are — Mal takes him down with a few well-placed moves. Saffron reacts as —

TWO MORE COPS — appear coming the other way. One of them is raising his SONIC RIFLE.

SAFFRON
<Wahg-ba DAN duh biao-tze.> [Son of a mother's whore.]

Mal drags her along, over the fallen cop. They round the corner just as BOOM! from the sonic rifle.

INT. FLOATING ESTATE - BACK ENTRANCE - DAY

They bolt down the glass corridor, the way they came in. Cops appear, coming after them. They push through the door, end up —

EXT. FLOATING ESTATE - BACK ENTRANCE - DAY

Saffron beelines for the security panel, hooks her device onto it, starts working. Mal braces himself against the door.

MAL
What are you doing?

SAFFRON
Shut up and stand back.

Mal backs away from the door just as her enabler BEEPS.

INT. FLOATING ESTATE - BACK ENTRANCE - DAY

A cop reaches for the door — but it pulls AWAY FROM him. We hear a KA-CHUNK as the door locks.

EXT. FLOATING ESTATE - BACK ENTRANCE - DAY

SAFFRON
Let's go!

She runs off. Mal regards the door and the POUNDING from the trapped cops for a tiny beat.

MAL
(impressed)
Good security.

He turns to join her as —

SAFFRON (O.S.)
Mal!

TWO MORE COPS, armed with sonic rifles, coming at them. Saffron is already spinning and kicking at the first one. Mal takes on the second one, hand-to-fist-to-face.

SAFFRON
(calls to Mal, as she fights)
Can I have my gun back now, please?

MAL
No!

He lays out the cop he's fighting. Then reaches down and grabs the fallen sonic rifle. Spins on Saffron and the cop she's still engaged with:

MAL (cont'd)
Move!

She dives out of the way as Mal fires a [CGI] SONIC BLAST. Second cop is down for the count. Mal tosses the sonic rifle aside. Saffron goes to grab it. Mal grabs her, yanks her from it.

MAL (cont'd)
Nope. Let's go.

And they do.

INT. FLOATING ESTATE - BACK ENTRANCE - DAY

One of the cops is trying to work the security code pad. No luck. The Sergeant calls into his COM.

POLICE SERGEANT
Subjects have exited the residence and are on the grounds. Does anyone have visual?

Off the Sergeant's frustration —

EXT. FLOATING ESTATE - DAY

Shuttle II flies away, unpursued.

INT. SHUTTLE II - DAY

Mal pushes buttons, engages autopilot (either burned in graphics or a voice saying as much), and heads into the back as he straps on his holster, back to normal.

Saffron sits on a crate, facing away from him, sullenly ignoring the welling in her eyes.

MAL
That must've been tough.

SAFFRON
Yeah, have yourself a great guffaw.

MAL
I mean it. Six years, you knew he was holding such treasures, you didn't move on him. I gotta figure that's a job you told yourself you'd never take. Til times got hard enough, and the one line you hadn't crossed...

SAFFRON
(turning, fierce)
My name's not Yolanda.

MAL
Never entered my mind that it was.

She looks away again. Her tone at first is worldly, bitter — but there is clearly more underneath.

SAFFRON
I tried. I actually tried. I thought, "This is a decent man. The genuine article."

MAL
A working man, struggling to get by with the barest necessities on his private floating island...

SAFFRON
Yeah, he had money. I thought it would help. That if I had everything... I wouldn't want...

MAL
Heinrich the Security Programmer?

SAFFRON
You know, I'd forgotten his name.

MAL
Addressing the itch of curiousness, you marry him too?

SAFFRON
No. I didn't kill him either.

MAL
I don't reckon you've killed many. Just put 'em in a position to die easy.

SAFFRON
I should've killed Durran.

MAL
Right. The one guy that don't have it coming. The man who knows you and still loves you, treachery and all. Can't have him walking about.

She does start crying now, balled up, not making any move toward Mal.

SAFFRON
You must be loving this.

MAL
Little bit. I seen you without your clothes on before. Never thought I'd see you naked.

She looks up at him with genuine pleading in her eyes.

SAFFRON
Can people ever change?

MAL
Depends on the person. I'm guessing the pain of this fades away, you'll just go back to being what you are.

SAFFRON
(small voice)
What is that?

He squats before her, takes her chin in his hand.

MAL
(not unkindly)

A brilliant, beautiful, evil, double-crossing snake. Cheer up, weepy: you've earned yourself a boat-load of hard cash today. You can question the meaning of life on a floaty island of your own for a while.

SAFFRON
You won't tell anyone about me breaking down?

MAL
I won't.

SAFFRON
Then I won't tell anyone how easily I got your gun out of your holster.

He looks down.

MAL
I take that as a kindness.

They rise, her with the gun pointed at his belly.

SAFFRON
You just may be the most gullible fool I have ever marked. And that makes you special.

MAL
You can riddle me with holes, Yolanda. Won't make what I just saw anything but truth.

SAFFRON
(almost convincing)
I played you. From minute one.

MAL
You got me at barrel's end, who am I to argue. What's your move?

SAFFRON
We'll be settling down in the desert. Leave you to set a spell. Oh, and speaking of naked...

MAL
No, now that's just low.

SAFFRON
Kinda evens things out, don't you think? Pants.

She cocks the hammer, he starts undoing his trousers.

MAL
Don't really see the benefit in all this. However I slip, you're not gonna catch my crew with their trousers down.

INT. SERENITY - BRIDGE - DAY

Wash at the controls. Zoe and Kaylee enter.

ZOE
We still clear?

WASH
Nobody's following.

ZOE
Good. Time to turn around. Bin'll be dumped by now. Let's get there before anyone else does.

Wash nods. Pulls on the ship controls. Frowns.

WASH
Can't.

ZOE
What?

WASH
Can't... turn.
(still trying)
Not getting any tug from the aft alternator —

KAYLEE
What? That don't make no sense...
(realizing)
Unless...

She turns and runs out, toward the —

INT. SERENITY - ENGINE ROOM

Kaylee goes right for the engine, Zoe and Wash following. She only has to look for a second before knowing what's up —

KAYLEE
Yep. <Tah-shr SUO-yo DEE-yure duh biao-tze duh MAH!> [She's the mother of all the whores in hell!] The filament in the grav-dampener's stripped.

WASH
Now, who could've possibly done that?

KAYLEE
I can fix it, but she must've put a timer on the motivator and wetwired the dampener with —

ZOE
What does that mean, Kaylee?

KAYLEE
We ain't gonna make the rendezvous. We have to land. Now.

Off their reactions, PRELAP —

MAL (O.S.)
That dirty, dirty whore...

CUT TO:

EXT. WASTELAND - DAY

MAL'S FACE staring up into the sky as CAMERA CRANES UP, the engines of the departing (yet unseen) shuttle whipping wind and dust around Mal.

As CAMERA CONTINUES TO PULL BACK, we see that Mal is very much naked. And standing in the wasteland where we first saw him in the opening. Mal stares at his bare feet and shakes his head as if to say "shoulda seen it coming".

EXT. MOON - DAY

A different wasteland-y part of the moon. The disposal bin sits near Shuttle II, its lid open. From inside the bin, we hear —

SAFFRON (O.S.)
Blaerghchh!

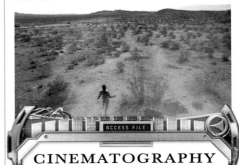

ACCESS FILE:

CINEMATOGRAPHY

Director of photography David Boyd on filming a naked Mal: "With Nathan, that stuff is just hilarious to do, because that guy has, for some reason, been given the ability to laugh at the most outlandish things and the most preposterous situations. My remembrances of working with him are just wonderful. That guy's fantastic."

Garbage comes flying out of the bin.

INSIDE THE BIN —

— is Saffron, digging through the trash, rummaging through moldy fruit, eggshells, and assorted sticky, wet rubbish. Her hair is matted — basically, she's covered in shit and doesn't look happy about it.

SAFFRON
Where the hell is it...

She keeps digging. Diggy, diggy, diggy — then she stops, throws her hands up in defeat.

SAFFRON (cont'd)
It's not here.

INARA (O.S.)
Looking for this?

She looks up to see Inara perched on the wall of some nearby ruins, beautiful as always, in her veil and bare midriff ensemble. She points to the Lassiter.

INARA
Wonder if it works?

Pulls the trigger. Nothing.

INARA (cont'd)
Ah well. Still worth a fortune.
(as she raises a Lugar)
Anyway, this one works fine.

SIMON
Can you move your arms and legs?

Jayne looks suddenly worried. Tries — cannot move anything below his neck.

JAYNE
Dah nod movin'!

SIMON
Do you want to know why?

He turns to Jayne, eerie calm on his face.

SIMON (cont'd)
Your spine. You hit it pretty hard when you fell.

JAYNE
(worried)
'Pine?

SIMON
Yes. So I gave you something to knock out your motor functions so you wouldn't wrench it when you came to. Should wear off in half an hour. You'll just be bruised.

JAYNE
'Pine okay?

SIMON
How much did they offer you to sell out me and River on Ariel?

Jayne pauses. Now he's worried.

Saffron makes a move; Inara points her Lugar.

INARA (cont'd)
Uh-uh.
(beat)
You know, I'm a little disappointed. Some of the crew's performances weren't quite as nuanced as they could've been. I thought they might tip the fact that we were playing you from the second Mal took you out of that crate.
(beat)
Oh, well. Guess not.

As she's said this, she's set aside the Lassiter and picked up a small REMOTE CONTROL. She aims it at the bin, presses a button — and the lid SLAMS SHUT on Saffron.

SAFFRON
Wait a minute, wait, you can't —
(SLAM! the lid shuts)
— mmmf mmfff ni ffmm do hmf!

INARA
You're not going to die, you big baby. The authorities will be here in a few hours to dig you out.

INT. SERENITY - INFIRMARY

Jayne fuzzily comes to, looks around. Simon is quietly notating some things, his back to Jayne.

JAYNE
Wuh guwwunoh?

SIMON
(not looking around)
You got knocked out.

JAYNE
Dih we gedda payoff? Dih we make the money?

(then)
Honey, you look horrific.

SAFFRON
What are you doing here?

INARA
Oh. Just my part of the job.

SAFFRON
What part of the job?

INARA
(matter of fact)
You know, I put on this big act and storm away in a huff, then I fly off, wait for you to doublecross Mal, beat you to the rendezvous spot and grab the loot before you can get to it.
(beat)
What, you didn't see it coming?

JAYNE
Das crazy talk.

SIMON
Then let's talk crazy. How much?

JAYNE
(looking beyond Simon, calls out)
Is anybody there?

River leans in from the doorway, looks at him calmly. It's not comforting.

JAYNE (cont'd)
(quieter)
Anybody else?

SIMON
You're in a dangerous line of work, Jayne. Odds are, you'll be under my knife again. Often. So I want you to understand one thing very clearly. No matter what you do, or say, or plot... No matter how you come down on us, I will never ever harm you. You're on this table you're safe. I'm your medic, and however little we may like or trust each other, we're on the same crew. Got the same troubles, same enemies and more than enough of both. Now we could circle each other and growl, both sleep with one eye open but that thought wearies me. I don't care what you've done. I don't know what you're planning on doing, but I'm trusting you. I think you should do the same, 'cause I don't see this working any other way.

He exits. We hold wide on Jayne, thinking on what Simon has said, as River's head pops in the doorway at the other end of frame.

RIVER
Also, I can kill you with my brain.

She pops back out, leaving Jayne to contemplate even more.

EXT. WASTELAND - DAY

ON MAL, who sits naked on a sheared-off stump of stone. He lifts his head, and utters the now familiar:

MAL
Yep... that went well.

REVERSE TO INCLUDE Inara, who has emerged from Serenity's open ramp and is now standing a few feet from Mal. The line is addressed to her.

INARA
You call this "going well"?

MAL
We got the loot, didn't we?

INARA
Yes, but —

MAL
Then I call it a win. What's the problem?

He stands, starts casually walking back to Serenity

NAKED MAL

Costume designer Shawna Trpcic: "Nathan was an incredible sport about having to be buck-naked in the middle of the desert surrounded by crew, because there was nothing we could do to cover him up — he just had to be all out there."

with Inara, who does her best to not glance at his naughty bits.

INARA
Should I start with the part where you're stranded in the middle of nowhere, or the part where you have no clothes?

MAL
All according to plan.

INARA
Really? I thought the plan was for me to act as a failsafe in case everything else went wrong. Like, for instance, if Saffron disabled Serenity and left you for dead.

MAL
Nonsense. You had a key role to play in this. How sad would you have been if you hadn't gotten to play it?

INARA
Heartbroken.

MAL
See? All according to plan.

They reach Serenity, where Zoe, Wash and Kaylee await. As Mal moves up the ramp —

MAL (cont'd)
Wash, take us out of the world. Zoe, contact

Brennert and Ellison, see if they're interested in fencing a priceless artifact for us.

Zoe and Wash just stand there, staring at his nakedity. Yes, I said nakedity.

MAL (cont'd)
What?

Zoe and Wash mutter "nothing", "I'll get right to work", etc., as Kaylee smiles at Mal, not at all thrown.

KAYLEE
Good work, Cap'n.

MAL
Thanks.

Kaylee goes off as Mal closes the ramp. As the ramp rises, Mal looks out at the wasteland with a certain fondness.

MAL (cont'd)
Good day. Good day.

The ramp shuts and we —

BLACK OUT.

END OF SHOW

FIREFLY-THAT-WASN'T

Unused Story Ideas

Jose Molina recalls: "When we started assigning the scripts, Ben had an episode that was called 'Blue Sun Rising' that we spent a couple of weeks breaking. The basic story is, our guys land in a junkyard on this planet, because a piece of the ship has broken, and this mom-and-pop operation helps them get back on their feet. It turns out Blue Sun is trying to build a freeway over their planet and want them off, but the planet's residents won't leave, and so Blue Sun send the Blue-Gloved Men after them — and the Blue-Gloved Men kill everything and everyone. So we knew what these guys were in terms of their job within Blue Sun and we knew that we wanted to introduce that Darth Vader sort of menace to the universe. Ben [Edlund] wrote a really cool, detailed beat sheet, about thirteen pages long. He had come in a couple of weeks earlier with this crazy idea about 'Jaynestown', with the whole beginning, middle and end, but because of the writer rotation, he was going to write 'Blue Sun Rising' and I was going to write what became 'Jaynestown'. Joss and Tim then decided that 'Blue Sun Rising' was maybe a little too heavy on mythology or maybe too dark. We decided to put a pin in 'Blue Sun

Rising', and so Ben inherited what should have been his in the first place and wound up writing 'Jaynestown'."

Any other unmade stories? "There was one that I actually pitched to Tim a few times when we were running low on ideas, which was where Kaylee had to go undercover in a heist as a Companion, and so Inara has to train her to be a girly girl. The idea was that our guys get caught in the middle of a robbery and thrown in jail and will be executed, and the only way of getting them out was for Kaylee to do what Inara did in 'The Train Job'.

"I remember Brett Matthews and I were talking about doing this episode which we loved and pitched to Joss. It was the first time that I've actually seen Joss go, 'That's too dark.' It starts with a standoff gone wrong and one of the members of the opposite posse is a pregnant woman. She draws on our guys and our guys, to save their own lives, have to kill her. Simon, being the excellent doctor that he is, saves the baby. Our crew is left to play out *Three Men and a Baby*, until we figure out what we are going to do with this baby. Well, we are who we are, so let's sell the baby. Then of course, we find a great home for the baby, but we've killed the mother and we've sold him for a profit. And Joss, I think wisely, went, 'that is really too bleak for our gang of marauders'. There were limits. If we'd gone a couple of seasons and the show was doing well and the network was giving us free rein, I think we would've possibly done that at some point, because Brett and I were very gung-ho on it. I remember having a conversation with him about a year after the show ended, he was about to do the *Firefly* comic book, and he was still interested in doing that story. So it's something that neither of us let go of, because it had such darkness and such heart."

Ben Edlund remembers some ideas for *Firefly* episodes that didn't make it to the screen: "I didn't have any that I had written. We were really burning our engines to just meet the demands of production as it occurred over every week, so there wasn't a lot of material ahead of us. I remember an idea for an episode — when we were talking about 'Trash', we had actually been, for some time before then, discussing a different episode, which may have eventually been used in one form or another. It was about going to a planet that was surrounded by mines left over from the war, and having the ship get caught by the Alliance. Basically, the feel-ing was that Mal had survived the war, and then they were flying by some Podunk [small-town] planet and they actually get clipped by a mine, ten years after the war has ended, and the ship goes down. Then they're stuck on this junked planet that's been kept complete-ly isolated because no one's come by to clean out the mines, and they find a whole adventure there. That was going to bring us about as close to a monster as we had gotten up to that point — some genetically-altered sol-diers that had been store-housed in an underground complex. That was going to be kind of interesting, but ultimately, I think, too big and too off-character for the period that we were chronicling at that point. Maybe something from that story might have gotten into a later episode, but mostly we were just burning the mid-night oil trying to figure out what story would fit *now*, to keep the train moving — the constant challenge in television production." ◀

❖ Opposite: Some of the scripts that *were* produced, signed by cast and crew.

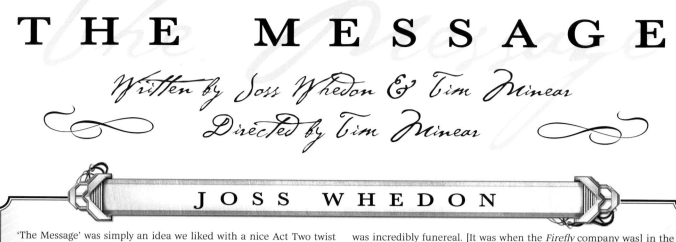

THE MESSAGE

Written by Joss Whedon & Tim Minear
Directed by Tim Minear

JOSS WHEDON

'The Message' was simply an idea we liked with a nice Act Two twist that also showed a little bit more of Mal and Zoe and the war, which is interesting to us. We managed to get a funeral scene that really sort of makes you feel a little bit of something when it's basically the funeral of a guy we don't trust and don't like and haven't known before this episode. We got to throw somebody in Simon's way with Kaylee, which is always nice. But there's a very emotional thing about people who are in a war together. And when somebody betrays that and it ends up killing them — that whole scene with Tracey at the end with Mal and Zoe, to me, that's what makes the whole thing work.

It was the last episode we filmed and therefore the funeral scene was incredibly funereal. [It was when the *Firefly* company was] in the middle of filming that episode that I was told we were canceled. [Prior to the filming of 'Trash', 'Heart of Gold' and 'The Message',] we were given an order for two or three more, instead of the back nine, which was not a good sign; and then right before Christmas, Tim was directing 'The Message' and I came on set and told the crew. We all went home. The next thing we had to shoot was the scene of Zoe and Mal laughing their asses off, talking about their friend who was dead, and in a way, there couldn't have been a more appropriate scene and they couldn't have been better in it, because we all had a friend who was dead. But the joy we got from it was so worth laughing about.

TEASER

EXT. SPACE BAZAAR - DAY

(Black, space-y day.) Ships land and take off from this decrepit but inviting old structure, clearly clapped together from several different ships and stations. We hold on it, silent but for a bit of intro music and a sudden, booming voice:

BARKER (O.S.)
We are not alone!

INT. BAZAAR - CONTINUING

It's a giant flea market/food court/carnival/bar/post office/whatever the hell anybody needs out here station. We see the scope of the place as we push in (low angle) towards a BARKER, standing in front of a small, curtained off space. He's talking from the top, very fast, selling hard.

[NOTE: This is not a large build — it's the size of a large closet, curtained off on all sides, with but one display.]

BARKER
Forget what you think you know. Forget what your mother told you when she tucked you in at night, forget the lies of our oppressive, cabalistic Allied governments! Behind this curtain lies the very secret they don't want you to see — the most astounding scientific find in the history of humanity. Proof! Of Alien life. Yes, go ahead and laugh, sir, but what you see inside this room will change your life forever! It will haunt your dreams and harrow — YES — your very soul. For six bits you can unlock — this lady wants to go, I cannot allow her to be near such wonder, such thrilling horror, unescorted! Who will go with her? Who will see the unholy

truth, the only captured specimen — in existence — of Alien life!

INT. BARKER'S BOOTH - CONTINUING

Hold a still frame on SIMON and KAYLEE, staring intently at something in a big jar that we can't see very well. Wait a beat.

SIMON
Yep. That's a cow fetus.

KAYLEE
Guess so... Does seem to have an awful lot of limbs...

SIMON
It's mutated. Most of the breeding on the outer planets was done by shipping DNA scrip instead of animals. The first herds were grown in labs, then

set loose. Every now and then...

KAYLEE
But cow? How do you figure?

SIMON
It's upside down.

She cranes her head upside down, looks. Nods, sagely...

KAYLEE
Okay, then. Cow.

SIMON
And I'm out twelve bits. I really know how to show a girl a... disgusting time.

KAYLEE
Oh, it's sweet. Poor little thing never even saw the

light of day, now it's in show business!

He looks at her admiringly.

SIMON
You manage to find the bright side to every single thing.

KAYLEE
(coming closer)
Also, we get the booth to ourselves for five whole minutes...

SIMON
(glances at jar)
We are not alone, remember?

KAYLEE
(taking his hands)
He won't squawk. Tell me more good stuff about me.

SIMON
(smiles)
Well, you're kind of a genius when it comes to machines... you always say what you mean, and your eyes...

KAYLEE
Yeah? Eyes, yeah?

SIMON
I don't know how to...
(joking)
Plus, every other girl I know is either married, professional or closely related to me, so you are more or less literally the only girl in the world.

Those famous eyes of hers darken considerably. She draws back.

KAYLEE
That's a hell of a thing to say.

SIMON
I was joking...

KAYLEE
No, no, I get it. Back on Osiris you probably had nurses and debutantes crawling all over you. But down here at the bottom of the barrel, there's just me.

SIMON
That is not even —

KAYLEE
Well, I'm glad I rated higher than dead bessie here. <Nee GAO-soo NA niou, TA yo shwong mei-moo?> [Why don't you tell the cow about its beautiful eyes?]

She is storming out just as WASH and ZOE are coming in. Simon watches Kaylee despairingly.

WASH
Oh my god, it's grotesque! Oh, and there's something in a jar.

He ogles the fetus as Zoe comes up to Simon.

ZOE
Scared her away again, did you?

SIMON
This may come as a shock, but I'm actually not very good at talking to girls.

ZOE
(not unkindly)
Why, is there someone you ARE good at talking to?

WASH
(in the background, to the jar)
Do not fear me. Ours is a peaceful race, and we must live in harmony...

INT. BAZAAR - CONTINUING

MAL and INARA walk through, talking.

INARA
Struck out again, did you?

MAL
It's like something from a fable! I've got a priceless artifact, the biggest score of my unseemly career, and no one will touch it.

INARA
The Lassiter is universally known, Mal. Fencing it has to be like... like fencing the Mona Lisa.

MAL
The Mona who?

INARA
You're out of your league. You should think about my offer —

MAL
I done that thinking, and you're to stay clear.

INARA
I know people in the highest ranks of —

MAL
Jabber jabber, I ain't listening. Just 'cause you helped on the job don't make you a crook, and I don't want you jeopardizing your career over this.

INARA
The career you abhor and look down on?

MAL
I don't want you in the way a' trouble. Take it as you like.
(calling out)
Amnon, how've you been?

They have reached a more official-looking section of the bazaar, with a sign reading: POST, FREIGHT and HOLDING.

AMNON DUUL, the postman, wears a sort of combination of a postal uniform and Hasidic wear. He

TIM MINEAR

Tim Minear is fuzzy on the actual inspiration for the episode, "I think Loni Perestere showed me this ice planet footage that he had acquired and I said, 'Can we do a thing where Serenity is flying through these snowy mountains?' and that may actually be where the idea for the episode came from. We just built the whole thing around that so we could do that chase. Loni had the material so we could afford to do it.

"That episode was harder in many ways. We started shooting and we didn't really have the script finished. The battle scene in the top of Act One wasn't written. Joss was supposed to write it and I was like, 'When are you going to write this thing?' He said, 'I'll get around to it.' And I said, 'But I'm shooting it!' To be honest, I was more focused on directing. I'm

not sure what I was trying to say except I was just trying for it not to be boring. My favorite thing was Mal's line, 'Someone's carrying a bullet for you right now, doesn't even know it.'

"It was kind of a spare parts episode in some ways. There were things we wanted to do and we built set pieces around the episode. The whole space mall was built from spare parts from every set we had done so far. We also talked about going to real snow, doing a location thing, but then we didn't and we ended up with fake snow on the stage."

The episode also introduced Jayne's now infamous hat from his mother. "We knew we were going to make him wear a stupid hat when we wrote it. Adam was all about the hat!"

is decent and more or less unflappable, and happy to see Mal.

AMNON
(shaking his hand)
Malcolm, an old friend's face is a balm in this age.

MAL
It's been too long.

AMNON
No, just about the right amount. Too much of you is less of a balm.
(to Inara)
I'm disappointed to see you haven't found a better berth by now.

INARA
I'm a little confused myself.

MAL
I read your wave. You're holding post for us?

AMNON
Got yourself a haul this time. You can sign for everyone?

MAL
Sure.

Amnon goes into a back room as Mal starts filling out a form.

BOOK arrives, with RIVER in tow. They both hold short sticks that dangle strings off the end. Each string runs through the middle of a ball of ice cream that is supported by a bowl shaped cookie attached (under the ice cream) to the string. They're sort of like little mace and chains, and eating them is not altogether convenient, since they swing a bit.

BOOK
Any packages for me?

MAL
Don't know yet.

RIVER
My food is troublesome.

JAYNE arrives, toting a couple of boxes of ammo.

JAYNE
Girl's a mind-readin' genius, can't figure out how to eat an ice-planet.

MAL
You get everything?

JAYNE
They didn't have rounds for the Buhnder, but we're ammoed up pretty good. Got a discount, too, on account of my intimidating manner —

Amnon returns, wheeling in a man-sized crate. He tosses a couple of smaller packages on the counter.

AMNON
This one's addressed to you and Zoe, Mal.

MAL
I don't remember ordering any parts...

He gives Amnon a hand, settling the crate and starting to open it.

AMNON
The little one's for Cobb.

Jayne hurriedly puts the ammo on the counter and takes the small package.

JAYNE
I got post?

BOOK
Might we all want to step back a few paces before he opens that?

INARA'S COSTUMES

Costume designer Shawna Trpcic: "Inara was taken from a lot of different cultures. I went to the past once again to find pictures of a lot of women in lingerie; I took from a lot of different periods, all the way back to Grecian times and all the way up to modern-day geishas. So we combined a bunch of them, and then I just took Morena Baccarin's body and designed on it. She was my Barbie doll, she has this incredible body; I had this little figure, and I would draw on it and just use my imagination, and then we'd collect amazing fabrics from all different sources and blend them to try to come up with her look."

JAYNE
Haw haw. It's from my mother.

During this, Inara finds a small package, squarish, addressed to her. She smoothly slips it beneath her outfit without anyone noticing, turns to see Kaylee arrive, looking glum.

INARA
(to Kaylee)
So, do aliens live among us?

KAYLEE
One of 'em's a doctor. No post for me?

Amnon shakes his head. Inara puts her arm around Kaylee, Kaylee putting her head on Inara's shoulder as Jayne tears open his package and pulls out a letter.

Zoe and Wash wander up with Simon trailing behind as Jayne reads, with the classic toneless hesitation of a slow reader:

JAYNE
"My dear boy. I hope you are well and that you get this soon in your travels."

AS JAYNE CONTINUES: Mal motions for Zoe to help him.

MAL
You order equipment?

ZOE
No sir.

JAYNE
"Thank you for the credits you forwarded, they have helped as Matty is still sick with the Damplung. He waves hello, and so does your father. He is in good spirits and there was layoffs but the foreman said no one can weld like a Cobb so he has employment still. I made you the enclosed" —

He digs in the box —

JAYNE (cont'd)
Ooh! Enclosed!

He reaches in and pulls out a woolly knitted hat with earflaps and a pompom. He is clearly moved. He puts it on, continues reading.

JAYNE (cont'd)
— "the enclosed to keep you warm on your travels. Hope to hear from you soon, love, mother."

He closes the letter, proudly adjusting his hat.

JAYNE (cont'd)
How's it sit? Pretty cunning, don'tchya think?

It's faintly ridiculous, but are you gonna tell him that? Anyway, Kaylee likes it, wistful as she is.

KAYLEE
I think it's the sweetest hat ever.

BOOK
Makes a statement.

JAYNE'S HAT

Costume designer Shawna Trpcic explains the genesis of Jayne's hat: "He had a World War Two pilot's hat in 'The Train Job' — it's a green canvas cap with flaps. I went to the production coordinator in the office — I saw her knitting something for her mom for Christmas — and I said, 'Look, I need a hat for Jayne.' My thing is the ombre — ombre is a way of dyeing something where you start dark and it gets lighter and lighter. That's the idea that I wanted. Elyse, the girl who sewed it for me, brought me different yarn samples, and we put it together from there, and she knitted it from the pattern using that World War Two fighter pilot's hat. And of course, it had to have a pompom on top. Joss said it shouldn't look really stupid, like we're trying too hard, but it should look like a labor of love. So I went to my grandmother's slippers that she used to make me every Christmas — they are goofy because they're these knit slippers with this giant pompom on them, but I love them, because they're from her. That was how we were supposed to see Jayne's hat. You can tell that he loves it because it's from his mom, and he doesn't even think about the fact that here he is, this hired killer, wearing a pompom on his head."

JAYNE
Yeah, yeah!

WASH
A man walks down the street in that hat, people know he's not afraid of anything.

JAYNE
Damn straight.

Mal and Zoe are just finishing unlocking the crate, trying to pry it open.

MAL
Well I hope we got us some fun hats too.

As he's saying it, they pry the lid off and we see the corpse of a young man lying, arms folded, inside.

Mal and Zoe look at him with somber recognition. Everyone goes very quiet, looking inside.

The last to bother is Jayne, who cranes his head into frame, hat still perched proudly, looking quizzically at the body.

JAYNE
What'd you all order a dead guy for?

As Mal and Zoe look at each other:

END OF TEASER

ACT ONE

INT./EXT. BUDDIST TEMPLE - NIGHT

Just inside the temple we see TRACEY, who is a green but gutsy private. Right now he's sweaty and tense. He looks out over the remains of a wall slowly, looking for enemies.

Light from the occasional explosion or far away burst of gunfire gives us a better view of the place — it's being held by about six Independents, all looking out in different directions.

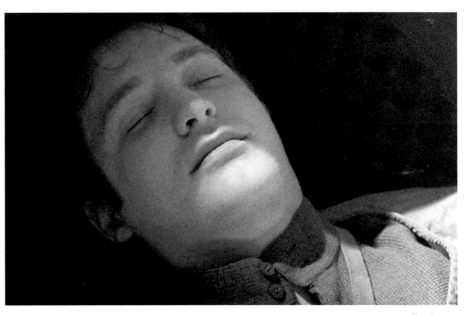

Tracey sees nothing. He takes a moment and lays down his weapon. Reaches into his bag and pulls out a can of beans. As he does, we see an Alliance soldier creeping towards him from the other side of the wall. Tracey doesn't see —

— til the guy's foot hits a rock — Tracey moves, scrambling for his rifle — too late as the Alliance soldier raises his —

CLOSE ON: The Alliance soldier — as Zoe calmly appears behind him and draws a knife across his throat.

ANGLE ON: Tracey — as a few blood splatters hit his face.

Zoe drops the soldier and enters, taking the extra rifle.

TRACEY
Thanks. Didn't know you were there.

ZOE
(stone cold)
That's sort of the point. Stealth, you may have heard of it.

TRACEY
I don't think they covered that in basic.

ZOE
Well, at least they covered "Dropping your weapon so you can eat beans and get yourself shot."

TRACEY
Yeah, I got a badge in that.
(off her look)
Won't happen again.

ZOE
It does, I'm just gonna watch.

TRACEY
Anything interesting out there, you don't mind my asking?

ZOE
(indicating)
'Bout thirty troops behind those buildings. Mortars, but no rollers yet. I expect they plan to pick at us a spell before they charge. They had two scouts sniffin', about ten yards out, but I took 'em down.

TRACEY
(impressed)
I didn't hear a single thing.

ZOE
First rule of battle, little one. Never let 'em know where you are.

Mal runs in, screaming and firing behind him, and dives over a wall for cover, lands nearby, bullets zinging over his head.

ZOE (cont'd)
Of course, there's other schools of thought...

Mal scrambles over to them, laughing.

MAL
Oh! That was bracing. They don't like it when you shoot at them. I worked that out myself.

ZOE
Did you find Vitelli?

MAL
Vitelli's out of it. That bumblebee laid down arms at the first sign of inevitable crushing defeat. Can you imagine such a cowardly creature?

TRACEY
Northwest quadrant's open, then?

MAL
Tracey. Ain't you been killed yet?

TRACEY
(looking sheepishly at Zoe)
No fault of my own, I promise.

MAL
(disappointed)
I really wanted your beans.

ZOE
They're gonna be coming right through here. They got rollers?

MAL
They got every damn thing. How's the Lieutenant?

TRACEY
He started screaming. All of a sudden. About his arms, where was his arms. We hadda go back and find 'em.

ZOE
What the hell hap —

TRACEY
He ain't even hurt! Got ten pretty fingers like the most of men, but he's screaming they're gone, crying. Then he ain't said a word in two hours.

MAL
(mournful anger)
These kids...

ZOE
Sir. Do we hold?

TRACEY
(breaking a bit)
I don't want to die here. Forgive me saying, but this rock ain't worth it. Not our lives.

MAL
Everybody dies, Tracey. Someone's carrying a bullet for you right now, doesn't even know it.
(smiles)
The trick is to die of old age before it finds you.

ZOE
We can still cut through to the 22nd at the school system. Make a decent stand there.

MAL
We can't do any good here. And I sure as hell ain't laying down arms. Zoe, you heard the Lieutenant give the order to join up with the 22nd?

ZOE
I did.

MAL
Round 'em up, then.
(to Tracey)
You also heard the Lieu —

TRACEY
I wouldn't rat you out, Sarge, hell I —

MAL
Ain't me I worry on. Lieutenant gets his mind back in order, he shouldn't have this on his record. Weren't his fault he couldn't take it.

TRACEY
That's more'n he woulda done for —

Mal raises a hand, intense, for quiet. Tracey doesn't get it, doesn't hear the growing whine of —

ZOE
SEEKER!

Things happen very quickly (or very slowly, depending on Mr. Minear). Zoe dives for cover as Mal pulls a flare from his belt that activates the moment he touches it, hurls it above his head —

— and a tiny missile zooms at the group, suddenly turning up, hitting the flair thirty feet up —

The explosion lights up the air, Mal also diving over Tracey as shrapnel rains down —

TRACEY
AAGH!

Mal is hit in the back and arm. He rolls off Tracey, who's taken it in the leg pretty badly.

TRACEY (cont'd)
Is it bad? Is it bad?

MAL
(ignoring his own wounds)
It's glorious.
(calls out)
We gotta move!

TRACEY
I can't...

MAL
Time to run!
(to Zoe)
Zoe! Get the Lieutenant!

TRACEY
Sarge, I really can't run here.

MAL
Well, you know the old saying...

He hoists Tracey over his shoulder and runs just as a tank bursts through the wall —

SMASH CUT TO:

INT. BAZAAR - CONTINUING (PRESENT DAY)

Close up of that same Tracey, all stiff and dead and blue.

After a moment, Mal slides the lid back over him.

MAL
This don't make any kind of sense. Zoe?

ZOE
I got nothing. But it's definitely Tracey.

WASH
You know this guy?

INARA
Is this a warning of some kind?

AMNON
(quietly)
Listen, Mal, you gotta get this thing out of my station.
(Mal starts to object)
Human transport on a postal route is very very illegal. Anybody even knows I took a corpse in, I'll lose my franchise.

MAL
Well who sent it to you?

AMNON
No return.

ZOE
How long has it been here?

AMNON
Near a week, that's why I waved you. If I'd known...

JAYNE
He don't smell.

MAL
I know. He's been decently preserved.
(to Zoe)
Give me a hand.

JAYNE
We're taking him on board?

MAL
We are.

JAYNE
Don't figure the percentage in that.

MAL
Don't strain your brain trying, then. Might break something.

Mal and Zoe haul the box up, start walking. Book moves to help —

ZOE
(stony)
We got him.

They cart him off, the others folding in behind, quietlike. Simon approaches, oblivious, hoping to win Kaylee into a conversation.

SIMON
What's going on? Did we get something fun?

A glare for Simon. River passes him, ice cream swinging —

RIVER
You are such a boob.

INT. SERENITY - CARGO BAY - A BIT LATER

The box is open again. Everyone is about.

JAYNE
How do we know he ain't plague-ridden or some such?

ZOE
We know.

WASH
We don't, actually. I mean, I respect you guys have a history, but... What are you doing?

Zoe is reaching in, pulling something from the corpse's folded hands.

KAYLEE
He's so young...

SIMON
(to Mal)
If you want me to do a proper autopsy —

KAYLEE
Cut him up?

MAL
Not just yet, thank you Doctor.

KAYLEE
(muttering)
Robot.

Zoe produces a FUTURISTIC DEVICE! That is a tape recorder — of the FUTURE! [Someone design this please.]

MAL
What do you got?

She turns it on. The voice stops them all. It is hesitant at first, and weak, as though the talker were straining for breath, but it soon settles into a rhythm...

TRACEY (V.O.)
Uh. Okay. Um, recording... Hi, I guess. It's me. Tracey. This is a message for Zoe, and for Malcolm Reynolds, and I really hope you all are the ones listening to it. Or, I guess I don't. I guess I hope I'm upright and telling you this tale myself, and we're laughing about how stupid I am, but that don't look likely.

EDITING

Film editor/associate producer Lisa Lassek: "*Firefly* has the best gag reel of any show I've ever worked on, and it's because of Nathan, he is hilarious. You could just give Nathan a camera and turn him loose and craziness would ensue. That *Firefly* gag reel is priceless. In 'The Message', where they're all standing over the corpse in the coffin and they're playing the tape that Tracey recorded, Nathan was everywhere. That was one of the best gags ever, because it was shot exactly as the shot was for the episode, which was a pan of everybody reacting. In one take, Nathan stayed ahead of the camera, so as it pans around Nathan is with everybody. And in every single one, he's got a different expression. It's the funniest thing ever."

We move over everyone as they listen soberly.

TRACEY
No, it's more probable I've gotten myself dead, which is a shame if you're me. I'll spare you the boring details, falling in with untrustworthy folk, makin' a bunch of bad calls... All that matters is I expect to be shuffled off, and you two are the only people I trust to get me where I'm going. Which is home. I'd like my body to be with my folks on St. Albans. We got the family plot there, and my mom and dad deserve to know I died. If you can come up with some heroical lie as to the how, I'd be... no. I'd just like to be able to lie with my kin, and for them to know that's what I wanted. It's funny. We went to war never looking to come back, but it's the real world I couldn't survive. You two carried me through that war. Now I need you to carry me just a little bit further. If you can. Tell my folks I wanted to do right by them, and that I'm at peace and all. When you can't run anymore, you crawl, and when you can't do that... well, you know the rest. Thanks, both of you. Oh. Yeah. Make sure my eyes is closed, will you?

A moment, and the tape ends. Everyone is quiet.

Wash rises, heads to the stairs —

MAL
Wash?

Wash turns back.

WASH
St. Albans ain't two days ride, we burn hard enough.

A moment, and Mal nods. Wash continues up and Mal turns to replace the lid again, says to Inara:

MAL
This might make your schedule a little —

INARA
It's all right.

He nods again, not much with the verbal thank yous right at this moment. He and Zoe lift the top together —

ANGLE: FROM INSIDE THE BOX as they cover it.

EXT. SPACE BAZAAR - MOMENTS LATER

Silent but for music, we see Serenity gently lifting off. It passes another ship — a slightly larger, ALLIANCE SHORT RANGE ENFORCEMENT VESSEL. It's basically an oversized, beat up squad car. As it lands right near where Serenity took off, the music changes to indicate this might not be wonderful.

INT. BAZAAR - MOMENTS LATER

We TRACK BEHIND three men as they stride through the bazaar. If they're cops, they're detectives, since they have no uniforms to speak of. The man in the middle is called WOMACK. He's

been around the block, and likely beaten up everybody on it. The other two, FENDRIS and SKUNK, aren't much different, but they clearly defer to Womack.

They make their way through the place with purposeful indifference. Pass the Barker:

BARKER
That's right, gentlemen, you've been told tales all your life, but Alien races exist among us, the proof is right inside, you'll be amazed and astounded. What is the government not telling us? Alien life! Six bits!

WOMACK
(to the others, an ugly growl)
It's fake. I seen it. It's a pig or some such.

ANGLE ON: Amnon. He is going through papers behind his counter. He arranges them carefully —

ANGLE ON: his papers

— as a badge is dropped on top of them.

Amnon looks up to see Womack standing right in front of him. Amnon hesitates, and before anything can happen Skunk is already going in his back room to search. Fendris is behind Womack, checking his rather large pistol and watching out for pain-in-the-ass innocent bystanders.

AMNON
Can I help you...?

WOMACK
You are an ugly-looking little quim, you know that?

AMNON
If there's a problem —

WOMACK
So you have to be asking yourself, ugly as you are, how repulsive-looking the guy that makes you his lady friend is gonna be. I mean, prison is a lonely place, and you sure as a hundred moons ain't gonna be pitching, so what kind of sorry-ass troll is gonna get blue enough to grapple with you? Shudder to think.

AMNON
I've broken no law.

WOMACK
Transportation of human cargo — especially dead cargo — through the Allied postal system is punishable by five to ten years on a penal moon. Plus, you don't know this yet, but you resisted arrest.
(off Amnon's terror)
Where's my body?

AMNON
I didn't... I don't...

WOMACK
The dead guy. He got shipped here.

Skunk comes out, shakes his head no.

WOMACK (cont'd)
And shipped back out, I guess. Where?

AMNON
I never saw a body. But there was a crate big enough for one. I did hand that over just a while ago.

WOMACK
Lovely. Who got it?

Amnon hands over the register, points to a name.

WOMACK (cont'd)
Malcolm Reynolds. And where would you suppose he's off to?

AMNON
I swear on my soul I don't know. But he just left. He captains a firefly, you should be able to capture them if you leave now.

WOMACK
Are you telling me to leave?

AMNON
No, no...

WOMACK
Relax, you've been great. I was only bluffing with that stuff about arresting you. Who needs that kind of paperwork? Skunk. Light him on fire.

Skunk sprays Amnon with lighter fluid he keeps in a cool container in his jacket. With swift, graceful motion, he holds up a suddenly lit match. Amnon backs into a huddle in the corner, utterly terrified.

Womack stands next to Skunk, over the cowering postman.

WOMACK (cont'd)
Tell anyone we were here, warn
(looks at the register)
"Malcolm Reynolds" that we're coming, and you'll wish we'd burned you. <Dong ma?> [Understand?]

Amnon nods frantically.

WOMACK (cont'd)
Boys... let's go find us a corpse.

He blows out Skunk's match.

END OF ACT ONE

ACT TWO

INT. SERENITY - ENGINE ROOM - NIGHT

Kaylee lies in her hammock, listening to the recording of Tracey's voice. She clearly has been doing this for a while, and has gotten awful misty about the lad.

TRACEY (V.O.)
All that matters is I expect to be shuffled off, and you two are the only people I trust to get me where I'm going. Which is home. I'd like my body to be with my folks on St. Albans. We got the family plot there, and my mom and dad deserve to know I died.

INT. SERENITY - AFT HALL - CONTINUING

Simon comes up, looking for Kaylee. He stops outside the engine room door. Sees her, hears the recording...

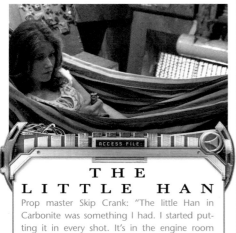

THE LITTLE HAN

Prop master Skip Crank: "The little Han in Carbonite was something I had. I started putting it in every shot. It's in the engine room twice, but it's most prominent in the galley. I started it, but Nathan wanted to do it too. He's a big *Star Wars* fan; *Star Trek* too — he does the best Bill Shatner impression."

TRACEY (V.O.)
If you can come up with some heroical lie as to the how, I'd be... no. I'd just like to be able to lie with my kin, and for them to know that's what I wanted.

Simon slowly slips away, realizing with regret he is unwanted.

INT. SERENITY - CARGO BAY - CONTINUING

Book stands at the head of the crate/coffin, bible in hand, head bowed. WIDEN to see that during his little silent service, Jayne is busily lifting weights. Jayne replaces the barbell in its holder, the metal noisily clattering. Book looks around.

JAYNE
Hey, I'm sorry, Preacher. Makin' too much noise?

BOOK
No, no, I was just... saying a few words. Don't know the boy's denomination, but...

JAYNE
It's good. Lord should oughta look after the dead.

Over the following, Jayne pats himself down with a towel — he's quite sweaty. Really been going at it.

JAYNE (cont'd)
You wanna do a set? I'll spot you.

BOOK
Not so terribly in the mood.

JAYNE
Most people is pretty quiet right about now. I guess the Captain and Zoe were summat bonded with the kid.

BOOK
It would appear.

JAYNE
Me, I see a stiff — one I didn't have to kill myself — I just get, you know, the urge to do stuff. Work out, run around, get some trim if there's a willin' woman about... Not that I get flush from corpses or anything. I ain't crazy.

BOOK
Makes sense. Looking to feel alive, I would venture.

JAYNE
For psychology, that ain't half dumb. My kind of life don't last, Preacher. So I expect I'm invested in making good sport of it whilst I can.
He puts on his hat as he says it.

As they continue talking, we come around to see River in the background, crawling gracefully onto the coffin. She stretches, catlike, moving her head about in an odd fashion, as though listening, then lies flat on her belly, arms out to her sides.

JAYNE (cont'd)
You gonna read over me when I'm taken down, Shepherd?

BOOK
Oh, I suspect you'll be around long after we're all —

JAYNE
(noticing River)
What the hell is she —
(at River)
What the hell are you doing?

BOOK
Oh. River, that might not be the best place to...

RIVER
I'm very comfortable.

They consider pulling her off... hesitate...

BOOK
(to Jayne)
I guess we do all have different reactions to death.

SMASH CUT TO:

INT. SERENITY - DINING ROOM - CONTINUING

Mal and Zoe are laughing their asses off. We widen to see Inara is with them, laughing as well. They've all had a few drinks, and continue to drink as they talk:

MAL
I really thought I was gonna die.

INARA
How could he possibly have even...

MAL
The Colonel was dead drunk. Three hours pissing on about the enlisted men, "They're scum, they're not fighters" — and he passes right out. Boom.

ZOE
We couldn't even move him. So Tracey just snipped it right off his face.

KAYLEE

"Bye now! Have good sex."

Jewel Staite says that *Firefly* creator Joss Whedon and show-runner Tim Minear have somewhat different styles as directors. "Joss is really specific. He has his vision mapped out and he gives great direction. I think Tim likes to go with the flow and see what happens and what we come up with. They're both really cool."

Minear directed a scene that Whedon has cited as being among his favorites: the partially improvised basketball game in 'Bushwhacked'. Staite is fond of it as well. "That was hilarious. We didn't really know what we were doing and we were running into each other. We were genuinely having a lot of fun and it didn't require much acting."

Of all the various relationships between the *Firefly* characters, did Staite have a favorite to play? "I would say the relationship with Book, because Kaylee was the first person that he met before he came onto the ship and they had this instantaneous bond. They're always really sweet to each other. I think everybody felt a little unrestrained with Book. He's full of great advice and he's such a strong, sage character; he's very experienced and I think Kaylee felt like she could really trust him."

In which episode do we learn the most about Kaylee? "I would have to say 'Out of Gas'. Because the revelation of how Kaylee got the mechanics job surprised even me. I had no idea they were going to do that until I read the script a couple of days before we were going to shoot it. I was totally shocked — but I loved that it was really shocking. Kaylee was this seemingly sweet and innocent girl and really, she's this very sexual being and totally unashamed of it. I thought that was really great. I had asked when I was first cast, 'What are her parents like, how did she get on the ship?' And they said, 'Oh, you'll see, we're going to do an episode about that,' so I just went with the flow, but never really knew

how naïve to play her. I started out thinking she was *really* innocent and she's not at all," Staite laughs.

Staite finds it difficult to narrow down her favorite experiences on *Firefly*. "If he ever finds this out, he's going to gloat about it, but I loved working with Nathan so much, because he makes me laugh so hard. But at the same time, I don't break character with him. He really does bring the best out of me somehow.

"I had to keep my weight up to play Kaylee for the series, and that was fun. I had to raid the craft service table about twenty times a day just to make sure I kept the extra twenty pounds on me.

"The cast in general, just being friends with them and being able to hang out off-set and really bond. I've worked on a lot of series and I never really had that with another cast — you get close and you become friends and say you're going to keep in touch, but no one ever really does. We actually did. That is one of my absolute favorite things."

Whedon announced *Firefly*'s cancellation during the shooting of 'The Message', "It was in the scene where Tracey has me in his grip just outside of the bridge. Alan was there and Gina and Nathan and poor Jonathan Woodward and me. Joss came up and told us all then. We still had another four days left to go and we had to buck up and just get over it, keep shooting. We all had been really stressed. It was a daily obsession: seeing the numbers and how many people were watching. It was just excruciating. So I was relieved that we finally had an answer. Even if it was a 'no', at least we knew it was a 'no', and we could move on now and figure out a plan B. But I don't remember the shooting of that episode being particularly sad. I remember us goofing off like crazy. We knew that they weren't going to fire us, because we were already canceled, so there was a lot of laughter and a lot of fun on that one."

Summing up, Staite says, "I had such a special experience on that show that everything I do, ever since the end of *Firefly*, I compare to that experience. And I don't think anything will ever be like that again. It's kind of this indescribable thing. It was a sort of bond that we had, and we knew it was really special, we all felt that way. But when we were filming *Firefly*, I had absolutely no idea that it would be one of those things that I don't think will ever really go away."

MAL
And you never seen a man more proud of his moustache than Colonel Obrin. In all my life I will never love a woman the way this officer loved that lip ferret.

ZOE
Giant walrussy thing, all waxed up...

INARA
Did he find out?

Another burst of laughter from Mal and Zoe.

MAL
The next morning, he wakes up, and it's gone. He's furious, but he can't actually say, you know, "Someone stole my moustache". So he calls out all the platoons —

ZOE
I thought he was gonna shoot us —

MAL
And he's eyeballing the men something fearsome, not a word, and he comes to Tracey... and Tracey is wearing the gorramn moustache on his face.

ZOE
He glued it on.

MAL
Staring the old man down, wearing his own damn... Oh god...

The laughter falters, Mal looking into his drink a moment. Inara looks at him sympathetically, tries to jump start the conversation again:

INARA
Well, the Colonel must have said SOMETHING to —

The SHIP ROCKS with the force of an explosion. They all start out of their chairs.

ZOE
Are we hit?

MAL
Too damn close —

And they are racing to the —

INT. SERENITY - BRIDGE - CONTINUING

Where Wash is piloting intently.

WASH
They're behind us. Fired over the port bow.

MAL
Warning shot?

WASH
They coulda hit us...

ZOE
Feds.

The screen comes to life, Womack's face on it.

WOMACK
This is Lieutenant Womack of Allied Enforcement. You are in possession of stolen goods and are ordered to cut thrust and prepare for docking.

MAL
The Lassiter.

ZOE
That was quick.

INARA
Think Saffron tipped them off?

Mal hits the screen com:

MAL
This is Captain Reynolds. I think there's been a mistake.

WOMACK
There's been a lot of mistakes, Captain. The latest of which is you taking that crate.

He looks at the others. "Crate"?

MAL
(to Womack)
We took in a lot of inventory today. If something got mixed in, we'll sure hand it back, but I don't think we're your men. Let me check through the cargo — is it marked at all?

WOMACK
You might wanna think twice about playing games with me. I will blow you into fragments.

MAL
You do that, your precious crate's gonna be in bitty shards. Now I got deliveries to make, Officer, so you just lock onto my trajectory and I'll see if there's anything here fits your description.

He turns off the screen.

WASH
Police procedure has changed since I was little.

MAL
They call back, you keep them occupied.

WASH
What do I do, shadow puppets?

BOOK
We'll take care of it.

ZOE
I don't get this. They're after Tracey?

MAL
Or there's something else in that box.

INT. SERENITY - CARGO BAY - MOMENTS LATER

Tracey's body lies on the floor as Mal, Zoe and Jayne go through both the crate and the box, looking for something. The others including Simon, Inara and River (minus Wash and Book) look on.

MAL
Anything?

JAYNE
(smashing planks)
Not unless this crate's made a' magical, wish-granting planks.

MAL
(to Zoe)
Check his pockets.

KAYLEE
That ain't right...

MAL
Neither's being blowed up. There's nothing about this sits well with me.

ZOE
Empty.

MAL
Well, they want this body for something, and I'm guessing it ain't a proper burial.

Looks around. No option. Looks to Simon:

MAL (cont'd)
Well, Doctor... I guess you are doing an autopsy.

INT. SERENITY - INFIRMARY - LATER

Mal, Zoe and Jayne watch as Simon prepares to open up the now naked (but sheet covered) body.

ZOE
You really think there's something in there.

MAL
Using corpses for smuggling is a time-honored repulsive custom.

JAYNE
Maybe it's gold!

ZOE
And maybe this was a friend of ours, and you wanna show a little respect.

JAYNE
I got respect. But I'm just saying... gold...

SIMON
He's been opened before.

MAL
How's that?

SIMON
It's good work. The scar's nearly invisible, but...

He traces his finger all the way down the chest.

MAL
Well, let's see what's in there.

He looks at Zoe, hating this. A tense moment. Simon takes his scalpel and starts cutting.

And Tracey SCREAMS.

END OF ACT TWO

ACT THREE

INT. SERENITY - INFIRMARY

Where we left off. Everyone backing away from the SCREAMING Lazarus. Tracey looks with horror to his bleeding chest, then to the man who holds the scalpel — Simon. Simon sees the blood, makes an instinctive move to see to the wound. All Tracey sees is the knife. He gives a PRIMAL CRY as he lunges off the table at Simon. They struggle, knocking shit over. Mal and Zoe jump into the fray. Mal calling to Jayne:

MAL
Get hold of him!

JAYNE
Spry for a dead fella!

Mal pins him to the floor, ends up sitting on top of him.

MAL
SETTLE! That's enough!

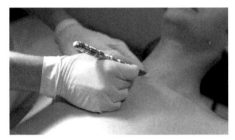

TRACEY
He was cuttin' on me, Sarge!

MAL
I know it! I told him to!

TRACEY
You told him to! What for?!

MAL
You were dead!

TRACEY
(coming back to him)
Hunh? Oh. Right. Suppose I was.
(sees Zoe)
Hey there, Zoe.

ZOE
Private.

MAL
You feeling a mite calmer now?

TRACEY
Yes, Sarge.

TRACEY (cont'd)
(then)
Sarge?

MAL
What?

TRACEY
I think I'm nekked.

A beat. Mal's straddling a naked man.

MAL
Okay. We're gonna get up off this floor, you're gonna stand like a person, cover yourself, and the Doctor's gonna tend to that gash.

Tracey nods. Mal gets off of him. He rises. Looks a bit sheepish. Pulls the sheet up around his waist as he sits on the edge of the table. As Simon starts to tend to the wound:

TRACEY
Sorry for jumping on you the way I did. I was a little confounded.

SIMON
Emerging from that state can be disorienting. Was it byphodine?
(clarifying)
The drug you took to make it appear as though you were dead. Do you remember what it was called?

TRACEY
Never did ask.

SIMON
(puts gauze to wound)
Hold that there.
(casually, to Jayne)
Bring that pan, please.

Jayne, not knowing why, brings a bedpan over. Simon positions Jayne's hand with pan in front of

Tracey without explanation, then moves to his med supplies.

TRACEY
Fella sold it to me said I'd be under a week or more. He told me I wouldn't dream. But I did. Dreamt of my family.

Simon has moved back to his patient, reaches out, repositions the bedpan as Tracey suddenly HEAVES forward (leaning forward so all spew is sound fx). Jayne reacts. Simon doesn't, was expecting it. Gives Tracey a shot:

SIMON
This should take the edge off the nausea.
(to grossed-out Jayne)
You can take that.

Simon goes about checking Tracey's vitals, hooking him up to the scanners and reading the monitor in the BG.

MAL
All right. Now you care to explain why it is you got yourself all corpse-ified and mailed to me? What're you running from?

TRACEY
Running to, not from. Just want to get home is all. That's all I ever wanted. 'Cept there's them took exception to that. To me leaving... while I's in possession of their property...

MAL
What'd you boost, Tracey? More important, who'd you boost it from?

SIMON
Captain... Captain, I don't mean to... I think we may have a medical emergency here...

They all look at him; he's looking at the monitor.

SIMON (cont'd)
This man... He appears to be in cardiac arrest...

MAL
What? Tracey, you having a heart attack?
(to Simon)
Don't look like he's having a heart attack...

TRACEY
(laughs)
Don't pay no attention to your machines, Doc. They'll fib to ya. Heart's just fine. Better'n fine. Runs a bit hotter'n normal, is all.

SIMON
(off monitors)
My god... it's not just the heart muscle... it's everything...

TRACEY
All the movin' parts. That's what I took, Mal. And that's what they want back.

MAL
Tracey — you want to explain what in the <TYEN shiao-duh> [name of all that's sacred] you're talking about?

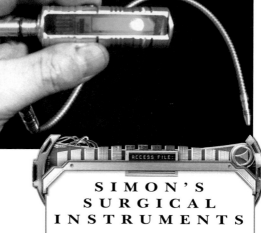

SIMON'S SURGICAL INSTRUMENTS

Prop master Randy Eriksen tasked Applied Effects with the job of making Simon's surgical instruments for the pilot show. Applied's Chris Calquhoun explains: "We were just told: 'medical tools', a scalpel and a bullet-grabber. A year after the first *Star Wars* movie came out I customized an X-Acto hobby knife handle, and I used to make all kinds of cool little tools and stuff that were based on the look I came up with like a zillion and a half years ago. I've incorporated the look into a couple of props since then, but never so prominently as in Simon's medical instruments. This is me 'going off' on the lathe. As well as the lathe work, there are some little milled parts too. The scalpel was originally designed with a laser cutter as shown in the design artwork, but was later changed to a more traditional blade." The colored bands are sections of silicone sleeving stretched over the handles. It is a more durable surface than paint and stands up to on-set rigors far better.

The scalpel and bullet-grabber were first, then the laser probe device was ordered: "I picked a style and made it fit in with the other instruments. I turned some aluminum tube and made an end-cap and fitted an LED, some batteries and a little switch on top. The graphic on the display is a 'geekness' flow chart — so you can tell how geeky you are in comparison to other sci-fi fans! It's too small to read on TV and I put it in just for fun."

Randy Eriksen on Simon's surgical tools: "Applied Effects made Simon's surgical tools, which were totally awesome. They were inspired by desperation. I was standing in Applied's shop talking to Chris and I noticed his X-Acto knife. I said that it was cool and we should just do them like that. We had a scalpel, a scope and a grabber. They are so good and you didn't really see them on the show much. They look much better in real life than they do on the screen. Then again, they *would* focus on something that we didn't pay any attention to and was awful and kind of embarrassing. Oh, you'd see that!"

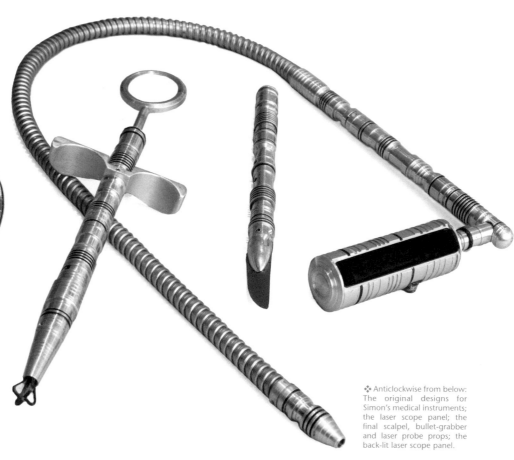

❖ Anticlockwise from below: The original designs for Simon's medical instruments; the laser scope panel; the final scalpel, bullet-grabber and laser probe props; the back-lit laser scope panel.

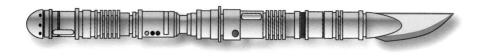

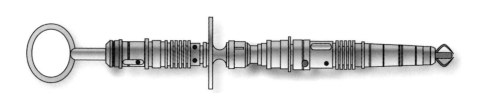

TRACEY
(distracted)
Sure, Sarge... sure...

Now the MONITOR really starts to go nuts, Tracey's heart beating ever faster. The others look from the monitor to him, then follow his gaze to...

KAYLEE stands in the doorway, staring at the man come back to life. They hold the look between them.

INT. SERENITY - COMMON AREA - (SHORT TIME) LATER

Mal, Zoe, Jayne, Simon, Kaylee and Tracey. Kaylee brings Tracey some water. They will have a silent connection throughout the following.

TRACEY
Thank you.

She smiles at him, takes a seat.

MAL
So your innards... ain't your innards?

TRACEY
Mine got scooped out, they replaced every bit.

JAYNE
Why'd you wanna go and do that?

TRACEY
For the money. They're paying me to transport what they stuck in.

ZOE
You're smuggling human organs?

TRACEY
But not from a person. I wouldn't do a thing like that. Grown in a lab. Only way they can be moved is in a person. Not sure why.

SIMON
Because the technology's not ready. The blastomeres are unapproved. Likely unstable. You're not just a carrier — you're an incubator.

TRACEY
Whichever. It ain't strictly legal, I can tell you that. I was supposed to be at the drop spot two weeks ago. A clinic on Ariel. They were to open me up, take the goods and put back my own workings.

ZOE
And you believed them? That they'd put you back together?

TRACEY
Sure. They want you to make as many runs as you're able. Hell, I met a fella, he's on his third already.

MAL
So what happened?

TRACEY
Well, truth is I had a —

SIMON
Change of heart?

A beat. Simon's amused. No one else is. Tracey continues:

TRACEY
A better offer. Another buyer, willing to pay three times the going rate. Enough I could get my folks off that rock they been forced to live on, set them up someplace nice, someplace warm, maybe one of the central planets.

MAL
But your "better offer" went south...

TRACEY
Got myself into a bit of a pickle, Sarge. The folks I was working for... they musta got wind what I was planning. When I showed up... my new buyer was dead. There was men there, waitin' for me.

KAYLEE
But you got away.

TRACEY
Only just. I knew they'd never stop looking for me so long as I was alive. Thought my chances'd be better if I weren't.

MAL
So you "died" and figured then they'd stop looking?

TRACEY
Yeah.

A SUDDEN BLAST from outside. The ship ROCKS with the impact. Tracey reacts with fear. As Mal rises —

MAL
Think maybe you figured wrong.

EXT. SPACE - CONTINUING

The police cruiser is behind Serenity, pacing. It lets loose with another ELECTRONIC BLAST.

INT. SERENITY - BRIDGE - CONTINUING

Wash and Book on the bridge. As Mal and Zoe and Jayne enter behind them:

WASH
I think they're about done being stalled, Ca —
(as he swivels)
GAHHHH!

He's just laid eyes on Tracey, who stands in the doorway with Kaylee. Book takes in the sight with interest.

WASH (cont'd)
Mal, your dead army buddy's on the bridge!

ZOE
He ain't dead.

WASH
Oh.

MAL
How close're we to St. Albans?

WASH
Five from atmo.

MAL
Pull up the terrain specs. Kaylee, take him out of here. And strap in.

Wash brings up terrain maps on the nav monitor. Mal starts paging through the maps on the screen as he grabs the radio mic, speaks.

MAL (cont'd)
This is Captain Reynolds —

WOMACK (ON VID)
Reynolds, I'm a dangerous-minded man on a ship loaded with hurt. Why you got me chattin' with your peons?

MAL
(shuts off mic)
Tracey, you go on below. Let us handle this —
(back into mic:)
Just seein' to some technical difficulties, Officer.

WOMACK (ON VID)
Not interested, Captain. I stepped over a lot of bodies to get to that one you got in your hold. You play this right, and yours won't have to be among them.

TRACEY
(scared)
Sarge...

ZOE
Private, the Captain ordered you off the bridge.

KAYLEE
Come on.

She starts to lead him away. Mal pages through maps.

MAL
We'd love to let you boys dock, but that last pop you give us knocked out our fore-couple. We're gonna have to park it if you want the tour.

FOREDECK HALL — Tracey heard that, turns back. Kaylee gently tugs him her way.

KAYLEE
It's okay. Captain'll take care of it. You'll see.

They have arrived at the door to her bunk, she pulls it open. Gives him a little push forward. He looks at her, unsure. But the total, guileless faith in her face persuades. He starts down the ladder to her bunk. She follows as —

BRIDGE

WOMACK (ON VID)
All right, Captain. We can do this on the ground just as easy.

Womack FITZES out. Mal looks at the blank screen.

THE CHASE

Visual effects supervisor Loni Peristere: "I loved working with Tim Minear on 'The Message'. We had discovered a new software program called Terragen that created virtual landscapes. It was so realistic that we thought it would be an interesting idea to show a demo of a fighter plane flying through a landscape to Joss and Tim, so they could maybe write it into an episode. We came up with this cat and mouse game, which was chasing down Serenity in a snowfield."

MAL
(to himself)
Yeah. Easy.
(clicks off, points to map)
There. Think you can do it?

WASH
Watch me.

Mal clicks over the feed on the mic, now when he speaks it's an internal SHIP PA.

MAL (AMPLIFIED)
Attention all crew. Sit down and hang on to something...

EXT. SPACE/ATMO - CONTINUING

As Serenity, followed by cops, dips down, heads for a PLANET.

SERENITY

breaking atmo, speeding up, taking a dive, as...

INT. SERENITY - KAYLEE'S BUNK - CONT-INUING

Kaylee is coming down the ladder into her room. As the ship heads into the dive, she is sent into Tracey's arms. He catches her. Holds her. They look at each other as —

INT. SERENITY - BRIDGE - CONTINUING

Jayne has great sea legs, he walks back onto the bridge (he stepped out during that intercut) with three guns. Starts prepping them, just in case.

Book is over at a secondary radio station, checking monitors. Zoe steps in by him.

ZOE
What is it?

BOOK
Just a little strange. There's a fed station near here, but our friends haven't made a transmission since they broke atmo...

As Zoe considers that...

Wash is all concentration, heading for —

EXT. PLANET - DAY

Serenity banks off now, heading for —

MOUNTAINS in the distance... the police cruiser banks easily, dogging them as —

INT. SERENITY - BRIDGE - CONTINUING

Wash grits his teeth —

WASH
Get ready for hard burn —
(leans on controls)
They'd be crazy to follow us in here.

Everyone hangs on, as

EXT. ICE CANYONS - CONTINUING

Serenity racing into the mountain range, then diving into snowy canyons. As the walls of the canyons start to close in and things get tight —

— the police cruiser pulls up sharply, leaving Serenity to go it alone.

Serenity thrillingly zooms through the twisty canyons.

INT. SERENITY - BRIDGE - CONTINUING

Wash lets out a breath.

WASH
Not behind us anymore —
(then, glancing up)
Oh. Didn't think of that...

EXT. ICE CANYONS - CONTINUING

Cops follow placidly just above the canyon, pacing. BELOW, Serenity is having a tougher time of it as it maneuvers through the ever precarious canyons.

INT. SERENITY - KAYLEE'S BUNK - CONT-INUING

As before. Tracey holds Kaylee.

TRACEY
You okay?
(she nods, their faces close)
So I can let go now?

KAYLEE
(only if you want)
You can...

They start to separate and another lurch throws them, they go to the bed, sitting, bracing. Tracey looks momentarily queasy.

KAYLEE (cont'd)
All this hard banking — when the gravity drive and actual gravity start working against each other, it tosses your lunch about a bit.

TRACEY
Your pilot's pretty wild.

KAYLEE
Oh, he could thread a needle with this bird. He's the best.

TRACEY
Good to know.
(tentative foray:)
So you two are —

KAYLEE
Sweeties?
(laughs)
Hell no, I got no... I'm not with any...
(too forward)
He's married to Zoe.

TRACEY
Zoe got married? I can't even get my mind around that. Next you'll be telling me she smiles and has emotions.

KAYLEE
She must have been such a stone-cold <SHIONG-tsan SHA-sho> [ass-kicking killer] during the war.

TRACEY
Nobody EVER messed with her. I think the Sarge was even a little afraid of her. And she got married. It's good. People making a life for themselves.

KAYLEE
What about you?

TRACEY
Mostly —
(another LURCH)
— stuff like this. Sorry to bring you all into it.

KAYLEE
Oh, danger is pretty much our business.

TRACEY
Still, if you got put in a bad spot at all, Kaylee... I think I'd be real unhappy.

Bing! Moment.

INT. SERENITY - BRIDGE - CONTINUING

Wash pilots, swinging the ship from side-to-side as he navigates the terrain.

WASH
Whoo! This kind of flyin' really wakes up a guy —

MAL
(teeth gritted)
Awake helps —

The ship SHUDDERS — one side brushed up against a mountain, as we can tell by Wash's

hard turn —

WASH
Whoa! Baby!

MAL
(nervous)
Wash —

WASH
Just a love tap —

EXT. ICE CANYONS - CONTINUING

Serenity goes behind a curve, disappears for an instant, reappears, then disappears again... then doesn't reappear.

The police cruiser circles, looking. No sign.

EXT./INT. ICE CANYONS/CAVE - CONTINUING

As Serenity backs into ice cave.

INT. SERENITY - BRIDGE - CONTINUING

Wash sets the ship down, starts flipping switches and the ship POWERS DOWN to dashboard light.

WASH
There. Now, I shut down main power, they might not read our auxiliary under all this.

MAL
And if they come down here and try to get a visual?

WASH
(looks around)
Well... she's not a small ship.

INT. SERENITY - KAYLEE'S BUNK - CONTINUING

TRACEY
(nervous)
We're not moving. Why aren't we moving?

KAYLEE
Probably part of some genius plan to give the feds the slip.

TRACEY
Yeah. Probably.

BOOM! A concussion ROCKS the ship. Tracey reacts, spooked.

TRACEY (cont'd)
What was that?

INT. SERENITY - PASSENGER DORM - CONTINUING

Simon and River sit, looking a bit nervous.

RIVER
Thousand-one, thousand-two, thousand-three —

SIMON
River?

RIVER
Shh. Counting between the lightning and the thunder. See if the storm is coming or going... Thousand-eight, thousand-nine —

INT. INARA'S SHUTTLE - CONTINUING

Inara is strapped into the pilot chair of her shuttle. She takes out the small SQUARE PACKAGE she picked up in the teaser, looks at it. Whatever's in it sits heavy with her.

ANOTHER BOOM shudders the ship, her shuttle with it. She's scared, but keeps her courtly manner about it.

INARA
That's enough, thank you very much — !

EXT. ICE CANYONS - CONTINUING

Where WE SEE the police cruiser drop a CONCUSSIVE DEPTH CHARGE.

INT. SERENITY - BRIDGE - CONTINUING

ANOTHER BOOM.

ZOE
Sounds like full-yield mag-drops.

WASH
I think they picked up a little triangulation in cop school —

MAL
Options?

WASH
Well, we're only good as long as the roof holds out. Direct hit above us, ship's electrics'll be fried. We'll have to climb out.

JAYNE
Or be dug out.

ANOTHER BOOM!

ZOE
Gettin' closer.

Book steps in by the Captain.

BOOK
Captain, there is another way.

They look at him.

INT. SERENITY - KAYLEE'S BUNK - CONTINUING

A L A N   T U D Y K

The last episode we shot was 'The Message'. I'm flying and trying to lose this cop and he has a better spaceship than me. If you watch that sequence you can see that, because the show was canceled, we abandoned the whole Wash calm thing and, in fact, that was closer to me in real life. I was totally Jerry Lewis. I went completely, 'Whoa! Wow! Whoa!'. Joss came on set that day and went over to Tim and said, 'So, the calm pilot thing... that's gone?' Tim was like, 'Yeah, that's gone. We're going for the funny.'

BOOM! The room shudders with the impact. Tracey moves to the ladder.

KAYLEE
Captain said to stay put.

TRACEY
I just want to see what's happening.

INT. BRIDGE - CONTINUING

BOOK
We're cornered, outgunned and it's only a matter of time before they find us — or what's left of us. Let's not wait for that to happen.

ZOE
What are you saying, Preacher?

BOOK
I'm saying we make good on what we said we were going to do. We call them, fly out of this canyon — and let them board.

During this we have CUT TO A SUBJECTIVE POV moving toward the bridge from the FOREDECK HALL.

JAYNE
Give ourselves up?

BOOK
It's our only choice.

MAL
We let them walk on this ship, we're taking an awful chance. These boys ain't playin', Preacher.

BOOK
Yes. I'm aware of that.

BRIDGE

Mal and Book hold a look between them. Mal is weighing this advice. Reading some world experience in Book's certainty.

The moment is interrupted by yet another, and much closer, CONCUSSIVE BOOM. This time ICE and ROCK rain onto the front window. They look up, react, as —

REVEAL

What they don't see behind them — TRACEY is at the door; he's heard it all. He looks ashen, betrayed... and now his gaze falls to —

 — one of JAYNE'S newly loaded GUNS, within arm's reach.

Tracey's face clouds over.

END OF ACT THREE

ACT FOUR

INT. BRIDGE - CONTINUING

Sweat-beaded brows, a beat of nervous silence, held breaths. Then from above a rolling

THUNDEROUS BOOM. The bridge vibrates with the O.S. explosion's force. A cascade of ICE CHUNKS clatters over the windshield and the nose of Serenity.

Wash lets out his breath, checking some of his dash monitors.

WASH
<Wuo duh MA.> [Mother-of-Jesus.] That one was really close...

Jayne turns from the debris still falling to the others. He's extra sweaty, falling prey to his cowardly side.

JAYNE
That tears it. I'm with the Preacher. I ain't gettin' snowed-in permanent on account of some jack-ass kid —

ANOTHER BOOM FROM ABOVE — throughout this scene, the depth charges are a slow, regular drum beat, adding rhythmic percussion to the tense-ness.

BOOK
(quiet conviction)
It's the only option, Captain.

Mal turns to Zoe. They exchange a look. Zoe gives a slight nod — "Can't think of anything else to do". Mal nods back.

MAL
Wash... Call the cops. Tell them we give up.

Wash nods and flicks the RADIO ON, preparing to call.

TRACEY (O.S.)
No.

ANOTHER BOOM.

Tracey edges the barrel of a gun into the FG, holding it on the others on the bridge.

MAL
Tracey, what are y —

TRACEY
I said NO! Those bastards up there are gonna pull this million-credit meat outta me and leave me bleedin' —
(turns gun on Wash)
Now turn off that radio!

Another depth charge EXPLODES, closer, louder. Jayne braces himself as more ICE SHARDS rain down on the ship.

JAYNE
Ruttin' twerp's gonna get us —

TRACEY
(loud, arresting)
Don't you move! No one move!
(gun back to Wash)
Power up! We have to run! NOW!

Book takes a slow step toward Tracey. Tracey

swings the gun at him, the model of panicky-guy-with-gun-in-over-his-head-and-ready-to-go-postal.

BOOK
Put that thing down, boy. You got no idea what —

TRACEY
Shut it, Shepherd! I swear to God I'll shoot you dead if you don't.
(manic, bitter laugh)
Sarge — Zoe — Why you listening to this bible-thumper?

ZOE
We've seen the man fight, Trace. Seen him think. And we trust him on both counts.

TRACEY
Yeah, well, you two were always lookin' for someone to spend your trust on... Didn't exactly get your war won, did it?

He turns to Mal, whose hands are slightly raised, eyes boring back at Tracey. ANOTHER BOOM.

MAL
Wash. Call the cops.

Wash's eyebrows raise; he points gingerly at Tracey's gun.

WASH
Um —

TRACEY
(to Mal, re: Wash)
I'll kill him. I'll put a hole right through him.

MAL
You mailed your ugly business to Zoe and me, Tracey, cash-on-delivery. I'll go to hell before I watch you turn and bite us for the favor —

ANOTHER BOOM, even closer. Ice, clatter, scary.

MAL (cont'd)
Wash, you call them up. Tell them we'll meet 'em topside.

TRACEY
No —

MAL
Do it.

Wash does that funny-under-pressure nod of his, turns to the radio, reaches for the switch —

TRACEY
NO!

Tracey swings his gun off Mal and fires a SHOT at the radio console. He misses, and it RICOCHETS off the railing above it, grazing across Wash's temple, throwing his head back.

Tracey stands, mouth open. For a moment we think he can't believe what he's done. But now we realize it's for another reason, this look of surprise... He looks down, and the camera tilts down, to his chest, where a BIG RED HOLE gapes. Fresh blood blooms there. He looks up at —

Zoe, who holds her gun at him, having got her shot off the instant he moved to fire on Wash.

TRACEY (cont'd)
You sh — You shot me...

Zoe cocks her gun, sending the spent shell flying.

ZOE
Damn right.

ANOTHER BOOM. A little dazed, but still standing, Tracey backs out of the bridge. Zoe covers him as she glances to Wash.

ZOE (cont'd)
Wash — ?

Wash dabs a finger at the bullet graze.

WASH
Ow?

It ain't critical.

INT. SERENITY - FOREDECK - CONTINUING

Tracey backs down the stairs into the foredeck, gun covering the door to the bridge.

ANOTHER DEPTH CHARGE shakes the ship.

Kaylee appears, emerging from her room.

KAYLEE
What happened!? I heard —

MAL
Kaylee! Get out of here!

Tracey turns on her, swings an arm around her, pulling her against him as a shield. Mal is at the bridge door, gun out.

TRACEY
Gorramn it, Mal.

He fires a wild shot toward the door, Mal ducks. Tracey herds Kaylee toward the exit to the cargo bay stairs —

INT. SERENITY - STAIRS/CARGO BAY

As Tracey pushes Kaylee down the stairs, her arm in his white-knuckled grip.

TRACEY
Kaylee, I'm sorry... I don't want to scare you... I just —

She sees the blood pouring down his shirt front.

KAYLEE
Blood...!

TRACEY
They shot me. They want to turn me in...

KAYLEE
No — they wouldn't —

ANOTHER BOOM.

TRACEY
Come on, Kaylee... You've got to fly me out of here. We'll take a shuttle and go —

They get to the catwalk, and he drags her toward Shuttle II's airlock.

TRACEY (cont'd)
They want to sell me off... You won't let 'em do it, will you? I mean, I thought — I thought we had a moment back there —

Kaylee digs in her heels at the shuttle's entrance.

KAYLEE
Tracey —

TRACEY
Didn't we have a moment back there?

ANOTHER BOOM.

KAYLEE
(scared but firm)
Tracey, take that gun offa me...

TRACEY
Kaylee, please —

KAYLEE
I ain't goin' anywhere with you.

MAL
Nobody's going anywhere, Private.

Mal walks down the stairs from above, gun trained on Tracey.

KAYLEE
Captain, what's happeni —

He pulls Kaylee back into shield position, gun now raised to her head. He's nothing but panic in a pair of pants now.

TRACEY
Don't make me do it.

ANOTHER BOOM. Mal gets to the catwalk, angry, but cool as cucumber slices. Zoe moves slowly down the stairs behind him.

MAL
Far as I can see, nobody's made you do anything. You brought this onto yourself. Got in over your head with these stone cold gut-runners, then you panicked, and then you brung the whole mess down on all of us...

As he was speaking, we saw Jayne, easing himself onto the catwalk across the bay, gun in hand, quiet like a kitty.

TRACEY
That ain't how it happened —

MAL
Oh yes, that's how it happened. And I'm startin' to think that trail of bodies Womack was talkin' about, I'm thinkin' some of that trail was left by you...

TRACEY
And you ain't left a trail of bodies, work you do? 'Cause your rep speaks elsewise.

MAL
Weren't bodies of people helping me out —

TRACEY
Oh, you're helping lots! 'Cause I needed a chest wound...

JEWEL STAITE

On being pulled along the catwalk: "There's a couple of hot spots on the railing. When the lights have been on all day and they've been hitting that same spot and you brush your hand against it, it's like-a-stove hot. That's why I'm holding my hands up in the scene with Jonathan Woodward, because I don't want to get distracted and put my hand on one of the hot spots and burn myself."

MAL
That can be seen to —

TRACEY
You think I'm stupid?

MAL
In every way possible.

TRACEY
You know why I picked you and Zoe? 'Cause you're saps. You're repped out as stone killers, but I still remember old Sarge with his stories and his homilies, honor and glory...

MAL
Maybe you shoulda listened.

TRACEY
What are you now? What are we now?

Mal looks up, around, then back to Tracey.

MAL
See there? Hear that quiet? Means the call's already been made.

TRACEY
(breaking up)
You — That call —
(sobs, gun at Kaylee's head)
That call means you just murdered me.

Mal flicks his eyes towards Jayne, who responds by LOUDLY COCKING HIS GUN. Panicky-panic, Tracey spins, trying to see where the sound came from, as Kaylee wrenches free. Mal FIRES, hitting him in the chest, inches from the first wound.

MAL
You murdered yourself, son.
(as Tracey sags, eyes wide)
I just carried the bullet for a while.

Tracey drops the gun, slumps to the catwalk floor. Zoe and Mal move briskly toward him, holstering.

WASH (O.S.)
Captain, they say we got two minutes before they start shelling again —

MAL
Get us up there!

Kaylee heads off.

KAYLEE
I'll get the Doctor.

Zoe and Mal look at Tracey, then at each other, eyes speaking: "There's no way in hell he's gonna make it."

EXT. PLANET - DAY

Serenity parked nose-to-nose in front of the cop ship, on a plain of glacial ice.

INT. SERENITY - CARGO BAY - DAY

The airlock doors slide open — the blinding glare of sun on snow — out of that, Womack and his two men emerge, walking up the ramp into the cargo bay, guns drawn.

Womack stops, confronted by Jayne, who stands in the middle of the bay, BIG GUN trained on Womack's head.

WOMACK
Well now... Somebody left their dog off the leash...
(cold low growl)
I been shot too many times to be scared by a gun, boy.

JAYNE
(keeping aim)
I hear you. Most ever'body I know's been shot least once. S'no big thing.

A voice trails thin from above.

TRACEY
Womack...

Womack looks up, sees Tracey propped up against the catwalk railing, sees the BLOOD dripping down through the grates.

WOMACK
Smith? You squirrely little piece a' go-se, that you?

TRACEY
(delirious chuckle)
I think I... I think I broke your junk...

Mal appears over the railing, gun on the cops as well.

MAL
Little problem during shipping.

Simon is by Tracey up on the catwalk, but there's nothing he can do.

WOMACK
Don't think I need to tell you folk the trouble you're in. Wetware smugglin', resistin', fleeing an officer a' the law... an' I'm sure a search of your ship'll come up with another few felonies.

Book walks out from behind some crates and stuff.

BOOK
You won't be searching the ship, Womack.

WOMACK
That so?

BOOK
It is. You won't be taking us in. Nor that boy who's dying up there. You're going to turn around, and just fly away.

WOMACK
You know, I'm authorized to kill as I like, Shepherds not withstandin'.

Book is so cool here it's making my hands sweaty.

BOOK
There's nine armed and dangerous desperados on this ship. You count in at three. Why is it you didn't call in for back-up?
(Womack skips a beat)
There's a fed station eighty miles from where you're standing.
(walks closer)
You got your command stripes at the Silverhold colonies. Puts you about eight solar systems away from your jurisdiction...

WOMACK
Listen here, Preach —

BOOK
And since you're running this job on the side, you took pains to keep your presence here secret. I don't imagine it'd bother anyone if we laid your bodies to rest at the bottom of one of these canyons.

Zoe cocks her gun from above. The cops lower their guns.

Womack looks up at the dying Tracey, at the various guns trained on him, crunching the numbers. Finally, he spits on the ground.

WOMACK
Damaged goods, anyhow.
(to his men)
Let's go, boys.

They start backing out of the bay. Jayne and Book slowly follow them, Jayne still aimed rock solid on Womack's face. As they get past the open airlock doors:

CINEMATOGRAPHY

Director of photography David Boyd: "That was done right out the back of the cargo bay, on a stage. Carey Meyer found a backing in the Fox library that I'm sure hadn't been unrolled for four decades, and it was just beautiful. I learned that day that artists back then made these things so not only could you front-light them, which I thought was all you could do with these painted backings, you could backlight them, too. They painted [the backings] so that you could actually make a sunrise. The paint used for the horizon, the land, was opaque, and the paint used for the sun, or the skyline, was translucent. And so here we had a snowstorm at a transitional time of the day, and we put up this wonderful backing, probably a hundred-and-twenty-feet long and forty-feet high, and made for this wonderful look, which was soft snow falling in a cool light and a far distant horizon. That was a great day."

WOMACK (cont'd)
Hat makes you look like an idiot.

This, oddly, hits Jayne. He frowns with affront.

Book hits the airlock button and the doors SLIDE
SHUT.

JAYNE
You either spent a lotta time dealin' with bad
cops... or bein' one.

BOOK
Maybe both.

Up on the catwalk, Tracey's life ebbs fast. He looks
up to Mal as Zoe enters frame, crouching by him.

TRACEY
So... That was the plan?
(Mal nods)
That —
(coughs)
That was a good plan.

MAL
I think so.

He looks to Kaylee, then to all gathered there.

TRACEY
You weren't far off about me bein' stupid... Never
could get my life workin' right, not once since the
war...

TRACEY (cont'd)
Sorry, Kaylee. Didn't mean to...
(scared)
Sarge?

MAL
Right here.

TRACEY
That stupid message of mine, trying to play you
guys... and now I'm... You'll do it? Get me home?

ZOE
Yeah.

MAL
You know the old saying...

Zoe brushes his hair from his face gently.

TRACEY
(sad little laugh)
"When you can't run anymore, you crawl... and
when you can't do that — "

Coughs again, this time a trickle of blood falls
from his lips.

ZOE
"You find someone to carry you."

Tracey nods, his eyes fluttering, dying.

Head slumps. Dead. Sad.

EXT. SNOWY HOMESTEAD - DAY

THE SNOW

Production designer Carey Meyer: "There were several different areas that got snow. We shot at the Universal backlot for one portion of that sequence. It was a small, English-looking town. First you go in with a crew and put cotton down on all the little horizontal surfaces and then, on the day of the shoot, you come in and spray foam, like soap suds, everywhere in the background. For the foreground of your shot, you actually have a truck that comes with huge blocks of ice. They chop them up into what looks like snow, and spread that around where you might have somebody walking, so you can really see their footprints. On stage, it's essentially the same processes, but you try to control it a little bit more so you don't have as much water — ice, actually — in your environment.

"For falling snow, if you're at an exterior that is environmentally sensitive, you end up using potato flakes or a cornstarch product, usually something that is biodegradable that you can get away with washing down a drain. If you're on stage, something like a synthetic plastic tends to hang in the air a little bit better and so that's usually what it is on stage."

Tracey's body is carried down the ramp by Mal and Zoe, the others in attendance. Before them is a homestead, a large EXTENDED FAMILY stands there awaiting their dead son.

ANGLE ON: Mal, Zoe and Kaylee (in particular) as they hand the body over. The coffin is open, the mother over it, fussing with Tracey's hair. Kaylee hands the tape recorder to the father. As they stand over the body...

TRACEY (V.O.)
Uh. Okay. Um, recording... Hi, I guess. It's me. Tracey.

END OF SHOW

MUSIC

Composer Greg Edmonson: "I got to make a musical comment, because there was no dialogue and so the music was free to tell a story that was not being told any other way. The end of 'The Message' had everybody together. They were all at the funeral and were bonding. Little moments — Simon stands and he takes Kaylee's hand, Jayne takes his hat off. There weren't too many moments in the show where you had all the characters together in a poignant scene like this. I didn't write that music for the Tracey character, I wrote it to say goodbye to the *Firefly* characters, who I desperately loved and didn't want to say goodbye to, but who I had to say goodbye to. The music was maybe too emotional for what the Tracey character deserved, but I didn't really write it for him."

MUSIC

An interview with Greg Edmonson

Greg Edmonson says of being hired to score *Firefly*, "It's really a miraculous tale. Everyone wanted to work with Joss. His track record is so good and he's so creative. For whatever reason he responded to the CD I sent in. So we had a meeting, and there you have it. It never normally happens that way. You usually have to jump through a lot more hoops, a lot of it happens because somebody is somebody's brother's cousin — in other words, the hiring decision is almost never made on the basis of music."

Filming had already begun at the time Edmonson came aboard, so the music team had to work hard and fast. "It was primarily a synth [synthesizer] show, for budgetary considerations and also time constraints. Probably about eight players on every show were live: the woodwinds, the guitars, the percussion, the violin, and when we used a cello, that was live. So the overdubs were live. That's fairly common in television."

Edmonson credits Whedon for much of *Firefly*'s unique sound. "One of the great joys of *Firefly* was that because Joss had created such a diverse universe, almost any kind of music could be appropriate, depending on the scene. It was a cultural melting pot, so almost anything could work. If there was a directive, it came from Joss and was, 'Let's not sound like every other TV show.' In the television world everyone always says that, and then most of them run away from the idea. Certainly there are common elements — we all have a limited number of musical instruments to choose from. But I so admire Joss's willingness to not just do what everyone else does. Sometimes, a producer or a writer might have a vision and then the studio gets scared and goes, 'We want it to be like this other show, because this is successful.' And you don't have the power to fight it. Joss had the power to make it be what he wanted it to be, and he did."

Some shows require music to fill in emotional holes; Edmonson says this was never the case with *Firefly*. "The acting and the writing were so good on this series that it didn't need music to tell the story.

❖ This page clockwise: River about to grab Kaylee's gun during 'War Stories', Inara during the pilot, the Reaver ship.

❖ Opposite: Tracey's funeral in 'The Message'.

Sometimes people go, 'Well, this scene was supposed to be like this, but it didn't really work out, so we need you to lead people by the nose with the music, so they come to the right conclusion.' *Firefly* was never like that. The writing, the directing and the acting were all spectacular. It felt like you were working on a feature every week."

Did the characters or Serenity herself have specific musical themes? "There was no reason for that," Edmonson replies. "Rather than a theme, we would use sounds. For instance, every time you saw Serenity in space, the one thing we *weren't* going to do was French horns going [makes a majestic noise], because that's like *Star Trek*. So any time you had a space shot, it was dobros, fiddles, those kinds of things, which gave it a unique character. For River we used a lot of ambient stuff, because we never knew what was going on in her mind, so she got lots of atmospheric piano and tinkly bells. For Inara's room, there was some Asian theme, because Inara was essentially a Buddhist. So it was more just specific instrumentation."

As for the metallic sound that introduced the Reavers, Edmonson says, "One of the things I think Joss was doing was making the anti-*Star Trek*. So the enemy ships were not necessarily some high-tech, gleaming piece of looks-like-a-shark; this was a rag-tag, very dangerous-looking thing. There was something on the temp music track used in editing, not like what I did, but something that made me think of it. When I heard this thing, it seemed to match the ship that we were looking at. It seemed more evil to do this than to play music that had some dark, horrific melody."

Edmonson had a unique perspective on the scenes; he saw everything before the music was added. "While composing the score I would watch the same scene over and over. I picked up nuances, and I was never disappointed. I would just look at a scene and say, 'What can I do to rise to the same level as the acting and the directing?'"

One of the most satisfying pieces of music Edmonson composed was also one of the saddest — Tracey's funeral in 'The Message'. "That little sequence meant a lot to me, because I was saying goodbye to these people. In fact, I wept at the end of that. I really put my heart into it. I wasn't putting my heart into it as opposed to not doing so on other things, it's just that my heart was desperately involved with *Firefly*.

"I've got to tell you, of all the things I have ever done in my life, nothing has ever lived on like this show has. I've never worked on a project that I've cared as desperately about as this one. It's amazing to me that it's still alive; it's amazing to me that people love something that I loved, and that's given me an even greater love for it." ◉

HEART OF GOLD

Written by Brett Matthews
Directed by Thomas S. Wright

BRETT MATTHEWS

Comic writer Brett Matthews (*Spider-Man*, *Daredevil*) made his television-writing début with 'Heart of Gold'. Matthews explains the episode's origin: "I originally pitched a Reaver-centric story that Joss really liked, and saw as a Christmas episode. But when the time came to do it, he decided he didn't want to overexpose the Reavers as they'd already featured heavily in 'Bushwhacked', and would again figure in the original pilot. Long story short, we needed a different episode and we needed it yesterday.

"It took a long time to settle on what story we were going to tell to fill a rapidly approaching slot. A lot of different ideas were bandied about before pulling 'Heart of Gold' out of the drawer, so to speak. It was the stock, Western-heavy episode we had always talked about doing — the crew of Serenity as *The Magnificent Seven/The Seven Samurai*. It may literally have been pitched in the writers' room on day one. The decision was eventually made that now was the time, and we got to work.

"As soon as we got the script to a point it could shoot, it was shooting," he remembers. "We're talking a matter of days, not weeks. The lion's share of the changes came afterward, in post, when Joss and Tim and the episode's editor, Sunny Hodge, had a little more time. A couple of things were shot and added to the episode at that point.

"The shadow puppet origin of the 'verse was something I got maybe too into, to the point where I actually scripted the entire thing, knowing it would ultimately be 'lost in translation'. Still, we tacked it on to the end of the script as an addendum and had the whole thing translated and read underneath the scene. You don't hear much of it, but it's there if you want it. If memory serves, Alan was the one constantly joking he wanted to find a place in the show for Balinese Puppet Theater. And, lo and behold, Joss took it to heart and did.

"Jayne in a whorehouse is pretty much fish in a barrel. One of my favorite little things — and I actually indicated this in the script — is that he doesn't let his favorite girl kiss him on the mouth when they start to go at it. You'll see the way Adam goes out of his way to avoid it and shakes his head. It's an in-joke, but I loved that *Firefly* was so specific and consistent that way. Like all of Joss's shows, it gives meaning to the canon.

"Morena really cried her guts out in the scene where Inara breaks down. She really got to that place. It was hard to watch in person, but beautiful.

"A couple of rooms in the Heart of Gold brothel set were wallpapered with old newspaper. I'm not sure if this reads onscreen, but it struck me as a neat idea and very much of the world. The stunt guys used full blank rounds for the scene in which the brothel gets shot up. They were beyond loud, and the splintering wood you see when they go off is not so much an effect.

"I really like the last scene, how wounded and blindsided and gut shot Mal gets by Inara and the way Nathan played it. A lot of actors wouldn't have surrendered to it the way he did, especially when playing a male lead. That moment was a bombshell, and is vintage Joss. Every one of his series delivers them."

TEASER

EXT. HEART OF GOLD BORDELLO - DAY

A plain but stately-in-its-own-way multi-storied wood-frame structure, alone and secluded on this pleasant moon.

A PRETTY GIRL (late teens) and PRETTY BOY (same age) are currently out front, hanging the laundry. Sheets. They giggle and laugh. Picture perfect country tranquility. They react to the SOUND of POUNDING HORSE HOOVES...

THROUGH THE BILLOWING SHEETS...

HORSES on the horizon. Coming up fast over a rise. And now, in between them, bouncing up INTO VIEW — A HOVERCRAFT, a badass SPACE JEEP, zooming over its buffeting hover-current.

The BOY AND GIRL register recognition. React —

PRETTY GIRL
Nandi! NANDI!

A BEAUTIFUL WOMAN, early thirties, NANDI, the madam of this concern, appears from the house. Sees the trouble approaching in the distance.

NANDI
Get inside.

But they are frozen to the spot as the riders and hovercraft get closer. Some other GIRLS are appearing variously at the door and windows. All of them are varying degrees of pretty — prostitutes.

NANDI (cont'd)
GO!

The frightened girl and boy head in. Nandi mentally runs through her options. There is only one: stand tough. The horses gallop up. She is immovable.

NANDI (cont'd)
We ain't open for business. It's the Sabbath. We don't do no trade on the Sabbath.

The HOVERCRAFT glides to a stop. Piloting it is RANCE BURGESS. A handsome, fancified imperious GENTLEMAN. But he's anything but gentle...

BURGESS
Shut up, whore.

NANDI
And you we don't trade with at all, Rance Burgess. You're no longer welcome in this establishment. You been told that.

BURGESS
Been told a great many things. I'm here for what's mine.

NANDI
Ain't nothing here belongs to you. You don't get gone, we'll be well within our rights to drop you.

BURGESS
Only rights you got are the ones I give you.
(to his men)
Find her.

The horsemen move to the door, push their way in.

NANDI
She ain't here. Girl left this moon more'n a month ago. It was you chased her off.

BURGESS
I got information says different.

Nandi is poker-faced. Some SCREAMING and CRYING from inside. Crying he recognizes. He smiles at the stone-faced Nandi.

BURGESS (cont'd)
We'll look to dealing with your prevaricatin' ways another time.

Rance's men now hustle a struggling GIRL out through the door — young PETALINE. She'd be the picture of scrubbed wholesomeness — except for the fact that she's very, very pregnant. 'Bout ready to pop. She's terrified. They force her to her knees.

BURGESS (cont'd)
Petaline. Good thing you didn't leave with my baby.

PETALINE
This baby ain't yours!

BURGESS
So you've been saying.

He nods to his men, who rip open Petaline's dress, exposing her belly. Rance pulls a FUTURISTIC HYPO DEVICE from his coat, plunges it into her belly. She winces and gasps in sudden pain. He brings the device away from her.

MUSIC

Composer Greg Edmonson: "The very last episode that I scored was 'Heart of Gold'. I put the music together for the opening sequence, and also the vocals, which are Indian. I didn't specifically record the vocals — I took vocals that I had access to and made it work. Again, the whole fun of this show, the opening shot — there's an establishing shot of a planet, and then we see this air glider racing across the desert, and then the whorehouse. So what are you going to do? The whole idea here is to say, 'We have a multi-ethnic world.' So as I looked at the scene, I thought, this is the perfect place — because we don't have a lot of big [dialogue or sound effects] things to fight — for the vocals to say, 'We're just in another place.' The reason for using vocals and making it sound ethnic was specifically to say, 'Even though we have a whorehouse, which might be interpreted as a Western thing' — and girls looking like this could have been out of a Western — 'I'm just trying to say, it's not exactly that.' And the foreign vocals are a real good way of putting some identity on it.

"The last scene in this episode was Inara telling Mal that she's leaving and then she walks off; that was the last *Firefly* scene that I got to write music for."

❖ Above: Burgess's DNA test device.

BURGESS (cont'd)
If this DNA is a match to mine — know I'll be back for my child.

Rance climbs on his hovercraft, his men to their horses.

BURGESS (cont'd)
And if you decide to close your legs for once in your life and that baby hasn't been born by the time I'm ready — I'll cut it out of ya.

They go. Nandi and some of the other girls move to Petaline, who's quietly sobbing. Help her to her feet.

NANDI
Shhh. Quiet, now. It's all gonna work out.

Among the whores helping to steady Petaline are CHARI, a petite and refined prostitute, maybe the prettiest one here, and HELEN, a more hardy whore. They watch the men leaving.

CHARI
He'll do it, too. He'll do what he says.

NANDI
No, he won't. We won't allow it.

HELEN
How we gonna stop him, Nandi?

NANDI
We'll get help. That's how.

CHARI
Help? There's not a soul on this moon'd go up against Rance Burgess.

HELEN
She's right. Ain't nobody strong enough. And even if there was — who'd help us?

CUT TO:

INT. SERENITY - DINING ROOM

MAL

in a wicked-cool CLOSE UP whips his gun at us with a stylish rack to the barrel. He's cleaning and checking it, looking casually heroic. Spread out on the dining room table are an assortment of his best guns and such.

INARA enters behind him. He doesn't hear her.

INARA
Hi.

MAL
BWAAA!

INARA
Sorry. I didn't mean to startle.

MAL
You didn't.
(repeating, as if he meant to, points gun)
BWAAA! That's a kind of a warrior... It's a... Strikes fear into...
(nothin')
Bwaa?
(then, fuck it)
You know, it ain't altogether wise, sneaking up on a man when he's handling his weapon.

INARA
I'm sure I've heard that said. But perhaps the dining area isn't the place for this sort of thing?

MAL
What do you mean? Only place with a table big enough.

INARA
Of course. In that case...
(rearranges guns)
Every well-bred petty crook knows — the small concealable weapons always go to the far left of the place setting.

Mal bridles at the term "petty crook". Before he can speak, WASH enters from the bridge.

WASH
Got a distress call coming in. Some folks asking for help.

MAL
Really? Folks asking for help? From us petty crooks?

WASH
Well...

MAL
(at Inara)
Maybe I should take that right away.

Mal makes to do that, but Wash stops him with:

WASH
Well, it's for her.

MAL
Huh?

WASH
They didn't ask for you, Mal. Call's for Inara.

INARA
I'll take it in my shuttle.

WASH
I'll send it back there.

MAL
This distress wouldn't be taking place in someone's pants, would it?

She throws a look, goes one way; Wash goes the other. Mal is left alone. A beat.

As Mal whips his gun back up into a heroic frame.

MAL (cont'd)
(all cool)
Bwaa.

BLACK OUT.

END OF TEASER

ACT ONE

EXT. SPACE

Serenity gently moving through the big black.

INT. INARA'S SHUTTLE - DAY

Inara sits at her Cortex screen, where WE SEE the live image of NANDI.

NANDI
Can't say I'm not a little ashamed, Inara, this being the first contact we've had since we parted in Sihnon.

INARA
Nonsense.

NANDI
I been meaning to answer the last few waves you sent. It's just... things do get a mite chaotic.

INARA
It's perfectly understandable.

NANDI
And now here I am, calling on you for a favor like this. Imposing on a past friendship.

INARA
It's not past. Never past. I want to help, Nan... I do. I just don't know if there's any way...

NANDI
Just speak to your people. That's all I ask.

INARA
Yes. Yes, I will. But so you know... they're not actually "my people". I'm a tenant. I just rent a shuttle on the ship.

NANDI
(after a beat)
You'll speak to them?

INARA
Yes.

NANDI
I'll wait to hear from you.
(then)
<TZOO-foo nee, mei mei.> [Blessings on you, dear sister.]

INARA
And you.

Inara touches the screen. Nandi's image FREEZES there. Inara sits there quietly contemplative for a beat. Then:

INARA (cont'd)
I suppose you heard most of that?

Mal appears, peeking around the corner at the entrance.

MAL
Only 'cause I was eavesdropping.
(then, no bullshit)
Your friend sounds like she's in a peck of trouble.

INARA
She is. There's no authority on that moon she can turn to. They're totally alone.

MAL
Some men might take advantage of that.

INARA
One man.

MAL
And she's lookin' for someone to come along and explain things to him?

INARA
That's essentially it, yes.

MAL
A whole house full of Companions... How they fixed for payment?

INARA
They're not Companions.
(then)
They're whores, Mal.

MAL
Thought you didn't much care for that word?

INARA
It applies. None who work for Nandi are registered with the Guild. They're —

MAL
Independent?

INARA
Yes.
(then)
If you agree to do this, you will be compensated. I'll see to it. I've put a little aside...

MAL
You keep your money. Won't be needing no payment.

INARA
Mal. Thank you. I'll contact Nandi at once.
(he smiles; she turns away)
But you will be paid. I feel it's important we keep ours strictly a business arrangement.

Her back's to him now, so she doesn't see the stung look.

MAL
I'll speak to the crew.

INARA
Good.

She never looks back. Off Mal, waiting a beat before he goes —

INT. SERENITY - CARGO BAY

Mal has EVERYONE assembled (except Inara). He's letting ZOE brief the troops. He's to the side, the silent commander.

ZOE
Those who have a mind are welcome to join. Those who just as soon stay on the ship can do that, too.

JAYNE
Don't much see the benefit in getting involved in strangers' troubles without an upfront price negotiated.

BOOK
These people need assistance. The benefit wouldn't necessarily be for you.

JAYNE
S'what I'm sayin'.

ZOE
No one's gonna force you to go, Jayne. As has been stated — this job's strictly speculative.

JAYNE
Good. 'Cause I don't know these folks. Don't much care to.

MAL
They're whores.

JAYNE
I'm in.

MAL
(moving off)
Wash — plot a course.

EXT. PLANET - DAY

Serenity lands amidst cover.

INT. BORDELLO LOBBY - DAY

Our gang files into the lobby. The girls are all hanging about, some making a bit of a show of themselves, draped about as if for customers; some more earnest or just curious. Inara is in the process of coming towards Nandi for a great big hug. Mal is behind her, waiting, as is Zoe.

As for the rest, they politely nod and greet the whores, Kaylee guilelessly, Simon politely, Book kindly, Jayne grinningly, Wash uncomfortably, River inquisitively. Much ad-libbing from them as have speaking parts. (Chari and Petaline are not present.)

INARA
Nandi, darling.

NANDI
It's so good to see you, mei mei...

INARA
You look wonderful.

NANDI
And you look exactly the same as the day I left. How do you do that out here?

MAL
Sheer force of will.

INARA
Nandi, this is Malcolm Reynolds.

NANDI
I appreciate your coming.

She shakes his hand, firmlike.

MAL
Any friend of Inara's is a strictly businesslike relationship of mine.

The dig is not lost on Inara, nor is her reaction lost on Nandi.

MAL (cont'd)
This is my first mate, Zoe. I'll introduce you to the rest in a bit. They're good folk.

JAYNE
(calls out from across the room, no 'tude)
Can I start getting sexed already?

MAL
Well, that one's kind of horrific.

Jayne has Helen by the shoulder, is pointing at her...

JAYNE
This one could sex me okay...

NANDI
He good in a fight?

MAL
'Bout the best.

NANDI
(calls out)
Helen, why don't you show our new friend what a Palastinian Somersault is.

Helen giggles. Jayne looks confused and excited.

JAYNE
Is that good?

ZOE
(ugh)
Can we talk business?

NANDI
(indicating lounge)
In here.
(to the others)
Rest of you, there's food and some liquor at the sideboard, make yourselves to home.

The four exit. We stay with the others.

JAYNE
(to Helen)
Just let me get a drink in me, and then we'll get to that Panatarian... thing you do.

Kaylee nudges Simon and Wash, indicates the two young men.

KAYLEE
Look, they got boy whores! Isn't that thoughtful? Wonder if they service girlfolk at all.

WASH
Let's not ask.

SIMON
Isn't there a pregnant woman I'm to examine?

WASH
(to Kaylee)
You'd really lie with someone being paid for it?

KAYLEE
(pointedly forlorn)
Well, it's not like anyone else is lining up to, you know, examine me...

JAYNE
(joining them)
Man, my John Thomas is gonna pop off and fly around the room, there's so much tasty here.

WASH
Would be you get your most poetical about your pecker.

Chari brings Petaline up to them.

CHARI
You'd be the Doctor?

SIMON
Yes. And this is Petaline?

PETALINE
Yes sir.

CHARI
She's feeling a mite weak right now.

SIMON
Well, let's get you lying down, take a look at you.

JAYNE
Now that's a plan!

He goes off with Helen, Simon goes to the back room with the two girls, River trailing.

We see Book making up a sandwich — he is approached by LUCY and EMMA.

EMMA
Shepherd —

BOOK
No thank you!

They smile a bit.

EMMA
We were hoping we might have a prayer meeting?

LUCY
We ain't had one in months, 'cept what Emma here reads out on Sunday.

EMMA
Last Shepherd to come by was springtime. He

only read the one passage, and he took it out in trade off both of us.

Book has no response.

Kaylee watches the girls chat up Book...

KAYLEE
Everyone's got somebody...
(wistfully)
Wash, tell me I'm pretty...

WASH
Were I unwed, I would take you in a manly fashion.

KAYLEE
'Cause I'm pretty?

WASH
'Cause you're pretty.

KAYLEE
Thank you. That was very restorative.

INT. BORDELLO - LOUNGE – DAY

Mal, Zoe, Nandi and Inara. Mid talk.

MAL
So I take it reason doesn't enter into this?

NANDI
Not with Rance Burgess. The man is a taker.

ZOE
You think the kid is his?

NANDI
(firm)
I think it's Petaline's.

INARA
But the blood test...

NANDI
Well, he did favor Petaline pretty exclusively, but she had others. Fifty-fifty, not that it matters. The man ain't fit to raise a cactus plant. His barren prairie shrew can't bear him an heir, so he takes it into his head to pull it outta us. That's not gonna happen.

MAL
(likes her strength)
I see that's the case.

NANDI
He means to burn me out, Mr. Reynolds. Besides the matter of his child, this is one of the few establishments around he doesn't own.

MAL
He sounds like a fun guy. I'd like to meet him.

NANDI
This won't be solved with talk.

MAL
I'm gonna fight a man, it helps to size him up.

NANDI
Well, he'll be at the theater tonight, that's a certainty.

MAL
Then so will I. Inara, think you could stoop to being on my arm?

INARA
Will you wash it first?

He smiles at the light dig, turns to Zoe.

MAL
Zoe, start getting the lay of the place: fortifications,

A D D E N D U M
(T H E A T E R   S H O W)

A CIRCULAR SHADOW representing Earth-That-Was fills the frame.

NARRATOR (Chinese)
<Man, man di, ren lei yong jin le da di de zi yuan. Huang wu le, ta wu ke gong yin.> [Little by little, the tribes used the Earth up. Barren, she had little left to offer them.]

Silhouetted shapes appear. SPACESHIPS. They radiate out from the shadow sphere, scatter in all directions. Leave it behind.

NARRATOR (continuing)
<Lue duo ze, man zai er chu. Chuang si ji, can shen de da di, shou du gan dao gu li.> [Swollen of her, they left. And for the first time since the Great Burn that birthed her, she was alone.]

The ships are gone now. A wisp of SMOKE wafts off the sphere, creates a snake of shadow.

NARRATOR (continuing)
<Di qiu wei ren lei de rou lin er tong ku liu lie, suan ku de lei shui, man liu le yi shi ji.> [The Earth cried, and terrible were her tears. Acid and caustic, the spawn of the tribes' rape. They flowed a century.]

The smoke INTENSIFIES, becomes shadowy FLAME.

NARRATOR (continuing)
<Hui mie zhi huo, ru tien jiang fu zhong yu lai dao.> [The fire that finally came did so as a blessing.]

The sphere SMOLDERS now, bits of it breaking up and disintegrating under the intense heat.

weak spots and whatnot. I'll slip into my Sunday best, and see what passes for entertainment in this town.

INT. THEATER - NIGHT

A CIRCULAR SHADOW representing Earth-That-Was FILLS THE FRAME. Silhouetted shapes appear. SPACESHIPS. They radiate out from the shadow sphere. We're witnessing some form of Balinese Puppet Theater. A nattily attired NARRATOR (speaking in Chinese: see addendum) presides before the backlit gauze screen across which the shadows play. It's the story of the destruction and fleeing of Earth-That-Was.

WIDER — Well-heeled PATRONS mill about as the show continues on a small stage in the BG. The theater itself is upscale, ornate in its own particular way. Asian and Pacific influences abound.

Mal and Inara enter, arm-in-arm. They're dressed to kill.

MAL
I'll never understand rich folk. All that money, this is what they do with it.

INARA
It's art.

MAL
It's puppets.

INARA
It's puppet art.

A waiter passes with a tray of strangely-colored drinks. Mal grabs one, takes a sip. His face immediately contorts.

MAL
<LAN-dan JIANG!> [Weak-ass sauce!] I swear to you, it's like money and good taste are inversely proportional.

INARA
That might make you the most tasteful man I've ever met.

MAL
Funny.

He swirls his colored drink. Eyeballs it.

MAL (cont'd)
Maybe you drink enough of this stuff, the puppets start makin' sense.

Inara smiles, enjoying him. It fades as her eyes lock on something beyond Mal. Off her reaction:

MAL (cont'd)
Found our boy?

Inara nods, and Mal turns to find Burgess lording over a particularly influential crowd. He's holding court, his guests laughing with disturbing frequency and force. On Burgess's arm is his wife, BELINDA. Pale and slight, she's dressed a cut above most every woman there, fiscally speaking.

Conservative excess.

MAL (cont'd)
I've a sudden itch to see how the other half lives.

Mal offers his arm to Inara, she takes it and they stroll up to where a conversation is in progress.

BURGESS
(midstream)
...So I explained to the boy: you take a clean woman's virtue, you take the woman. And that's for life. Boy said his vows right then and there. Took very little persuading on my part.

Burgess pats his laser pistol which hangs conspicuously on his belt. LAUGHTER from the assembled. And now Mal is among them, laughing LOUDER and LONGER than any of them. Finally everyone's staring at him.

MAL
Nice to know there're some places left in the 'verse where old-fashioned values still mean a thing.
(to Inara)
Isn't that right, dear?

INARA
(forced smile)
Mmmm.

BURGESS
I don't think I know you...

MAL
(hand extended)
Name's Malcolm. Malcolm Reynolds.

Burgess takes Mal's hand. They shake. Mal doesn't let go as he leans in a bit closer, says:

MAL (cont'd)
And might I just say? She is quite a beauty.

Mal releases Burgess's hand. Burgess looks at him.

BURGESS
Thank you.

He unholsters his laser gun, offers it up to Mal.

BURGESS (cont'd)
You ever have an occasion to handle one, Mr. Reynolds?
(offering it)
Silk trigger active return bolt laser.

Mal takes the laser pistol, looks it over.

MAL
Lighter than it looks. Thought it'd have more heft to it.

BURGESS
Don't let that fool you. Won't find technology like that short of Alliance. And even their issues don't yet have the auto-target adjust. Had that one crafted special.

MAL
Didn't think firearms such as this were generally

legal — for a private owner, I mean.

BELINDA
My husband makes a distinction between legality and morality, Mr. Reynolds.

Mal glances over at Belinda, holds her eyes for a beat.

MAL
I've said that myself.

BURGESS
Bending one unjust law is a small thing when it comes to protecting one's family.

MAL
I think I understand you.

BURGESS
(smiles)
And as you say — she is a beauty.

MAL
She sure is.
(hands it back)
'Course, I was referring to the lady.
(nods to Belinda)
Ma'am.

Mal steers Inara away. The others watch them go.

Now Burgess's FUTURE CELL PHONE BEEPS. He takes it out of his pocket, his eyes still on the retreating Mal —

BURGESS
Yes?

EXT. TOWN - NIGHT

Mal and Inara exit the theater hastily. Mal walks quickly, looking to put distance between himself and the theater.

INARA
Well?

MAL
Well what?

INARA
You said you wanted to look him in the eye. You've done that. So what's the plan?

MAL
Plan is — we get back to Serenity and we get off this rock just as fast as we can.

Mal hasn't slowed his pace. Off Inara, surprised —

INT. THEATER - NIGHT

Burgess is in a private-ish corner speaking on his future cell phone. Belinda joins him, expectant.

BURGESS
(into cell)
And there can be no mistake? Good.

Beat. Burgess snaps the cell shut. Mulls.

BELINDA (O.S.)
Rance?

BURGESS
The DNA matches. The child's mine. And Belinda — it's a boy.

PUSH IN on Belinda. Registering that.

BELINDA
A son... A son.
(then)
Come first light, you ride over there... and you get me my boy.

BLACK OUT.

END OF ACT ONE

ACT TWO

INT. BORDELLO LOBBY - NIGHT

Mal stands in the center of the bordello's lobby, his finery from the previous scene taken down a notch. The crew and the staff of the Heart of Gold surround him.

MAL
We run.

Nandi takes this with stoic calm, but some of her girls GASP with surprise.

MAL (cont'd)
Math just don't add up. Our weapon store ain't exactly overpowerin' at the moment, and I don't much like what we'd be up against...

The Serenity crew looks a bit surprised by this as well.

MAL (cont'd)
Nothing worse than a monster who thinks he's right with God. We might turn Burgess away once, but he'll keep comin' — won't stop til he gets what he thinks is his. So we —

NANDI
Captain Reynolds, I understand. You have your people to think of, same as me. And this isn't your fight.

MAL
Don't believe you do understand, Nandi. I said "we run".
(Nandi gives no response)
We. My people. Your people. And whatever bits of precious you got in this place you can't part with. We load up Serenity and leave Burgess in the dust.

Nandi steps closer to Mal, all strength and resolve. Despite the audience of listeners, she and Mal talk with intimate intensity, as if they're the only ones there.

NANDI
Captain Reynolds... It took me years to cut this

piece of territory out of other men's hands. To build this business up from nothing.

MAL
Nandi —

NANDI
It's who I am. And it's my home. I'm not going anywhere.

MAL
He'll kill you.
(re: her people)
Kill every last one of them, it comes to that. And he'll sleep well that night.

NANDI
And how well will you sleep, Captain?

Mal has no answer for that. Nandi holds her stare on him as she calls to her staff.

NANDI (cont'd)
Any of you want to take up the Captain's offer, you do it, with my blessing.

Behind her, much head shaking by the whores. No one's going anywhere. Nandi turns to Petaline, voice gentle.

NANDI (cont'd)
Petaline, that means you, too.

Petaline sits in an overstuffed chair, sweating, clearly uncomfortable. Simon takes her pulse.

PETALINE
No, Miss Nandi. I ain't leavin' the Heart of Gold. Ain't leavin' you...

Nandi turns back to Mal.

NANDI
Rance Burgess is just a man... And I won't let any man take what's mine. I doubt you'd do different, in my position.

Eyes still locked on each other, a stalemate of personal cool, until Mal shakes his head slightly.

MAL
Well, lady, I must say —
(admiring smile)
You're my kinda stupid.

He turns to Zoe and the rest of his crew.

MAL (cont'd)
Y'heard my points of contention with this thing. But I got a lifetime of good night's rest to consider, so I'm goin' back on that.
(glances at Inara)
There's still money in the job, for them that want to throw in —

Jayne, arm around Helen, shrugs.

JAYNE
Hell, he ain't expectin' much of a fight. We might catch him with his drawers low.

MELINDA CLARKE

I remember doing *Firefly* at Halloween, because I missed Halloween when my daughter was two [laughs]. Somehow I always end up getting these characters who are madams or dominatrix [recurring character Lady Heather on *C.S.I.: Crime Scene Investigation*] or in science-fiction. Ultimately, these women are not stupid; they're businesswomen and they're highly evolved in their way of thinking and don't make excuses for what they do. In a society where people might look down on that kind of position as abnormal, the writers always kind of revere them as being much more intelligent than your average female.

I have no idea why I get these roles. Maybe it's my eyes or the way I look, but it's the furthest thing from the real me. It's interesting that people consider me sexy or very strong, because my husband would say that I'm a wimp and looking pretty haggard every morning [laughs].

Lady Heather and Nandi, they're like mothers, taking care of their girls; I think it's just an intuitive thing that happens, that women will do naturally.

You always hope that every show is going to be full of amazing people, but I've got to say that *Firefly* had some of the *most* amazing people and was one of the most harmonious sets I've ever seen. They really, truly loved being at work and laughed hysterically at every moment and appreciated each other. It was really a joy to see how much they loved working together.

Mal raises his eyebrows. Zoe checks the chamber on her gun, cocks it.

ZOE
(nods)
He'll probably ride in by daylight, but I figure a three point watch, say, four hour shifts, be on the safe side.

WASH
(nods, mock expertise)
Three-point, four-hour, should do it.

Mal gives a slight smile, then Book steps up.

BOOK
I'm fair handy with a hammer, Captain.

MAL
That so, Shepherd — ?

BOOK
Been following the footsteps of a carpenter for some time now. I think I can do something about our fortifications.

Mal looks over the rest of his people, Kaylee smiles and nods, Simon looks up from Petaline, then back to his task. We feel Mal take understated pride in knowing them.

MAL
Okay then...

His strategy wheels start turning, as UNDERSTATED "GET SHIT DONE" MUSIC starts to build.

MAL (cont'd)
We start shootin', they'll most like try to burn us out, save their sweat and bullets. Nandi, what's the water supply here?

NANDI
Underground well. Pump that draws it up's antiquated, but it don't break down.

Quietly, off to the side of the action, Petaline stops with a jolt. She puts a hand to her belly.

MAL
Kaylee — think you can swing an upgrade for

their waterworks?

Kaylee moves closer to him, beaming happily.

KAYLEE
I'll talk to Serenity, see what she's got we might use.

MAL
Good. And we'd better find some —

River is suddenly at their side.

RIVER
It's starting.

Kaylee gives a little STARTLED JUMP, unseen by Mal.

MAL
That's a sure fact. But time is on the enemy's side, so —

PETALINE
(pained yelp)
Dr. Tam — !

Mal sees Petaline, who Simon helps to her feet as she pants with contraction.

MAL
Oh — It's starting — Okay.
(a little panicky)
It's starting! — No one panic — It's gonna be fine —

Simon leads Petaline toward the bordello's back room, nodding to Mal.

SIMON
I got this one, Captain.

Mal looks around at everyone else, they smile, at the brink of chuckling, at his display. He CLAPS his hands, resuming his heroical authority:

MAL
Come on, people! Let's get to work.

BOOK'S COSTUME

Costume designer Shawna Trpcic: "We went through a few different designs trying to come up with our nondenominational and yet recognizable preacher. He was more like a pastor than, say, a Catholic priest, but we wanted people to recognize him because at one point Book says, 'I thought the outfit gave it away,' about what he does. So we ended up with a blend of a lot of different religious leaders. The grey was to echo the Alliance colors. And when I could, I showed off his body, I threw a t-shirt on him, because the guy is in incredible shape."

INT. BORDELLO LOBBY - BALCONY - DAY

Book wields a hammer, boarding up windows. Lucy and Emma, the "church" whores, assist.

EMMA
The girls and I've been talkin', Shepherd.

He stops, turns to face her.

EMMA (cont'd)
We've been discussin' what we'd like said over us if we should happen to fall —

BOOK
No.

Book reaches out, places a hand on her.

BOOK (cont'd)
I only bury the dead, child. And no one here is going to die. Not a one of you.

He smiles and the tension disappears. Lucy returns it.

SMASH TO:

INT. BORDELLO - UPSTAIRS ROOM - DAY

JAYNE
Now, there's people gonna die.

Jayne sits in front of a large window, its field of view panoramic. Across from him, Helen sits attentively.

JAYNE (cont'd)
Ain't no way 'round that. And with people dyin' comes guts and screamin' and that can bring on all sorts of screwed-up behaviors, a person's not used to it. When the time comes, most important thing is you keep your wits about you. Clear?

Helen nods. Jayne reaches over to a nearby table strewn with weapons and ammunition.

JAYNE (cont'd)
These here are my favorites, and you're to keep 'em comin' til there ain't no more to be had. I shoot, I run out, you just hand me the next biggest and so on. Is there an understanding here?

HELEN
Yes.

JAYNE
All right, then. Let's get to work.

Giggling, Helen hops on top of Jayne, straddles him. She plants wet kisses all over. Jayne craning his neck to keep his mouth out of reach.

EXT. BORDELLO - DAY

Wash sweeps a pile of dry earth over a wood-and-rope contraption, securing and camouflaging the device.

WASH
All I'm saying is we're living pretty deep in the rough and tumble, and I don't see that changing any time soon.

Zoe rises behind him, a large spool of wire in her hands.

ZOE
Nor do I.

She crouches, begins to wind the wire between one of two stakes buried deep in the ground, some fifteen feet apart.

WASH
Well, I'm not sure now is the best time to bring a tiny little helpless person into our lives.

Wash lies flat, secures the wire to the stake. He takes a pair of WIRECUTTERS and cuts the wire.

THE BROTHEL

Production designer Carey Meyer: "We needed to find this brothel out in the middle of another deserted planet and we ended up with a location that was great for shooting. We found this house — we'd been getting a lot of feedback from Joss and the studio that this whole Western concept wasn't really playing as well as anybody had hoped and so we had been given a directive to try to make it less Western. We ended up covering the entire house with something that looked like tin foil, essentially, which were those silver space blankets — you know, the little packages that you might keep in the glove box if you were in danger of getting stranded in your car, to keep your body warm. The blankets were very thin, silver, reflective Mylar sheets. It felt a little bit like the Apollo spaceships, they were covered in a lot of that sort of material.

"We also had this laser gun, because it was at this point they decided they had to have lasers in our world as well, and a floating hovercraft. So we completely sheathed this whole house in this tin foil material and had explosives behind it, so that when the laser whipped across the house, a large streak of flame would be blown up on the side of the house. It just ended up being a little comical, and I remember Joss referring to it as 'the Jiffy-Pop mansion'. It was very funny."

ZOE
That excuse is getting a little worn, honey.

WASH
It's not an excuse, dear. It's objective assessment. I can't help it if it stays relevant.

Zoe stands, starts kicking dirt over the lines of their trap.

ZOE
I don't give a good gorramn about relevant, Wash. Or objective. And I'm not so afraid of losing something that I won't try havin' it. You and I would make one beautiful baby. I want to meet that child one day. Period.

WASH
And this beautiful baby of ours, you don't mind that it's going to grow up on a spaceship?

ZOE
Worked fine for me.

Beat. Wash considers, nods.

EXT. TOWN - DAY

Burgess stands in the street, jacket swept back behind his holstered LASER PISTOL, tumbler of whiskey in one hand. He takes a swig then FAST DRAWS, firing THREE SHOTS from his laser. Just before the third, we CUT TO:

ANGLE ON TARGET DUMMY

A stuffed burlap dummy, tied to a rough wood tripod. The last LASER BEAM sears into its head, IGNITING IT. HOLD ON the dummy as it bursts into FLAMES.

INT. BORDELLO - NANDI'S ROOM - EVENING

Mal looks out the window. We can't see what he sees, but we hear a cluster of gunshots, followed by the barking of Jayne:

JAYNE (O.S.)
That ain't nothin'! Y'all are pulling, not squeezing like I said. Next one doesn't hit that board is giving up a special treat, <dong-MA?> [you understand?]

Mal closes the window, smiling a little.

MAL
That man is gonna use up all our credit 'fore we've earned it.

NANDI
Well, after you've saved our lives you can do some chores, maybe.

She is getting a box from her bottom drawer. As they talk she lays it on the bed, pulls out a few fancy looking pistols.

MAL
I'm a fair hand with a mop.

NANDI
So your legend tells.

(chuckling)
Truth is, I expected a whole lot more of you to be taking payment in our trade.

MAL
Well, we're an odd conglomeration. Got a preacher, a married fellah, and the Doctor... Well, he'd have to relax for thirty seconds to get his play, and that'd be more or less a miracle.
(re: guns)
These are fetching little pieces. They work at all?

NANDI
Don't got many rounds for the Chaplain there, but the rest'll be of use.
(picks one up)
This is my favorite.

MAL
What's its history?

NANDI
Violence and crime, sad to say. What about you?

MAL
Similar.

NANDI
No, I mean, when are you planning to avail yourself of some of our trade? My girls is clean and kind-spirited.

MAL
Well, I got the job in mind. After, I'm sure I'll... trade. They're a fine bunch.

NANDI
You ain't looked at one of 'em as long or as lovin' as you looked at those pistols. You're not sly, are you? 'Cause I got my boys...

MAL
(totally comfortable with the question)
Sly? No. I lean towards womanfolk. Just one thing at a time. Never like complications.

She smiles, knowingly.

NANDI
I'm certain of that.

MAL
Something to be smiling at?

NANDI
I trained as a Companion, remember? I read people pretty well.

MAL
Well, that's nice for you.

He's examining the weapons, deliberately.

NANDI
She's a hell of a woman, ain't she?
(off his look)
Inara.

MAL
(casual)
Oh. Yeah. She's a cherry-blossom, no denyin'.
(still looking at gun)

SIMON

"Well, my sister's a ship, we had a complicated childhood."

At the time he auditioned for *Firefly*, Sean Maher was something of a Fox television veteran: he had had the title role in the teen cop series *Ryan Caulfield: Year One*, which was pulled off the air after episode two; he played Neve Campbell's boyfriend in seven episodes of *Party of Five*; he was on the short-lived financial drama *The $treet*. But the Pleasantville, New York native says he hadn't done science fiction before, partly because it hadn't interested him. However, Joss Whedon and the *Firefly* universe won him over: "Joss made my character and this universe so unique. That is the first thing I was attracted to when I read the pilot. It was like nothing I had read before. It was so unique and like a world of its own. Everything about it was so complete and well thought out, so that it was this altered world — there was no element that was missing. Everything about it... The characters were so rich and flawed. I was always drawn to the relationships between them and their dynamics because it was so fresh. Someone was asking me the other day about what archetype I would compare Simon to and I really couldn't think of anything. In that regard, each character, Simon included, is a character of their own."

Maher found his close relationships with his fellow cast members very helpful to him in his portrayal of Simon Tam: "Initially, as an actor, there are times when you read a script and you worry you will never draw parallels between yourself and this character. It sort of happens with me that when I start rehearsing and working with the other actors I discover those similarities. My love for my sister after working with Summer, and the crush I have on Kaylee after spending a lot of time with Jewel. In this particular project, the dynamics of the characters were all attributed to the other actors, and that is when I started finding all the similarities between myself and Simon." As much as he enjoyed playing Simon,

Maher concedes there's another *Firefly* character he would have liked to play: "Jayne!"

When Zac Hug (www.BrilliantButCancelled.com) asked Maher how he felt about the cancellation, he said at the outset, things were somewhat mysterious. "We were not told much. I think we were strung along for a little while, because they were on the fence about what to do with us. We all took it really hard. It was a big blow; it was awful."

Like many of his *Firefly* colleagues, Maher says the dedication of the fans to the show came as a welcome surprise. "We would not be here without them. That's how important they are. I always say, 'Why are we here? — Joss Whedon and the fans.' There was support from the very beginning. They were always there. There was always a small group and it just grew and grew and grew. It was inspiring to us and it kept driving us. It was nice to know that someone was out there actually getting what we were trying to say."

Maher feels that the movie *Serenity* is a rightful continuation of the series *Firefly*. "The tone was very similar in terms of the wit and the humor, and the lightness of the dynamics between the characters. There's an overwhelming sense that the stakes have been raised. Summer had to be even more tormented than she was before, in the series, in questions of her sanity and how she reacts to everything, so I just built off of what she gave me. It was really a lot of reacting to her and wanting to keep her character safe. There was a greater sense of urgency for me to figure out what was going on with her and to put an end to this pain that she was in."

Zac Hug asked Maher if he would want to be part of a continuation of *Firefly*, "If there's a sequel, or anything these people want to do, I'm there. We always joked about taking the show on the road, as a side show act: 'Let's drive cross country and do *Firefly* episodes on stage!' It's a wonderful group of people."

What would Maher like to see happen if Simon and Co. have more adventures? "If Joss takes requests — I think Kaylee should be barefoot and pregnant, shaving Simon's head, telling him he just looks too pretty." ☉

'Spect you know her better'n I do, comin' up together and all.

NANDI
Imagine I do. She ever tell you why she left Sihnon?

MAL
Never asked.

NANDI
Yes you did, and I don't know my own self. I was gone long before. And I'll tell you, it was a shock, her leaving. She was special. There's forty women in House Madrassa and you'd pick her out in a second. Coulda been House Priestess, few years time.

MAL
Is that right.

NANDI
Had her eyes on it, too. Very focused. She's like you, more than a little.

MAL
And how exactly is that?

NANDI
She hates complications.

A moment between them. A small understanding.

MAL
They do crop up though, don't they?

NANDI
Such is life.

INT. BORDELLO - BACK ROOM - NIGHT

Petaline is in bed, letting out an impressive YELL. She's sweaty and breathing hard. Inara is by her side, mopping her brow supportively.

Simon is at the foot of the bed, looking under the tent of sheet they've rigged up. River looks over his shoulder, completely agape.

SIMON
You're not completely dilated yet. Should be pretty quick but don't try to force it. These contractions are still preliminary.

PETALINE
What's he saying?

INARA
It's gonna be a little while, sweetie.

PETALINE
But it hurts! Child wants to be born, I know it.

SIMON
(to Inara)
Can you grab the green vial from my bag. We can dull the pain some.

Inara crosses, pausing by Simon, whispers —

INARA
How many babies have you actually delivered?

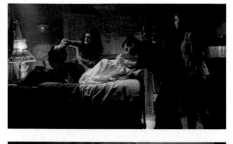

SIMON
As the primary? This would be the first. You?

INARA
My first too.

RIVER
(looking even closer)
Mine too.

They look at River a moment.

SIMON
Gonna be a long night.

Inara gives him a peck on the cheek for luck.

INARA
You'll do great, Doctor.

RIVER
(still staring)
Who do you think is in there...?

Petaline huffs and puffs...

DISSOLVE TO:

INT. BORDELLO LOBBY - NIGHT

Book is standing with his bible, about half the whores standing or kneeling before him.

BOOK
...Forgive us our trespasses, as we forgive those who trespass against us, and lead us not into temptation, but deliver us from evil, for thine is the kingdom, the power and the glory, Amen.

WHORES
Amen.

They rise, some squaring away tools and weapons and such.

BOOK
Not much more we can do tonight. I think it best we all get some rest. Is there... is there a room I can lay down in?

EMMA
(sweet but sly)
Alone?

They all look at him, guilelessly sexy. He waits perhaps a bit much of a beat.

BOOK
Alone.

They laugh, and he smiles along with them.

BOOK (cont'd)
Thank you.

INT. BORDELLO - NANDI'S ROOM - NIGHT

It's very late, and Mal and Nandi are on the couch. He throws back a shot. They've both been drinking a while.

NANDI
It was the dulcimer.

MAL
The dulcimer drove you out of Sihnon. What, did you kill a dulcimer in a terrible passion?

NANDI
(smiles)
Actually, yes.

MAL
And that dulcimer's family is looking to get even. I get it.

NANDI
I was at practice. You never stop practicing, you know, not a true Companion. Some baroque piece, and the instructor keeps saying "You're playing it, not feeling it". And the fifth time he said it I took the damn thing and smashed it into kindling. And that's when it occurred to me that a Companion's life might just be a little too constricting.

She crosses to the dresser to pour two more shots.

NANDI (cont'd)
So I trucked out to the border, learned to say "ain't" and came to find work. Found this place.

MAL
It's a nice place.

NANDI
It was a dungheap. Run by a pig who had half the girls strung out on drops. There's no Guild out here; they let men run the houses, and they don't ask for references. We didn't get along.

MAL
Where's he at now?

NANDI
(sitting)
Let's just say he ain't playing the dulcimer any-more either.

They clink glasses. Knock 'em back.

MAL
You are a remarkable woman, you don't mind my saying.

NANDI
Long as it's you saying it, and not my fine rice wine.

MAL
It takes more'n a few drinks to render my judge-ment blurry. What about you? Am I getting any prettier?

NANDI
By the minute.

She is so sweetly seductive that they hold on each other a moment. Then he breaks it, all conscience.

MAL
(rising)
I should check the barricades, make sure every-one's ready to —

NANDI
Everyone's asleep. Well, them as can, night before a fight.

She heads for the dresser, to pour again.

NANDI (cont'd)
Can you?

MAL
What?

NANDI
Sleep?

Another beat, as that loaded question settles in. Mal's reply is intimate in tone as well, as he steps forward.

MAL
Miss Nandi, I have a confession to make.

NANDI
Maybe I should get the Shepherd.

MAL
Well, I ain't sinned yet, and I'd feel more than a little awkward having him here when I do.

NANDI
You expect to accomplish something sinful then, do you?

MAL
If I'm overstepping my bounds, you let me know.

NATHAN FILLION

Melinda Clarke in 'Heart of Gold', another amazing casting job. She's an amazing actress. I loved learning more about Malcolm Reynolds through other characters, and Nandi was a big one. It was the first time Malcolm could actually feel along the lines of something he needed to feel for so, so long. Of course, it was a little bit misguided not being Inara and all. He's a human being and it's hard for him to let himself be a human being.

NANDI
<jen mei NAI-shing duh FWO-tzoo> [Extra-ordinarily impatient Buddha], Malcolm, I been waiting for you to kiss me since I showed you my guns —

They're kissing. It's soft, but not without heat. He pulls away, looks at her.

NANDI (cont'd)
You okay with this?

MAL
I'm just waiting to see if I pass out. Long story.

NANDI
I want you to bed me.

MAL
I guess I mean to.

A small beat, as he strokes her hair.

NANDI
I ain't her.

MAL
Only people in this room is you and me.

She hands him one of the newly filled shotglasses, takes one herself.

NANDI
So, my child... How long has it been since your last confession?

MAL
Longer than I care to tell.

NANDI
You gonna remember where everything goes?

MAL
Let's just say I plan to take it real slow.

They drink. They kiss. They sink to the bed.

INT. BORDELLO - NANDI'S ROOM - NIGHT

It is later, and they are in the act. They are both naked, him sitting up at the foot of the bed and her astraddle, sheets pooled about the lower portions of them and clever camera work con-cealing the more interesting details of the upper. Their movement is slow, deliberate — and not quite so rhythmic as to be entirely spe-cific. They are drenched in sweat.

He runs his hands along the side of her head, his thumb sliding indelicately into the corner of her mouth, Nandi biting down lightly, eyes clos-ing, then opening again, near startled, as his hands slip to her hips and they look at each other with something resembling need.

She brings his head to her breast, still moving, eyes wet with tears not spilt.

EXT. TOWN - NIGHT

BURGESS
So the whore's got herself a champion, has she?

He is standing in the light of a couple of torches, on the balcony of a two-story building, couple of his men behind him. He looks over the railing a moment, amused. Looks back to the person he's addressing.

JOSS WHEDON

There's one more edict of the network — 'For god's sake, no Western.' And then we saw the dailies from 'Heart of Gold' and went, 'Oh, we're in trouble. Oh, we're in so much trouble.' We did a lot of re-shoots on 'Heart of Gold' just to explain why it was so Western because we thought the network was going to kill us. The network *was* going to kill us, but we didn't know that it was going to happen right away at that point. 'Heart of Gold' really was, let's *do* a Western — let's do *Rio Bravo*, let's do the siege, and let's let poor Mal get some play and see how that affects Inara. It was again throwing everybody into a different kind of situation — 'Let's help a bunch of nice whores and get ourselves into kind of a classic Western scenario.' Then we realized that we were being told not to make a Western, and we weren't really sure what to do about it.

BURGESS (cont'd)
This great man got a name?

REVERSE to see CHARI is the one feeding him info. Why, she's a TURNCOAT!

CHARI
Reynolds. Malcolm Reynolds.

BURGESS
(thoughtfully)
Yes, I've met the man. How many does he have with him?

CHARI
Just a few, and only two real fighters besides his-self. But they got the girls stirrin' for a battle.

BURGESS
Well, I certainly wasn't counting on a battle.

He turns out over the railing, addresses his men.

BURGESS (cont'd)
Seems the Heart of Gold has got itself a few mercenaries. I guess we'd best call the whole thing off!

As he says this, the camera pans over to take in the view of the men — and they number at least thirty, many on horseback, all total bad-asses. A ROAR of laughter meets Burgess's statement.

Burgess grins, turns back to Chari.

BURGESS (cont'd)
Earned yourself quite a bag of silver, little kitten. Got a few more chores in mind afore you get it, though.

CHARI
I'm ready.

He motions for her to come closer, puts his arm around her as he addresses the men.

BURGESS
Now Chari here, she understands a whore's place, don't she?

General assent and applause.

BURGESS (cont'd)
But Nandi, and those others, they spit on our town. They've no respect for the sanctity of fatherhood, for decency or family. They got MY CHILD held hostage to their decadent ways and

that I will not abide!

More cheers.

BURGESS (cont'd)
We will show them what power is! We will show them what their position in this town is! Let us all remember, right here and now, what a woman is to a man!

He turns to Chari, no longer smiling.

BURGESS (cont'd)
Get on your knees.

She looks startled. Looks out at all the men watching. But Burgess is unwavering, and she hesitantly sinks out of frame.

ANGLE: THE MEN

There is a pause. Then an uproarious cheer.

END OF ACT TWO

ACT THREE

EXT. BORDELLO - DAWN

The sun creeps over the horizon. The MORNING OF.

INT. BORDELLO - NANDI'S ROOM - DAWN

Mal and Nandi are asleep together in a tangle of sheets, in a tangle of limbs. Content.

Sunlight streams in from the horizon, cutting her across the eyes. She blinks awake. She looks at him sleeping awhile.

INT. BORDELLO LOBBY - MORNING

Mal is coming quietly out of Nandi's room, doing up his shirt, just as Inara is coming from the back hall. He stops, totally busted.

MAL
Um...

INARA
Well.

She is startled, but doesn't seem shocked. That doesn't stop Mal from excusifying:

MAL
I was just, um, I had to tell Nandi about the... It's near time to... Big fight today.

INARA
Mal. Please.

MAL
Hey, no, I've got, I've been up thinking...

INARA
(sincerely)
So you took to bed with Nandi. I'm glad.

MAL
Thinking and pondering the — Glad?

INARA
Yes! She's a dear friend, and probably in need of some comfort about now.

MAL
Well, I...

INARA
(amused)
One of the virtues of not being puritanical about sex is not being embarrassed afterwards. You should look into it.

MAL
Well, I just... didn't want you to think I was taking advantage of your friend.

INARA
She's well worth taking advantage of, I sincerely hope you did.

MAL
So you're okay. Well, yeah. Why wouldn't you be?

INARA
I wouldn't say I'm entirely okay. I'm a little appalled at her taste.

Smiling, she turns and exits, leaving him come-backless.

INT. BORDELLO - UPSTAIRS ROOM - MORNING

The sun's a mite higher now. Jayne stirs, stretches, as does Helen. Then he rolls over and goes back to sleep.

INT. BORDELLO - BACK ROOM - MORNING

We see Petaline, having dozed off. Track across the room to find Inara sitting on the floor in the corner. Sobbing her eyes out.

EXT. PLAINS - MORNING

Wash and Kaylee trek toward Serenity, which looms in the distance (for one — and only one — shot). Wash sips coffee from a lidded MUG. He has a PISTOL holstered at his side.

Mal's voice comes in over Wash's RADIO HANDSET.

MAL (O.S.)
Wash — are we there yet?

Wash pulls his radio off his belt and answers.

WASH
All but. Nice day for a last stand, innit?

MAL (O.S.)
Nope. Plan to make a healthy few stands after this one. Just hopin' for some air support from your quarter, is all.

WASH
(nods)
Couple of low fly-overs, engines tipped earthward at full blast, should give our guests something other than killin' you to think about.

MAL (O.S.)
What I like to hear... Out.

Wash clicks off his radio and clips it back to his belt.

KAYLEE
Captain seem a little funny to you at breakfast this morning?

WASH
Come on, Kaylee. We all know I'm the funny one.

INT. BORDELLO - MORNING

Mal walks behind some of the women, who stand in position at the bottom floor lobby windows, holding rifles. He himself is now armed for battle. He wears a RADIO EARWIG.

MAL
You ladies all locked and loaded?

LUCY
Yes, sir.

MAL
Good. Remember, shoot the man, not the horse. Dead horse is cover, live horse is a great pile of panic.

He stops as a TRANSMISSION crackles in over his earwig:

JAYNE (O.S.)
(lewd chuckle)
Whoa now, girl, that's just plain dirty —

He holds a finger up to the women, and hits the transmit switch.

MAL
Jayne — You aware your radio's transmittin'?

INT. BORDELLO - UPSTAIRS ROOM - MORNING

CLOSE ON RADIO HANDSET — which sits in a twist of bedspread. Jayne's hand enters frame, fumbling for it.

MAL (O.S.)
'Cause I ain't feelin' particular girlish or dirty at the moment.

Jayne picks up the radio and speaks into it as he untangles himself from Helen. He's dressed for war. She, not so much.

JAYNE
Oh, uh, just up here waitin', Captain. Ready one-hunnert-percent.

He grabs his weapon and looks out his window.

MAL (O.S.)
Better be.

Jayne gives Helen a sharp, businesslike nod, and she nods back.

EXT. PLAINS - ELSEWHERE - MORNING

A beat of quiet. Then the FAR-OFF SOUND of horses as a cloud of dust rises on the horizon. SMASH CUT TO —

— MID-THUNDER with the MERCENARY HORSE-MEN surging forward at full gallop, flanking Burgess's hovercraft.

Burgess pilots the hovercraft, expressionless, behind stylish mirrored goggles. Over his face, PRE-LAP Petaline's SCREAM OF PAIN —

INT. BORDELLO - BACK ROOM - MORNING

CLOSE ON Petaline, who writhes in the throes of a contraction.

PETALINE
(continued scream)

Her legs are up and spread apart, concealed by a sheet. Inara holds her hand.

Inara leans in toward Petaline's face.

INARA
You're stronger than this thing, honey. I can feel it in your grip...
(Petaline SCREAMS again)
Petaline, look at me —

Petaline looks up at Inara, who catches her eyes in an intense, almost hypnotic stare.

INARA (cont'd)
This is just a moment in time... Step out of it and let it happen...

Nandi enters, stopping at Inara's side.

NANDI
How is she, Doctor?

Simon speaks from a counter a short distance away, as he fits a VIAL OF MED into his HYPO-GUN.

SIMON
She's at ten centimeters. Not long now.

Nandi turns to Inara. They share a subtle exchange of looks. This should be cut to show they're communicating via expression alone — Companions wordlessly reading each other.

Nandi smiles sadly, rests a hand on Inara's shoulder. Inara turns to Simon, sees he's still engaged, then quietly:

INARA
Nandi, believe me, I'll be fine.

❖ Below: Burgess's hovercraft.

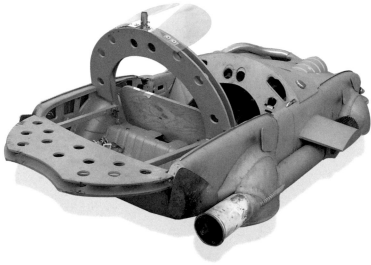

They share a look and Nandi exits.

EXT. BORDELLO - MORNING

BINOCULAR POV — of Burgess and his riders, charging forward in the distance, trailing a plume of dust.

INT. BORDELLO LOBBY - MORNING

Mal, now standing on the interior balcony, lowers a slim pair of BINOCULARS. He is not at all pleased.

MAL
Zoe, Jayne — you seein' this?

JAYNE (O.S.)
Gotta be thirty men out there.

ZOE (O.S.)
Confirm that. Plus a mounted gun on that hovercraft.

JAYNE (O.S.)
What's that you said about runnin' for it?

Mal takes a moment, visibly adjusting to the new odds. He lifts up his RIFLE.

MAL
All right, folks — We got no shortage of ugly ridin' in on us. But that don't change the plan.

Nandi climbs the stairs, gun in hand, addressing the whores.

NANDI
Anybody here goes down, you drag 'em to the back, then get back to shooting. Only way to help them is to finish this.

She cocks her rifle then turns to Mal, smiles at him sweetly for a quick beat.

NANDI (cont'd)
Morning.

Mal smiles back.

INT. SERENITY - CARGO BAY - DAY

Kaylee and Wash enter through the SMALL

INT. BORDELLO LOBBY - CONTINUING

Mal calls to his troops.

MAL
Fire!

They all swing out and unleash a BARRAGE OF FIRE from their positions. One WHORE is caught by a shot and falls.

Nandi sees this and bristles, aiming another shot —

NANDI
<Wang bao DAHN — > [Dirty bastard sons-of —]

She FIRES.

EXT. BORDELLO - CONTINUING

A HORSEMAN takes it in the neck and flops off his horse.

INT. SERENITY - CARGO BAY - DAY

Wash and Kaylee under fire. Wash is trading shots with his pistol as THREE OF BURGESS'S MEN work their way along the upper catwalk. Wash and Kaylee fall back behind different crates, finally getting close to the door that leads to the COMMON AREA.

WASH
GO!

Kaylee darts out, Wash behind her, fires a FLURRY OF SHOTS to cover their exit.

They get through the door.

The men race down the stairs after them. CAMERA FINDS the radio.

MAL (O.S.)
Wash — Where the hell is my spaceship!?

EXT. BORDELLO - CONTINUING

Horsemen criss-crossing, SEVERAL get hit by GUNFIRE from the whorehouse, dropping from their steeds.

A HORSE GOES DOWN, crashing into the FG and throwing its rider.

The REST RETURN FIRE.

Burgess angles the hovercraft, flying parallel with the house front, still a ways off. He lifts his laser and FIRES a CONTINUOUS BEAM.

The BEAM sears along the front of the house, wavering between the second-storey windows and the eaves of the roof, which already started SMOKING.

INT. BORDELLO LOBBY - CONTINUING

As the LASER BEAM traces a RED-HOT LINE along their barricade, FLASHING through the gun-slits as Mal and the others hunker away.

DOOR. Kaylee closes the door behind them; something's not right — She scans the bay as they start for the stairs. Mal CRACKLES IN over Wash's radio:

MAL (O.S.)
Wash — gonna be tradin' injuries in under two minutes. Like my sky a little less empty —

WASH
Copy that, Mal. We —

Kaylee sees SHADOWY FIGURES on the catwalk above, and tackles Wash just as GUNFIRE rains down at them, SPARKING off metal.

Wash slams down behind some metal crates, Kaylee on top of him. The radio skitters off into open floor; unreachable. But they have cover for the moment. Wash looks up into her face.

WASH (cont'd)
I told you, Kaylee — I'm a married man —

Kaylee knits her brow at him as another SHOT ricochets off their cover.

KAYLEE
(flatly)
You ain't all that funny.

EXT. BORDELLO - DAY

The hovercraft HUMS forward, just ahead of the horsemen.

Lead horse SNAPS A TRIPWIRE, and the ROPE springs up out of the dirt, singing taut, catching THREE RIDERS in the throats and pitching them off their horses. The other riders duck, some slide sideways in their saddles, clearing the line.

Burgess calls back to KOZICK, the man on the craft's large MOUNTED GUN.

BURGESS
Open her up, Kozick —

Kozick nods, cranks back a lever and starts shooting — MASSIVE MACHINE GUNFIRE flares.

INT. BORDELLO LOBBY - CONTINUING

Mal sees it coming and swings behind his shielding.

MAL
Cover!

The women do the same, just as a HAIL OF MACHINE GUNFIRE rips through everything that isn't fortified.

MAL (cont'd)
(into earwig)
Jayne — I believe that's our first hurdle. Think you might —

EXT. BORDELLO - CONTINUING

Kozick, FIRING AWAY, is plugged in the chest and FLIPS BACKWARD off the hovercraft.

INT. BORDELLO - UPSTAIRS ROOM - CONTINUING

Jayne pulls his eye away from his sight long enough to speak into his radio:

JAYNE
Think I might, Cap.

Mal looks up, where he sees SMOKE pouring in from a TORN UP PATCH OF CEILING.

MAL
Ruttin' lasers —
(into earwig)
Book — Zoe — Second hurdle —

EXT. BORDELLO - CONTINUING

FIRE HAS BROKEN OUT on the front facade of the whorehouse. PAN/TILT to what looks like a PILE OF BARRELS AND TARPS on the ground in front of the house.

ZOE (O.S.)
Copy that, sir —

The tarps are thrown away, revealing Zoe and Book. Book holds the hose, Zoe covers his back with her rifle. He starts up the hose, and A HISSING JET OF WATER sprays up toward the wall.

A HORSEMAN turns toward them, leveling his gun at Book. Zoe FIRES, taking him out.

BOOK
Thank you —

Book catches sight of a PAIR OF RIDERS behind Zoe, taking aim. He swings the hose around, BLASTING them off their horses with its powerful stream.

ZOE
Don't mention it —

INT. BORDELLO LOBBY - CONTINUING

Mal, Nandi, and the others continue BLASTING AWAY. Petaline's SCREAMING comes in from the back room.

INT. BORDELLO - BACK ROOM - CONTINUING

Simon is in position, Petaline is bearing down hard and SCREAMING between breaths. River is fascinated and smiling.

PETALINE
(screams again)

SIMON
That's it, Petaline, one more push —

She bears down.

SIMON (cont'd)
That's the shoulders... Good —

EXT. BORDELLO - CONTINUING

The horsemen are in chaos now, riderless and wounded horses stymie their efforts to fire on the house. Our guys are kicking ass!

INT. BORDELLO LOBBY - CONTINUING

Up on the balcony, Mal talks into his earwig as he scans the battlefield.

MAL
Jayne — I lost visual on Burgess —

JAYNE (O.S.)
Same here —

A BOY WHORE falls away from a window down the line, bloodied by a gunshot. Mal RETURNS FIRE.

INT. BORDELLO - SIDE OF HOUSE - CONTINUING

Burgess's hovercraft is up close to the house, and he's leaping off it to the ground. A BULKHEAD CELLAR DOOR swings open. Chari is there, and ushers Burgess inside.

INT. SERENITY - DINING AREA - CONTINUING

The three mercenaries move through the dining area, grim-faced, covering it with their guns, cursorily checking its nooks and crannies for their prey.

A DOOR LOCKING SHUT calls their attention to the aft corridor.

They see Wash at its end and raise their guns.

WASH
(that weird Robert Mitchum "hoot!" from *Night of the Hunter*)

Wash darts into the engine room, narrowly missed by their FIRE as they move into the AFT CORRIDOR.

Kaylee pops out of a CLEVER HIDING PLACE and swings the door shut behind them, then locks it.

INT. SERENITY - AFT CORRIDOR - CONTINUING

Before they can react, Wash swings the ENGINE ROOM DOOR shut as well, locking it. The passage leading off from the middle of the corridor is BARRED BY ITS DOOR [which we have not seen yet in the series — a Carey issue]. They're trapped.

INT. SERENITY - ENGINE ROOM - CONTINUING

Wash peers in through the thick glass porthole, issuing adrenaline-charged laughter.

WASH
Got you, you <niao SE duh DOO-gway.> [piss-soaked pikers.]
(laughs again, then realizes he's trapped in the engine room)
Nobody's going any... where...

He massages the headache his brilliant scheme has occasioned.

INT. BORDELLO - BACK ROOM - DAY

Simon lifts up a SWADDLED BABY, purple, newborn, squealing. Inara and River look on. Petaline is near delirious from childbirth.

SIMON
It's —

RIVER
It's a boy. Healthy.

A DOOR behind Inara opens, and Burgess is there, laser covering them.

BURGESS
Mornin', Petaline...

INT. BORDELLO - LOBBY - CONTINUING

Nandi hears PETALINE'S SCREAM first:

PETALINE
Rance! NO!

Mal is caught in the ebbing FIREFIGHT, but Nandi races down the stairs, toward the rear hall.

INT. BORDELLO - REAR HALL - CONTINUING

Burgess backs out of the back room, where Petaline screams. He's got the BABY in one arm, laser pistol in the other. Nandi appears behind him, entering from the lobby, confronts him.

NANDI
Most of your men are dead, dyin', or run off, Rance.

BURGESS
Don't matter none. Got what I came here for.

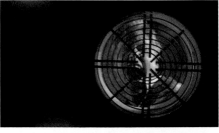

NANDI
Ain't leaving here with it.

BURGESS
This is my blood, woman.

Burgess gestures toward the baby with his pistol.

Suddenly a slim arm snakes a nasty curved RAZOR in under Burgess's chin from behind, digging its tip into the side of his throat, DRAWING BLOOD. It's Inara, accompanied by two ND whores, as cold dead serious as we've seen her.

INARA
(re: blood dripping down his neck)
No. This is your blood.
(nods to a whore)
Now you give over that child nice and slow, or I'll spill more than you can spare.

Burgess complies, wincing at the wound, handing the baby over to a whore, who backs out of the scene to safety.

As this happens, Burgess takes the pause to ELBOW Inara hard in the stomach. As she staggers back, he FIRES his laser from the hip, searing straight through Nandi's chest.

Mal gets to the lobby end of the hall, just as she drops, dead.

END OF ACT THREE

ACT FOUR

INT. BORDELLO - REAR HALL - DAY

The WHORES shout in alarm. They can't believe Nandi has fallen. Even Burgess seems surprised at what he's done. Mal moves to the fallen Nandi — as Burgess turns and runs for a side door, escaping.

Mal touches Nandi. She's stone dead. He shares a look with Inara, there's murder in both their eyes. He hears the O.S. THRUM of the hovercraft

❖ Below: Inara's knife.

starting up and turns for the front door.

EXT. BORDELLO - CONTINUOUS

ANGLE ON FRONT DOOR

The front door slams open and Mal stalks out, eyes forward.

Without dropping a beat, Mal PLUGS a horseman off his horse, and swings up into the saddle just as the man finishes falling.

Burgess's hovercraft rumbles out from behind the house, heading out for the plains.

Mal spurs the horse hard, and it tears off —

MAL
Hyah!

EXT. OPEN LAND - DAY

A WIDE LANDSCAPE SHOT of Burgess speeding away in his hovercraft and Mal in pursuit, his horse kicking up dust as he whips and spurs it into a breakneck gallop.

Burgess sees Mal behind him and stands in his craft, steering with one hand as he turns back. He FIRES his laser —

The LASER BEAM cuts the air by Mal's head. Mal whips a burst of speed out of his horse as another BEAM sears past him.

Mal is closing in on the hovercraft, an easy shot. Burgess takes careful aim, and pulls his trigger. We hear a RAPID BEEPING. Burgess checks the display screen on his gun —

LASER GUN

The LCD screen flashes "CHECK BATTERY".

Burgess GROWLS, looking up just as Mal flies from his horse, tackling Burgess off the hovercraft.

They slam into a hard roll on the plain as the hovercraft drifts off aimlessly in the BG.

Burgess has had the wind smashed out of him and writhes on the ground. Mal ain't much better, but drags himself to his feet using sheer force of will.

He grabs Burgess's shirtfront and hauls him up, pulling his pistol from his holster, bringing its barrel up to Burgess's head.

MAL
You're gonna pay for what you took.

BURGESS
(still out of breath)
She was a whore.

Mal seethes with vengeful fury, he's about to pull the trigger, but then — he flips the gun in his hand and smashes the butt across Burgess's face. Burgess collapses, unconscious.

❖ Above: Burgess's laser pistol battery read-out.

MAL
That don't enter into it.

CUT TO:

EXT. BORDELLO - DAY

Mal and Zoe watch as Inara finishes tying the kneeling Burgess's hands behind his back.

THREE MEN CRASH INTO FRAME, as Jayne dumps the bruised and bloodied Serenity-crashers before the bordello steps, Kaylee and Wash close by. Burgess's other men are also tied up.

BURGESS
(calling out)
PETALINE! YOU BRING MY BOY OUT, RIGHT NOW! YOU HEAR ME? I WANT TO SEE MY SON!

Petaline appears at the bordello door, the baby nursing at her breast. All eyes watch as she descends the steps and approaches Burgess.

PETALINE
Rance... this is Jonah.

(beat)
Jonah, say hello to your daddy.

BURGESS

smiles like a proud papa. He's actually moved at the sight of his son.

Petaline raises her free hand in which she holds Nandi's favorite gun. She aims it at Burgess's head.

PETALINE (cont'd)
Say goodbye to your daddy, Jonah.

Burgess blanches.

CLOSE PETALINE: Camera looking up the business end of the gun, she fires.

Petaline looks up from Burgess's dead body, icy —

PETALINE (cont'd)
Anyone else wanna try and take what's mine?

She scans the rows of Burgess's bound men; every last one avoids eye contact.

PETALINE (cont'd)
Go on, then. Go home. Next time I see any of you... you best be coming to get your wick wet. You pay up front from now on... and for god's sake, tip a girl once in a while — especially you, Milo.

Milo nods quickly: whatever you say, Petaline. The men start rising to their feet. Petaline indicates Chari —

PETALINE (cont'd)
You go with 'em. You got no place here.

Chari is about to speak, before she can:

PETALINE (cont'd)
You let 'em in the back door, Inara seen it, now go.

CHARI
You can't just make me —

CLICK. Petaline cocks the hammer of her pistol. Chari shuts up, breaks eye contact, falls in step with Burgess's men as they walk away.

Mal approaches Petaline, indicates Burgess's body —

MAL
We'll dispose of that for you.

PETALINE
Thank you, Captain.
(beat)
Emma?

Emma (Book's churchy whore) appears at Petaline's side.

PETALINE (cont'd)
Get the spade from the shed.
(beat)
Our Nandi's gonna be buried proper.

HIGH ANGLE

As the crowd disperses, we HOLD for a long moment and PRELAP:

LUCY (V.O.)
(singing)
Amazing Grace, how sweet the sound...

EXT. HILLTOP - DAY

LONG SHOT: A score of mourners have gathered around a makeshift cross beneath a large oak. This is a fusion of BUDDHIST and CHRISTIAN ceremony. A number of mourners are dressed in

white robes, with Tibetan prayer beads draped over their clasped hands.

Lucy sings in a simple, quiet voice. (Think Margo Timmins.)

LUCY
That saved a wretch like me/ I once was lost, but now am found/ Was blind but now I see...

Lucy continues to sing. One by one, Nandi's staff step up to the wooden cross marking her grave. At its foot is a low Asian-looking table, on which sits a bowl of smoking incense. They bow as they drop pinches of incense into the bowl.

SIMON AND RIVER

Alongside a couple of the girls, their faces a solemn mask.

LUCY
'Twas Grace that taught my heart to fear...

ZOE, WASH AND JAYNE

Zoe and Wash hold hands. Jayne looks at his feet.

LUCY
And Grace my fears relieved/ How precious did that Grace appear...

BOOK

holds the bible to his chest, a tearful Emma with her hands wrapped around his arm.

LUCY
The hour I first believed...

PETALINE

Baby in her arms, the stolid look of one who's been to war on her face.

LUCY
Through many dangers, toils and snares/ We have already come...

INARA

steps up to the small table, dressed in a white shawl, beads draped, and drops a pinch of incense into the bowl. She bows to it and turns away.

MAL

His arm paternally around Kaylee's shoulder, comforting, as tears roll down her face.

Inara takes in the entire gathering now: the unit that is Serenity's crew standing side by side with the bordello gals. She stands slightly apart from all of them.

LUCY
T'was Grace that brought us safe thus far...

Lucy's singing continues as we —

CUT TO:

MORENA BACCARIN

I love the scene in 'Heart of Gold' where I tell him I'm leaving. It is the first genuine moment between them when they're *honest* with one another, because she is going to go. When I first read it, I remember running to Joss going, 'What is this scene — I'm leaving the show?' but he said, 'Don't worry.' I think, had we gone on, they were planning to do something where they would show me in the Companion training house, like they did in the movie.

EXT. SPACE

Serenity exits atmo and glides silently into the black.

LUCY (V.O.)
And Grace will lead us home...

INT. SERENITY - CARGO BAY - NIGHT

Mal and Inara stand on the catwalk outside her shuttle. They are contemplative, subdued.

MAL
I think those girls'll do all right.

INARA
She taught them well.

MAL
Yeah.

A beat.

INARA
I'm... I'm glad that you were with her. Her last night. I am.

MAL
I ain't. Hell, I wish I'd never met her. Then I wouldn't've failed her.

INARA
That wasn't the way of it.

MAL
It's a kindness, but nothing you say'll convince me different.

INARA
Well, I'm still glad.

A small beat.

MAL
So you weren't before?

He's looking at her direct. She looks away.

MAL (cont'd)
Inara, I ain't looking for anything from you. I'm just feeling kind of truthsome right now. Life is too damn short for ifs and maybes.

INARA
I learned something from Nandi. Not just from what happened, but from her. The family she made, the strength of her love for them. That's what kept them together. When you live with that kind of strength, you get tied to it, you can't break away. And you never want to.

They're getting closer to each other, Mal's eyes locked on hers.

INARA (cont'd)
There's something that I... that I should have done a long while ago. And I'm sorry — for both of us — that it took me this long.

A beat.

INARA (cont'd)
I'm leaving.

Another moment, and she goes past him into her shuttle.

He doesn't move.

END OF SHOW

VISUAL EFFECTS

An interview with Loni Peristere

From the beginning, Joss Whedon had a unique vision for how he wanted to portray space in *Firefly*. He wanted it to be a character, as alive and complex as Mal and as ephemeral and daunting as River — it was to be an equal with the cast, enfolding Serenity into its limitless, black embrace. Finding a visual effects team to 'get' that vision would seem difficult in theory, but Whedon just turned to the team that he'd already been working with for six years, Loni Peristere and Zoic Studios, to get it absolutely right.

Peristere was brought onto the project even before a script had been written, and he vividly recalls how Joss pitched him this new series. "It was just before Christmas time, several months before we were to go to pilot. He said, 'After the break, I am going to start working on this pilot and I think you are going to like it. It's set in the future, but it's centered around characters out of our past and the present. It takes place on a spaceship and I think that might interest you.'" Detailing the concept, Loni remembers Joss said, "'I really want to do something different with space. I want to get away from placid, calm imagery and I want to use space as a character, and the ship as a character. I need to feel the camera is always important in the story, when we are inside the ship *and* outside the ship. With that in mind, think about 3D in a different way. When you are designing the sequences for my show, I really want

❖ Right from top to bottom and below: Scenes from 'The Message'.

❖ Opposite page left: A scene from 'The Train Job'.

❖ Opposite page right: The green screen before and after shots of Mal and the Torturer during 'War Stories'.

❖ Opposite page bottom: Serenity arrives in Ariel City.

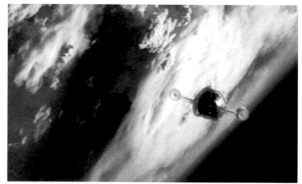

you to think about the photography as if you were trying to find the story with me, on the outside in space, the same as if you were on the inside with the characters.'"

With that concept driving him, Peristere says he threw himself into finding the look of the show's effects shots, which was to be a revolutionary departure from the sedate, measured style of the past. "I started taking a look at voyeuristic ways of looking at exteriors and objects in motion. I started watching things like NASCAR and air shows, documentaries about science and space exploration, anything where

there wasn't a plan for photography. I decided that that was going to be my approach to pitch to Joss. So instead of having cameras in these magical places that just happen to be there to catch the spaceship, I thought we should have rules. The main rule should be: if you are photographing a spaceship, you should know where you are shooting it *from*. If you are the 'camera spaceship', you can be just like a helicopter, you can fly around the ship and there must be an operator that tries to keep the ship in frame, if that is important. So there is always a camera operator in space, and there is always a placement for a camera on the ship, with options that would mirror options you would have using aerial photography in real life.

"So I made a compilation for Joss where I literally took every single space scene I could think of from

movies and TV series, put them all on one DVD and called it 'Firefly Research'," Peristere continues. "We sat down and watched it and Joss said, 'You had so many cool things on there and some things I hadn't seen in a long time — but that's not what the show is about,'" he laughs. Then Peristere showed him some documentary footage, with its whip pans and crash zooms, as an example of the style he was aiming for. "Joss just said, 'I have no idea what you just showed me, but I'm sure it will look good!'" And with that, Whedon entrusted Loni and his team with the task of making his ideas translate to the screen.

"I did illustrations, storyboards or animatics so Joss got a better idea of what I was talking about," Peristere remembers of the initial stages. Whedon was soon giving him a lot of latitude when it came to ideas for shots. "We'd had such a great partnership for such a long, long time, but I had always wanted to participate more. He knew I was hungry, and with *Firefly* he was happy to give me this fun gift to design some really cool sequences. He gave me the keys to the car, and I was very excited to have that opportunity. Joss would really challenge us every episode to do something that seemed impossible. When I got the script, he would write things like, 'a great space battle ensues', which was very curt; and then sometimes put, 'Loni will think of something cool here.' In every instance, he would write it knowing there would be a solution that we would have to come up with to make that show work, and that's what we expected. He knew he should always be pushing us, or it wouldn't be fun."

Peristere says the Reaver chase scene in the pilot was the key moment when he knew he had achieved the right look for *Firefly*. "When I got the script, I immediately ran rampant with our shot designer Neil Smith and we put together the animatics of the Reaver chase sequence. I showed the sequence to Joss, Lisa Lassek, David Solomon and David Greenwalt and they all said, 'That's awesome!' It was a great feeling, because it let us know that we were on the right track. Solomon even said, 'You are going to win an Emmy!' and he was right!" Zoic Studios won a richly deserved Outstanding Special Visual Effects Emmy in 2003 for *Firefly*, which forever sealed the series' place in television effects history. ◁

❖ Above: Serenity takes off towards the end of 'Heart of Gold'.

❖ Opposite page top: Serenity in space.

❖ Opposite page middle: The Ariel City junk yard.

❖ Below: A sequence from the Reaver chase during 'Serenity'.

OBJECTS IN SPACE

Written & Directed by Joss Whedon

JOSS WHEDON

"The most difficult villain for me in *Firefly* was Jubal, and the most rewarding. That whole thing was the best experience I could ever have had. I had been trying to break the story, and it was about River, and her powers discovered, and, oh, the not-very-interesting stories we were going back and forth on. I called Tim in desperation and he said, 'Well, can't you just have Bobba Fett?' [Minear mispronounced Boba Fett, of *Star Wars* fame.] And I said, 'Who's Bobba Fett, first of all? And you call yourself a nerd? And second of all, thanks. Bye.' Because it just clicked. And when I got to 'Objects in Space', I had the idea of this character, and I had the idea of River and what I had to do. I said, 'This will write itself. Like 'Our Mrs. Reynolds' did. I'll just be sitting here waiting for it to write itself. Any minute now, it will start to write.' And then I realized that I was in... Hell [laughs]. I had a couple of things that helped me. One of them was *The Minus Man*, which is a movie that I think has an extraordinary portrait of a serial killer, just the main character's comical observations. The other was — and this has worked for me on all my shows when things are hard — walking the set. I went one weekend, just walking the set and doing everything that River did and everything that Jubal did, climbing up on the ladder, standing on the railing. The physicality of the thing clued me into his *perception* of the physicality of the thing and ultimately what the episode was going to be about: the ecstasy of being, the idea of imprinting meaning on objects and that two people who really step out of the norm are very similar, but because what they bring emotionally is completely opposite, they ultimately are very different. That came from physically being there in the space, and once it unveiled itself, it was an extraordinary experience — but it was a long time coming."

Did Whedon expect the audience to respond to 'Objects' on an existential level? "Well," he replies, "ultimately, you try to reach people on the level of, 'Ooh, this is entertaining, this guy's a badass — ooh, he's menacing Kaylee, oh, he's got a cool outfit and wait a minute, *is* River the ship?' Because it's science-fiction — we don't *really* know the parameters — we found out she's psychic and that's weird. Is it possible that she's the ship. It was, 'Let's have as much fun as possible, and let's bring the team together as a family.' Beyond that, the meaning that it had was extremely important for *me*, and I know it was extremely important for a lot of the people who watched it, but I am sure there are equal if not greater numbers of people who just said, 'Ah, it was a fun one.' If people come out feeling that you've written an essay, then you have made bad TV. I do these things because there's something I want to say or feel and I make sure that not only is the show entertaining, but that what is entertaining about it is wrapped up in whatever it is I'm trying to say."

TEASER

EXT. SPACE - NIGHT

Not just 'cause it's dark in space, but because it's evening cycle for those in Serenity, which happens to glide into frame. We are above and behind it, and we glide with it a bit, keeping pace.

CLOSE ON: the top of Serenity as the camera goes THROUGH it, into the labyrinth of wires and pipe and spaceship innards, moving about rabbit-fast, twisting and turning, ending up looking down through a grating at:

INT. RIVER'S ROOM - EVENING

RIVER, sleeping.

Cut to EXTREME CLOSE UP on River's closed eyes. There is talk, chatter from every shipmember, like static in her head, rising slowly. The noise builds until —

A MAN'S VOICE
We're all just floating...

Her eyes snap open. That voice could've been in the room with her.

She rises, sits on her bed. She wears a dress, no shoes, seems to be in a slightly dreamlike state. (No huge change there, but we may do something with the lens occasionally to accentuate that.) Laughter pulls her from her room.

INT. PASSENGER DORM - CONTINUING

She moves slowly, finds KAYLEE and SIMON on the couch. Kaylee is lying with her legs (her feet are also bare) over the sitting Simon, innocently intimate. Laughing.

KAYLEE
You couldn't possibly have!

SIMON
I wish I was lying. I just — we'd all just made surgeon, that was it. We were the elite, the world was ours, you know —

KAYLEE
So you had to be naked.

SIMON
Naked, yes, and on top of the statue of Hypocrates, and — Can you just picture me?

KAYLEE
Naked? I'll have to conjure up — it'll be tough.

He smiles at her, and she taps his chin with her toes playfully.

KAYLEE (cont'd)
So the feds came?

SIMON
There were no feds. Until I started singing.

KAYLEE
(laughing)
Oh no! What'd you sing?

SIMON
This is not funny. This is a morality tale about the evils of sake.

River has been watching them the whole time. They suddenly turn to her, the laughter draining from their faces.

SIMON (cont'd)
(to River)
I would be there right now.

There is coldness in his voice, and Kaylee looks at her with an expression that matches.

And then, oddly, there's a JUMP CUT to the two of them laughing again, as though that moment never happened.

River looks mildly confused, then starts up the stairs.

SIMON (cont'd)
It was either that or the national anthem. Reports vary.

KAYLEE
Do you remember any of it?

SIMON
I remember talking them out of telling my father... or paying them out of telling my father. I'm fuzzy on aspects...

INT. AFT HALL/DINING ROOM - CONTINUING

River comes into the hallway, touching the walls as she goes, looking at her hands. She finds BOOK and JAYNE, also in mid-conversation. Jayne is cooking scallion cakes on the griddle. Book is at the table.

JAYNE
So, like... never?

BOOK
Well, no.

JAYNE
Not ever never?

BOOK
Some orders allow Shepherds to marry, but I follow a narrower path.

JAYNE
But, I mean, you still got the urge, right? They don't cut it off or nothing...

BOOK
(smiles)
No, I'm more or less intact. I just direct my energy elsewhere.

JAYNE
You mean like masterbatin'?

BOOK
I hope you're not thinking of taking orders yourself...

JAYNE
That'll be the day.

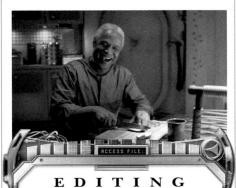

EDITING

Film editor/associate producer Lisa Lassek: "Joss and I often talked about getting inside River's head. In 'Objects in Space', the entire opening of the show is from her perspective. We gently increased that feeling, so at the beginning you're in reality just watching Simon and Kaylee talk, so that when it jumps into what River's perceiving, and then jumps back out, you're surprised. As she moves through the ship, it gets more and more surreal and we get more and more into her head. We did the same thing with the sound design. It started out normal and then we got progressively more into her space. One of the most tantalizing clues about Book's background is in what he says, because it seems to come out of left field, something like, 'I don't care if you're innocent or not.' We get a clip of what he's thinking; we've never seen Book be so aggressive and scary. This is a perfect example of something laid almost in the background that, if you watch the entire series and then the movie, ends up becoming really meaningful."

During all this, River wanders unnoticed right between the two of them. She turns to look at Jayne, who looks back guiltily.

JAYNE (cont'd)
I got stupid. The money was too good.

She turns, looks at Book, who is in her face, fiercely angry.

BOOK
I don't give half a hump if you're innocent or not! So where does that put you?

JUMP CUT back to reality — the men are laughing, Book still sitting, and River has walked between them unnoticed. She heads to the foredeck hall as the men continue:

JAYNE
It ain't impossible! Saint Jayne, it's got a ring to it.

BOOK
I'm just trying to remember how many miracles you've performed.

JAYNE
I once hit a guy in the neck at five hundred yards with a bent scope, don't that count upstairs?

BOOK
Oh, it'll be taken into consideration...

JAYNE
Well, you make that sound kinda ominous...

INT. FOREDECK HALL/BRIDGE - CONTINUING

River moves into the foredeck hall, is about to turn right when she sees WASH and ZOE on the bridge. The door is half shut and they are a ways away, but she is suddenly awash in their energy.

Which is different than anyone else's, seeing as how Zoe is sitting on Wash's lap, facing him, smooching him. Their clothes are on (it's the bridge, already), but though they are playful, their energy is intense, their eyes locked.

We see them as River feels them, VERY CLOSE up, wide angle lens roving around them, sweat and smiles and the sound of the ocean, waves breaking as River nearly staggers back with it, suddenly perturbed to be in that intimacy.

She moves away, hugging the wall, down into:

INT. CARGO BAY/INARA'S SHUTTLE - CONTINUING

And now she's coming down the steps as MAL and INARA are in quiet conference at the entrance to her shuttle.

INARA
I've put out a few waves to some old acquaintances — I may even be able to find something in New Melbourne, if you need the shuttle free.

MAL
Only thing you're gonna find in New Melbourne is fish and fish related activities. Unless you got

an overwhelming urge to gut sturgeon — and who hasn't, occasionally —

INARA
But it's a layover point for almost every planet this side of the system, and I could... I just don't want to draw this out.

MAL
You decided when you're gonna tell the others?

INARA
I... no. I appreciate your not saying anything.

MAL
I don't. So make up your mind.

River stops near the entrance. Inara looks at her, says:

INARA
I'm a big girl. Just tell me.

Pan over to Mal, who is looking away from us.

MAL
None of it means a damn thing.

That ocean noise again, and River looks pained,

nothing is as it should be here. She stumbles down the steps in a jumbled series of jump-cuts...

She walks along the floor of the cargo bay, steps on something.

ANGLE: HER FOOT

steps on a branch. She gingerly steps off it, then bends over to look at it, her head coming into frame, staring.

ANGLE: FROM HIGH ABOVE we see the entire cargo bay floor around her is littered with branches and leaves.

She picks up the branch. It's smallish, curved to fit well in her hand.

She studies it, uncertain.

RIVER
Just an object.
(looks up)
It doesn't mean what you think...

She smiles comfortingly —

Jump-cut to reality — Simon and Kaylee are standing in front of her, yelling — Mal yelling as well from above...

SIMON
River you know that's not to be touched!

KAYLEE
Everybody just be real calm already —

MAL
Get it away from her —

SIMON
Just put it down!

River looks confused at the sudden cacophony. Looks down at her hand — and there is a BIG DAMN GUN in it. Pointed at Simon and Kaylee, the latter of whom looks shit-scared.

River lowers the gun, looking grouchily confused, as Simon comes to take it from her. She looks

over at Kaylee, who fades out to the passenger dorm, unable to deal.

RIVER
Kaylee...?

SIMON
What were you thinking? Where did you get ahold of this?

Mal is down with them by now, takes the gun from Simon, checks it.

RIVER
It was in my hand...

MAL
Fully loaded, safety off. This here's a recipe for unpleasantness, does she understand that?

She turns to him.

RIVER
She understands. She doesn't comprehend.

MAL
Well, I'm glad we've made that distinction. No touching guns, okay?

RIVER
No touching.

She moves off, quickly.

SIMON
River —

RIVER
It's getting very very crowded!

And she's out. Mal looks at Simon.

MAL
Thought she was on the mend.

SIMON
The medications are erratic: there's not one that her system can't eventually break down, and you have to recalibrate —

MAL
I want a lot of medical jargon thrown at me, I'll talk to a doctor.

SIMON
You are talking to a doctor.

MAL
Yeah, okay — point is, coulda been you she mighta shot just then. The doctor, as you just made note of. And who exactly could fix you? Not nobody. We're still in deep space, Doctor, corner of No and Where. You take extra care with her. 'Cause we're very much alone out here.

EXT. SPACE - CONTINUING

Serenity continues on, as the camera comes around to see that there is another, smaller vessel RIGHT behind and above it. Sleek, quiet.

They're not so much alone out here.

END OF TEASER

ACT ONE

EXT. SPACE - CONTINUING

We move in on the smaller craft as it hugs Serenity's wake. Move in closer to see the windshield, and a single figure inside the cockpit. (It's way too small to be called a bridge — if Serenity is a family van, this is a Harley.)

INT. EARLY'S SHIP - CONTINUING

He's called EARLY, and for the next while, he will say not a word. He merely goes about his business with quiet, intense efficiency. His business is hunting.

He watches the ship below him as readouts come over the windshield "screen". Among them:

— Serenity heat-scanned with infrared, showing a

small model of the ship with heat signatures indicating where everyone is.

— A blueprint of Serenity that shows her layout, names the rooms, shows points of egress, lists components and operating systems.

— A graph of two lines coming together that then flashes: TRAJECTORY SYNC COMPLETE. LOCKED ONTO FLIGHT PATH.

While he works the controls beneath these readouts, the camera pans over to see a picture stuck to the hull near his head. A picture of River — the one the Blue Hands sported in 'The Train Job'. Around it are a warrant showing River with the legend, FUGITIVE, and at the bottom, REWARD 200,000 CREDITS, Alliance Bond Standard. WANTED ALIVE.

There's also a picture of River and Simon, and a beat up picture of an older black woman with a dog on a lawn.

Early takes the first picture of River off the wall, stares at it a moment, returns it. Then slips out of his seat.

INT. BRIDGE - EVENING

Wash is at the helm, Zoe beside him. He's talking, but also concentrating on his readouts.

WASH
Little River just gets more colorful by the moment. What will she do next?

ZOE
Either blow us all up or rub soup in her hair, it's a toss up.

WASH
I hope she does the soup thing. It's always a hoot and we don't all die from it.

ZOE
That poor kid...

WASH
(looking at screen)
Yeah, she's definitely... got... funny.

ZOE
Something wrong?

WASH
I'm just getting a weird heat bounce off our wake.

ZOE
Engine flux?

WASH
Sensor probably got turned around. I'll climb up top when we hit land.

Over this last exchange, Jayne and Mal enter, talking.

MAL
The lockers were sealed. We both know —

JAYNE
I don't leave my guns around, Mal. And I don't leave 'em loaded.

MAL
Well, somehow she got her hands on your hardware. Suppose she took up something with hull-piercing bullets?

JAYNE
Bullets is soft lead, Mal. Even Vera could barely breach hull and she's the best I got! Anyhow, let's direct this conversation in a not-Jayne's-fault direction. I didn't make her crazy. Hell, I didn't want her on the damn ship.

MAL
(in his face, quiet)
Is that the direction you want this conversation to go in?

Jayne looks guilty, covers...

JAYNE
I just don't like taking a lashing for what I ain't the cause of.

ZOE
Where's River at now?

MAL
In her room, which I'm thinking we bolt from the outside from now on.

WASH
That's a little extreme, isn't it?

JAYNE
Anybody remember her coming at me with a butcher's knife?

WASH
(remembering fondly)
Wacky fun...

JAYNE
You wanna go, little man?

WASH
Only if it's someplace with candlelight.

ZOE
Sir, I know she's unpredictable, but I don't think she'd harm anyone.

JAYNE
("Hellooo...")
Butcher's knife...

ZOE
Anyone we can't spare. I mean, far as we know, the girl's never even picked up a gun before.

KAYLEE
That ain't so.

She's standing in the doorway; looking upset. They give her their attention.

MAL
Kaylee, you got something to say?

She looks at him, not sure where to start.

EXT. SPACE - LATER

We are close on Early's ship, near the bottom as a door slides open and he glides out. Pushes a few keys as it shuts, then looking down, steadies himself a moment —

And pushes off, floating down toward Serenity. We pull out wide to show the three objects: the big ship, the smaller ship, and the tiny man floating rapidly from one to the other.

Close on the top of Serenity as he hits the top, landing gently as possible. He walks, slowly and deliberately, pulling his feet up with the slight effort of disconnecting magnets. Walks to the window. Very slowly, looks in.

INT. DINING ROOM - CONTINUING

We see his head — briefly — by the fore window, looking in at the group that contains everyone save River.

KAYLEE
It was when... when the Captain and Wash got took by Niska.

MAL
Ain't like to forget that any time soon.

KAYLEE
Well, we all went in, me too... Didn't make much account of myself, I'm afraid.

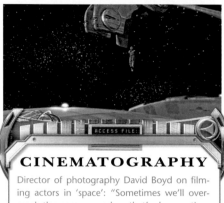

CINEMATOGRAPHY

Director of photography David Boyd on filming actors in 'space': "Sometimes we'll over-crank the camera, and so that's slow-motion; sometimes the actors, in conjunction with that, can move a little slower, a little more controlled. We also had the shots in wide of the character arriving onto the outer shell of the ship, and that's just done with wires; the speed of that and the way that it is done physically sells the fact that there's weightlessness out there. To have that going on as part of the work day is just plain fun, because all of those things have to come together in a perfect way for it to be believable."

MAL
(touches her head)
I got no problem with the notion of you not killin' nobody, Kaylee. Take it as my own fault that you were put in such a spot.

SIMON
What's this got to do with River? She wasn't even in that fight.

KAYLEE
Well, no, she was. I got pinned down, there was three guys and I couldn't... and then River comes up and she looks out, sees 'em all. They was spread out, you know, had some cover, but she just looked for a second and... She took my gun. Closed her eyes. Killed 'em.

SIMON
She shot them?

KAYLEE
All three dead in an instant. With her eyes still closed.

JAYNE
Well that's <FAY-FAY duh PEE-yen.> [a baboon's ass-crack.] You saw it wrong.

KAYLEE
Not a jot. And it weren't autofire, or luck... She just... She just did the math.

ZOE
You understand how that sounds...

JAYNE
What? She killed them with mathematics. What else could it have been.

KAYLEE
You couldn't've done it, Jayne. Nor you, Captain; not nobody can shoot like that that's a person.

SIMON
So River's not a person?

As they continue, the camera moves suddenly down to the floor, THROUGH the floor, pipes and wires visible, to the ceiling of:

INT. CARGO BAY - CONTINUING

Where River is standing directly below them, feet on the railings of the catwalk, ear as close to the ceiling as she can get, hearing every word. Or sensing them.

KAYLEE (O.S.)
Please don't be mad...

SIMON (O.S.)
I just want to understand what you're saying here. I thought River was your friend.

INT. DINING ROOM - CONTINUING

KAYLEE
She is. But Simon... the way she... right after, she looked at me and smiled, like nothing was wrong. Like we were playing.
(to the group)
Scared me.

There's a moment, as the group takes this in.

BOOK
Could be she saved your life, Kaylee.

KAYLEE
I'm all aware of that, I'm not trying to —

SIMON
She probably didn't even know what was going on! Thought it was a game.

JAYNE
Later on you can explain to me how that's a comfort. Might have to use some'a that math we been hearing about...

MAL
(running over Jayne)
What we got here to deal with is the larger issue. And the larger issue is we got someone on board this ship might be a danger to us.

Now the camera moves UP, again through pipes and wires, through the hull, to:

EXT. TOP OF SERENITY - CONTINUING

Where Early kneels, holding a listening device to the hull. The voices are coming through, somewhat static-y.

MAL (O.S.)
It's not a question of whether we like her... some of us have grown attached...

INT. DINING ROOM - CONTINUING

MAL
Kaylee, I know you have or you'd've spoken up sooner, which by the by you should have. I find River pleasant enough myself. But she's got an oddness to her, and it ain't just her proficiency with fire-arms. Girl knows things she shouldn't. Things she couldn't.

JAYNE
Are you saying she's a witch?

WASH
Yes, she's a witch, Jayne. She has had congress with the beast.

JAYNE
She's in congress?

WASH
How did your brain master human speech? I'm just so curious.

INARA
<BEE-jway, neen hen BOO-TEE-TYEH duh NAN-shung!> [Shut up, you inconsiderate schoolboys!] This isn't a joking matter. This is about your — about our lives. And River's.

MAL
Thank you.

SIMON
She's deeply intuitive, it's true she has a —

MAL
I don't think she's just intuitive, Doctor. I think she's a reader.

ZOE
Psychic?

WASH
Is that even remotely possible?

MAL
(to Simon)
You tell me. You been studying what they did to her.

SIMON
They've definitely altered the way she reacts to things, even the way she perceives... but I'm not...

WASH
Psychic, though? That sounds like something out of science fiction!

ZOE
You live in a spaceship, dear.

WASH
So?

JAYNE
(suddenly more uncomfy)
Back up a sec. You're saying she might really read minds?

MAL
Or near enough. Am I the only one thinking along those lines?

BOOK
No.

JAYNE
I don't like the idea of someone hearing what I'm thinking.

INARA
No one likes the idea of hearing what you're thinking.

BOOK
The Alliance could have any number of uses for a psychic. Any government would.

ZOE
A psychic or an assassin...

SIMON
She's just a kid.

His voice is quiet, but it stops them.

SIMON (cont'd)
She just wants to be... a kid.

MAL
I wish it were that simple.

JAYNE
Yeah, and if wishes were horses we'd all be eatin' steak. What do we plan to do about this?

MAL
Well, that's the question.

SIMON
I don't think she'd ever hurt any of us.

MAL
Maybe you're right.

He looks around, at all of them.

MAL (cont'd)
Well, I ain't making a decision on anything til I've thought on it awhile. It's late.

Looking at Inara:

MAL (cont'd)
We hit New Melbourne in three days time. We'll see who... We'll think of what to do by then. Let's get some rest.

Simon turns and goes quickly out the back. Kaylee follows.

INT. AFT HALL - CONTINUING

He is rounding the corner as she stops him.

KAYLEE
Simon —

SIMON
I gotta go check on my assassin.

KAYLEE
Simon please don't be mad at me. I had to say something.

He turns to her.

SIMON
I'm not mad at you. I just... She loves this ship. I think it's more home to her than any place she's been.

KAYLEE
What about you?

SIMON
I'm... I thought the hospital was home. I was really making a difference there... and embarrassingly large stacks of money, and I could've... I would be there now if she hadn't... if they had just left her alone.

KAYLEE
Is it so bad here?

SIMON
I don't even know if the Captain'll let us —

RIVER

"Also, I can kill you with my brain."

Of all the actors on *Firefly*, Summer Glau was the only one without any previous acting experience. With wide-eyed wonder and sheer terror, Glau admits the early days of the series were an intense learning curve for her. "I was very, very nervous. The first table read where we worked as a group, I didn't know what a table read was! I barely knew how to follow the script. They send you rewrites all the time and you have to put them into your original script and I didn't know how to do it!"

Part of her comfort with the role and her new vocation came from her rapport with Whedon. Taking the actress under his wing, Glau admits he helped push her creatively to trust her instincts and her talent. "Joss was so good at coaching me and getting a performance out of me," she smiles. "I need a lot of reassurance. I'm the kind of actress that comes on set every day thinking, 'What am I doing here? I have no business being here.' Joss is so good at bringing out the best in me. He never would give a lot of direction before a scene. He wanted to see what I would do with it and then he would talk me through it, finding things that would inspire me or get me going in the right direction. I think that everyone would probably say about Joss, that he sees things in his head exactly how he wants them. He is such a strong leader. You go on set and things go so quickly because he is really good at getting us on the right track. Also, our chemistry as a cast and a team has been incredible from the beginning. We were just meant to be together. Everybody has such strong ideas about their characters and I think from the pilot everyone was bringing so much to the table."

Over the season, Glau says discovering River's history was incredible to portray. "Everything was shocking. Whenever we got a script, it would usually be late at night when we were working on another episode. It would be so hard to focus on finishing out the episode we were on because we were all dying to know what would happen to us in the next script! River was just shocking every week: I got to dance in 'Safe'; in 'War Stories' I ended up

shooting people; and in 'Objects in Space' I fly somebody else's ship. It was spectacular. I got to do so many things that I never dreamed I'd do in my life."

With only half a season produced, Glau says the cancellation of *Firefly* was a devastating reality check about Hollywood, but also an incredible introduction to the tenacity of Whedon's fanbase. "When we were doing it, we were in our own world. Afterwards, when we got canceled, I went home to Texas for Christmas. It was just gone and over, all of a sudden. My mom went online to look at the message boards and I thought, 'Nobody is going to be on them anymore.' But they were just flooded with people saying, 'We are going to save this show, we aren't going to let go, and we are going to petition and riot!' This is when I realized it's powerful to be part of Joss's universe. The things that he creates are so special and beloved. His fans are so dedicated and I couldn't believe how they kept us alive. I think they made our movie. Joss created miracles all along and it was a miracle that he wanted to stay behind us, because god knows he could have moved on ten times over. But our fans love him and what he creates so much and it's a really special thing to be part of."

Now years after cancellation, Glau is still in awe of the support of those fans and what they give to her personally. "I'm constantly touched by the fans and the things that they've gotten for us or written to us. I get a lot of mail from people who suffer from depression or have schizophrenia or some kind of other mental illness and River has brought them comfort. I think the show as a whole teaches you about family and loving things unconditionally and being part of a team. River fights so hard to contribute to her family. Simon always said, 'River loves this ship. She just wants to stay here and be a part of this.' If the series continued, you would have seen more of what you saw in the film, which was River defeating the demons and things that haunt her mind and being able to go back to the people that care about her — her new family on Serenity. I think that is why people love the story and want more of it. It's a story about love and loving something that doesn't make sense. Mal is always looking at River and asking himself why he is keeping this liability on board when she isn't part of his family or his crew, yet he can't walk away from her. I hope that's what people remember about our story and keep with them." ⊙

KAYLEE
No, but, isn't there anything about this place you're glad of?

He looks at her. Something passes between them, something that draws them closer —

BOOK
G'night, you two.

He passes right through the moment and blows it completely. Simon and Kaylee go back to being awkward.

SIMON
Uh, I —

KAYLEE
No, yeah —

SIMON
Good night.

KAYLEE
Don't let the space bugs... bite...

He goes. She looks after him, feeling like the queen of Lame-donia. A beat, and she heads into the engine room, muttering:

KAYLEE (cont'd)
Space bugs...?

INT. DINING ROOM - NIGHT

It's later, and the Captain sits alone. He thinks a moment, then exits, killing the lights.

INT. FOREDECK HALL - CONTINUING

He goes to his door and kicks it in, starts climbing down. The camera moves away from him to the exterior hatch Simon and River used in 'Bushwacked'.

It opens.

Early comes quietly down, looking about him. Pulls off his helmet. And pulls out his gun.

END OF ACT ONE

ACT TWO

INT. RIVER'S ROOM - NIGHT

River is lying in her bed. She senses something, pulls the covers over her head.

INT. FOREDECK HALL - CONTINUING

Early looks around the hall. No one around. He holsters his gun, moves back to the hatch, puts his helmet in there and seals it shut.

He comes back into the hall and bumps into MAL, who's headed back to the dining room. Mal is completely taken by surprise — and Early is a blur, a little bit ninja as he pops Mal in the throat to keep him from screaming, gets in close and punches a nerve cluster in Mal's back. Mal pushes

him off and swings, connects only glancingly —

INT. WASH AND ZOE'S ROOM - CONTINUING

Zoe stirs — is something going on upstairs?

INT. FOREDECK HALL - CONTINUING

Early slams his foot into Mal's face, slamming the back of his head into his own ladder, Mal starts to drop — and Early shoots forward, GRABS him by the shirt, keeping him from falling.

INT. WASH AND ZOE'S ROOM - CONTINUING

Zoe rolls over. Nothing.

INT. MAL'S ROOM - CONTINUING

Early lowers Mal gently into the room, letting him drop the last of the way, unconscious. Closes the door from above.

INT. FOREDECK HALL - CONTINUING

He goes to the com and locks the rooms from the outside — this involves punching buttons by the com and hitting some graphics, the legend PRIVATE QUARTERS LOCKED coming up and a little red light appearing over each door. Except Kaylee's. He comes to Kaylee's room and the door is open. He listens a moment — nothing — then looks down the length of the ship.

INT. ENGINE ROOM - LATER

Kaylee is lying on her back, working under the engine. She yawns, goes back to work — hears something.

She sits up, looks out into the dark of the hall. Maybe a little unnerved. It's dark in here, most of the light comes from the lamp she's working by, and the hall itself is pitch.

KAYLEE
River...?

She stands, looks. Nothing.

She turns back to the toolbox, squats down to toss in a part, comes back up and Early is RIGHT behind her. She spins to see his face staring impassively, inches from hers.

She gasps, stumbles back. She's up against the wall here.

EARLY
I like this ship.

She says nothing. Looks frantically around.

EARLY (cont'd)
Serenity. She's good-looking. I mean she looks good.

KAYLEE
How did you get on...?

EARLY
It strains the mind a bit, don't it? You think you're all alone... Maybe I come down the chimney, Kaylee, bring presents to the good girls and boys. Maybe not, though.

He comes closer to her. She shrinks closer to the wall.

EARLY (cont'd)
Maybe I've always been here.

KAYLEE
What do you want?

He looks at the turning engine, mesmerized.

EARLY
That's her beating heart, isn't it? You pull off any one of a thousand parts, she'll just die. Such a slender thread...
(still looking at the engine)
Have you ever been raped?

A small beat —

KAYLEE
The Captain's right by —

JEWEL STAITE

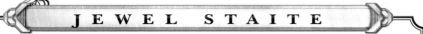

The scene where Early corners me in the engine room and basically threatens to rape me was probably one of the most emotional scenes in the whole series for me.

EARLY
The Captain's locked in his quarters. They all are. There's nobody can help you. Say it.

KAYLEE
There's... There's nobody can help me.

EARLY
I'm gonna tie you up now. And you know what I'm gonna do then?
(she can't answer)
I'm gonna give you a present. Get rid of a problem you've got. And I won't touch you in any wrong fashion, nor hurt you at all, unless you make some kind of ruckus. You throw a monkey wrench into my dealings in any way, your body is forfeit. Ain't nothing but a body to me, and I can find all unseemly manner of use for it. Do you understand?

KAYLEE
(tiny voice)
Yes.

EARLY
Turn around and put your hands behind your back.

She slowly does, terror on her face, as he pulls out a thin roll of tape. Pulls a strip out, says:

EARLY (cont'd)
Now tell me, Kaylee... Where does River sleep?

INT. PASSENGER DORM/SIMON AND RIVER'S ROOMS - NIGHT

Book exits the bathroom, in his sleepwear, towel over his shoulder, kit in hand. It's dark here as well, though there are safety lights enough to keep one from bumping into shit.

Book heads for his room, hears something at the top of the stairs. Turns back that way, looks up.

ANGLE: up the stairs — is complete blackness.

BOOK
Hello?

Nothing. He turns to go, hears another sound. Starts up the stairs, merely curious.

Early SLIDES down the handrails on both hands, shooting down at Book with both feet out, catching the Shepherd in the face at two steps up, sends him flying back as Early lands gracefully by him.

ANGLE: SIMON

wakes, hearing the thumps. There is silence after, but he's not satisfied. He climbs out of bed (he's just wearing drawstring pants) and opens his door, looking out at:

ANGLE: the hall where Book got slammed — is now empty. Simon looks around for a sec — then crosses to River's room to check on her. He slides the door open —

ANGLE: RIVER'S ROOM is empty.

SIMON
River...

He comes back into the hall, stands between the two bedrooms, not sure what to do... and the camera finds Early PERCHED on both ladders above him, almost spider-like.

Simon almost has time to look up as Early drops, lands straddling Simon's head, holding the ladders and swinging the Doctor up and SLAMMING him to the ground.

Simon's in pain, but Early comes over him and Simon GRABS him, throws him as he himself gets up, ready for a fight — but Early comes up with his weapon pointed at Simon.

EARLY
Doctor Tam, why don't you sit yourself down?

SIMON
Rather die standing.

EARLY
The intention is not for you to die. The warrant doesn't specify any particular need for you to be alive, but...

Early waves the gun. Backed into the curved corner of the hall, Simon sits on the steps. Early peers into the rooms.

EARLY (cont'd)
Where's your sister?

SIMON
Are you Alliance?

EARLY
(not understanding)
Am I a lion?

SIMON
What?

EARLY
I don't think of myself as a lion.
(smiles)
You may as well, though: I have a mighty roar.

SIMON
I said "Alliance".

EARLY
Oh. I thought —

SIMON
No, I was...

EARLY
That's weird.
(beat)
Where's your sister?

SIMON
I don't know. Who do you work for?

EARLY
This is her room.

SIMON
Yes.

EARLY
It's empty.

SIMON
I know.

EARLY
So is it still her room when it's empty? Does the room, the thing have purpose? Or are we... What's the word...

SIMON
I really can't help you.

EARLY
The plan is to take your sister, get the reward, which is substantial. "Imbue." That's the word.

SIMON
So you're a bounty hunter.

EARLY
That ain't it at all.

SIMON
Then what are you?

EARLY
I'm a bounty hunter.

SIMON
That's what I said.

EARLY
Yeah, but you didn't say it well. I'm named Early. I'm known to some — probably not your set, though. She sleep with anybody?

SIMON
River?

EARLY
Yeah, she grapple with any of the crew? Might be in their quarters?

SIMON
No!

EARLY
Maybe she does that you don't know about.

SIMON
This is insane. I'm not gonna help you find her in any case.

Early holds up his gun — not pointed at Simon, just observing it.

EARLY
I think this is very pretty. I like the weight of it.

SIMON
I thought the intention was not to kill me.

EARLY
You're missing the point. The design. Of the thing. It's functional. The plan is not to shoot you, the plan is to get the girl. If there's no girl, then the plan... well, it's like the room. You are gonna help me look for her.

SIMON
I don't think my last act in this 'verse is gonna be betraying my sister.

EARLY
You're gonna help me because every second you're with me is a chance to turn the tables, get the better of me, and it's the only chance your sister has. Maybe you'll find your moment. Maybe I'll slip. Or you'll refuse to help me, I'll shoot your brain out, and then I'll go upstairs and spend some time violating the little mechanic I got

trussed up in the engine room. I take no pleasure in the thought but she will die weeping if you cross me.

SIMON
(quietly)
You're out of your mind.

EARLY
That's between me and my mind. Let's start with these rooms.

ANGLE ON: BOOK, whose unconscious form is slumped in the other hallway. Simon (having grabbed a shirt) comes upon him quickly, checking to see he's not dead.

EARLY (cont'd)
He's not killed. Be a while before he comes to, but he'll mend.

SIMON
And which part of your plan dictated the necessity of beating up a Shepherd?

EARLY
That ain't a Shepherd.

Simon looks at Early, unsure if this is just more of his off-centerness. Early is looking down the hall.

EARLY (cont'd)
Open the rooms.

INT. INFIRMARY/PASSENGER DORM - A BIT LATER

The infirmary doors open. Simon steps in, Early behind, gun still held on the Doctor.

SIMON
She wouldn't come in here anyway. She hates this room. You see, Early, the people you're planning to sell her to cut up her brain in a lab like this. Tortured her. Teenage girl. Not some bandit on a murder run, just an innocent girl —

EARLY
You ever been shot?

A small beat.

SIMON
No.

EARLY
You oughta be shot, or stabbed, lose a leg... to be a surgeon. You know? Know the kind of pain you're dealing with.

What seemed like a threat becomes more like a distant observation — not that Simon is particularly comforted by this.

EARLY (cont'd)
They make psychiatrists get psychoanalyzed before they can get certified, but they don't make surgeons get cut on. That seem right to you?

Simon has no answer.

INT. CARGO BAY - MOMENTS LATER

The two of them enter the big, darkened bay. Early pulls out a small, powerful flashlight, shines it about. The locker with the spacesuits is near him, and the door is ajar. He moves to it — swings it open, gun at the ready. It's empty (except for a couple of spacesuits).

Early steps into the middle of the room, looks about at it.

SIMON
Come on out, River, the nice man wants to kidnap you...

EARLY
Shhh.

He looks at the walls, holds his arms out, moving them up parallel to the slanted walls.

EARLY (cont'd)
I like the way the walls go out. Gives you an open feeling. Firefly's a good design.

He motions with his gun for Simon to go upstairs. Heads up after.

EARLY (cont'd)
People don't appreciate the substance of things. Objects in space. People miss out on what's solid.

They reach the landing as he speaks, and he looks out over the room. Simon stands by him, unnoticed. He could just give a little shove —

And Early's gun is in his face, Early not even looking at him.

Richard Brooks
=EARLY=

MAMA

helmet from FX mouse

Back

front

Nov 12 Nov

ZIP front

silver

chin guards
New rock
MOD:
ROXANA
MICHAEL
Color:
ITALI NEGRO
Y ANTIC
ACERO

Hera

Boot
New rock
MOD: 373C #. 114
SOLE: PLANNING MICRO # B
A CERO PUNK COLOR
Color: ITALI NEGRO
Y ANTIC
ACER

Shawna Trpcic
=Firefly= ep 11

Back

SHOULD LOOK AND
FIT LIKE DARE DEVIL
OR X-MEN

H 310·822·6518
C 310 962 1813

Richard Brooks
6'3" 195 lbs
44L
35/35
14 shoe
7⅞

EARLY'S SPACESUIT

Chris Gilham of Global Effects: "The bounty hunter leather suit was something that the wardrobe department already had made. The helmet was a variant of the *Firefly* helmet but with parts re-sculpted and different details. We wanted to give the impression that they might have been made at the same factory. This one was painted with a silver undercoat which had areas peeling off to make it look like it's an aluminum helmet underneath. We bought a bunch of cast resin parts from another FX company which had closed down, and there are two details on the helmet we can't identify, one on the forehead and one on the chin. They could be part of Johnny Five from *Short Circuit* or even from *Aliens*. The two discs on the neck are from *Armageddon*."

Costume designer Shawna Trpcic: "One of my favorite guest characters was the bounty hunter, Early. I took his costume from everywhere from the *X-Men* to *Daredevil* to spacesuits — I did a lot of research on spacesuits to make sure that it looked like it could be airtight and he could actually survive. The helmet has the shape of the Alien's head in the *Aliens* movie, it's pointed in the back. Then there's the side-slung gun, which is Han Solo — I wanted to echo Mal, because if Mal just took one step further, he could end up doing something like that."

EARLY (cont'd)
It's not your moment, Doctor.

Simon takes a step back. Early points his light at Inara's shuttle.

EARLY (cont'd)
Companion lives there?

SIMON
Yes.

EARLY
Let's visit.

INT. INARA'S SHUTTLE - LATER

Inara is sitting up in bed. Simon stands near the entrance of the room, looking tense.

Inara, vulnerable and more than a little confused, looks from him to Early, who is peeking in the back room, gun trained steadily on Inara.

INARA
This is pointless, you know that.

EARLY
Two-hundred thousand seems fairly pointed to me. Money like that, I could retire, not that I would. What's life without work?

INARA
This is a smuggling ship. I've been here a year, I couldn't name all the places she might hide.

EARLY
I don't have a year.
(to Simon)
Your sister's becoming a real annoyance.

SIMON
I feel for you.

He heads to the exit, herding Simon ahead of him, talking to Inara.

EARLY
I'm not gonna waste my time threatening you, because I think you believe that I will kill people if someone upsets my plan. I'm gonna seal you in,

though. You just sit.

INARA
You can still walk away from this. I know you're tired.

He violently pistol-whips her, pointing the gun back at Simon as she feels the blood on her lip.

EARLY
Don't go visiting in my intentions. Don't ever.

He moves to the entrance. Before he shuts the door:

EARLY (cont'd)
(to Inara)
Man is stronger by far than woman. But only woman can create a child. That seem right to you?

He shuts the door on her.

INT. BRIDGE - LATER

Simon comes up the stairs from the front of the bridge while Early stands at the very front, looking down into the space, gun trained on Simon. He steps over to the middle with Simon, his manner tenser and the gun held with both hands at arm's length.

EARLY
(calls out)
All right! That's all the hide and seek I got time for!

INT. MAL'S ROOM - CONTINUING

Mal stirs, the voice barely reaching him.

INT. WASH AND ZOE'S ROOM - CONTINUING

She does the same.

INT. JAYNE'S ROOM - CONTINUING

He's sleeping right through it.

INT. BRIDGE - CONTINUING

EARLY
Now I know you're on this ship, little girl, so here's how this goes!

He points the gun at Simon's temple.

EARLY (cont'd)
You show yourself, and we finish this exchange, or your brother's brains'll be flying every which way.
(to Simon)
You understand, I'm sort of on a clock here, it's frustrating —

RIVER (O.S.)
You're wrong, Early.

He looks around, what the fuck — but realizes she's just coming over the com.

He speaks in a more normal voice, knowing she can hear him.

EARLY
I'm not wrong, dumpling. I will shoot your brother dead if you don't —

RIVER (V.O.)
Wrong about River. River's not on the ship. They didn't want her here, but she couldn't make herself leave, so she melted. Melted away.

INT. MAL'S ROOM - CONTINUING

He is hearing this also, and is more than a mite confused.

RIVER (V.O.)
They didn't know she could do that... but she did.

INT. WASH AND ZOE'S ROOM - CONTINUING

Even Wash is waking up... as Early's voice also sounds on the general com.

EARLY (V.O.)
Not sure I take your meaning there...

The two of them look at each other.

INT. BRIDGE - CONTINUING

RIVER (V.O.)
I'm not on the ship. I'm in the ship.

Simon looks almost as perturbed as Early.

RIVER (cont'd; V.O.)
I am the ship.

SIMON
River...

RIVER (V.O.)
River's gone.

EARLY
Then who exactly are we talking to?

RIVER (V.O.)
You're talking to Serenity. And Early... Serenity is very unhappy.

Early looks over at Simon, a bit freaked. Simon just shrugs. What are you gonna do?

END OF ACT TWO

ACT THREE

INT. ENGINE ROOM - MOMENTS LATER

Kaylee is sitting in the corner, hands tied behind her back, legs tied together. She hasn't moved since Early left her, she's so scared. After a moment...

JOSE MOLINA

One of our more veteran actors, who has been in everything under the sun, said that it was the rare time in his career that he would walk onto a set and he would talk to people and he could tell, at the time that they were doing the work, that people realized they were working on something special. Usually, you do a job, you go in, the product comes in and you go, 'Wow, that was pretty cool, I was a part of something great.' But in the middle of doing it, people were aware that this was something special.

Another moment I remember: I'm sure you'll hear this from every other person you talk to, but this cast was such a rarity and so fantastic to work with. I remember one time, about two-and-a-half months into production, Nathan called Gareth Davies, the producer, to book some time with him. And Gareth called Joss to go, 'Uh-huh, here we go. So it begins. This guy is going to talk to me because he has some problems.' And the entire reason Nathan was calling Gareth was because he wanted to sit down with him to tell him what a great time everybody was having and how happy they all were to show up to work every day, and what a joy it was to work on the show. Believe me, [an actor setting up a meeting to thank a producer] has never happened in my, or anybody else's experience, before or since. These guys were fantastic.

RIVER (V.O.)
Kaylee?

The voice is quieter, more intimate — this is not being broadcast for the public.

RIVER (cont'd; V.O.)
Kaylee, can you hear me?

KAYLEE
River...?

RIVER (V.O.)
You're afraid.

KAYLEE
(near tears)
He tied me up... I don't know where he came from, he just...

RIVER (V.O.)
It's okay. Gonna be okay.

KAYLEE
Is he gone?

There is a small beat.

KAYLEE (cont'd)
(panicked)
Is he coming back?

RIVER (V.O.)
He's not gonna hurt you, Kaylee; he's only visiting.

KAYLEE
I told him where you were, I'm sorry, I didn't know what —

RIVER
Shhhh... I'm fine. Only I need you to do something for me. Gotta be brave.

KAYLEE
I'm tied up, I can't —

RIVER
Got tools. Something sharp. Don't be scared. I'm right here.

INT. BRIDGE - CONTINUING

Early and Simon are very still. After a beat:

EARLY
Where'd she go?

SIMON
I can't keep track of her when she's NOT incorpo-really possessing a spaceship, don't look at me —

EARLY
That's some nonsensical crap! Ain't nobody can do that.
(to the air)
You're somewhere on this boat! Somewhere with a com, playing games!

Her LAUGHTER filters over the com. It's somewhat unsettling.

EARLY (cont'd)
That's somewhat unsettling.

RIVER (V.O.)
Early, Mr. Jubel Early, bounty hunter... Can I call you Jubel?

Okay, freak time. How'd she know that?

EARLY
Ain't nobody calls me that.

RIVER (V.O.)
Your mother does. I'm sorry. Did. She's gone now.

EARLY
That supposed to scare me? Bringing up my mother?

RIVER (V.O.)
You're a liar.

A beat.

RIVER (cont'd; V.O.)
I don't think your intentions are honorable.

EARLY
Well, no, I'm a bounty hunter, it's not generally considered "honorable" so much as... I live by a code, though, which I think is worth —

BOOK

"You can't fix the bible, River."

Despite the fact that *Firefly* only lasted for an abbreviated season, one thing that has become legend was the amazing chemistry and rapport amongst the cast — a fact that is rare indeed in Hollywood. Having worked on more than fifty television series during his long career, Ron Glass admits that connection to the cast, among many other things, made *Firefly* a truly unique experience. Talking about the group dynamic, he offers, "When you sit around the table for a family dinner, you connect with all the people in your family, but you don't want to spend the same amount of time around each individual, all the time," he chuckles. "It was kind of like that. There were some people that you immediately feel more simpatico with than others, but the most significant thing for me was that I was really impressed with the commitment and the potential and the excitement that everybody seemed to feel toward the project and their individual characters. I think that kind of thing happens from the top down and that's really to Joss's credit that he was able to generate that kind of commitment and enthusiasm from people. I also think that because Nathan was the Captain, that his particular personality was just ideal for the character he was playing. His own commitment and willingness to do anything and for however long, helping to keep everyone's spirits up, was contagious. It made it easy to fall in line, whether it was in the script or just on the set. The tendency was to support wherever he was leading and that is pretty unusual. It wasn't a drag to do it," he laughs. "It was a pretty seamless experience as far as the chemistry and the devotion to the material. That is part of the reason it was so hard to let go. You want to hold onto that type of experience because it feels good."

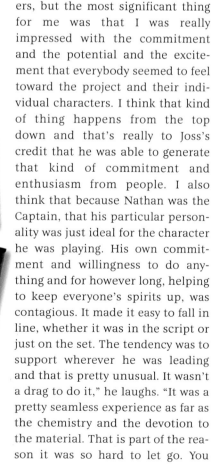

Of all the characters on the series, Shepherd Book was arguably the least revealed. His history was left largely unexplored, save for the occasional cryptic hints or comments the character would dangle from episode to episode. Alternately frustrating and engaging for fans, Glass admits he felt the same way. "Whenever I had a conversation with Joss about Book's background, he was generally as mysterious and evasive as what you saw played," he chuckles. "At times that felt a little aggravating, but ultimately it made it really, really interesting for me every time I saw a new script. It was intriguing! I still maintain and harbor great curiosity about how this character would have unfolded had the series continued. It was an uncertain thing for me and was at times unsettling, but it always remained exciting and adventurous. It was like two sides of a sharp sword, which ultimately I came to really enjoy and appreciate."

The legacy of the show has been the life it still maintains, even years after cancellation. The cast has traveled the world meeting fans who adore the show, and the actors that brought it to life. For Glass, that outpouring of support has truly been the least expected but most welcome aspect of the show. "It's a unique experience out of the many years of experience that I have had. It will always be singular and special and really close to my heart. I still have the opportunity to do conventions and meet people one-on-one and hear what they have to say. I get to have a human exchange between myself and the other person. It's very fulfilling and at the same time, it's an unusual honor to be able to thank people in person for their tremendous support. I like to let them know how much I really appreciate the response they have had for the whole work and towards me individually. One of the things I have really felt is how there is so much gentleness amongst these *Firefly* fans. There is a gentleness and respectfulness that is really humbling to be in the presence of. I've never had this kind of experience before and I might never again. In the moment, it's very special and I am really very honored to be a part of the whole thing."

RIVER (V.O.)
You hurt people.

EARLY
Only when the job requires it.

RIVER (V.O.)
WRONG. You're a bad liar. You crawl inside me uninvited and you hurt my crew. I see everything that passes —

EARLY
I only hurt people 'cause they keep getting in the way of finding you!
(to Simon)
Tell her!

SIMON
What am I, your advocate?

EARLY
(thrusts out gun)
You are starting now.

SIMON
(to River)
He's really very gentle and fuzzy. We're becoming fast friends.

She giggles again.

EARLY
You folk are all insane!

SIMON
Well, my sister's a ship, I just have issues going way back.

EARLY
Does anybody care that I have a finely crafted gun pointed at this boy's head?

RIVER (V.O.)
I care.

EARLY
Then are you gonna come out, stop me from doing what I don't want to? You gonna be smart here, River?

There is no answer.

EARLY (cont'd)
River?
(beat)
Serenity?

INT. MAL'S ROOM - CONTINUING

He's shaking off the beating he took, pulling himself up.

MAL
(groggy)
What in the hell is going on here?

RIVER (V.O.)
I need you to do me a favor, Captain.

MAL
There was a guy, he was very blurry. You gotta be careful... How come there's a guy on board and how come you're all of a sudden the ship?

RIVER (V.O.)
I know you have questions...

MAL
Yeah, that would be why I just asked them —

RIVER (V.O.)
But there isn't a lot of time. Captain, I need you to trust me.

MAL
Am I dreaming?

RIVER (V.O.)
We all are.

The Captain rolls his eyes.

RIVER (cont'd; V.O.)
Don't make faces.

He looks around. That was creepy.

INT. AFT HALL - CONTINUING

The door opens slowly and Kaylee peers out, still very afraid. A moment, then she starts down the hall, hugging the wall.

INT. BRIDGE - A BIT LATER

Early is getting a little more hyper.

EARLY
Just gotta think here...
(turns to Simon)
You know, with the exception of one deadly and unpredictable midget, this girl is the smallest cargo I have ever had to transport and by far the most troublesome. Does that seem right to you?

SIMON
What'd he do?

EARLY
Who?

SIMON
The midget.

EARLY
Arson.
(beat)
Little man loooved fire.

INT. FOREDECK HALL - CONTINUING

Kaylee peeks out around the corner. She can just see a piece of Early. She ducks her head back, then braves it, comes around and works the console.

GINA TORRES

On whether she misses *Firefly*: "You know, not so much, because I get to see the people that I worked with. That was the biggest joy for me, to meet and get to work with Nathan and Morena and Jewel and Alan and Adam and we're in touch and we love each other a great deal, so that's great. So I don't miss it so much, because I still have them in my life."

The red lights over the rooms go out.

Kaylee bolts down toward the cargo bay.

INT. WASH AND ZOE'S ROOM - CONTINUING

They are talking with River's voice.

ZOE
I can take this guy out.

RIVER (V.O.)
He's faster than you. All of you. And he's wearing armor.

WASH
What about his face? Is his face wearing armor?

RIVER (V.O.)
No touching guns. You just have to sit and be good. He'll leave soon.

Wash looks at Zoe.

WASH
This is all very surreal. I hate surreal.

INT. MAL'S ROOM - CONTINUING

He is standing right under his ladder, waiting.

RIVER (V.O.)
It's soon now. Are you ready?

MAL
How do you know what this guy's gonna do?

RIVER (V.O.)
I'm very close to him. He doesn't even see it.

MAL
Okay, but —

RIVER (V.O.)
Go now.

INT. BRIDGE - CONTINUING

The lights go completely out in the bridge and the hall. We may or may not see Mal scrambling up his ladder and disappearing around the corner in the far background as Early looks around, NOT seeing him.

Now Early's very freaked.

RIVER (V.O.)
You're not welcome here anymore, Early.

EARLY
And you think I'm gonna leave here empty handed?

BEN EDLUND

Firefly really came at the right time in my life, helped restore my faith in television and just having the opportunity to work with a Joss, a Tim, a Jose and everybody was really, really valuable and important for me.

RIVER (V.O.)
I know it.

EARLY
Yeah, you know me real well.

RIVER (V.O.)
Wish I didn't. You like to hurt folk.

EARLY
It's part of the job.

RIVER (V.O.)
It's why you TOOK the job. Not the chase, not the money... Power. Control. Pain. Your mother knew. Sadness in her when she waved goodbye, but she's relieved. Saw darkness in you. You're not well.

EARLY
You'll be wanting to shut up now.

RIVER (V.O.)
Big golden retriever, sitting on the lawn. Never took to you. Smell on you, the neighbors' pets, you did things to 'em... Cleaned up after. Shined and polished. Everything in here gleams.

Realization dawns on Early.

EARLY
Well, I'll be a son of a whore. You're not in my gorramn mind. You're on my gorramn SHIP!

EXT./INT. - EARLY'S SHIP - CONTINUING

We push in on River, who is in fact sitting in the pilot's seat of Early's ship, spacesuit on and helmet off. She is giggling again.

RIVER
It's very interesting. All these buttons...

INTERCUT THE TWO LOCATIONS:

EARLY
Okay, we're not touching those, okay?
(to Simon)
How the hell did she get on my ship?

SIMON
At this point, I'm as lost as you.

RIVER
Can see everyone from here. Wave to mommy. Put the gun away.

EARLY
(not putting it away)
Okay, I'm putting it away...

SIMON
No he's not.

He glares at Simon. Puts it away.

EARLY
I'm putting it away 'cause we're all reasonable people, don't want to be doing anything rash, fiddling with any dials.

RIVER
You're not right, Early. You're not righteous. Got issues.

EARLY
No! Or, yes, I could have that, you might have me figured out, that... Good job, I'm not a hundred percent — Are we gonna be reasonable?

RIVER
Talk too much.

EARLY
I'm flawed in that way, I sometimes go on, it's been said —

RIVER
It's okay, Early. I'm going with you.

Now it's Simon's turn to be unhappy.

SIMON
River, what are you —

RIVER
Don't belong. Dangerous. Like you.

INT. WASH AND ZOE'S ROOM - CONTINUING

They listen in, somber.

RIVER (V.O.)
Can't be controlled. Can't be trusted. Every-

body could just go on without me, not have to worry.

INT. PASSENGER DORM - CONTINUING

Where Kaylee is tending a groggy Book, also hearing this.

RIVER (V.O.)
People could be who they wanted to be, could be with the people they wanted... Could live simple. No secrets.

We move in on Kaylee, the words clearly affecting her.

INT. BRIDGE INTERCUT WITH EARLY'S SHIP - CONTINUING

The realization of what she's saying truly hits him.

SIMON
(quietly)
No...

RIVER
And I'll be fine. I'll be your bounty, Jubel Early. And then I'll just fade away.

Early smiles. Heads for the door.

EARLY
Well, finally something goes according to —

Simon throws himself at him, they clatter to the ground, tussling —

RIVER
Simon?

Early throws him off, pulls out his gun — and fires. Simon's eyes go wide.

River starts screaming.

END OF ACT THREE

ACT FOUR

INT. BRIDGE - CONTINUING

Early stands, looking at Simon, who's shot in the upper thigh. He holds his hand over the spilling wound, face blanching.

EARLY
See? That's what it feels like.

He takes off —

INT. FOREDECK HALL - CONTINUING

Takes a moment to make sure no one is waiting in the hall —

EARLY
You just hang tight, darlin'... Early's on the move.

Comes down the steps just as Simon launches himself at him, flying, knocking them both down, getting a couple of blows in before Early recovers enough to ninja his face.

Early takes off, rounding the corner —

EARLY (cont'd)
Spirited boy...

SPACE EFFECTS

Visual effects supervisor Loni Peristere: "I really liked working on 'Objects in Space'. We played with the quiet of space and how alone our crew could feel when they're being invaded. The only way to get rid of the nemesis was to go outside and kick him into space. I loved playing that sequence between the two vessels tied together, with the threat and jeopardy of the vastness of space. I loved that sequence on the top of Serenity. Making that feel real was a challenge and fun.

"We had a wonderful shot at the beginning where we approach Serenity from the back and enter in through the engine ducts and the vent shafts and the next thing you know we are in River's room. I loved that CGI helped tell that story. We were creating effects to create tension — it was great storytelling."

ANGLE ON SIMON trying to shake it off.

RIVER (V.O.)
Simon...

SIMON
River don't let him.... Don't let him do this...

RIVER (V.O.)
Have to.
(quieter)
Have to.

EXT. TOP OF SERENITY - CONTINUING

Early comes out the hatch, helmet on. He looks up to see his ship following perfectly, smiles.

EARLY
You made the right move, darlin'. Best for you to go with old Early.

MAL
You think so?

Early turns awkwardly (magnetic boots) to see

Mal, suited up and cabled to the ship, right behind him.

MAL (cont'd)
Some of us feel differently.

Mal double palms him in the chest, an inelegant move, but the force of it sends Early flying off the ship, gone, just like that, long gone.

Mal watches him go a moment, then looks up. After a long beat, River floats down to him. He steadies her as she lands. Looks at her affectionately.

RIVER
Permission to come aboard?

MAL
You know, you ain't quite right.

RIVER
It's the popular theory.

MAL
Get on in there. Give your brother a thrashing for messing up your plan.

RIVER
(going down)
He takes so much looking after...

INT. INFIRMARY/PASSENGER DORM/CARGO BAY - LATER

(This is possibly a one-er.)

Simon is on the table, talking Zoe through pulling

out his bullet. He watches her progress on the screen...

SIMON
To the left — your left. Now, very gently, pull that aside.

ZOE
This is really not my area of expertise, Doctor. I tend to be putting these into people more than the other thing.

WASH
(to Zoe)
Can I mop your brow? I'm at the ready with the fearsome brow mopping.

SIMON
You got the bullet. Okay, I'm gonna pass out for a minute, but you're doing great.

We find Mal and Inara at the entrance, watching.

MAL
So we live to fight another day.

INARA
Any chance that <SHIONG-mung duh kuang-ren> [violent lunatic] might survive?

MAL
Air he had left... chance'd be one in about... a very big number. Ain't odds I'd play. How's your lip?

He touches her face to look and she pulls away. They look at each other a moment, and she goes off into the cargo bay, where we find Book and Jayne coming downstairs to do some weights. (Jayne going first, Book spotting.)

BOOK
I just feel such a fool.

JAYNE
Yeah, all those years of priest training and you get taken out by one bounty hunter.

BOOK
Don't get me wrong — I gave him a hell of a fight.

JAYNE
Epic, I'm guessing.

BOOK
There'll be poems and songs, you just wait.

JAYNE
Hey, at least you got some play. I missed every damn thing.

We are moving off them to find the girls, Kaylee and River, sitting in the corner. They are playing, of all things, jacks. It's Kaylee's turn, and she's tellin' a tale, the ease between them returned...

KAYLEE
And then his folks come by to fetch him, and it turns out he's fourteen years old!
(they both laugh)
I mean, he must have been some kind of genetic experiment, 'cause I swear he was... My daddy whupped me so hard...

SUMMER GLAU

My favorite episode is 'Objects in Space'. It's a special, special memory for me working with Joss. It's the one episode when I got to work every day. I just felt like an important part of that episode. It was one Joss wrote and directed and there are so many images from it that I think about all the time and mean a lot to me. I loved working with Richard [Brooks], who played Jubal Early. He was fantastic, but that suit was really loud and smelled really bad. I felt so bad that he had to wear that. It was this huge, purple, leather suit!

There were some moments of River's physicality that I really worked hard on in that episode. River communicates a lot with her face and body. She's not good at talking to people: what she says never makes sense. So with 'Objects in Space', I really felt like her physicality was important to her expression. Joss said that there were things that he noticed after shooting it that he didn't even realize I was doing: ways that I was moving and touching the ship. He said that it really added to the episode.

The one mistake I wish I had never made started the 'Summer Blame Game'. It was the end of 'Objects in Space', and Jewel and I are sitting on the floor of the cargo bay, playing jacks. It was this long shot that everybody was in and it was a oner — where they move the camera through the entire ship and it's very complicated and delicate. I was the very last shot of the scene and they went through the whole scene perfectly and they come to me at the very end and I have one line! I'm looking at the ball and I don't remember to say my line. Nathan was all the way in the other end of the ship and I could just hear him say, 'Summmmer! You ruined the whole shot!' So now it's a game — when anything wrong happens to anybody, it's my fault. It was so funny, when Nathan was working on *Buffy*, playing Caleb, and somebody messed up something, he yelled my name and I'm not even on that show!

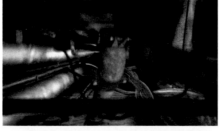

She misses —

KAYLEE (cont'd)
Dyah! I'm at fours. Let's see you match that.

RIVER
(seriously)
I can win this.

KAYLEE
I'm hearing a lot of talk, genius. Come on. Show me what you got.

River looks at the ball in her hand.

CLOSE ON the ball, as she contemplates it. The solidity of the thing. We might notice it has a similar coloring to the moon we saw at the beginning of the show.

CLOSER STILL as she throws it down, camera goes slowly with it. It hits ground but the camera keeps going down, through the ship one last time, and out the bottom to:

EXT. SPACE - CONTINUING

Looking up at Serenity and panning left as she rockets away into the distance.

EXT. SPACE - ELSEWHERE - LATER

We see him, floating, turning slowly in space.

His helmet comes into view, his face amusedly resigned.

EARLY
Well... Here I am...

Tiny, alone, he floats.

END OF SHOW

ALSO AVAILABLE

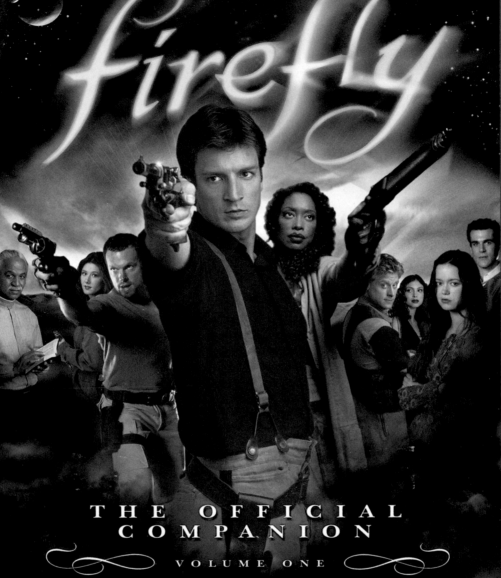

CREATED BY JOSS WHEDON

firefly

THE OFFICIAL COMPANION
VOLUME ONE

❖ The uncut shooting scripts for the first seven episodes.

❖ Part one of the in-depth interview with Joss Whedon.

❖ Stacks of rare and previously unseen imagery.

❖ Exclusive commentary from the cast and crew.

❖ Mal's pistol and Browncoat.

www.titanbooks.com